W9-DCJ-196

CONTEMPORARY ROUMANIA

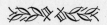

STANFORD BOOKS
IN WORLD POLITICS

GRAHAM H. STUART, *Editor*

❧

The Law and Procedure of International Tribunals
by JACKSON H. RALSTON

The Washington Conference and After
by YAMATO ICHIHASHI

The Public International Conference
by NORMAN L. HILL

The Politics of Peace
by CHARLES E. MARTIN

The Governance of Hawaii
by ROBERT M. C. LITTLER

International Arbitration from Athens to Locarno
by JACKSON H. RALSTON

Greece Today
by ELIOT GRINNELL MEARS

International Understanding: Agencies Educating
for a New World
by JOHN EUGENE HARLEY

The International City of Tangier
by GRAHAM H. STUART

Liberalism in Mexico, 1857–1929
by WILFRID HARDY CALLCOTT

Progress in International Organization
by MANLEY O. HUDSON

Contemporary Roumania and Her Problems
by JOSEPH S. ROUCEK

Carmen Sylva Place, Bucharest

Contemporary Roumania
and
Her Problems

A Study in
Modern Nationalism

By JOSEPH S. ROUČEK

Professor of Social Science, Centenary Junior College
(Hackettstown, N.J.)

1932
STANFORD UNIVERSITY PRESS
STANFORD UNIVERSITY, CALIFORNIA
LONDON: HUMPHREY MILFORD
OXFORD UNIVERSITY PRESS

STANFORD UNIVERSITY PRESS
STANFORD UNIVERSITY, CALIFORNIA

LONDON: HUMPHREY MILFORD
OXFORD UNIVERSITY PRESS

———

THE BAKER & TAYLOR COMPANY
55 FIFTH AVENUE, NEW YORK

MARTINUS NIJHOFF
9 LANGE VOORHOUT, THE HAGUE

THE MARUZEN COMPANY
TOKYO, OSAKA, KYOTO, SENDAI

———

To

PROFESSOR NICOLAE IORGA

The Grand Old Man
of Roumania

PREFACE

For the last few years the Kingdom of Roumania has been continually in the public eye. Probably no other state of southeastern Europe has received so much attention. Undoubtedly much of this has been due to the dramatic changes in its dynastic and political affairs which have been following each other with spectacular frequency. Then there have been the frequent stories of anti-Jewish demonstrations in Roumania. The protagonists as well as the antagonists of the country have been voluminously expressing their opinions.

It is difficult to pick an impartial way among the exaggerated reports, decorated as they are for public consumption. One becomes more and more impressed with the feeling that the spectacular has crowded out all sober understanding of Roumania as a nation and as a people, if indeed such ever existed. The editor of a leading American magazine wrote some time ago to the author: "There are a great many questions about which there is more or less a mystery in the story of Roumania." And his first question touched upon the noisiest, though relatively unimportant, problem of Roumania: "In the first place, what is the secret of the anti-Semitism in Roumania?" Notice that the words "mystery" and "secret" are used.

An explanation and analysis of these "secrets" is attempted in this work—and no claim is laid in it to the spectacular or the flashy in its revelations. It is an attempt to explain the basis of Roumanian life and politics, to separate the fundamental from the merely spectacular. The author hopes it may be recognized as an impartial treatment of the Roumanian problem. Whatever conclusions are presented herein take account of both sides of the question. We might hear again the editor mentioned above: "We receive many manuscripts in which the Roumanians are praised to the skies and numerous others in which the ruling classes in Roumania are pictured as fiends and as moral perverts. What we are after, however, are the facts and the object of this letter is to ask whether you are in a position to ascertain the truth and to present the facts unassailably, as a chapter of history."

The author lived for many years in Europe and has twice revisited Roumania. His most recent visit was in the summer of 1930, shortly after the return of Prince Carol. He tried by personal investigation to study Roumania as a foreign observer. He went there as a friend of the country, but a critical friend. That fact may point to a weakness in this narrative, but there is no practical alternative, for the hostile observer is subject to even graver limitations.

Roumania is indeed an interesting country to study. Dusty and somber plains mingle in it with magnificent mountains, stately rivers, and rich pasture lands. It is one of the few countries of Europe where one can find the peasant in his original costume, which lends charm and color to the landscape.

The backbone of Roumania is agriculture. This fact will explain to us in the subsequent pages many Roumanian problems of the past and of today. But the natural wealth of Roumania is not derived from agriculture alone. Under the surface lies one of the greatest deposits of oil in Europe, in addition to an abundance of natural gas, gold, silver, lead, iron, copper, and many other minerals. And immense forests will supply the building requirements of the country and of the neighboring states for generations to come.

What is remarkable is that despite this natural wealth Roumania cannot be considered a rich country. These riches are only beginning to be used. The promise, however, is great. From this standpoint Roumania is a country of the future. While, for example, with the World War, England passed the zenith of her greatness and glory, based on economics, the day of Roumania is still to come. And its beginning can be reckoned from the horrible days of the World War. This world struggle left Roumania ruined, depleted in man power and in resources. On the other hand, the armistice saw materialize the centuries-old dream of the Roumanian—the birth of Greater Roumania.

Roumania has written one of the most epochal stories of the world's history. As proud descendants of the Roman colonists in Dacia, the Roumanians until the nineteenth century carried the yoke of foreign and feudal oppression. Their rise to independence is a story of nationalism—and the aspects of this nationalism are the primary objects of this study. Foreign invasions and continual wars of the past could not make the Roumanian give up his dream. The past tells in another respect as well; Turkish domination left its impress on the country, and, though the Turks are gone, the bad features of the heritage from them are still discernible.

Only a part of the Roumanian nation was included in the borders of the newly established kingdom in the nineteenth century. The other part lived in the neighboring states, and its largest branch, the Transylvanian Roumanians, carried on its nationalistic struggle against the denationalizing policy of the Magyar masters. It is a matter of interest to note that Transylvania contributed largely to the regeneration of modern Roumanian nationalism, just as these Transylvanians today contribute to the regeneration of modern political life of Greater Roumania.

While the World War united all branches of the Roumanian nation, it brought a series of great problems, which increased in intensity with its people's sudden realization of nationalistic aspirations. This battle-scarred, valiant nation had to recover from the devastation of 1916–18 and to find the means of conserving its statehood against openly hostile neighbors. On the one side, Roumania has been one of the foremost bulwarks against the spread of Bolshevism. On the other, Hungary is still showing its irreconcilability. In this often unfriendly atmosphere Roumanian diplomacy has met difficulties with dispatch and success, even when opposed by powerful states. The problem of minorities is still very troublesome.

Underneath the current life of Roumania, there has been going on since the World War a remarkable transformation. During the World War, the agrarian reform cut the ground from under the feet of the landlord, who, from his strong political position before the war, was nearly eliminated from the political arena. The National Liberals, under the leadership of the great family of Brătianus, whose name has been associated with the creation of the kingdom, with the victory of the war, and with the coronation of the royal family as sovereigns of Greater Roumania, played a great part in the development of the nation. But with the creation of Greater Roumania, they were pushed to the political Right of Roumanian politics, where they tried in vain to stem the rising tide of the strongest power of Roumania—the peasant. The peasant, who carried the burden of centuries on his shoulders, was the last to receive any benefits from the political fortunes of his independent country. But the great reform of 1917 was ample recompense. In the ensuing years the peasant had to consolidate forces with his brethren from the new provinces in order to push to the front of national politics his interest in agrarianism, while the Liberals were following their emphatic insistence on a policy very near to mercantilism. The strife was bitter. No large political middle class of Roumania provided a buffer between these two forces. Ultimately the peasant was given a chance to try his abilities in political leadership and he held the captaincy of the state for more than two years. But the new experiment was not very successful, because Roumania was caught in the wave of depression sweeping the countries of the world. But the new and fresh political vigor of Roumanians runs parallel to that of King Carol, who is also young and is trained in the new democratic methods of the present times. His residence abroad gave him new points of view, and allowed him to see matters in a different perspective. He is evidently convinced that for some years the energies of the political leaders of Roumania have been too much absorbed by party controversies, and his heart is set on his task—a fact which makes him extremely popular with Roumanians.

The United States has a large interest in the Kingdom of Roumania. The investments of American dollars in Roumanian enterprises leads us to borrow the paraphrasing of Dr. Max Winkler of the lines of Wilhelm Mueller, the great Grecophile:

> Without thee, O dollar, what would'st be, O Europe?
> Without thee, O Europe, what would be the World?

And Roumania is fully aware of the importance of the American dollar to her. Large loans and investments in Roumanian enterprises are proving helpful and constructive to both parties. The rising prosperity of Roumania will mean growing markets for American products. Mr. George Boncescu, a Roumanian economic and financial expert, calls our attention to this possibility: "Individual and collective prosperity will cause Roumania to become an attractive market for the exchange of goods with other countries. The industrial products of America, agricultural machinery, automobiles, oil drilling equipment, and so forth, could thus find ready buyers among the 18,000,000 potential Roumanian customers, and would help to solve some of the difficulties confronting her home industries in search of new markets abroad."

The author is fully aware of the shortcomings of the volume. An apology is in order for the large number of quotations and citations throughout the book. They have been put in intentionally. Because the affairs of Roumania are such a controversial subject, the views and arguments of other authorities have seemed to be essential, despite fact that the criticism may be made that many references choke creative thought or are more ornamental than needful.

This manuscript was completed in March 1931, but technical reasons prevented its immediate publication. The most important details have been brought up to date whenever possible.

Books and material in the foreign languages, inaccessible to the average English reader, namely, those in Roumanian, Russian, and Czechoslovakian, have been omitted. A select bibliography is included. It might be well to emphasize the material which has proved to be most helpful, or has most influenced the author: R. W. Seton-Watson's volumes on the pre-war conditions of central and southeastern Europe have been a source of information and inspiration to everyone who has dealt with that section of Europe. They are: *Europe in the Melting Pot; Corruption and Reform in Hungary; German, Slav and Magyar; Racial Problems in Hungary; Roumania and the Great War; The Rise of Nationality in the Balkans.* David Mitrany's contribution to a volume, entitled *The Balkans,* treating Roumanian history up to the World War, is both illuminating and fair, as is his latest standard volume *The Land and the Peasant in Rumania.* Professor Iorga's numerous literary contributions are of course well known throughout Europe and America. A mass of information on pre-war Roumania can be gathered from two official English publications: the Admiralty Handbook, *Rumania;* and a somewhat larger volume of the same title in the Foreign Office Handbooks Series. The United States Department of Commerce issued a similar economic treatment down to 1924 in its *Rumania: An Economic Handbook.* In 1926 C. G. Rommenhoeller published a large volume, *La Grande-Roumanie. The Near East Yearbook, 1927,* and *The Near East Yearbook, 1931–32,* edited by H. T. Montague Bell, contain much-needed reliable information. In September 1931, when this volume was being completed, N. L. Forter and D. B. Rostovsky published *The Roumanian Handbook* (London). The annual editions of *Les Forces économiques de la Roumanie,* published by the Banque Marmorosch, Blank & Cie., of Bucharest, contain current statistics and a summary of the year's progress, as does the *Compass Finanzielles Jahrbuch, 1930,* edited by G. Leonhardt. The same applies to the *Annuaire statistique de la*

Roumanie, edited by the Institut de Statistique Générale de l'État at Bucharest. The economic policy of the National-Peasant Government is treated in Dr. Virgil Madgearu's *Rumania's New Economic Policy.*

C. U. Clark's *Greater Roumania,* published in 1922, was a pioneer in its field after the World War. Clark's volume on *Bessarabia* is also very valuable. H. F. Armstrong's two volumes, *The New Balkans* and *Where the East Begins,* have proved to be as popular as his occasional articles in *Foreign Affairs,* of which he is the editor. On foreign policy, A. J. Toynbee's *Survey of International Affairs* volumes are of great scholarly value. While R. Machray's *The Little Entente* collected considerable material, J. O. Crane's *The Little Entente* is of much greater interest and value.

Two issues of current periodicals must be consulted: the *Völkermagazin* of May 1929, and the *Manchester Guardian* of November 28, 1929, each having a collection of excellent articles by different authorities.

For current events the best source of information and statistics is a quarterly review, *Roumania,* published by the Society of Friends of Roumania, 36 West Forty-fourth Street, New York City, and here quoted by permission. The *Central European Observer,* edited formerly by Aleš Brož and now by Dr. Karel Kraus, for the Orbis Publishing Company, Prague, Czechoslovakia, is most useful; the same applies to the *Near East and India, L'Europe Nouvelle* and *L'Europe Centrale. Current History* has a monthly summary compiled by an impartial authority, Dr. F. A. Ogg, of the University of Wisconsin. Nor can we overlook the publications of the Foreign Policy Association of New York City and occasional surveys of *The Economist* (London), which reprinted the *Economic Survey of Roumania* in pamphlet form in 1929. *The Annual Register* is especially valuable, as well as Mallory's *Political Handbook of the World.* Dr. Isaiah Bowman's *The New World* and also the *Encyclopaedia Britannica* are well known. Weekly *Commerce Reports* of the Department of Commerce, summarized in the *Commerce Yearbook, 1930,* Volume II, are of course, indispensable to all those interested in foreign trade. Among the Roumanian periodicals useful in keeping abreast of current events are *L'Indépendance Roumaine,* the official organ in French of the National-Liberal Party of Roumania, and the *Argus,* which has a weekly French edition devoted to commerce, industry, and finance.

I must express my personal thanks to at least a few of the many who have helped me with my task. First of all, Mr. Carol A. Davila, Roumanian Minister to the United States, Mr. George Boncescu, Financial Counsellor, and Mr. Frederick Nano, Counsellor of the Roumanian Legation, Washington, D.C., have been untiring in their efforts to supply all material at their disposal and to make my visits to Roumania profitable. Mr. I. Rosenthal, a member of the Roumanian Legation, with residence in New York, former editor-in-chief of the *Dimineaţa* and *Adevârul,* two of the largest Roumanian newspapers, has spent many an hour discussing particular problems and providing the most valuable material. Mr. Horia Babes, secretary of the Society of Friends of Roumania, which operates under the Presidency of Dr. Wm. Nelson Cromwell, has always helped very cheerfully. In Roumania, Mr. Eugen Filotti of the Presidency of the Council of Ministries and Professor Alexandru Marcu of the Foreign Office have shown admirable patience despite my steady demand for their services. Professor Iorga made every effort to acquaint me with the cultural life of his country and Mr. I. Pangal was always ready to introduce me to the leading personalities of Roumania and gave all the help he could.

Finally, to Dr. Wallace S. Sayre of New York University goes the credit for its editing. President Robert J. Trevorrow and Dr. H. Graham DuBois of Centenary Junior College, Hackettstown, N.J., were most kind in arranging my teaching schedule so that I might spend many hours in the New York Public Library.

The reader will note that the Roumanian names are written in the Roumanian style. English equivalents of accents and cedillas used in Roumanian orthography are as follows:

â, î—has no exact equivalent in English. It is pronounced somewhat like French *u.*

ă, ĕ—as *e* in fath*e*r.

ş is pronounced *sh,* as in *sh*all.

ţ is pronounced *ts* as in *ts*ar.

c when it precedes *e* and *i* is pronounced *ch,* as in *ch*urch; otherwise it has the sound of *k.*

g when followed by *e* or *i* is pronounced *dj,* as in *g*eneral; otherwise as in *g*reat.

u is pronounced *oo,* as in t*oo.*

It is of course understood that the author is entirely responsible for the shortcomings and limitations of the book.

Joseph S. Roucek

Centenary Junior College
  Hackettstown, N.J.
    September 1931

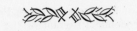

TABLE OF CONTENTS

PART V. CONCLUSION

LIST OF ILLUSTRATIONS

MAPS

CHRONOLOGY

A.D. 101–105—Roman Emperor Trajan defeated Decebal, King of Dacians, a tribe of the Thracians, and colonized the province

271—Emperor Aurelian abandoned Dacia

3d to 7th centuries—Barbarian invasions. Only the Slavs, assimilated completely in the 12th and 13th centuries, left their impress on Roumanian civilization

9th to 12th centuries—The Magyars settled in the higher Danubian plains. About 1100 the Magyars extended their authority over Transylvania. Subsequently Szeklers, Flemish-Germans, and Saxons colonized in Transylvania

13th to 14th centuries — Wallachian and Moldavian principalities founded

14th century—Debrotici the Despot (who gave his name to the Dobrogea) made himself Prince. Soon after his death (1386) the Turks conquered the province and dominated it for four and a half centuries. The Turks forced the principalities to submit to their suzerainty

16th century—A period of decadence for the principalities; a series of contentions for the Wallachian and Moldavian thrones. Sultan Suleiman completed the Turkish conquest of Hungary. Transylvania paid tribute to the Turks, though it kept its autonomy under a Magyar noble. Mihaiu the Brave (1593–1601) succeeded for a brief time in uniting Wallachia, Moldavia, Bessarabia, the Bukovina, and Transylvania

1594–1610—Austria dominated Transylvania. The Thirty Years' War ended this domination

17th to 18th centuries—Economic, social, and political decay of the provinces. In the second half of the 17th century books were printed in the Roumanian language. The Phanariote régime (18th century). At the end of this period, Hellenic classicism and French culture began to penetrate the provinces. Social and administrative reforms

1699–1876—Transylvania under Austria. At the end of the 18th century a school of Roumanian writers was founded, aiming to prove the Latin origins of the Roumanian people and their language

1774—Austria received Bukovina

1775-1846—Bukovina incorporated with Galicia

1812—The territory between the Prut and the Dniester, named Bessarabia, annexed by Russia

1821—Roumanian princes restored in the principalities and the Phanariotes removed. This is the period of national regeneration, led by Transylvanian teachers

1829-1834—Russian protectorate over the provinces

1846—Bukovina became an autonomous province of the Austrian Empire

1848—The Hungarian revolutionists annexed Transylvania for a time. The revolution in the provinces was unsuccessful

1856—The Treaty of Paris returned three counties of Southern Bessarabia to Moldavia, though Russia received them again by the Treaty of Berlin, 1878

1859—Colonel Cuza elected ruler of Wallachia and Moldavia. The union was acknowledged in 1861 by the Powers and the Porte

1866—Cuza overthrown. Carol I (1866–1914) elected

1867—Transylvania given to Hungary by the "Ausgleich"

1877—May 10. Roumanian independence proclaimed. The Treaty of Berlin, 1878, recognized Roumanian independence

1881—Carol I crowned King

1913—Roumania joined the Second Balkan War. The frontier of Dobrogea extended by the Bulgarian cession

1914—October 10. King Carol I died

1914-1927—King Ferdinand I

1916—August 17. Roumania signed a secret treaty with the Allies and agreed to enter the World War

1917—June. Article 19 of the Roumanian Constitution amended, enunciating the expropriation principle on which agricultural reform was to be carried out. The modification of the Constitution was promulgated on July 19, 1917

1918—May 7. Peace of Bucharest signed

1919-1920—Treaties of Versailles, Neuilly, and Trianon signed

1921—Little Entente Treaties signed, with Czechoslovakia on April 23, and with Yugoslavia on June 7. A defensive pact signed with Poland on March 4

1922—October 15. The coronation of King Ferdinand and Queen Marie as rulers of Greater Roumania

1923—March 26. The new Constitution adopted

1926—January 4. A provisional Council of Regency appointed in place of Prince Carol, who had resigned. The National-Peasant Party formed

1927—March 9. Italy ratified the Bessarabian Treaty
       June 20. King Ferdinand died; Mihaiu proclaimed King
       November 24. Ion I. C. Brătianu died
1928—November 10. The National-Peasant Party came into power
1929—February 9. The Litvinoff Pact signed
1930—June 6. Prince Carol returned to Roumania and was proclaimed
       King on June 8
       October. The First Balkan Conference
       December 22. Vintilă I. C. Brătianu died. During this year the
       Hague and Paris agreements settled the optants' problem and
       the problem of Eastern reparations
1931—April 18. Professor N. Iorga appointed Prime Minister
       October. The Second Balkan Conference

PART I

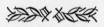

HISTORICAL DEVELOPMENT TO 1918

CHAPTER I

OUTLINE HISTORY TO 1878

Aʙᴏᴜᴛ two thousand years ago the Dacians, of Thracian origin, had their center in what is today known as Roumania. In the first century B.C. their power extended as far as the regions of the Moldavia of today and the Black Sea. The Romans were annoyed by their plundering incursions. Two expeditions of Emperor Trajan conquered Dacia; and Sarmisegetuza, their capital, a lovely spot in Transylvania, was taken by assault.

Here we have the origins of the Roumanian nation. The Roumanian people of today claim to be the direct descendants of the old Roman colony of Dacia. What remained of the Dacian population completely amalgamated with the settlers and colonists who spoke Latin. Thus the birth of the Roumanian race may be dated between A.D. 101–102 and A.D. 105–106, when the legions of Rome completely crushed the brave mountaineers of this country. Subsequent Roman colonization was concentrated in the regions of the Dacian strongholds, in the Oltenia of today, in Eastern Banat, and in Transylvania, for gold and other mineral wealth induced many colonists to settle in this Roman province.

After the conquest, immortalized in the reliefs of Trajan's column at Rome and those of the Adamelissi's Monument in the Dobrogea, Dacia rapidly became a flourishing province, its chief town being Apulum (Alba-Iulia).

Although under the strain of the barbarian invasions Dacia was finally evacuated in A.D. 271, the Roman government withdrawing its soldiers and officials, the populace remained. Many of them perished under the swords of the successive waves of invaders who swept over these regions. But a remnant survived by taking refuge in the Carpathian Mountains or to the south of the Danube. The spreading of the Slavs over Dacia, and later on beyond the Danube, from the seventh century onward, divided the Roumanians from

3

the Romans. They are expressly mentioned by the Byzantine chroniclers of the events that took place at the end of the tenth and the
beginning of the eleventh centuries. They are called by the Byzantine historiographers *Vlachs,* a Slavonic word, of the same origin
as "Welsh," the name given by the Germanic peoples to the Roman-
ized Gauls. In the Roumanian Dobrogea of today, there appeared a
few little political organizations on the right bank of the Danube
under the protection of the Byzantine Empire.[1]

In the Carpathians the descendants of the Roman colonists continued the old Roman way of living. The barbarians—Goths, Huns,
Gepides, Avars—could rarely reach the heart of their regions. Only
the Slavs introduced alien elements into the Roumanian language.
But we must notice that there has been a lively historical controversy about what happened during these invasions. The opposing
thesis supports the Magyar contention that the Magyars were in
possession of Transylvania and the Banat long before the Roumanians, and that there is no proof that the former Hungarian territory
was inhabited by the Roumanian nation before the thirteenth century.[2] But today it is generally agreed, outside of Hungary,[3] that

---

[1] N. Bănescu, *Historical Survey of the Rumanian People,* p. 11. Bănescu supports this statement especially by an article of N. Iorga, "Les Premières cristal-
lisations d'Etat des Roumains," in the *Bulletin de la section historique de l'Académie Roumaine,* 5–8e année, Janvier 1920, pp. 33–46.

[2] For a summary see C. U. Clark, *Greater Roumania,* pp. 47–49. The best
exposition of the Roumanian thesis is N. Iorga, *Histoire des Roumains et de leur
civilisation,* Cultura Națională, Bucharest, 1922. The Magyar view has been recently revived by Benedetto Jancsó, "Critical Remarks on the Early History of the
Roumanian People," reported in the *Social Science Abstracts,* January 1931, III,
27.

[3] Oscar Jászi makes a very interesting comment regarding this point in his
The Dissolution of the Habsburg Monarchy, p. 306, note 5. According to Jászi,
Dr. John Karácsonyi, a canon of Nagy-Várad, a member of the Hungarian
Academy, and an acknowledged historian, wrote in 1912 a pamphlet, "A Hundred
Thousand Evils and a Million Woes for an Error." Jászi comments: "According
to this distinguished author the whole dangerous Magyar-Rumanian controversy
was due to a historical error committed by the Italian scholar Bonfini who, in a
famous book written in the fifteenth century at the court of the great Hungarian
king, Matthias (himself of Rumanian origin), made the thoughtless remark that
the Rumanians of Transylvania are the remnants of the Roman population of the
ancient Dacia under Trajan. The book of Bonfini had a wide circulation and in
the eighteenth century fell into the hands of some Rumanian youths who completely lost their heads and, animated by the fallacious myth of having an older
and nobler origin than the Magyars, claimed equal rights with them. This doctrine,
however, was erroneous because the Rumanians did not come into the country
until 1182 and therefore cannot have the same rights as the Magyars. Now Dr.

the original inhabitants withdrew to the stronghold of the Carpathians and there preserved their ways and customs, for even today
the villagers there wear Dacian dress and build their homes just as
they did when the Emperor Trajan found them.

The populace lived at that period in patriarchal organizations,
under the mild paternal authority of their local leaders. The land
was held in common. *Voevodes* ("captains of armies"), or at still
earlier date, *knezes* (lesser chiefs), were the terms used by the
Roumanians for their *domni,* elected or hereditary, who administered justice and even led them in war. The people and their local
leaders did not make claims to political independence from the domination of the Asiatic and Slavic invaders in the northern Danube
basin. This explains partly why their more developed neighbors
failed to pay much attention to them and why no more detailed
records were left. When the authority of the Magyar chiefs, who
had become apostolic kings, was extended in the Transylvanian up-
land, the Roumanian leaders could no longer maintain themselves.

In 1224 the Hungarian king Andreaş II granted special privileges to little groups of Germans, settled in the center of the country
or at its borders. At the same time the Catholic bishopric was
founded in southwestern Moldavia and groups of Magyars, the so-
called Szeklers, were established at the passes of the mountains. At
the other end of the Carpathians the city of Severin was founded in
1230 with a bishop of its own for spreading Catholicism.

This resulted in the Roumanians' first attempt to organize as a
political entity. They had been Christianized from Rome, but they
later established relations with Byzantium and thereafter held to

Karácsonyi was convinced that by his important historical revelations the whole
Magyar-Rumanian conflict would be eliminated, because the Rumanians instructed
by him concerning the real facts, namely, that they were in the Hungarian state
only for the short period of 800 years and that they hadn't so distinguished a
pedigree as that light-minded Italian had asserted, would be brought to their
senses and would recognize that they can have only a subordinate rôle in Hungary." It is worth while to quote also the following: "In this manner this serious
and scholarly man and with him the feudal society conceived the complicated
economic, social, and psychological problem of nationality struggles to be exclusively an issue of historical right, accepting the naïve theory that the Rumanian
went into the Revolution in consequence of the erroneous teaching of Bonfini.
(By the way, the historical thesis of Karácsonyi is more than doubtful. Besides,
the Slav inhabitants of Hungary constituted the earliest population of the country
and therefore the theory of 'historical right' expressed by Karácsonyi would have
meant a Slav hegemony in Hungary!)" Quoted by permission of the University
of Chicago Press, publishers.

the Greek-Orthodox faith. The spread of Catholicism around 1290 forced many leading families to leave Transylvania, who established the two principalities of "Muntenia" (Mountain Land), commonly known as Wallachia and Moldavia. Wallachia lay compactly between the Carpathian Mountains and the Danube; Moldavia extended eastward from the Carpathians toward the Dniester River.

The beginning of independent Wallachia dates from the second half of the thirteenth century. The province was a fief of the Hungarian kings of the House of Arpád. The internal difficulties of Hungary gave to Basarab, who ruled as vassal of Hungary over the province of Oltenia and whose dynasty firmly established the Roumanian state, an opportunity to free it from Hungarian domination. The Hungarian kings attempted to reduce Basarab again to dependency on Hungary, but the Wallachian princes were for the most part able to defend their independence until the fourteenth century, though occasionally they acknowledged Hungarian overlordship.

The second Roumanian principality, Moldavia, was founded in the period of retreat of the Tartars, who had occupied the country for a century (1241–1345). The region enjoyed national autonomy. King Louis of Hungary wanted to extend his dominions beyond the Carpathians. The defense of the territory was intrusted to the Roumanian Prince Dragoş and his son, Sas. About 1360, another Roumanian prince, Bogdan, also from Maramureş, decided to follow the example of Basarab, and at the death of Sas he snatched the heritage from the sons of the dead leader. He became the first independent Prince of Moldavia.

About a century afterwards, both principalities were rent by internal struggles. The rivals often called in foreign aid—Hungarians, Poles, and Turks. Then two men appeared who dominated their epoch: Vlad the Impaler (1456–62) in Wallachia, and Ştefan the Great (1457–1504) in Moldavia.

Wallachia acknowledged the suzerainty of the Sultan in 1393. In 1411 the country had to submit to further tribute, on the basis of which the relations between Turkey and Roumania rested until 1877. Vlad came to the Throne three years after the fall of Constantinople and was able to oppose the Turk for a few years. Then the Turkish domination prevailed.

Ştefan the Great fought during his long reign for the independence of his country against the Turks, the Hungarians, and the Poles. In those times of the fearful attacks of the Turks he was the only bulwark that stayed the onslaughts against Christianity. But, disappointed, on his deathbed Ștefan advised his son Bogdan to make voluntary submission to the Turkish suzerainty.

A long period of decadence followed in each principality. A series of worthless princes fought each other. Following the victorious battle of Mohács (1526) the Turks began to encroach more and more openly upon Roumanian territory and to interfere in the elections of the princes.

But the same century was fortunate in another sphere. Roumanian culture did not follow in the wake of political decay. Intense activity was displayed in the monasteries, which gave to Roumania her first literary monuments. Books of liturgy, theological treatises, commentaries, etc., were composed. The first printing press was set up. A similar fertile religious activity was noticeable in Transylvania. Protestants tried to attract the Roumanian peasants by publishing religious books in Roumanian. The famous monastery of Argeș was built. Even today it attracts students for its paintings, which are of surpassing artistic value.

At the end of the sixteenth century, one of the most important figures of Roumanian history appears on the scene: Mihaiu (Michael) the Brave (1593–1601) succeeded for a brief space of time in uniting and freeing all the Roumanian provinces—Moldavia, Wallachia, and Transylvania. The documents of the time speak of him as "Prince of the whole land of Hungro-Wallachia, of Transylvania, and of Moldavia." To him goes the glory of uniting all of Roumania under one scepter, as it never was again till 1918. The great emotional significance which attaches to his name and his exploits is readily seen in the following quotation from Professor Bănescu: "By uniting under his sceptre the three sister countries Michael for a moment unconsciously realized the dream which in later days the Rumanians greatly cherished."

With Mihaiu the Brave and his contemporaries in Moldavia the old national dynasties passed and the era of decay commenced. At first the Sultans were contented to make the provinces tributary, permitting them to select their own princes, religion, laws, and institutions. But gradually the situation grew worse. Corruption and intrigues became capital factors in the choice and election of the rulers. The lower classes groaned under the exorbitant taxes. The nobles depended upon the good will of influential officials at Constantinople.

The principalities of Moldavia and Wallachia contained at the end of the sixteenth century only about half of the Roumanian nation. The second half lived on the other side of the Carpathians, in Transylvania. This second half, peasant for the most part, was undergoing similar hardships. The dissatisfied nobles of Transylvania were leaving the territory and thus depriving the masses of the Roumanian population of all moral and political support. In addition, a part of the nobility had already been won over by their Hungarian masters. The subsequent denationalization prevented the weak Roumanian remnants from asserting their claims against the Magyar upper classes.

Another factor, as has been said, in Transylvanian history was the existence side by side, almost from earliest times, of four nations, viz., the Szeklers, the Magyars, the Saxons, and the Roumanians. The Magyar and Saxon lords kept the Roumanians in strict feudal subjection. Frequent revolutions (1387, 1437, 1514) were useless and only made their situation worse.

Occasionally some of the Trans-Carpathian Wallachian and Moldavian princes tried to improve the lot of their compatriots in Transylvania. The Hungarian kings were in good relations with a part of the nobility there and frequently granted them feudal holdings. Thus the nobles assumed the right to intervene in the affairs of their feudal lands, from time to time protected the political and religious interests of their subjects, and aided in the exchange of Greek-Orthodox priests, who went to Moldavia and Wallachia for their ordination. This policy marks the beginning of the first consciousness of national unity on the part of the Trans-Carpathian and Transylvanian Roumanians. Thus was produced and encouraged a feeling of unity and of one national culture on both sides of the Carpathian Mountains.

The reign of Mihaiu is the culminating point in the mediaeval history of Roumania. Several Wallachian and Moldavian princes tried to follow in Mihaiu's footsteps, but in vain, for their countries were headed for political and cultural decadence under Turkish influence.

At the end of the seventeenth century the Porte was intervening more and more in the administration of the principalities. The freedom of the elections of the princes was being gradually restricted; the dubious policy of Constantin Brăncoveanu (1688–1714), in Wallachia, and the rebellion of his Moldavian contemporary, Dimitrie Cantemir (1710–11), led by the Porte to assume the right to appoint the ruling princes. The provinces became mere Turkish dependencies. In order to get as much money as possible out of the country, the Porte farmed out the administration to rich Greeks of Phanar, merchants and bankers inhabiting the quarter of Phanar or lighthouse quarter of Constantinople, the so-called Phanariotes. They were not called *voevodes,* but simply *gospodars* (administrators). These Greek applicants for the Throne had to pay great sums for the appointment and when on the Throne were naturally determined to get as much as possible from the country. The Porte, in turn, changed the Phanariote rulers very frequently to increase its income. For example, from 1716 to 1821 Wallachia had 37 and Moldavia 33 *gospodars.*

It is true that the principalities enjoyed far greater privileges than Serbia and other Turkish provinces. There were always a local administration, local law-courts, and a local law-code. But the Phanariote period, which lasted from 1711 (1716) to 1821, was a heavy economic strain upon the provinces. The anti-Greek hatred engendered by the financial exactions still remains in Roumania today. Many *boiars* and peasants emigrated at that period. The high clergy were chosen from among the Greek priests only. Commerce and business went into the hands of the Greeks, Armenians, and Jews. Greek culture also brought the many Oriental customs which we still meet in Roumania today. The literary movement, which had been so active under the last national princes, almost disappeared, and only a few chroniclers continued to write the sad events of their time but did not reach the high level of their predecessors.

An occasional Greek ruler tried to improve the condition of the peasantry. For example, the reforms of Constantin Mavrocordat, about 1750, allowed the serfs to buy their liberty and limited the amount of produce and the number of days of work which their lords could demand.

The rule of the Phanariotes also marks the loss of two important provinces, Bukovina[4] and Bessarabia.

---

[4] Many races have in turn occupied this forest land, lying about the headwaters of the Seiret, the Prut, and the Moldava. Before 1775 Bukovina formed a part of Moldavia, without any special name. The name of Bukovina (meaning "forest of beech") was given to this part of Moldavia by the Austrians following its annexation by the Treaty of Kuchuk-Kainardji of May 12, 1774, notwithstanding the protests of the Moldavian *boiars.* It was constituted an autonomous province, was later incorporated with Galicia (1786–90), and then once again its autonomy

This was a period dominated by the problem of the Turks. Austria and Russia were each willing to join in driving the Turk out of the principalities, but desired to substitute their own rule for that of the Porte. Russia especially was to become a dangerous neighbor. She was drawing nearer and nearer to Roumania at the end of the seventeenth century, and was to exercise a grave influence on Roumanian destiny. Thus it happened that the weakened principalities became a prey to the ambitions of the neighboring states. The Peace of Passarowitz (1718) gave Oltenia (Wallachia west of the Olt) and the Banat to Austria. The ambition of Austria to annex all Roumania was checked by Russia, who began to entertain the notion of having the principalities under Russian protection. But in the Peace of Belgrade (1739) Austria had to restore Oltenia and Russian Moldavia, the *boiars* of which had made formal acceptance of Russian suzerainty on condition of autonomy. During the Russo-Turkish War of 1768–74, the Russian armies overran the principalities. And although by the Treaty of Kutschuk-Kainardji (1774) Turkey recovered Wallachia and Moldavia, and Austria received Bukovina, which she held until 1918, Russia secured a position which made her the acknowledged protector of the principalities, and obliged the Porte to give promise of protection to the Christian religion. After that the oppressed minorities naturally looked to the Slav giant as their active champion. The Russian Minister Resident at Constantinople was now given the power to intercede in favor of the principalities, and the first Russian Consul, in domineering attitude, appeared at Iaşi and Bucharest. In 1802 Russia obtained a decree from the Porte by which every *gospodar* was to hold office for at least seven years unless the Russian Minister was satisfied that there were sufficient grounds for his deposition.

Finally, the Russo-Turkish War, 1806–12, was ended through the peace signed at Bucharest by the Turks, who ceded to Russia the eastern half of Moldavia, the region between the rivers Prut and Dniester, called then Bessarabia (after its southern part, which had

was restored. At the end of the Napoleonic Wars, the territory was again united with Galicia for administrative purposes. The Roumanians were denationalized, and commerce and farming passed into the hands of foreigners, chiefly Jews from Galicia. The immigration of Ruthenes, Poles, and Germans was encouraged. However, certain ties of intercourse had persisted between the *boiars* who had emigrated and those who had remained in the territory, and this facilitated the Roumanian national movement of the nineteenth century and its penetration into Bukovina.

formerly been under the sway of the Basarabs). The Russian protectorate proved to be even more oppressive than that of the Turks,
though after the annexation the Russian Government allowed the
inhabitants a high degree of autonomy in their local administration and put Scarlat Sturdza, a member of an old Moldavian
boiar family, at the head of the temporary Russian government.
But after 1825 the autonomy was rapidly reduced and was suppressed entirely in 1828. Steps were taken to encourage the immigration of compact groups of Russians, Bulgars, Germans, etc.,
in order to denationalize the territory and aid in its economic development. The Roumanians could hold a compact position in the
middle of Bessarabia[5] only.

There was, nevertheless, one cloud with a silver lining in all this
overhanging shadow of subjection of the principalities. The Phanariotes, usurious and tyrannical as they were, brought with them into
this rude country all the leavening influence of French literature and
culture. They were, in that manner, the precursors of modern Roumania much as the Norman nobles were the civilizers of England
after the Conquest. By example and by precept they encouraged
education and learning, and the more fortunate Roumanians were
not slow to follow. The contact with French civilization roused in
them the sleeping Latin spirit, and the younger generation flocked
to Paris, drawn there also by liberal ideas. In addition, some com-

[5] Bessarabian history and her present status have been discussed in numerous
publications, most of them being written from a propagandist standpoint. The
following might be mentioned: A. Babel, *La Bessarabie* (Paris, 1927); C. U.
Clark, *Bessarabia* (New York, 1927); H. F. Armstrong, "The Bessarabian Dis-
pute," in *Foreign Affairs,* 1924, II, 662–67; J. Okhotnikov & N. Batchinsky, *La
Bessarabie et la paix Européene* (Paris, 1927); C. Rakovsky, *Roumania and
Bessarabia* (London, 1925); C. Uhlig, *Die Bessarabische Frage* (Breslau, 1926);
A. Popovici, *The Political Status of Bessarabia* (Washington, 1931); I. G.
Pelivan, *Les Droits de Roumains sur la Bessarabie* (Bucureşti, 1919); *L'Union
de la Bessarabie a la mère patrie la Roumanie* (Paris, 1919); J. Toporul, *La
Situation de la Bessarabie et de Bukovine comme elle se présente au point de vue
du droit public et international* (Léopol, 1926); etc. From the historical standpoint, we do know that Trajan's conquest of Dacia in the second century did not
extend to Bessarabia. Then for centuries, like the rest of eastern Europe, Bessarabia suffered from barbaric invasions and occupations, to emerge from the Dark
Ages with a distinct Roumanian life and culture as part of the domains of the
reigning House of Basarab, to which it owes its modern name. In the fifteenth
century Ştefan the Great of Moldavia subdued Wallachia and absorbed the territory between the Pruth and Dniester, whose Black Sea littoral came under Turkish
rule before the end of his reign. The Turks called their part Budjak, and this,
with the Moldavian northern part, the whole of what is known as Bessarabia,
passed to Russia.

Carol II, King of Roumania

pensation in culture came at this time also from Transylvania under the impulse of the national conscience, which had been awakened there among the Roumanians.

The period of national regeneration, which culminated in the proclamation of the independent Kingdom of Roumania, was begun by the Transylvanian Roumanians. This branch of the Roumanian nation tried to improve its material, political, and cultural lot by occasional but futile revolutions. A number of them, in order to improve their sad plight, entered into the so-called "Union with Rome" (1700), passing over to the Catholic Church, and a Catholic bishopric was instituted for them with its see at Blaj. This new church made every endeavor to raise the culture of its people. Theological schools were created at Blaj, and thence the pupils passed to the high Catholic institutions, to "Saint Barbara" of Vienna, and the colleges of Rome. There they had the opportunity to study original documents, and to learn from authentic sources the history of their country, with all the unity of their race implied. From their labors sprang the Transylvanian school and a cultural renaissance which, combined with the influence of the French Revolution, finally urged the Roumanians to revolt against their rulers with such violence that they secured (1821) the recall of the Phanariotes and gained the nomination of native-born princes as rulers.

The contemporary general situation was eloquently described by Dr. R. W. Seton-Watson:

What could be more gloomy and uncompromising than their situation in the middle of the eighteenth century, the two principalities ground under the heel of the Sublime Porte and of his jackals, the corrupt Phanariot Princes; the Roumanians of Transylvania subjected by the dominant Magyars to all the rigours of political and religious helotry? Yet at the very nadir of the national fortunes the voice of History sounded in their ears. A handful of priests trained in the despised Uniate rite which the Jesuits had devised for their further enthralment, saw with eager eyes the array of captive figures on Trajan's Column in Rome, and invoked memories of ancient Dacia and their Roman ancestry. . . . . The historical chroniclers composed by the younger Micu, Sincai and Peter Maior, uncritical and even fantastic as they were, and only circulating in manuscript owing to unfavorable political conditions, none the less secure to their authors the right to rank among the founders of Roumania.[6]

[6] *The Historian as a Political Force in Central Europe,* an inaugural lecture, November 22, 1922, published by the School of Slavonic Studies, University of London, King's College, 1923, p. 29. Quoted by permission.

The outstanding Transylvanian leader, who dared to use his position to protest publicly against the oppression of the Roumanians, was Bishop Ion Innocent Micu, "Baron Klein." The Austrian Government thought that he would prove a docile instrument in the task of appeasing the Wallachians, but this was not the case. In 1735 he made his proclamation to his people, whose sole leader he considered himself to be:

We have been the hereditary masters of this land of kings since the time of Trajan, long before the Saxon nation came into Transylvania, and we have to this day in it whole estates and villages which belong to us. We have been crushed by burdens of every description and by age-long misery inflicted by those who were more powerful than we.[7]

The efforts of Micu were not appreciated by the Hungarian leaders, who answered by insults and false assumptions to the petitions of the bishop for granting to the Roumanians the status of a constitutional nation. For example, the Transylvanian Diet replied in 1725 that there was no Union,

for these Wallachs are altogether ignorant and confirmed schismatics. . . . . They cannot be called a nationality, for they are nothing but a horde of peasants, all serfs, tramps, fugitives, half-savage if not altogether so, given over to all evils and crimes, hostile to the Catholics and the Catholic faith.[8]

The only result of the efforts of Klein was the recognition of the Transylvanian Roumanians as "natives" at the insistence of Maria Theresa. But practically it meant very little, because the Magyars and Germans were able to continue, by various means, their special privileges.

The growing antagonism between the Habsburgs and the Magyars brought in its wake some improvements. Joseph II was somewhat popular among the Roumanians for his reforms, especially his decree of August 22, 1785, abolishing serfdom, though this social right was lost again in 1790. Joseph was shocked by the abuses of the revolt of Nicolae Ursu Horea, who suffered the horrible penalty of the wheel. In 1791 the Emperor received favorably the famous memorandum of Roumanian wrongs, the *Supplex Libellus Valachorum*. This "book" was the foundation, until the World War, of national Roumanian demands. It maintained that the Roumanians

---

[7] N. Iorga, *A History of Roumania,* p. 205. Quoted by permission of T. Fisher Unwin, London, publisher.

[8] Quoted in C. U. Clark, *Greater Roumania,* p. 134.

were the oldest inhabitants of Transylvania and protested that while
being the most numerous of the population, they carried the heaviest
burdens of the land without any rights; to equalize conditions they
demanded that their clergy and laity should be treated on a par with
the Hungarians and the Germans; that Roumanian officials should
be employed in the Roumanian districts; that the Roumanian language should be used altogether in Roumanian districts and concurrently in others; and that there should be a Roumanian Assembly.

The Government of Vienna, however, referred the Roumanian
representatives to the Transylvanian Diet at Cluj, which, as might
be expected, rejected the demands *in toto*.

But the growth of nationalistic consciousness was evident. Under
the influence of the writings of the "knight errants in the service of
their national ideals" the pride of the subjected people was stimulated. Samuel Micu, Gheorghe Șincai, and Petru Maior were the
national awakeners.[9] The late Professor H. M. Stephens of the
University of California calls the movement "one of the most remarkable facts in modern European history, and it is largely due to
the labours of its [Roumanian] historians."[10]

These new leaders did not limit their work to Transylvania only.
Many of them settled on the soil of Moldavia and Wallachia with
the express purpose of awakening this second branch of their nation,
which was still dominated by Greek culture. Thus, for example,
Gheorghe Lazăr settled at Bucharest in 1816 and founded the first
Roumanian school. But the first steps were hindered by suspicions
and hostility, especially in religious circles, to whom the innovations
seemed dangerously revolutionary. Years of patient effort were required before a part of the Roumanians of the provinces understood the efforts of Lazăr and began to found schools with teachers
imported from Transylvania. The Roumanian language, which so
far had been the language of the peasant and of the lower classes,
was becoming more appreciated and more widely used in the principalities.[11]

[9] For a sketch of Roumanian literary history, see C. U. Clark, *Greater Roumania*, pp. 351–74, and L. Feraru, *The Development of Rumanian Poetry,* The
Institute of Rumanian Culture, New York, 1929.

[10] "Modern Historians and Small Nationalities," in *Contemporary Review,*
1887, LII, 107–21.

[11] The movement had its subsequent repercussion in the Bukovina. Certain
nobles, especially the Hurmuzachi family, took over the Roumanian tradition. Sev-

In 1821 there broke out in the Roumanian principalities the Greek revolution under the leadership of the *Hetairai,* the Greek brotherhood for the liberation of Greece from Turkey. Its leader was a Greek aristocrat named Alexandru Ypsilanti. On March 6, 1821, his force crossed the Prut and occupied Bucharest.

But he was disappointed in the Roumanians. He had summoned them to rise against the Sultan, hoping that religious motives would outweigh national feelings. Tudor Vladimirescu raised the banner of revolt at the head of some peasant bands, but the attempt of Ypsilanti to attract him to his side was a failure. Under the circumstances the revolting Greeks and Roumanians were both dispersed and the revolution came to an end. But the outbreak was not without good results. Turkey placed national princes again on the Throne of the principalities.

While the Greek influence was declining in the principalities, that of Russia was growing. The Phanariotes had been dangerous mostly economically; the Slav giant loomed as a future danger to Roumanian national existence. However, since the Turks were a more concrete and immediate menace, the Roumanians welcomed the Russian soldiers in 1828, when another war broke out between Russia and Turkey. The Treaty of Adrianople (1829) granted virtual autonomy to the principalities, the right of Turkey as suzerain being limited to monetary tributes and the right of investiture of the princes, who were to be elected by national assemblies for life. But the most important point was that the Sultan agreed to ratify all the administrative measures which had been drawn up during the Russian occupation. The Russians were entitled to keep a garrison in the principalities until the full payment of the war indemnity by the Sultan. Thus the occupation was prolonged to 1834, and lasted in all some six years. All the time the utmost efforts were made to establish the influence of the Tsar upon a permanent basis. An enlightened Russian general, Count Kisseleff, whose influence was felt in the improvement of the bureaucracy and the law courts, administered "Règlement Organique," the new constitutional law. It

eral leaders of the uprising at Iași in 1848, including those who subsequently shaped Roumania, Kogălniceanu, Cuza, and the poet Vasile Alexandri, found a refuge at the seat of the Hurmuzachi family. But the subsequent reactionary measures of the Austrian Government forced more spirited intellectuals to emigrate to Roumania, and the National Party, composed of landowners, officials, and members of liberal professions, could muster little resistance to the denationalizing policy of the Austrian Government.

provided for a Legislative Assembly composed of *boiars* and clergy and a special assembly to choose the prince in each province. But when Kisseleff left the country, "the liking for Russia passed away to be replaced finally by the two sentiments which always most swayed the Rumanian heart: love for their country, and affection towards France."[12]

French culture was planted in Roumania by the Phanariotes, who had to know this diplomatic language and usually employed French secretaries and tutors. As French culture was popular in Russia during the Russian occupation, French began to be spoken in Roumania by the Russian officials, who could not understand the native language.

The "Règlement Organique" meant in reality that the Roumanians exchanged for the phantom of Turkish suzerainty the stern reality of a Russian protectorate. Politically, it meant the continuation of Russian supervision over the administration of the provinces. The measure was not really a constitution in our modern sense. The prince and the *boiars* were made to act as a check upon each other. The nation was separated into two sharply divided classes—the nobles and the people. The administration was left entirely in the hands of the *boiars,* who paid no taxes and had the privilege of occupying all state positions. All financial burdens rested upon the peasant and small tradesman.

But there were also practical benefits derived from the Russian occupation. For the first time Roumanian law recognized the principle that some limit must be set to litigation; magistrates were made irremovable, sanitation was enforced, new tribunals were created, and a petty court was established in every village.

To aid the political and cultural renaissance, the economic development of the principalities was going on apace. The Treaty of Adrianople opened the Black Sea to international traffic, allowing the agricultural produce of Roumania to find an outlet into Western Europe, which immediately began to take interest in Roumanian conditions.

National sentiment was quickening. The "Règlement Organique" became the subject of frequent attacks. In 1829 one of the Roumanian revolutionists, Ion Eliade Rădulescu, founded the *Curierul*

---

[12] D. Mitrany, "Rumania: Her History and Politics," in Nevill Forbes, A. J. Toynbee, D. Mitrany, D. G. Hogarth, *The Balkans,* p. 267.

Românesc (Roumanian Courier). In 1833 Câmpineanu reorganized the *Societate Filarmonică,* which disguised political activities as cultural interests. The youth, coming from the schools and higher institutions, dreamed about nationalistic ideals and political freedom. The conviction that the Roumanians were the descendants of Trajan's legions, the sons of Mihaiu the Brave and of Ştefan the Great, who were to return the old glory to their land, to gain its freedom and unify all the national branches, found reflection in the writings of Rădulescu, Dumitru Bolintineanu, and Nicolae Bălcescu.

These young nationalists began to emphasize the doctrine that Russia, with her Bessarabian policy, and Austria, with her stranglehold upon Transylvania, Bukovina, and the Banat, were the real enemies of Roumanian nationalism, and that Turkey, satisfied with nominal control of Moldavia and Wallachia, was much less to be feared. The House of Habsburg and the Tsar were growing in strength, while the "Sick Man of Europe" could put forth only a palsied hand to stay the rise of the Roumanians into a new nation.

Russia and Austria were not unaware of this shift in attitude. They were uneasy about these revolutionary activities. But their repressive measures only made matters worse. They attempted, however, to strike directly at the root of the trouble. Shortly before 1848 the higher institutions of learning of Bucharest and Iaşi were dissolved. But the movement found another means of expression.

Prompted by the magnanimous ideas of the young men who had studied in the West, an advanced reform party arose. A strong Unionist Party succeeded in 1847 in abolishing the tariff walls between Wallachia and Moldavia, and tried to secure the election of Sturdza also to the throne of Wallachia. The undercurrent of uneasiness and the desire for recognition of the national integrity and unity of the principalities steadily increased. When the revolution broke out in 1848, it spread rapidly over the country, but was put down quickly because of the lack of any organized or definite program on the part of the nationalists. The Moldavian insurrection was broken up by the Russian troops; in Wallachia the masses were won over by the promise of extensive agrarian reforms, but the landowners were alienated and the flight of Prince Bibescu, who refused to accept the project of a constitution drawn up by the revolutionaries, brought Russo-Turkish intervention. The provisional revolutionary government did not last long and a Turkish army quelled the movement in Bucharest after a fight with the fire brigade, which was then the only organized force in Wallachia. The reactionary settlement of Balta Liman of 1849 provided for the occupation of the principalities by the Turkish and Russian troops. However, the newly appointed princes, Barbu Ştirbey in Wallachia and Grigore Ghica in Moldavia, continued the work of restoration. The joint military occupation continued until 1851, and was followed in 1853–54 by Russian occupation alone. The Russians retired in June 1854, but the Austrians took their place until the conclusion of the Crimean War.

The expatriated leaders who later were to play the most important part in the political history of Roumania, though scattered throughout the capitals of Western Europe, worked unceasingly for the cause. I. C. Brătianu,[13] C. A. Rosetti, Ion Ghica, and others endeavored to influence French public opinion in favor of the autonomy of the principalities. In this they received the enthusiastic and invaluable assistance of such sympathetic Frenchmen as Edgar Qiunet, Michelet, Saint-March Girardin, and others, who took their part and pleaded the Roumanian cause.

The Transylvanian revolution was a bloodier one. The Roumanian peasants had long remembered the torture of Horea, whose body had been broken on the wheel at Alba-Iulia in 1784. Their opportunity came when the Hungarians revolted against the Austrian Emperor in 1848, and they took up arms under Avram Iancu against their oppressors. However, when Vienna crushed the Hungarians with Russian help the Roumanians asked vainly for their rights, and were sacrificed again to the Hungarians. In the subsequent period they organized strongly their cultural life through Andreiu Şaguna, Orthodox metropolitan at Sibiu (Hermannstadt).

It was Roumanian good fortune that the views of Napoleon III of France coincided with the nationalistic principle propounded by the Roumanian agitators abroad. At the Paris Congress of 1856 the union of the principalities was suggested as a barrier against the Russian expansion. Finally, the treaty of March 30, 1856, gave back to Moldavia three of her districts in southern Bessarabia, at the mouth of the Danube. Great pains were taken in the treaty to define the position of the principalities as being "under the Suzerainty of the Porte and under the guarantee of the contracting Pow-

[13] I. C. Brătianu, *Mémoire sur l'Empire d'Autriche dans la question d'Orient,* Paris (Impr. de Voisvenel), 1855; *Mémoire sur la situation de la Moldo-Valachie depuis le Traité de Paris,* Paris, 1857.

ers," no one of which was to exercise any "exclusive right" of protection. A European commission was to regulate freedom of navigation on the Danube. Article 23 of the treaty stipulated that the principalities were to decide on their future themselves. For that purpose two *divans ad hoc* (assemblies) were elected, whose wishes were to be embodied, by a European commission, in a report for consideration by the Congress. In spite of the corrupt Turkish and Austrian influence, the assemblies met in 1857 and voted clauses summing up their national claims, the first of which was the union of both countries to form a single state.[14] On the basis of these desires, the second Congress of Paris of 1858 decided that Moldavia and Wallachia should henceforth form the "United Principalities," but were to have two princes, two national assemblies, and two governments, admitting only as common institutions a central commission at Focshani for the preparation of laws of common interest, a sole Supreme Court of Appeal, a customs, telegraphic, and monetary union, and the union, in special cases, of the armies of the two principalities.

It seems that this detailed scheme of government, which neither united nor separated the two peoples, for the time being worked out very well from the standpoint of the local authorities. But the National Party was determined to elude all the restrictions on complete union by electing the same person as prince of both principalities. This plan adopted, they selected Colonel Alexandru Ion I. Cuza as the leader to occupy both positions. His election on January 17 in Moldavia and on February 5, 1859, in Wallachia was the next step taken by the principalities toward realizing their union. The Porte appealed to the powers. A Conference of Paris, which met in April 1859, stated that the Convention of Paris had been violated, but recognized the double election of Cuza as an exceptional case. Cuza thus became ruler, but the union was not recognized by his sovereign, the Sultan, until later. In 1861 the powers and the Porte, by a firman of December 2, recognized the union for the life of Prince Cuza, and the union of the principalities was formally proclaimed.

[14] For an excellent discussion of diplomacy of this period see T. W. Riker, "The Concert of Europe and Moldavia in 1857," in *English Historical Review,* 1927, XLII, 227–44; T. W. Riker, "The Pact of Osborne," in *American Historical Review,* 1929, XXXIV, 237–49 (reprinted in *Roumania,* April 1929, pp. 53–66); W. G. East, *The Union of Moldavia and Wallachia.*

The reign of Cuza lasted seven years (1859–66). Certain of his drastic reforms stirred up much opposition. In general, the Prince accomplished two great reforms in his reign. First of all, the secularization of the great estates of the monasteries, in 1863, recovered for the state as much as a fifth part of the whole country, which had been alienated into the hands of the Greek monks through the old custom of dedicating the monasteries of the country to the other great monasteries of the East. Secondly, with the help of his Premier, Kogălniceanu, he promulgated on August 26, 1864, the Rural Law, which made the peasants the owners of the land they cultivated. Furthermore, Cuza introduced a series of educational reforms. The Universities of Iaşi and Bucharest were founded in 1860 and 1864, respectively.

The strong opposition of the ruling classes forced Cuza to dissolve the National Assembly in 1864 and to introduce universal suffrage in an attempt to use the peasant vote against the other fractious political parties. But the good intentions of Cuza failed to materialize and, as we shall see in the chapter on "The Agrarian Reform," the reform benefited the upper classes more than the peasants. The personal vices of the Prince, the unconstitutionality of his acts, and financial distress forced Cuza to abdicate on February 23, 1866.

Since among the wishes expressed by the *ad hoc* assemblies there was a provision asking for the enthronement of a foreign Western dynasty, in order to prevent the possible pretensions of the old princely dynasties, the parliament immediately proclaimed Count Philip of Flanders as Prince of Roumania. He, however, declined the honor. A new election was then held by the parliament which, confirmed by a plebiscite, declared for Prince Charles of Hohenzollern-Sigmaringen. Brătianu went up to Düsseldorf to offer him the Crown, and, on its acceptance, accompanied the young Prince on his incognito journey to Roumania. On May 8, 1866, Prince Carol landed at Turnu-Severin, "the very place where, nearly eighteen centuries before, the Emperor Trajan alighted and founded the Roumanian nation."

Carol was presented with a difficult internal situation. The economic condition of his people was miserable as a result of the former régime's shortsightedness, waste, and negligence. New reforms were needed, but the treasury was empty. The Paris Convention of 1858 was still valid, and Turkey was unwilling to give up her privileges accruing from the commercial treaties. The hasty reforms of Cuza resulted in an unruly spirit. Carol's German spirit of discipline and order could not immediately find satisfactory expression. Furthermore, Carol was new and could not exercise much influence over the governing class. However, he began his rule by appointing a strong cabinet under Lascăr Catargiu, a Moldavian Conservative, who held the positions of Premier and Minister of the Interior; I. C. Brătianu (Liberal, Wallachian) became Minister of Finance; Petru Mavrogheni (Conservative, Moldavian), Minister of Foreign Affairs; Ion Cantacuzino (Center, Wallachian), Minister of Justice; Constantin A. Rosetti (Extreme Left, Wallachian), Minister of Cults and Public Instructions; General Ion Ghica (Right, Center, Moldavian), Minister of War; and Dimitrie A. Sturdza (Center, Moldavian), Minister of Agriculture, Commerce, and Public Works.[15]

A new constitution was unanimously approved by the constitutional convention on July 11, 1866. It resembled the constitution of Belgium more nearly than any other, and was framed by a constituent assembly elected on universal suffrage, and, except for the modifications of 1879 and 1884, was in force until 1923. It provided for a lower house and a senate, and conferred on the prince the right of an absolute and unconditional veto of all legislation. The right of initiative rested either with any chamber or with the prince. The executive power was intrusted to the prince and his ministers, the latter alone being responsible for the acts of the government. Nine executive departments were established.

Of subsequent importance was the provision regarding creed and religion. It provided that "religion should not be a bar to naturalization. As for the Israelites, a special law is to regulate their gradual admission to citizenship." The opposition used the anti-Jewish sentiment to force the convention to state in the constitution that only foreigners belonging to Christian sects could acquire citizenship.

The Coalition Cabinet resigned after the ratification of the constitution, and Ion Ghica was appointed the new Premier.

The political parties of Roumania were from the outset personal parties, supporting their candidates for the Throne. In the Phanariote period a national party grew up, opposing Greek influence. Its various factions came to be known as "Russian," "Austrian," etc.,

[15] C. U. Clark, *Greater Roumania*, p. 67.

according to the states to which these factions looked for support
of their aims. With the accession of Cuza the whole problem
changed and the problems of internal politics created the Liberals
and the Conservatives. Cuza failed to affiliate with either party, and
both parties combined to depose him. When Prince Carol began
his reign, both parties formed a sort of *union sacré* and formed a
coalition ministry for the introduction of the new constitution. After
that the political strife broke out again. The Liberals, led by C. A.
Rosetti and Ion Brătianu, advocated radical reforms. The Conservatives—the Whites—were headed by Lascăr Catargiu and used all
their power to oppose the liberal measures of the opposing party.

Very soon the cabinets were succeeding each other in rapid
succession. Prince Carol became a subject of frequent attacks, the
politicians hammering at his foreign origin. The existence of famine
and cholera added to the difficulties. In March 1867 the lower house,
by a majority of three, passed the laconic resolution: "The Chamber
inflicts a vote of blame on the Government." Crețulescu, a moderate
Conservative, became the Premier, and Brătianu entered the government as Minister of the Interior. He soon proved to be the leading
spirit of the cabinet. The reorganization of the army was now
undertaken, and a concession was granted for the construction of
the first Roumanian railway. A less judicious decree was a measure
directed against all vagabond foreigners, actually aimed at the Jews.
Brătianu, though immensely popular, had to resign with the whole
cabinet in July 1869. In September, Prince Carol married Princess
Elizabeth of Wied, more widely known and celebrated under her
literary name of Carmen Sylva. Before the year closed, the army
was reorganized, a rural police was created, and another railway
concession was granted to a foreign syndicate, which subsequently
led to grave political complications.

The Franco-Prussian War nearly forced the abdication of Carol.
Bucharest anti-German street riots of March 1871 led the Prince to
inform the government of his intention to abdicate, but Lascăr
Catargiu's supplications and promises made Carol keep the crown.
By the time the newly elected parliament met in May 1871 the anti-
German feeling had subsided and Catargiu succeeded in uniting the
different sections of the Conservative Party. The Prince was wel-
comed most enthusiastically in the parliament.

The Conservative Ministry under Catargiu lasted until 1876 and
introduced many reforms. The revenues were increased by the stamp

taxes and the tobacco monopoly. The Rural Credit and the Urban Credit Banks with local capital were established. Commercial treaties were concluded with Austria and Russia in 1875. These compacts were of such high political significance to Roumania, then struggling to gain recognition from other states which would solve the indignity of her continued forced tribute to the Porte, that she made heavy economic sacrifices in order to secure the status of "contracting party" with the great states of Austria and Russia. The church became an independent organization through a law establishing the Holy Synod in 1872.

Catargiu's Ministry was succeeded by an administration of General Florescu, and, a month later, by the so-called "Ministry of Conciliation" under Iepureanu, which resigned almost immediately, being unable to stem the tide of popular passion for the impeachment of Catargiu. The Liberal Cabinet of Brătianu, which then came to power, was destined to govern the country through the eventful years of 1877 and 1878.

Russia had long been preparing for a new Balkan war in order to regain her prestige lost in the Crimean War. When a new war broke out between Russia and Turkey in 1877, Roumania concluded a convention with Russia on April 16, 1877, according to which Bucharest promised to the Russian army "free passage through Roumanian territory and the treatment due to a friendly army." Russia, on the other hand, undertook to respect Roumania's political rights, as well as "to maintain and defend her actual integrity." However, when Roumanian aid was offered to Russia the Roumanian Government was told that no help was necessary and that Roumania could continue to exist only "in the shadow of the Russian army."

But when the Russians suffered two disastrous defeats at Plevna, the Tsar called on Carol for help. Prince Carol took over the supreme command of both armies, and Plevna capitulated in November 1877. Meanwhile on May 10(22), 1877, the Roumanian Assembly proclaimed the independence of their country, which was recognized by the Treaty of San Stefano and, finally, though upon conditions, by the Treaty of Berlin.

The subsequent behavior of the Russians created a feeling of deep and lasting resentment among the Roumanians. The Treaty of San Stefano of March 3, 1878, recognized Roumanian independence, but created a Greater Bulgaria, which had been given the key to the

Dobrogea, the coveted fortress of Silistra. Furthermore, Roumania
was given to understand that Russia would appropriate Bessarabia.
The Congress of Berlin of 1878 sanctioned the Russian demands.
Roumanian independence was acknowledged by the Treaty of Berlin
on three irritating conditions. For the loss of Bessarabia, Roumania
was forced to console herself with most of the Dobrogea, which was
offered in exchange. Another article of the treaty provided for the
abolition of Article 7 of the Roumanian Constitution, which gave
the right of citizenship to Christians only.[16] As a third condition of
obtaining independence, Bismarck insisted that Roumania should buy
the Roumanian railways, which were owned by German speculators.

When Roumania promised compliance with these provisions,
which she did very reluctantly indeed, she was recognized in return
as an independent principality by the powers enforcing the conditions.

On March 26, 1881, the country assumed, without objection on
the part of any of the powers, the style of a kingdom. On May
22 of the same year, King Carol I was crowned King of Roumania.

---

[16] A specially elected Assembly repealed Article 7 of the Roumanian Constitution on October 18, 1878. It thus became possible for the Roumanian Jews to become naturalized and to hold the land. It was also decided to admit to
naturalization the 883 Jewish soldiers who had served in the war; for civilians a
special vote of the legislature with a two-thirds majority was required for each
individual case. The attitude of the Roumanians was based on their hate of Jewish
shrewdness in gaining control of the land as money-lenders. See F. Rey, "La
question Israélite en Roumanie," in *Revue générale de droit international public*.
1903, X, 460–526; "Un Aspect particulier de la question des minorités: les Israélites
de Roumanie," *ibid.*, 1925, XXXII, 133–62.

CHAPTER II

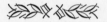

INTERNAL POLICY, 1878–1914

THE internal policy of Roumania during the years 1878–1914 was characterized by efforts to reform and improve internal conditions, both political and economic. Kisseleff, who had administered the principalities from 1829 to 1832, had attempted to bring order out of the chaos rooted in the country from the Turkish domination and the Phanariote rule. The Princes of Wallachia and Moldavia, who had followed him, had made the same effort. The revolution of 1848 interrupted these plans, however, and from that time to 1878 internal improvements were subordinated, on the whole, to foreign and other urgent problems. With the independence of the kingdom now an acknowledged fact, the country could, after 1878, devote its full time to domestic problems.

Up to the World War politics of the kingdom were dominated mostly by Brătianu and his Liberal Party, which had evolved from the National Party of 1848. Only occasionally were the Conservatives at the helm of the state.

Brătianu headed the ministry up to 1888 during the demoralization of the Conservatives, exercising after 1876 an almost dictatorial power. Numerous reforms were introduced. The National Bank, the National Savings Bank, and the Farmers' Credit Bank began their operations in the '80's; building and public works were encouraged. Some changes were introduced into the constitution. Three electoral colleges were formed instead of four, and the number of deputies and senators was considerably increased. Trial by jury was guaranteed for press offenses, except those committed against the royal family and foreign sovereigns; and the payment of members of the parliament during the session was arranged.[1] In

---

[1] These constitutional changes estranged the two leaders of the Liberal Party, Brătianu and Rosetti, the latter considering the new measures too moderate in their democratic character.

1882 and 1885 the Patriarchate of Constantinople recognized the independence of the Roumanian Church and the Catholic Church established an archbishop at Bucharest and a bishop at Iaşi.

The opposition to the Liberal Government became so violent in 1887–88 that the Conservatives threatened a revolution in favor of Prince Bibescu. Brătianu resigned in 1888 as Premier, his fall being partly due to the intrigues of his brother, Dumitru.

From 1888 to 1895, except for a short interval, the country was governed by a coalition of the Old Conservatives under Catargiu and G. G. Cantacuzino and the Junimists, a body of Young Conservatives who took their name from a club formed in Iaşi in 1874 and whose leaders were the intransigeant partisans of the Germans. Chief among the latter group were P. P. Carp (in the words of Professor Iorga "a Junker brought by some chance to the banks of the Danube"), T. Rosetti, and Titu Maiorescu.[2]

Under the Conservative ministries of T. Rosetti (1888–89) and G. Manu (1889–91), the treasury was put on a gold basis and the Roumanian currency was circulated at par. The judicial status was fixed by having judges confirmed in their tenure of office. The state assumed the control of the entire railway system. In 1891 another Conservative Cabinet was formed under Catargiu, which lasted four years. The public debt was converted; several judicial reforms were carried out; foreign capital was invited to participate in the development of the country's resources by the passage of a mining law; a state commercial marine service was established; public instruction reforms were passed; and commercial treaties were concluded.

Brătianu died in 1891; his brother Dumitru lived only one year as the head of the united Liberal Party. Dimitrie A. Sturdza was proclaimed the Liberal leader. He began a campaign in favor of "Roumania for Roumanians." Foreign concessions were denounced. In 1895 his party came into power. Sturdza's Liberal Cabinet (1895–99) toned down its anti-foreign pronouncements, but could not harmonize its own inner dissensions. As a result, the Liberal Party split up into factions called after their leaders—the "Sturdzişti," the "Aurelianişti," and the "Flevişti." A few of the most important measures promised in the Liberal program were passed,

---

[2] The Junimists favored a revision of the communal law in the sense of decentralization, the introduction of a gold standard, and the amelioration of the situation of the peasantry and artisan class, and had a leaning toward the Central Powers.

the reform of public instruction being the most noteworthy. The government finally fell, amid scenes of disorder in Bucharest, its downfall being due largely to a supposed impotence of policy toward the Austro-Hungarian Government on the problem of the Roumanian schools in Transylvania. That very evening, in 1899, the Conservative chief, Lascăr Catargiu, died.

The new Conservative Government of Cantacuzino had to deal with a serious economic and financial crisis, but saved itself by raising a loan in Berlin in 1899. When the Junimists and Carp failed to support the cabinet in February 1901, Sturdza headed the new Liberal administration and averted the impending bankruptcy of Roumania by a policy of strict economy and frugality. The Conservatives returned in January 1905, floated the conversion loan, and had to face the agrarian uprising of 1907 caused by the failure of former laws to free the peasant from the large landowners and by the heavy indebtedness to the Jewish money-lenders. Sturdza's Liberal Cabinet kept office from March 1907 until 1911. It restored order, granted new facilities for agrarian credit, reduced the land tax on small holdings, and abolished the system by which public lands were leased to middlemen. The costs of the reorganization of the army and of the agrarian reform were met by various taxing measures. In 1909 Sturdza had to give up the leadership of his party because of ill health and Ion I. C. Brătianu took his place at the helm of the government until 1911, when he gave way to the Conservative Cabinet of P. P. Carp, whom the death of G. G. Cantacuzino placed at the head of the Conservative Party.

Meanwhile Brătianu's party commenced to search for a new program. The Liberals began to advocate a single electoral college. The Government of Carp was reconstructed, in April 1912, under the critical assaults of the Liberals and of the followers of Take Ionescu. Maiorescu became Premier. Take Ionescu was the most prominent figure of the new cabinet. A clever man, gifted as an orator, he was known as *Gură de aur* (Golden Mouth).

The Government of Maiorescu concluded the victorious peace with Bulgaria. But when the World War broke out, Brătianu was back in office and had a program of numerous reforms, foremost among them being an agrarian law based on the expropriation of large landowners, and universal suffrage; the events of the war, however, forced the nation to devote all its time to foreign affairs and finally to active participation in the great conflict.

CHAPTER III

FOREIGN AFFAIRS, 1878–1914

THE aggressive and ungrateful Russian policy at the Congress of Berlin was a grave mistake, remembered by Roumania ever since. Its direct result was, paradoxically enough, to turn Roumania toward the Central Powers for recognition and friendship, despite the fact that in the final analysis Roumanian foreign policy had to tend toward the future acquisition of the territory inhabited by her nationals in Austria-Hungary. Roumania needed to consolidate her position, and in order to achieve peaceful development of the country she had to acquire the solid foundation of international and peaceful understanding with some great power. No understanding with Russia seemed to be possible for years to come. King Carol naturally remembered his heritage, and his outlook was thoroughly and sympathetically German.

However, the relations with the Austro-Hungarian Monarchy were from the beginning not on too friendly a footing. Bucharest disliked the Austrian diplomacy, which aimed, during the negotiations on the question of the Danube (1881–83), to acquire a preponderant influence on the lower Danube. Side by side with the Danubian Commission established by the Treaty of Paris, first from the Delta of Galaţi, and subsequently at Brăila, the Dual Monarchy —although it did not even own land on the reach of the river— claimed the presidency of the second Commission, to which the supervision of the waters of the Danube from Brăila to Orşova was to be confined.

Furthermore, Austria-Hungary, who, to flatter Roumanian patriotism and initiate the work of friendship, had been the first, in 1875, to consent to the conclusion of a trade convention with her neighbor (then still a vassal of the Porte), would not now make concessions in her favor. Consequently on the Roumanian side an autonomous tariff was applied, inaugurating a customs war. This was hardly likely to draw closer the bonds between the two countries.

On the other hand, the question of the Transylvanian Roumanians did not press immediately upon the Roumanian Government, for it could still be said that "at the most it occupied public opinion to the advantage of the opposition parties when they were at the end of their resources." The formation of a National Roumanian Party in that province had hardly influenced the attitude of the government, though the Roumanians beyond the Transylvanian Mountains felt the growing denationalizing policy of the Hungarians. The "Ausgleich" of 1867 left them entirely at the mercy of the Magyars. The problem of races and languages was henceforth decided in a summary manner, and the Hungarian minority after 1867 was steadily attempting the impossible—the assimilation of the majority. The Magyars were determined to magyarize the Roumanians in Transylvania early and thoroughly, and so refused to make any concessions. The law of 1868, which guaranteed "equal rights of nationalities," was admirable theoretically, but practically it was no more than a dead letter.[1] A large part of the Roumanian intelligentsia kept up the agitation against the oppressive measures and some of the most spirited members migrated to Roumania, where they agitated public opinion.

Dr. Oscar Jászi has emphasized, in his standard volume, *The Dissolution of the Habsburg Monarchy,* the inability of the Magyar nobility and the ruling class to understand the problem of the Hungarian nationalities from the economic, cultural, and social points of view. For the Magyars the question at issue was solely one of historical rights.[2]

An excellent statement of this Magyar conviction is given in the following remarks of Dr. Jászi:

From this point of view it could not be contended that the Magyars as the conquering race had special rights over the country beside which the nationalities could have played only a tolerated rôle in state life. The right

[1] For excellent descriptions of the problem see the works of R. W. Seton-Watson and especially (Scotus Viator), *Racial Problems in Hungary.* The attempt of the Magyars to form a unified national state is admirably described by Dr. Oscar Jászi in his *The Dissolution of the Habsburg Monarchy.* See also A. C. Popovici, *La Question Roumaine en Transylvanie et en Hongrie.*

[2] See Jászi, *op. cit.,* Part V, chapter iii, "The Chief Tendency of the Hungarian National Struggles: The Move toward a Unified National State," pp. 298–343.

of conquest, based on the sword, was always hidden more or less consciously behind the doctrine of Magyar supremacy and the unified national state. That the old feudal society at the beginning of the modern era was entirely hypnotized by this historical point of view of force will surprise no one who knows that this conception remained unaltered in the Magyar ruling class until the end of the monarchy and thereafter.[3]

Hence it is only natural that the Magyar ruling class looked with horror at the economic and political awakening of the Roumanians and hated them as serfs. Its attitude was characterized by the following lines of verse:

> Under human form, wild animal, murderous Wallachian,
> Old dog, biting Actaeon, snapping at his master,
> Sprung from a mountain rat, suckled by a shabby wolf . . . .[4]

Let us note that the expression "Wallachian" (Olág) was used by the Magyar upper classes intentionally instead of "Roumanian" in order to repudiate the Roumanian claim that they were descendants from the Roman colonists.

The inability of the Magyar ruling class to understand their problem of minorities was, in the last analysis, the fundamental reason for the final separation of the Transylvanian Roumanians from Hungary at the end of the World War. Before the war, the Roumanians, as well as other nationalities settled in Hungary, were not animated by any desire for secession but aspired for no more than administrative autonomy, liberty for the development of their language and culture, and an adequate national representation in the state organization. But the Magyar rulers considered such demands a kind of high treason. In 1891 the Roumanian leaders were brought to the courts because they committed the great crime of desiring to submit to the Emperor at Vienna, in the form of a memorandum, the grievances of four million loyal subjects. The procurator who conducted the prosecution was decorated. In 1894 the Roumanian National Party was dissolved as "unconstitutional" by an administrative act of the Hungarian Government.

The echo of this intolerance did not pass unnoticed by the Roumanians in the Old Kingdom, who began to pay more and more attention to the affairs of their brethren in Transylvania. In 1892 a "Liga Culturală" (Cultural League) was founded and, under the

---

[3] O. Jászi, op. cit., p. 306. Quoted by permission of the University of Chicago Press, publishers.   [4] Ibid., p. 300.

Dr. Nicolae Iorga   Dr. Nicolae Titulescu
Dr. I. G. Duca   Dr. Constantin Argetoianu

leadership of Professor Iorga, established branches all over the territory, having for its goal the cultural and national unification of all Roumanians.

In spite of the irresponsible policy of the Hungarian Government toward the Roumanian nationals, the Roumanian kingdom was being inevitably drawn into the orbit of the Central Powers. The personal sympathies of the King had much to do with it. Many prominent statesmen, as Sturdza, Maiorescu, Carp, and others, who had been educated in Germany, now stood at the helm of the Roumanian state. Many army officers were trained in the German military academies. A great number of students were attracted by the German universities. German schools in Roumania exercised a considerable influence. The *Evangelische Knaben- und Realschule,* controlled directly by the German Ministry of Education, was attended by more students and pupils than any other school in Bucharest.[5] Austrian and German investors supplied large loans to Roumania.

In the summer of 1883 King Carol visited Germany. Bismarck took this occasion to suggest a Roumanian alliance with Austria. The subsequent negotiations are well described by S. B. Fay in his valuable *The Origins of the World War:*

As Austria responded favorably, Bismarck had two long interviews with the Rumanian Premier, whom he found "more declamatory than businesslike." M. Brătianu was very eager for the kudos which would come from an alliance with Great Powers. He was loud in his denunciation of Russian intrigues in Austria as well as in Rumania and Bulgaria. At the prospect of Austro-German backing, his chauvinistic imagination began to build castles in the air in which the Italian conquest of Nice, Savoy, and Corsica should be but the prelude to Rumania's acquisition of the Danubian Delta and Bessarabia. He had to be brought down to earth by energetic reminders from Bismarck and Kálnoky that the proposal under discussion was to secure peace, not conquests; the contracting powers ought mutually to promise that they would refrain from all acts of provocation which might disturb the peace; if, contrary to their efforts, any war should break out, it would be time enough later to discuss the division of the spoils.[6]

Finally, a purely defensive kind of alliance was signed on October 30, 1883, between Austria-Hungary and Roumania, which pro-

[5] D. Mitrany, "Rumania: Her History and Politics," in N. Forbes, A. J. Toynbee, D. Mitrany, D. G. Hogart, *The Balkans,* p. 302, note 1.

[6] S. B. Fay, *The Origins of the World War,* New York, 1929, I, 88–89. Quoted by permission of the publishers, The Macmillan Company.

vided in substance that if Roumania or the Monarchy were attacked without provocation on their part, the contracting powers would assist each other against the aggressor. Because of the wish of Emperor William, Russia was not named in the document, but the negotiations showed that the statesmen signing it had Russia in mind. Germany signed an agreement on the same day with the same obligations, and Italy adhered to the agreement in 1889, which was renewed from time to time with slight modifications.[7] It was never submitted to the Roumanian parliament for approval, which might have been difficult to procure.

Notwithstanding the secrecy of the treaty, and despite a subsequent tariff war with the Habsburg Monarchy and differences on the question of the Danube control, Roumania remained until the Balkan Wars a faithful member of the alliance of the Central Powers. The alliance guaranteed international safety to the kingdom in that period and enabled her to consolidate her internal affairs without serious foreign disturbances. On the other hand, the Roumanian leaders hoped to effect certain occasional relaxations in the treatment of their nationals in the Dual Monarchy, though in this respect the union was unnatural and prejudicial to the general national aims.

The alliance had its repercussion on the economic side. Capital was needed for the reconstruction of roads, docks, agricultural credit, and railways. Austrian and German investors supplied most of the funds, though in the '90's French participation became increasingly important.[8] German capital financed the government purchase of railroads and founded in 1895 the "Banca Generală Română," which handled the financing of commerce and the development of Roumanian industry. Austrians established the "Banque de Crédit Roumain"; both Austrian and German capital shared with French capital in the "Banque Marmorosch Blank," and German financiers held shares and directorships in many Roumanian petroleum companies, which united in 1907 to form the "Allgemeine Petroleum Gesellschaft." Other German companies were interested in the lumber and textile industries, and German mechanics, executives, and engineers participated in the industrial development of the country.[9] "It was thought that the growth of financial and business

---

[7] The treaty was renewed for the last time on February 5, 1913.

[8] H. Feis, *Europe the World's Banker, 1870–1914*, p. 269.

[9] See *ibid.*, chapter xii, "The Financing of the Balkan States," pp. 268–72.

interests within Roumania would bind that country to Germany in political affairs." But, "the financial and industrial connections with Germany did not shape Roumania's ultimate political decisions."[10]

Bulgaro-Roumanian relations could not be described as very friendly. Bulgaria failed to abolish the fortifications on her frontier in accordance with the Berlin Treaty and the occasional Macedonian troubles had ill effects on the political atmosphere. The Dobrogea was still considered by some Bulgarian writers as "Bulgaria Irredenta." However, as long as the Balkan equilibrium and the balance of power was stable, there was no immediate danger of a conflict, despite the fact that diplomatic relations were strained to the breaking point in 1905 and 1908.

Greece and Roumania maintained friendly relations, with brief interludes, since the foundation of their modern states. In 1892, however, temporary brief rupture took place owing to a legal dispute in connection with the property of the brothers Zappi in Roumania. But the former friendly relations were soon restored. In 1905 another *impassé* was reached. Roumania was interested in the solution of the Macedonian question and when in 1905 the Porte granted official recognition to the Kutso-Vlachs as a separate nation in Turkey, this act offended Greece, who considered her Macedonian aspirations slighted by this concession. Diplomatic relations between Bucharest and Athens were broken off in 1905, 1906, and 1910. The matter, however, was satisfactorily solved, and in 1913 Greece and Roumania joined forces against Bulgaria.

Friendly relations between Serbia and Roumania existed from the date of their emancipation. In 1868 a treaty of "perfect and sincere friendship and understanding" was signed by both states. In 1885 Roumania refused to become a Serbian ally against Bulgaria, but in 1913 and in 1916 Roumania found herself twice allied with her southern neighbor.

Roumania did not participate in the First Balkan War of 1912. But the result of the war upset Roumanian public opinion. It was feared that the Balkan equilibrium would be disturbed and that Bulgaria would dominate the Balkans. The Roumanian Government hinted to her Central European allies that they exert pressure on Bulgaria for compensation. The hesitating part of Austria-Hungary offended Bucharest. Germany was more willing to acquiesce in the

[10] *Ibid.*, p. 270.

Roumanian demands for compensation. Russia profited by the situation by approving the Roumanian participation in the Second Balkan War. When the Bulgarian schemes for a Balkan hegemony materialized in the Bulgarian attack on the Serbs and Greeks, the Roumanian army overran northern Bulgaria. By the Treaty of Bucharest, signed on August 10, 1913, Bulgaria lost to Roumania the province of Southern Dobrogea with a territory of 7,659.8 square kilometers (2,971.3 square miles). This resulted in deep resentment in Bulgaria because of the economic value of the ceded territory.[11]

The events of 1912 and 1913 changed fundamentally the Roumanian attitude toward the Triple Alliance. By the end of 1913 Roumania was estranged from the Central Powers. The alienation was first felt directly when, in 1912, German investors began to sell their securities.[12] Still, the large 1913 Roumanian loan, needed for military expenditures, was issued mainly in Berlin. But the line of action followed by Vienna in the Balkan Wars could not satisfy either Bulgaria or Roumania and led to a clearly perceptible bitterness between Vienna and Bucharest, which enabled the Roumanian protagonists of the Entente to have their government look more favorably on Russia and the Allies. The agitation in favor of the Hungarian Roumanians became more and more active and Roumanian public opinion turned against the compromising policy of the Habsburg Monarchy. Austria was suspected of giving only slight assistance to the demands of Bucharest against Bulgaria and of being "more Bulgarian than the Bulgarians."[13]

When Roumania had acquired the South Dobrogea territory, Vienna began to fear a "Greater Roumanian movement" and sent a note to Bucharest in which the recently concluded treaty was described as a "preliminary arrangement."

Russia saw her chance to win Roumania and took immediate advantage of the situation. Public opinion noted with approval that Petrograd finally had joined with Germany in preventing a revision

---

[11] See L. Pasvolsky, *Bulgaria's Economic Position,* Institute of Economics of the Brookings Institute, Washington, D.C., 1930, pp. 52–53. Pasvolsky claims that it was "agriculturally the best-developed part" of pre-war Bulgaria. While the territory comprised about 8 per cent of the area of pre-war Bulgaria, it produced, on the average, about 20 per cent of the cereal crops of Bulgaria.

[12] H. Feis, *Europe the World's Banker, 1870–1914,* p. 269.

[13] S. B. Fay, *The Origins of the World War,* I, 478.

of the Bucharest Treaty.[14] The Russian ministers at Bucharest emphasized the Transylvanian problem and studiously ignored the Bessarabian question. When a new Russian minister arrived at Bucharest in January 1914, he was warmly welcomed. Crown Prince Ferdinand and his son Carol, who was educated under Iorga's nationalistic and anti-Austrian influence, were invited by the Tsar to visit Russia. The Tsar and his family returned the visit in June at Constanţa. Brătianu and Sazanov even went on a walking tour to Transylvania.[15]

In vain did Tisza undertake negotiations with the Roumanians in Transylvania and in vain was Count Czernin sent to Bucharest. Berlin was unsuccessful in its efforts to change the unfortunate policy of Vienna. The Kaiser hoped that Tisza would grant concessions to the Roumanians in Hungary. But the Austro-Hungarian statesmen lost their chance and paid heavily for their mistakes in the days to come.

In 1914 Roumania was conscious of her growing importance in the diplomatic chessboard of Europe. Though the secret treaty was again renewed on February 5, 1913, public opinion favored the Allies. When the World War came, the mind of Roumania was in general made up.

[14] S. B. Fay, *op. cit.*, I, 480–81.
[15] *Ibid.*, pp. 487–88.

CHAPTER IV

POLITICAL AND NATIONAL UNIFICATION

W HEN the conflagration of 1914 burst into flame along the valley of the Danube and spread rapidly over all Europe, Roumania balanced uncertainly on the borders of neutrality. The impressive military strength of Germany, the powerful influence of German and Austrian capital over Roumanian economic life, and the natural leanings of their German-born King—all these were arguments for an entrance into the war as allies of the Central Powers. On the other hand, Serbia had earned popular Roumanian sympathy, while Bulgaria was looked upon with suspicion. But the great and determining factor in Roumania's turning toward the Entente was the entrancing vision of "România Mare," to be made possible by freeing and uniting with the Old Kingdom that "unredeemed" half of the Roumanian people who lived in subjection to their ancient enemy, the Austro-Hungarian Empire. The lure of Bessarabia was also evident, but those who favored the Allies contended that the difference between Transylvania and Bessarabia in area and in number and quality of the population was such that no hesitation was admissible.

Before the war began, Roumania was approached from both hostile camps.[1] Germany offered Bessarabia and Russia offered Transylvania to Brătianu; at the same time Austria was offering special arrangements for the Roumanians of Austria-Hungary. But the public opinion of Roumania had been estranged by the repressive Hungarian policy in Transylvania and by the Bulgarophile leanings of the Dual Monarchy after the Second Balkan War. King Carol had to inform Vienna and Berlin that his country in case of a con-

---

[1] B. E. Schmitt, *The Coming of the War,* II, 274, 418, 424; see also a scholarly and detailed discussion in H. N. Howard, *The Partition of Turkey, 1913–1923,* pp. 166–76.

flict would probably not go to war on the side of the Central Powers.[2]

Germany was fully aware of the alienated Roumanian attitude and urged the Hungarian statesmen to modify their intolerant policy toward the Roumanians. However, Tisza refused to make any concessions despite the German pressure.[3] Wilhelm then appealed directly to Carol, and his government offered the bait of Bessarabia.[4]

King Carol of Roumania, however, was deeply attached to the German cause. On August 3, 1914, at 5 : 30 P.M., he summoned to his palace in Sinaia a crown council, at which the government and the opposition leaders were fully represented. Besides Brătianu and the members of the government, the former premiers Rosetti and Carp, the President of the Chamber, Marghiloman, leader of the Conservatives, and two associates, Take Ionescu, the Conservative-Democratic leader, and two associates, and the Crown Prince Ferdinand, were present. The King's proposal to join the Central Powers was favored by Carp alone. Brătianu refused to give up his policy of neutrality, and Marghiloman and Maiorescu preferred to wait. Filipescu was for intervention against Austria-Hungary. It was finally agreed that the *causus foederis* was not involved, since Austro-Hungarian action was aggressive, not defensive. The decision was announced to the Powers next day. King Carol was "so overcome by spiritual and bodily anguish that he could no longer think,"[5] and died on October 10. He was succeeded by Ferdinand.[6]

The country was divided and agitated. The Germanophiles, weak in numbers but strong in influence, included many outstanding politicians in their ranks, as Petru Carp, Al. Marghiloman, and Professor Stere. This group was afraid of the possible domination of the

---

[2] Schmitt, *op. cit.*, II, 419; S. B. Fay, *The Origins of the World War*, I, 479, 491.

[3] G. P. Gooch, *Recent Revelations of European Diplomacy* (New York, 1930), quotes J. Baernreither's *Fragments of a Political Diary:* "It was in vain that William II urged greater consideration for the Roumanians at Budapest."

[4] For the Roumanian negotiations see Schmitt, *op. cit.*, II, 418–31.

[5] Quoted by Schmitt, *op. cit.*, p. 429.

[6] As King Carol had no heirs, a family pact had been signed at Sigmaringen in November 1880, upholding Article 83 of the Constitution, according to which the succession to the Throne passed, in the absence of direct male heirs, to the ruler's oldest brother and his descendants. Prince Leopold had thus become heir to the Throne. He had subsequently renounced his rights in favor of his sons, the oldest of whom, Prince Ferdinand, had been formally proclaimed heir apparent on March 18, 1889.

Dardanelles by Russia, which would mean Russian economic domination of Roumania. They pointed out, on the other hand, that Roumania might acquire Bessarabia in the event of Russian defeat. Russian help, in case Roumania would join the Allies, could never be very effective anyhow and the German military strength was an assurance to them of the coming victory of the Central Powers. Their Germanophile influence was strengthened by numerous agitators, sent from Berlin, who flooded Roumania with propaganda and succeeded in affecting influential press-editors of Bucharest.

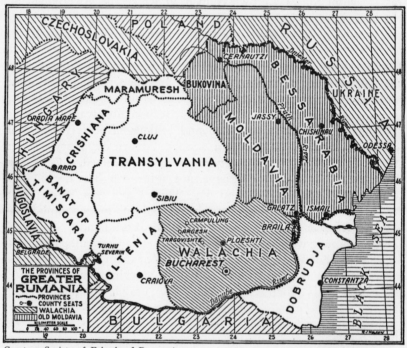

Courtesy Society of Friends of Roumania

The opposing group was led by Brătianu, who, though he was aware of the dependence of the banking and financial enterprises of his country on the support of German capital, could not fail to see the pleasant possibility of enlarging his country and absorbing the Roumanians included within the borders of the Dual Monarchy. He was supported openly by Professor Iorga, Take Ionescu, and Filipescu. These leaders were convinced that the aim of the Central Powers was to reduce small nations to their domination. Roumania by joining the Austro-Hungarian-German coalition would thus also support automatically the anti-Roumanian policy of Hungary. The liberation of Transylvania was preferred by them to that of Bessarabia. It was taken for granted that it would be hard to acquire Bessarabia even in the case of Russian defeat. Furthermore, most of the intelligentsia had always been strong in French sympathies; the Latin origins of both nations were remembered and the help France had given to Roumania during the Crimean War was again emphasized.

King Ferdinand was inclined to favor the Allies. Although, like his predecessors, he was bound by ties of friendship and blood with the sovereigns of Austria-Hungary and Germany, he understood that the interest of Roumania dictated joining the Allies.

The negotiations with the Allies were lengthy, lasting from the autumn of 1914 to August 17, 1916. Meanwhile Brătianu was feeling his way very carefully. He signed a neutrality treaty with Russia in September 1914 and a defensive agreement with Italy. A British loan was negotiated in January 1915; the Italian agreement was renewed in February of that year. Germany tried hard to keep Roumania on her side. Wilhelm sent the leader of the German Catholic Party, Dr. Erzberger, to Bucharest in the second half of 1915, but Erzberger's promises were considered insufficient by the pro-Allies group.[7]

The trend of public opinion in Roumania was evident when Roumania refused to allow the passage of munitions for Turkey in 1915. Henceforward, all that the Central Powers could exact from Bucharest were food provisions. When Italy entered the war in May 1915, public excitement increased. Vienna and Berlin had indeed not been wanting in offers to Bucharest after Italy's entry into the conflict, but had made their concessions conditional on the active intervention of Roumania on their side. But the government of Roumania would not agree to this, for despite the great military successes of the Central Powers, their final victory seemed to them doubtful. Bucharest continued to insist on important cessions of

[7] When Erzberger begged Tisza to "grant concessions to his Roumanian subjects, he was sharply snubbed for his pains" (G. P. Gooch, *op. cit.*, p. cxiii). While in Vienna, Erzberger tried to win the leaders of the Transylvanian Roumanians to his plans. Maniu, A. Popovici, and V. Goldiş asked for complete autonomy and wanted to have the promise announced by an Imperial manifesto, signed by Tisza and guaranteed by Wilhelm. The absolute refusal of Tisza brought the good intentions of Erzberger to naught.

territory in Bukovina and Transylvania in return for neutrality. The Austro-Hungarian Government was not to be moved from its resolve to refuse even the demands of the German Imperial Government and Conrad von Hötzendorff.

So when the waning vigor of the Brussiloff offensive in Galicia and Bukovina made the Tsarist Government more amenable to the Roumanian demands, Roumania signed a secret treaty with Russia, France, England, and Italy on August 18, 1916. On August 27 a crown council decided for war and the declaration of hostilities was presented in Vienna.[8]

For the services to the Allies, Roumania was to be rewarded by the cession of the Bukovina, Transylvania, the Banat, and the plain of Hungary as far as the Theiss River.

Two points deserve our special attention. By Article 6 of the treaty, Roumania was promised "the same rights as the Allies in all that concerns the preliminaries of the peace negotiations," as well as the full participation in the discussions of the questions which were to be decided by the Peace Conference. Brătianu did not want to have the disappointments of 1878 repeated at the future peace gathering. On the other hand, Article 5 pledged both parties to the agreement "not to conclude a separate peace or general peace except conjointly and simultanously." This last clause proved to be a fateful undertaking on the execution of which the validity of the whole treaty was to depend.

[8] Gooch, *op. cit.,* pp. 131–32, points out that "Roumania's diplomacy from the outbreak of war to her entry into the struggle must be studied in the Austrian Red-Book, *Diplomatische Aktenstücke betreffend die Beziehungen Oesterreich-Ungarns zu Rumänien in der Zeit von 22 Juli, 1914, bis 27 August, 1916.* The well written dispatches of Czernin vividly describe the attempts of the Prime Minister Brătianu to postpone action till he could secure his maximum terms, and be reasonably sure which side was going to win. The King is described as a tool in Brătianu's hands. The last and most sensational telegram, written after the breach had occurred, reveals that on August 24, 1916, Russia sent an ultimatum to Bucharest, offering Transylvania, the Banat, and the Bukovina as the booty, and strengthening the appeal with a threat of invasion with 100,000 men. It was for Roumania to choose whether the troops should come as friends or as foes. It is Czernin's opinion that the calculating Brătianu would have preferred to wait a little longer. A full and vivid account of the debate at the Crown Council at Cotroceni, which decided to abandon neutrality, was written the same evening by one of its members, and is reproduced in Raymond Récouly's *Les Heures tragiques d'avant Guerre.*" (Quoted by permission of the author and Longmans, Green & Co., publishers.) *La Roumanie,* Take Ionescu's organ, of March 6, 1921, contains a dramatic account of the sitting of the council. Numerous documents concerning this period can be found in *Le Monde slave,* 1928, 5th Year, No. 9, pp. 423–71; No. 3, pp. 422–51.

The subsequent military operations need not be described here. It is sufficient to say that the Roumanians failed to receive the expected aid from their Allies, and that the entry of the country into the war was untimely. The Russian and Italian offensives were already slackening. The Germans were abandoning their efforts at Verdun, and could concentrate their forces against Roumania. While the Bulgarians, under Mackensen, attacked from the south, the Austro-Hungarian-German armies under General Falkenhayn drove from the west and north. After numerous and heavy fights, in which the Roumanian army, inferior as to numbers and armament, showed its epic heroism, the enemy invaded the land. Bucharest fell into the hands of the foe on December 7, 1916, and by the end of the year all Roumania, with the exception of a small section in the northeast, was a prize of the Central Powers.[9] The government and parliament installed themselves in Iaşi, in Moldavia. For two years, the enemy forces combed the country clean of all resources, and typhus added to the misfortunes of the refugees in Moldavia. The Russian help evaporated into thin air with the accession of the Bolsheviks to power, and the disintegration of the Russian army turned its soldiers into pillaging bands. But in spite of the disadvantageous conditions, the Roumanian forces were able to re-establish themselves morally as well as materially, so that in the summer of 1917 they won the brilliant victories of Mărăşti, Mărăşeşti, and Oituz. At Mărăşeşti particularly, the battle was one of the most desperate, considering its length, the number of troops employed, and the fierceness of the onslaughts. The result was that the Germans were compelled to abandon their hope of crushing all Roumania by force of arms.

Meanwhile, in December 1916, Brătianu invited Take Ionescu and other Conservative leaders into the cabinet. Filipescu had died. The parliament met at Iaşi and enthusiastically approved the prosecution of the war to a finish. The policies of universal suffrage and the division of big estates were proclaimed under the influence of the Russian Revolution. The territory was full of Russian agitators, but they had little influence on the populace, conservative peasants, who accepted the King's promise of land reform. The parliament convoked a constituent assembly, and this body in June 1917 amended Article 19 of the Constitution regulating the position of

[9] For a good discussion see D. W. Johnson, "The Conquest of Roumania," *Geographical Review* (1917), III, 438–56.

private property in the country. The right to expropriate for reasons of public utility already existed. The Constitutional Amendment of Iaşi, as it is called, extended this principle to expropriation for reasons of national utility. The original proprietors were left, in general, 500 hectares at most for each separate estate. The Conservatives forced a compromise which fixed the area to be expropriated at 2,000,000 hectares, and, moreover, made the government abandon its intention of expropriating the subsoil.[10] All inalienable lands and all lands belonging to foreigners, absenteeists, corporations, and institutions were to be completely expropriated. The dispossessed proprietors were to be compensated adequately for their losses. However, the continued occupation of the greater part of the country by enemy forces made it impossible for this program to be applied forthwith.[11]

Side by side with this development in the Old Kingdom events were moving rapidly in Bessarabia. On October 20 (November 2), 1917, the first congress of all Moldavians in Russia assembled at Chişinău. It created a "Sfatul Ţării" (Council of the State), for the administration of Bessarabia until the election of a constituent assembly. The council opened its sessions on November 21 (December 2, according to the new calendar) and appointed a council of directors (ministers), a provisional government, and published a manifesto announcing that the Moldavians, on the basis of their historical rights and in conformity with the principle of self-determination of nations, constituted themselves an autonomous republic. On January 24, 1918, this autonomous republic declared its complete independence. On December 27, 1917, the Sfatul Ţării asked both the Russian general headquarters and the Roumanian Government for armies. The Roumanian military forces entered the territory at the beginning of 1918. On the night of January 23–24, 1918, the independence of the Moldavian Republic was unanimously

---

[10] The expropriation of the subsoil was carried through in the Constitution of 1923.

[11] The modification of the constitution was promulgated by decree No. 721 on July 19, 1917, published in *Monitorul Oficial,* No. 93, of July 20, 1917. It contained only the enunciation of the principles on which the reform was eventually to be carried out. The law for expropriation was to be passed within six months after the end of the war with the two-thirds majority required for amendments to the constitution. The actual agrarian reform received its first legislative expression in the shape of successive decree-laws. See D. Mitrany, *The Land and the Peasant in Rumania,* p. 122, note 1.

proclaimed. By an agreement with Russia of March 9, 1918, Roumania agreed to withdraw her troops, but before the step was carried out, the union with the Kingdom of Roumania was proclaimed[12] on March 27, 1918, on certain specified conditions.[13] During the night of November 26–27, 1918, the union was made unconditional and the assembly was permanently dissolved.[14] Bessarabia became a part of Roumania. As a result, the Soviet Government suspended diplomatic relations with Roumania and confiscated the gold reserves of Roumania, sent to Russia for safekeeping.

While Bessarabia was returning to her mother country, the lower part of Roumania was ruthlessly exploited by the Austro-Hungarian-German armies. It became a colony of the Central Powers especially in the economic sphere. Wheat and petroleum were goods needed desperately by them. Roumania was governed with an iron and, even more, a grasping hand.[15]

Possibly the greatest deteriorating influence on the economic situation of the occupied land was the banknotes circulated by the occupying armies to the amount of about two milliards of lei by the enemy's administration.[16]

When the Russians asked for an armistice in the autumn of 1917,

[12] The vote was 86 to 3, 36 abstaining. This Sfatul Țării had 85 of the peasant class, of its total membership of 138; 5 of the large landowning class (who, fearing the Roumanian agrarian laws, had withdrawn early), 103 Moldavians, 13 Ukrainians, 7 Russians, 6 Jews, 5 Bulgarians, 2 Germans, 1 Pole, and 1 Armenian. For other details see C. U. Clark, *Bessarabia,* and A. Popovici, *The Political Status of Bessarabia* (published for the School of Foreign Service, Georgetown University, by Ransdell, Inc., Washington, D.C., 1931).

[13] The retention of provincial autonomy; the respect of the rights of minorities in Bessarabia; the continuation of the life of the assembly until such time as it should have elaborated a system of agrarian reform, etc. The document can be conveniently found in C. U. Clark, *Greater Roumania,* pp. 198–200.

[14] The assembly passed, before it was disbanded, an agrarian law expropriating from all large landowners all their estate surpassing 250 acres. The law was voted on November 27, 1918, and promulgated by royal decree on December 22 of the same year. It was very drastic.

[15] The economic importance of Roumania was, for example, recognized by Ludendorff, who writes in his "Memoirs": "As Austria could not supply us with sufficient oil, and as all our efforts to increase production were unavailing, Roumanian oil was of decisive importance to us" (quoted by L'Espagnol de la Tramerye, *The World Struggle for Oil,* New York, 1924, p. 102). For the best discussion of the economic administration of Roumania by the Central Powers, see G. Gratz and R. Schüller, *The Economic Policy of Austria-Hungary during the War.*

[16] C. D. Creangă, *Les Finances Roumaines sous le régime de l'occupation et de la paix Allemande.*

the Roumanians were forced to sign a similar document on November 26, 1917.[17] Brătianu hesitated to violate the Treaty of Alliance of 1916 and sign a separate peace. But the King and the high command hoped to save by negotiations at least the nucleus of the army and to gain time. Averescu took Brătianu's place on January 29, 1918, and went to Bucharest to negotiate, where he learned the fantastic demands of Count Czernin. He was succeeded by Marghiloman, who on March 5, 1918, formed his Germanophile cabinet. Count Czernin was determined to punish the Roumanians for their "treason," and rejected Germany's advice for moderation.[18] On May 7, 1918, Marghiloman affixed his signature to the document which is known as the Peace of Bucharest.[19] The treaty itself pos-

[17] The war diary of the Archduke Joseph, published by the Hungarian Academy of Science in Budapest, under the title, *The World War as I Saw It,* Volume V, makes a sensational assertion: "In an entry in the diary for July 10, 1917, a secret offer to Joseph to become King of Roumania was made by Marghiloman, Titu Maiorescu, and Prince Stirbey. The Archduke Joseph was considered as an excellent choice because he was related to the ruling houses of Bavaria and Bulgaria. It was also expected that he would be able to settle the problem of Transylvania. Joseph discussed the plan with Count Czernin in Carlsbad. The result was that he refused to accept, giving as his reason that he was too deeply attached to his own fatherland, Hungary." For other interesting bits see a review in *Central European Observer,* February 27, 1931, IX, 127–28.

[18] Notice, for example, the "Memorandum of the Austro-Hungarian Minister for Foreign Affairs, Count Ottokar Czernin, to Emperor Charles of Austria" (presented in the summer of 1917, six months before the negotiations of Brest-Litovsk), as quoted in K. F. Nowak, *The Collapse of Central Europe,* pp. 353–60:

"Thanks to our geographical position, it is realized to some extent in Berlin that we have a first claim upon the Balkans, and here lies the wide sphere in which we may look for and find compensation for our terrible sacrifices. . . . . We must have Roumania; we must have Wallachia and the whole of Moldavia to the Sereth. The eastern part of Moldavia we must offer to Russia; the northern Dobrudja should fall to Bulgaria, while the small remaining section may constitute the new, small Roumania, and may so fulfil the double purpose of forming a wedge between Bulgaria and Russia and controlling the mouths of the Danube, which we should ourselves have great difficulty in holding.

"Roumania is an object worth milliards. It would be bringing owls to Athens to enlarge on this point. There is sense in acquiring an object worth milliards; it is something worth while; and even if at first our Vienna pothouse politicians and our Hungarian desperados oppose the plan they are unlikely to carry the day. In practice there is no solution that will be received with the unanimous applause of the entire Monarchy . . . . [Roumania] would have to be attached to the Monarchy as an Imperial domain and would have to be governed autocratically. . . . ." Quoted by permission of E. P. Dutton & Co., Inc., publishers.

[19] G. F. de Martens, *Nouveau Recuiel générale de traités* (ed. H. Triepel, Leipzig, 1920), Troisième Série, Tome X, pp. 856–70; the text is also reprinted in summary in H. W. V. Temperley, *A History of the Peace Conference of Paris,* III, 49–50, and in C. U. Clark, *Greater Roumania,* pp. 223–25.

sesses historical interest only in view of the subsequent defeat of the Central Powers.[20] However, it is important to note that the Allied Governments used this pact for assuming that the provisions of the secret Treaty of 1916 had become invalid, though the document was never ratified by the King and the parliament.

In November 1918, as a result of events in the western theater of the war, the German domination of Roumania collapsed. The Cabinet of Marghiloman had to resign on October 24. General Coandă was called to power by the King. War was redeclared. On December 1, the King formally entered the liberated Bucharest by the side of Brătianu, who was appointed to the head of the government on November 29.

The new Ministry was faced with grave tasks of an internal and international nature. The country had to be unified in one political whole with the provinces which had been a part of other states and now were joining the Roumanian kingdom. On November 28 the National Assembly of the Roumanians of Bukovina proclaimed the union of Bukovina with Roumania and asked for military protection. With the exception of the Ruthenians, all minority groups agreed to the new political amalgamation.

It was inevitable that the Transylvanian Roumanians would also join the kingdom of Ferdinand I. The unfortunate denationalizing Magyar policy, with its vexatious control of the Roumanian church and the exclusion of the Roumanian intelligentsia from the state life and local administration, bore fruit. After the dissolution of the Hungarian forces, the National Party of the Transylvanian Roumanians directed the affairs of their territory and proclaimed through Dr. Vaida-Voevod that the Hungarian Government no longer had the right to settle their affairs. During the revolution in Budapest the delegation of the National Party formed the so-called "National Roumanian Council," under the direction of Maniu, which formally demanded from Count Károlyi's Government the

---

[20] Roumania was deprived of the whole line of the mountains and all access to the sea, and divided the Dobrogea between Bulgaria, in the south, and a condominium, which would be exploited by the Germans, in the north of the province. The country was to lose the possession of its railways, wheat crops, and petroleum wells, for an indefinite period. German troops were to remain for a long time in the country to see that these onerous engagements were carried out. Practically, Roumania was reduced to a mere land of exploitation by the Central Powers. See G. Gratz and R. Schüller, *The Economic Policy of Austria-Hungary during the War,* Part III, "The Peace Negotiations at Bucharest," pp. 139–206.

surrender of executive powers in twenty-three Transylvanian counties. Local branches were organized in the departments, and the people were forming national guards against disorders. In vain did Dr. Oscar Jászi, a member of the Hungarian Cabinet, journey to Transylvania and propose the federation of the Hungarian nationalities on the Swiss basis. The Council, ignoring Jászi, asked Bucharest for Roumanian troops and called an assembly at Alba-Iulia to decide on the allegiance of the province. On December 1, 1918, this Assembly, composed of the delegates from Transylvania, the Banat, and Hungary, solemnly voted for the union of Transylvania and the Banat with Roumania.[21]

In March 1919 Károlyi resigned rather than acquiesce in the military convention which deprived Hungary of her provinces. The discontented elements under Béla Kun attacked the Roumanians in April and in July, 1919. The successful counter-offensive brought the Roumanian army to Budapest, which it entered on August 4, 1919. The occupation lasted until November 14, and throughout this period the Roumanian Government was in conflict with the Supreme Council of Paris, which repeatedly demanded the withdrawal of the Roumanian army. It is commonly asserted that the Roumanians were entirely at fault in this invasion of Hungary and particularly in their occupation of Budapest. But such an attitude fails to consider that the obstreperous Béla Kun struck first at the Roumanians in his attempt to appease opposition at home. When the Allies failed to act firmly with Béla Kun, the Roumanian Government considered itself justified in a determined counter-attack. If the old bitterness between Magyar and Roumanian, intensified by the Magyar oppressions during the war, was reflected in this first opportunity of the former serf to avenge his wrongs, the disinterested historian must observe that it was most natural that it should be so. Whether the Hungarian accusations of the Roumanian exactions during the occupation of Budapest are right or wrong, it must be remembered that the Hungarian has always been governed by universal hatred against everything Roumanian, and this fact somewhat reduces the force of his frantic denunciations.

[21] The National Council was dissolved in 1920. A meeting representative of the Saxons of Transylvania held in January 1919 declared for the union with Roumania in cordial terms. The Szeklers took an entirely different line and offered a bitter opposition to the Roumanian troops as they advanced through the province. The Magyar bishops, Catholics, Calvinists, and Unitarians, refused their allegiance until well into 1921.

CHAPTER V

ROUMANIANS AT THE PEACE CONFERENCE

WHEN the Peace Conference opened at Paris, the Roumanian case was handicapped beforehand by numerous factors. There was a general feeling against Roumania, as well as against other "succession states," that it was a backward country. Brătianu, as chief delegate of the Roumanian Government, could not understand the leaders of the Allies. Clemenceau was personally prejudiced against Brătianu and seems to have communicated his feeling to other delegates. Brătianu, on the other hand, was determined not to cancel the provisions of the secret treaty and resented the possibility of having his country again relegated to an inferior status as at the Conference of Berlin in 1878. Hence the secret Treaty of 1916 had stipulated that they should be treated as equals; but now this provision evaporated into thin air. Brătianu felt out of place and could not form practical contacts. His plea for full membership in the Supreme Council on the basis of the Treaty of 1916 was refused. Moreover, Roumania was allowed only two delegates, whereas Belgium and Serbia, though smaller geographically, were each allotted three. Further friction was due to the occupation of Budapest and Brătianu's refusal to sign the minorities treaty.

It was not until February 8 that Brătianu appeared before the Council of Ten to argue the Banat question.[1] After long discussions, Roumania received Transylvania, Maramureş, Bukovina, and the eastern part of the Banat.[2]

Brătianu vainly protested against the final decision of the Peace

[1] H. W. V. Temperley, *A History of the Peace Conference of Paris,* I, 249–50, 257–58; IV, 226. The territorial claims were handled by the Commission on Roumanian Territorial Claims. See Temperley, IV, 226–30, also Part I, p. 211, and chapter ii, Part II, pp. 133–35.

[2] The secret Treaty of August 17, 1916, gave the Banat to Roumania, but Serbian public opinion and policy, for both ethnic and strategic reasons, were unshakably opposed to it, and the Banat problem embittered the relations of both countries.

Conference. The minorities treaty proved to be the most objectionable feature of the peace treaties.

The minorities treaties are of extraordinarily great importance in international relations, and have conditioned Roumania's foreign relations in every aspect to the present day. As will be seen more fully hereafter, they were adopted chiefly through the efforts of President Wilson and Colonel House and their advisers of the American delegation, David Hunter Miller and Professor Manley O. Hudson, induced so to do chiefly by the American Jewish delegation led by Louis Marshall and Judge Julian W. Mack, who aided in their drafting. Lloyd George, Clemenceau, and Orlando supported them with the co-operation of their own aides, Headlam-Morley, Philippe Berthelot, and Signor Martino, as well as Lord Robert Cecil and Adatci of Japan, who were influenced by leading Jews of England and France.[3]

The program expressed in the notes of the Allies of December 30, 1916, and January 10, 1917, deals with the idea of self-determination for small nations as do the Fourteen Points of President Wilson. In these and other documents it is taken for granted that the principle of self-determination of small nations is vastly more important than a system for the protection of minorities. Some valuable suggestions, like that coming from "L'Organisation centrale pour la paix durable," in 1915, had very little influence on the international settlement of the minorities question.

The most important initiative was the action started by the Jewish organization. Already a long series of international congresses had been invoked by them to secure "equal rights," beginning with the Congress of Vienna in 1814–15.[4] If we disregard their ambitions

[3] The best discussion can be found in L. Feinberg, *La Question des minorités à la Conference de la Paix de 1919–1920 et l'action juive en faveur de la protection internationale des minorités* (Paris, 1929) ; Dr. Zd. Peška, "Otázka Národnostních Menšin na Pařížské Mírové Konferenci" ("The Question of the Nationalistic Minorities at the Paris Peace Conference"), in *Zahraniční Politika* (monthly, Orbis Publ. Co., Josef Chmelař, ed.), February 1930, IX, 212–26 ; M. J. Kohler, "The Origin of the Minority Provisions of the Peace Treaty of 1919," in L. Luzatti, *God in Freedom*, pp. 751–94. The last author, especially, draws heavily upon unpublished material.

[4] See M. J. Kohler, "Jewish Rights at the Congress of Vienna and Aix-la-Chapelle," in *American Jewish Historical Society Publications*, 1918, No. 26, pp. 33–125 ; M. J. Kohler, "Jewish Rights at International Congresses," in *American Jewish Yearbook, 5678 (1917–1918)*, pp. 106–60. M. J. Kohler & S. Wolf, *Jewish Disabilities in the Balkan States* (New York, 1916) ; L. Wolf, *Notes on the Diplomatic History of the Jewish Question* (London, 1919).

for the Palestine home, nowhere could they ask for territorial self-determination. Whatever this principle meant for other nations, for them it meant protection and equality of minorities rights.

The Jewish agitation was felt in influential and leading circles. Already in November 1915 the "Poale Sion," a Jewish socialistic organization, presented a memorandum to the International Socialistic Office,[5] and the socialistic conference of the neutral states of August 1916 at The Hague passed a resolution asking the autonomy for the nationalistic minorities.[6] As early as April 7, 1915, President Wilson assured Simon Wolf, chairman of the board of delegates of the Union of American Hebrew Congregations, of his deep interest in this cause,[7] and on May 29, 1916, the President wrote to him to assure him of his "determination to do the right and possible thing at the right and feasible time with regard to the great interests you so eloquently allude to in your letter."

From 1916 to 1918 there gathered about thirty Jewish congresses in Europe and elsewhere, and most of them asked for equality in the lands where Jews had settled. When the Paris Peace Conference opened its sessions, the city was visited by numerous Jewish delegates, who formed a "Comité des Délégations Juives" on March 25, 1919, composed of the representatives of eastern European Jews, the "Alliance Israélite Universelle," the British Joint Foreign Committee, and the Union of American Hebrew Congregations. The most important memorandum was presented at the Conference on May 10, 1919,[8] and its suggestions, on the whole, were embodied in the minorities provision in its modified form.

As the authors of the peace treaties were interested in insuring future peace—besides guaranteeing their victory and domination—they tried to exclude from the peace treaties the elements of future wars. The principle of self-determination proved capable of many interpretations. Furthermore, the results of the war proved that the attainment of national independence and unity was not a sure preliminary to international peace. Self-determination had to find its limits in the conditions of existence and the vital interests of society.

---

[5] *Die Juden im Kriege,* Denkschrift des Jüdischen Sozialistischen Arbeiterverbandes Poale Sion an das Internationale Sozialistische Bureau (Haag, 1915).

[6] N. Feinberg, *La Question des minorités, etc.,* p. 25.

[7] M. J. Kohler, in L. Luzatti, *God in Freedom,* pp. 753–54.

[8] Reprinted by Feinberg, *op. cit.,* Annex B; also in E. Cohen, *La Question juive devant le droit international public* (Paris, 1922), p. 275.

It was also conditioned by the size and geographical configuration of the area and by its economic resources. It was not—nor will it be in the future—possible to carry into effect fully and consistently the principle of the self-determination of all sections of the various nations and to make the frontiers of the new states coincide everywhere with the ethnographical boundaries. Consequently considerable national minorities remained in existence even after the war.

Some extreme proposals were propounded. Thus, for example, Wilson and Cecil suggested that an article should be incorporated into the treaties making possible future territorial changes in the interest of the self-determination principle.[9] But a co-author of the Covenant of the League, D. H. Miller, suggested that such a provision should be supplanted by minorities provisions.[10] In addition, many Allied statesmen were skeptical about the ability of new states to govern themselves. The most evident proof of this state of mind is seen in the proposal of General Smuts, who suggested some sort of international protectorate over the states born out of the Austro-Hungarian and Turkish territories.[11] However, the plan was severely criticized, as it was evident that such states as Roumania or Czechoslovakia could not be limited in their sovereignty, having already been recognized as fully sovereign members of the family of nations. The proposal took the form of the mandate system.

Definite mention of the minority problem can be found in the second draft of President Wilson of the Covenant of the League of Nations, written about January 10, 1919.[12] Nothing was said, however, about "religious" minorities and the proposal was limited to "new states" only. Wilson's third proposal of the Covenant,

[9] The second Wilson proposal for the League of Nations, of January 10, 1919, read: "The contracting Powers accept without reservation the principle that the peace of the world is superior in importance to every question of political jurisdiction or boundary."

[10] See D. H. Miller, *The Drafting of the Covenant* (New York, 1928), II, 71, and I, 52. He says: "That the territorial adjustments made by the Peace Conference will not satisfy all claims, is the only thing now certain about them. Such general provisions as above mentioned will make that dissatisfaction permanent. . . . . As the drawing of boundaries according to racial or social conditions is in many cases an impossibility, protection of the rights of minorities and acceptance of such protection by the minorities constitute the only basis of enduring peace."

[11] Reprinted in D. H. Miller, *op. cit.*, II, 23. This plan had a strong influence on Wilson, who adopted a substantial part of it for his own second plan. See Miller, I, 40; R. S. Baker, *Woodrow Wilson and the World Settlement*, I, 424.

[12] See M. J. Kohler, in Luzatti, *God in Freedom*, pp. 764 ff.

written about January 20, 1919, adopted again the previous plan, but mentioned religious minorities. As the plan of Cecil mentioned nothing about minorities, though he received the proposals of Wilson, it is evident that the English delegation was not anxious to establish a system of international protection of minorities. However, Wilson would not give up his proposal. The basis of further discussions between February 3 and February 13, 1919, was the so-called Hurst-Miller draft in the commission on the League of Nations, in which Roumania was represented. A rather unwelcome proposition came from the Japanese delegation, which offered the so-called Japanese "equality" clause, stating that "matters of religion and race could well go together." Then the negotiations for the inclusion of a minority clause in the Covenant of the League of Nations came to naught.

But this failure did not definitely settle the whole problem. It was the Jewish influence which again brought about renewed consideration of the minority clauses. When early in April Marshall and other Jewish delegates learned that the Roumanian commission of the conference had drawn up treaty clauses approved by the Superior Territorial Commission for submission to the Supreme Council, which did not suit their demands, Marshall and Wolf addressed a communication of protest to the Peace Conference, and Marshall arranged with Colonel House to have the desired modifications discussed with the legal advisers of the United States peace delegation. From that time on Marshall and Judge Mack acted in concert with Dr. Miller and Professor Hudson in drafting the minorities provisions, as well as with Colonel House and President Wilson on occasion.[13] There was no unity, however, among the Jewish delegations. Some of the eastern Jewish delegates went so far as to insist not only on "national Jewish rights," but understood by them the creation of an international Jewish parliament, to pass laws for Jews the world over, and Jewish official representation in the League of Nations. Others wanted to be made at least a special political entity in various east European states.[14]

The matter was referred to the "Committee on New States and the Protection of Minorities" created on May 1. But the German delegation was to be handed the text of the Peace Treaty on May 7,

[13] M. J. Kohler, *op. cit.*, p. 775.
[14] *Ibid.*, pp. 775–76. For bibliography see *ibid.*, p. 776, note 55.

and it was impossible to include in it the provisions concerning the protection of Polish minorities. Under these circumstances an ingenious device was adopted. The Treaty with Germany contained an article in which Poland promised to accept subsequent minorities articles.[15]

President Wilson ruled soon after the appointment of the committee that Roumania was to be treated as a "new state" in view of her large prospective accessions of territory. The work was then done expeditiously, so that the draft treaty with Poland was ready for submission to the Council of Four on May 14, and was communicated on May 21 to the Polish representatives. On May 23 a similar document was sent to Brătianu and subsequently to the Czechoslovak, Yugoslav, and Greek delegates.

The smoldering opposition of the small states culminated in a protest made in the plenary conference of May 31, 1919, which was styled by the press a "revolution of the small powers."[16] It was one of the few occasions when a real issue was discussed. Brătianu, supported by Paderewski, and in a modified degree by Kramář and Trumbić, protested against the fact that the minorities provisions implied the establishment of two categories of countries—countries of the first class, which, in spite of having certain groups of minorities, were placed under no obligations; and countries of the second class, which had been obliged to assume extremely onerous obligations.[17]

The main point which was put forward was that the states concerned were willing to accept any general regulations which were accepted by all states belonging to the League of Nations; but they were not ready to grant the principle of legal inequality, which, fur-

[15] Article 93 of the Versailles Treaty reads as follows: "Poland accepts and agrees to embody in a Treaty with the Principal and Associated Powers such provisions as may be deemed necessary by the said Powers to protect the interests of the inhabitants of Poland who differ from the majority of the population in race, language, and religion."

[16] *New York Times*, June 3, 1919, Vol. LXVII, No. 22.410, pp. 1–2; C. T. Thompson, *The Peace Conference Day by Day*, pp. 386–87; H. W. V. Temperley, *History of the Peace Conference*, V, 128–32; J. S. Rouček, *The Working of the Minorities System under the League of Nations*, pp. 32–41.

[17] When a suggestion was made to Italy that minorities guaranties ought to be given the 400,000 Germans who were transferred to Italy, "the Italian delegation felt that it was entirely inconsistent with its position as a principal power to have any such suggestion made." See M. O. Hudson, "The Protection of Minorities and Natives in Transferred Territories," in E. M. House and C. Seymour, Editors, *What Really Happened at Paris*, p. 474.

thermore, infringed the cardinal principles of state sovereignty. It was pointed out that a clause imposing general recognition of religious toleration, as a part of the draft of the League of Nations Covenant, on all members of the League, had in fact been rejected, and the question could be asked why an obligation which the great powers refused to undertake themselves should be imposed upon others. This inequality would give rise to difficulties of both a political and a moral character. The countries were divided into two groups, one of which had certain obligations to which the other was not subject. If the rights of minorities were to be recognized in certain countries, the same should apply to all the countries of the world.

The answer was given in the speech of President Wilson, so much debated in the American 1920 presidential campaign, in which he insisted that the United States could share the responsibility of the territorial adjustment only if assurance were given that conditions would be maintained which would not lead to new oppressions and renewed conflicts. To this line of reasoning Brătianu answered that if this protection of minorities was, indeed, indispensable, or desirable, it should not be restricted to the countries of central and eastern Europe, but should be extended to all without exception.

The outcome was that the continued dissatisfaction of the Roumanians and Yugoslavs led them to take a very determined stand with reference to the contents of the treaties themselves, and for this reason their signatures were withheld until some time after the principal powers had signed. That this attitude did not frustrate altogether the attempt to give special protection to minorities is due principally to President Wilson, "whose interest in the policy was keener than that of his colleagues on the Supreme Council."[18]

After Brătianu returned to Bucharest, the relations of his Government with the Supreme Council were strained for the next six months, more particularly over the occupation of Hungary mentioned above. The Premier resigned on September 27, 1919, and the Văitoianu Cabinet was unwilling to sign the peace treaty, even though faced by an ultimatum from the Supreme Council. Elections were eventually held. The National Party of Transylvania, under Maniu and Vaida-Voevod, the Peasant Party of Bessarabia, and the National Party of the Union of Bukovina were united in their

---

[18] M. O. Hudson, in House and Seymour, *op. cit.*, p. 215.

representation. The result was surprising. The Liberals lost heavily. A certain number of Socialists appeared.

In the last days of November a firm note was sent to Bucharest from Paris. On December 2, just previous to the expiration of the ultimatum, King Ferdinand directed Dr. Vaida-Voevod, of well-known democratic tendencies, to form a cabinet consisting of the Transylvanians, Old Roumanians of the Peasant and Socialist parties, including Dr. Lupu as Minister of the Interior, and for a very few days even General Averescu, who, however, resigned on December 17.

Roumania's decision to sign the peace treaties came as a dramatic accompaniment of the departure of the American peace delegation from Paris on December 9. It was seven o'clock in the evening. Outside waited the automobiles that were to take the Americans to the station. There came a telephone inquiry whether or not Mr. Polk would sign the Roumanian treaty before his departure. He replied in the affirmative.[19] The treaty was then signed by Polk, White, and General Bliss in the Hotel Crillon. The Roumanians signed the treaty on the following day, as well as the Austrian and Bulgarian treaties.[20]

The signature of the peace treaties fixed definitely the territorial boundaries of Roumania in relation to her neighbors. Only the acquisition of Bessarabia needed more definite legal basis. However, on March 3, 1920, in view of the Roumanian Government's compliance with the Allies' demands on the evacuation of Hungary, and the signing of the minorities treaties, the Supreme Council issued a statement in which it pronounced itself in favor of the union of Bessarabia with Roumania and expressed its desire to conclude a treaty in recognition of this.[21] The treaty was eventually signed on

[19] *Current History,* 1920, II, 10.

[20] The peace treaties can be found in Carnegie Endowment for International Peace, *The Treaties of Peace,* 2 volumes, New York, 1924; *Treaties, Conventions, International Acts, Protocols and Agreements between the United States of America and Other Powers, 1910–1923,* Vol. III, Washington, 1923, compiled by W. M. Malloy, under the resolution of the Senate of August 19, 1921 (Sen. Res. No. 130, 67th Congress, 2d Session).

[21] "After taking into full consideration the general aspirations of the populations of Bessarabia and the Moldavian character of that region from the geographical and ethnographical points of view, as well as the historic and economic arguments, the Principal Allied Powers announce themselves, therefore, in favor of the reunion of Bessarabia with Roumania which has now been formally declared by the Bessarabian representatives, and are desirous to conclude a treaty in recog-

October 28, 1920, between the British Empire, France, Japan, and Roumania.

Thus Roumania realized her nationalistic ambitions and transformed herself into "România Mare" out of the fortunes of the war. While her old area included 53,244 square miles, the territory added by the peace treaties had an area of 60,634 square miles. The population figure of 1912 was 7,234,919; but today the greater nation occupies more than 113,000 square miles and has about 18,172,000 population, the area being equal to the combined states of New York, New Jersey, Pennsylvania, Delaware, Maryland, and Connecticut, or about equal to Norway or Italy.

Thus the whole Roumanian nation, separated for over one thousand years, became a political unity, though some of its nationals are still left in southern Russia, eastern Hungary, Czechoslovakia, Yugoslavia, and northwestern Bulgaria. The former Roman Dacia, built up by Emperor Trajan, came out of her historical grave, after fifteen hundred years, to live again.

On the other hand, the people of Greater Roumania were presented with staggering problems. To unify the new provinces with the old country, to fuse all new people in a new state, to counterbalance the effects of their long separation, to rebuild the robbed and ruined state and repair the damages of the war, to educate the newly enfranchised masses of the people, to execute agrarian, economic, and political reforms, to exploit the vast Roumanian natural wealth, to form a stronger middle class, to solidify the international position of Roumania—these were mighty tasks confronting the Roumanian people in their new "România Mare."

nition of this as soon as the conditions stated have been carried out. They consider that in this reunion the general and particular interests of Bessarabia should be safeguarded, more especially as regards its relations with the neighboring countries, and that the rights of minorities in it should be guaranteed on the same terms as those residing in other parts of the Roumanian Kingdom . . . ."; see H. W. V. Temperley, *Survey of International Affairs 1920–1923,* p. 501; C. U. Clark, *Bessarabia,* pp. 227 ff.; A. Popovici, *The Political Status of Bessarabia,* chapter ix, "Roumanian Bessarabia," and chapter x, "Diplomatic Negotiations Relating to Bessarabia after Her Union with Roumania," pp. 170–223; A. Boldur, *La Bessarabie et les relations Russo-Roumaines,* chapter xii, "L'Indépendance de la Bessarabie et la reconnaissance internationale juridique," pp. 170–82.

PART II

POLITICAL LIFE

CHAPTER VI

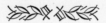

CHARACTER AND BASIS OF ROUMANIAN POLITICS

The Mind of the Peasant

THE foundation of the Roumanian nation is the peasant, who has evolved beyond his pastoral stage and is now mainly engaged in agricultural pursuits. He still shows many traces of the centuries of oppression which have been his lot. In the words of the eminent historian, Professor James T. Shotwell:

History has many examples of the hard endurance of sects or peoples under persecution, the most notable being the Jews. But no more remarkable instance of mere vitality and dogged persistence can anywhere be found than that furnished by this [Roumanian] people, so long lost sight of by history itself.[1]

The almost continuous invasions of Goths, Huns, Magyars, and Slavs in the distant past never succeeded in uprooting these peasants, who survived under such terrible conditions that as late as 1917 they could be described as semi-feudal.[2] While the West was passing through the great renaissance of art, literature, and science, from the fifteenth to the nineteenth centuries, the Turk laid his heavy hand on the Danube and the Balkan regions. Thus the transformation of political institutions toward democracy and nationalism was delayed and Roumania was left an anachronism in modern Europe. But the Turk was not the only one who imposed his domination on the Roumanian. The mercenary Greek or feudal rulers went hand in hand with other foreign oppressors. In Transylvania the Magyar followed his violent anti-Roumanian policy, which, for that matter,

---

[1] J. T. Shotwell, "Roumania and Its People," in the Society of Friends of Roumania, *Bulletin,* October 18, 1926, pp. 27–32.

[2] The reader is referred to D. Mitrany's *The Land and the Peasant in Rumania,* a historical survey of the land and farmers of Roumania of surpassing interest and importance.

was directed against other minor nationalities as well. In Bessarabia the Russians tried very hard to make the Roumanian population forget its national traditions and loyalties.

The results naturally left their impress on the people. The less pleasant side of the picture is well described by Professor A. I. Andrews:

> The years of Turkish and alien control left their blight upon the Roumanian principalities—the years of self-repression that followed Turkish rule, years when Roumanians had to face disappointments, when every "friend" appeared time and time again to be a selfish enemy disguised, when the Roumanians, flattered and caressed when needed (1877), were tossed aside ignominiously as soon as they had become inconvenient. Such years were not fortunate in some results, even if absolutely essential to the vital needs of Roumanian aspiration. There is venality enough in the bureaucratic organizations of other countries without the excuse of Turkish tutelage that the Roumanian could present. There is graft enough, waste enough, in other Governments, extortion enough without other countries being able to point to anything like Phanariot rule as a school for such accomplishments. If Roumanian officials of all ranks have been in the past more or less justly accused of "living on their wits" and of practising the wisdom of the serpent, it is because the Great Powers did their best to force Roumanian leaders of the past to practice any methods that might save their nation.[3]

The most amazing characteristic of the Roumanian people is that they have been able to maintain their language, culture, and religion throughout centuries in spite of war and servitude. Through all these thousand years and more they not only preserved but even intensified their faith in themselves. The peasant has preserved his ways and customs so remarkably that even today the villagers wear Dacian dress and build homes just as when the Emperor Trajan found them. The concrete evidence of this characteristic in politics is intense nationalism and patriotism and conservatism. The peasant clings to slow evolutionary methods and shrinks from radical changes. Dr. Mitrany observes that

> this conservatism is practical rather than sentimental, however, and an extremely reactionary ministry or an intolerable general situation, like the continued general paralysis of trade, might conceivably lead to a change.

On the other hand, the peasant is not very fond of politics. For him the main interest is the land, and he believes politics should be

---

[3] A. I. Andrews, "Historical Impressions of Roumania," in *Roumania,* April 1929, pp. 5–13.

left to those who do not have to work for their living.[4] In fact he is rather suspicious of his new privilege and power, which often had been turned against him. He is distrustful of strangers, but is a most hospitable fellow when he is sure that the visitor can be trusted. In fact his hospitality sometimes reaches the extent of American methods of "treating." There is an air of plaintive melancholy about him, due to long subjection and oppression; but in spite of it, he frequently possesses grace and inherent dignity. His folk-songs betray alike pathos and imagination. His family integrity is shown in the marked affection for the father and by the fact that, even when existing in direst poverty, a family welcomes every new addition— frequent in nearly every case.

The trait of obstinacy, which nurtured and preserved Roumanian civilization through hostile centuries, is still evident in the peasant. He is hard to convince, and it takes time to make him see a new point of view. He does nothing without reflection, and often the reflection is long. Slow as he is to make up his mind, he is also slow to change it. He remembers well and does not forget. Motives are a matter of indifference to him. Deeds and results are the things that he is looking for. He does not look for trouble, and when one looks into the blue eyes of the peasant one cannot imagine him fighting. Once brought, however, to recognize that necessity, he goes through the greatest hardships to win a cause. When he is sure that he has been wronged, his revenge is cruel. His dances are not bois-terous, neither is his voice loud; but he delights in colors, and some of his songs impress the listener with a suppressed passion, which is reflected in the beautiful peasant art. There are no warmer-hearted people in Europe, nor any more charitable, courteous, and polite. They are quite satisfied with their social standing, and for them the land is the chief form and source of wealth.

Hand in hand with conservatism, tradition shapes the life of the peasant. A Roumanian folk-proverb says that "the stone which rolls all the time will never be covered with pleasant green moss," and old moss is very much appreciated by the Roumanians.

---

[4] The author tried to engage a number of Roumanian peasants in a discussion of politics. The most interesting reply, or rather response, came from a peasant woman in a village near Vălenii-de-Munte. When her husband was asked what he thought of the political situation, his wife quickly stepped up and made the following answer: "He is not going to tell you about politics because he is interested in his work and must work for his family." Her caution evidently was mixed with prudence and an unwillingness to have the provider of the family go into the political game.

Traditions made sacred by centuries of observance and handed down from generation to generation still give the peasants many pagan beliefs and rituals. The old chronicles mention the Roumanians as a people "which, though professing the Christian faith, is yet nevertheless given to the practice of manifold pagan rites and customs, wholly at variance with Christianity." But the upper classes never have been appreciative of the external practices of their church and the peasants escaped its domination because the use of the Slavonic and then of the Greek language made the substance of its teachings largely foreign to them.

From one point of view the methods of the Roumanian church are fundamentally opposed to Protestant methods. Religion in the East does not take on a theological aspect, but an aesthetic one, the religious idea being expressed there mainly in an ecstatic way. The duty of the church is conceived to be to provide an environment in which the people will feel, not think, religiously. Consequently, music and color and incense are used, the underlying idea being that religion rejects appeals to reason, and consequently sermons and theology have no place in the services. The country priests are not learned men, in general, but through their voice and appearance they provide the atmosphere in which religious feeling is fostered. The philosophy of the Roumanian church is that beautiful environment is more apt to suggest good thoughts and good action than a theological sermon. On the other hand, the Catholic church of Transylvania stimulated the pride of the oppressed people and called forth a great response also beyond the Carpathians when its young devotees studied the Roumanian language, proving its Latinity, and did historical research on the origins of the Roumanians.

Thus we may describe the Roumanian peasant as a person possessing in a remarkable degree the qualities of patience, perseverance, and endurance, with the capacity for laborious effort peculiar to an agricultural race. He is not apt at assimilating quickly the externals of civilization, but the tenacity and determination with which he pursues his national and personal aims lead to final and lasting results. He is industrious and orderly, but phlegmatic as to business. The tranquillity of his village and farm has been invaded by political agitators, and the peasant does not seem overjoyous about it. A young Roumanian student summarizes this attitude: "Roumanian peasant knows how to work the fields, to believe in God, to love the King, to respect the law, to love his country, to fight, if necessary, and to die if it is for the good of the country; but he cannot understand why there are so many speeches and conflicting points of view in politics. If everybody is so interested in the happiness of Roumania, why do they not work all together in a healthful and useful co-operation? We see that the Roumanian peasant in his simple manner of understanding gives us the best solution for a good government!"

The peasant finds a way out of this confusing world of politics by centering his loyalty upon the royal house. The portraits of the King, of the Queen, and of princes and princesses of Roumania bedeck the walls of almost every peasant cottage in the country. The King personifies, for them, their nation and all its real or imagined glory. The peasant is now rather hopeful. Things are, after all, somewhat better than before—and the new King has all their confidence. The King's influence thus has been paramount because he represents sentiment and something that is larger than politics.

The Upper Classes

Roumanian national feeling was greatly stimulated early in the nineteenth century through contacts with France. Young Roumanians found their inspiration in the writings of Hugo and Lamartine, and in the courses which were given by Michelet, Mickiewicz, and Quinet. French laws and institutions have been imitated, and the great majority of the present leaders have been trained in Paris. This class looks upon politics as a profession and nearly all of them are inevitably drawn into it. The principle of free selection for government posts is continually bringing in new blood, and most Roumanian administrators today are young men highly trained in cultural or professional subjects abroad. Because of the radical changes which each new government makes in the administrative positions, the political game[5] is highly exciting and assumes spoils aspects comparable to those current in the United States. The campaigns of the opposition to the government are featured by extravagant charges and attacks. Meetings of protest are frequently held

[5] Maude Parkinson mentions an interesting practice of the pre-war elections in her book, *Twenty Years in Roumania* (New York, 1922), pp. 35–36: "By some means or other, names of people long ago dead are inserted in the register, and, as a man remarked in my hearing at one election, 'In my father's lifetime he never had a vote, but now he is dead they are giving him one.'"

and processions follow. Canvassing is thorough, and as the election approaches meetings become more numerous and excitable. Then, just as quickly, the excitement subsides.

The same love of ornament seen in the peasants' costumes and embroideries is reflected in the luxurious and expensive mode of life of the upper classes. Usually they reach the limit of their income, but they are energetic at times and confident always in the harvest of the future.

SOCIAL DIVISIONS

On the eve of independence there were at one end of the social scale in Roumania the large group of servile peasants and at the other a small number of privileged landowners and a few professional men and urban traders. The interpolation of foreign domination over a period of several centuries with its subsequent alien administration between the mass of the peasants and the few landlords, in addition to the backwardness of economic life and the patriarchal system of life, created no middle class. When Roumania was transformed into a national state, the sudden demands of self-government absorbed all the educated and trained people into the service of organizing the state. With the expansion of towns and the growing demand for manufactured goods, the absence of money and labor markets, in addition to the aversion of the landed people to the business of trading, left the economic functions of trader and economic *entrepreneur* largely to foreigners and Jews. The liberal professions and public office became the ambition and livelihood of every upper and middle-class Roumanian. The new bureaucracy, basing its desire on mercenary and often on individual motives, now joined with great zeal in the new nationalism, hoping thereby to retain control of the political machine and thus also to retain their positions.

When the thorough agrarian reform was accomplished during the World War, the landlords lost everything, as there was no buffer middle class between them and the peasants, who had now begun to be welded into a conscious social class. The remaining members of the ruling class found themselves with an exhausted social program and were forced to look for a new program in the attributes of the nationalistic policy of the state, which they controlled. But gradually their policy over-reached itself; and with the political consciousness of the peasants at length established and aided by the disintegrating influence of events, the peasant masses came to the fore and for a short time assumed the leadership of the state.

Character of Roumanian Politics

Throughout this period the political power and the central point of political gravity was almost entirely in the hands of the Crown, the politicians, and the state officials. The most important political factor was the King, who assumed the policy of arbitrary absolutism out of necessity. The internal and foreign conditions of the new state and the inexperience of the masses made this quite mandatory. Before the war, King Carol I had maintained the Crown in a strong position as arbiter of the parties. He possessed the constitutional power of absolute veto and of dissolution of parliament, in addition to the power to appoint and dismiss his ministers. He had often been instrumental himself in changing the government, thus supplementing to a certain extent the will of a people young and as yet unused to govern itself. Once in power by the appointment of the King, his government often formed its majority in parliament by influencing the elections. Thus the Crown became the supreme arbitrator in the affairs of the kingdom, notwithstanding the fact that the method imposed on the sovereign the very difficult task of interpreting popular opinion and movements. But obviously this political method could be relaxed only with the progressive education of the masses and with the increased representation of the lower classes. But a rapid change toward more direct democratic methods did not seem very practicable considering the unfavorable conditions of the new state and the nearness of reactionary and unfriendly monarchies.

During the pre-war years the King alternated the Liberals and the Conservatives in power, though the Liberals came in for a larger share of the favors. Each party held its adherents together by a judicious distribution of favors and lucrative positions, which practice even today imposes on Roumania the burden of supporting a disproportionately large bureaucratic class. King Ferdinand, who succeeded to the throne on the eve of the World War, did not maintain the total aloofness of the Crown. He found in the late leader of the Liberal Party, Ion Brătianu, his principal collaborator. The war and the difficulties at the beginning of the post-war period accentuated the closeness of this collaboration.

In order to understand the part that the Brătianus played on the political stage of Roumania, we must recognize that the dominating characteristic of Roumanian politics in its present stage of evolution, as well as before and after the World War, is the presence of strong political personalities. The moving spirit in politics found expression not in the programs of political parties but in men using their extraordinary abilities or strong measures. The political parties have until recently been centered not around certain definite programs but around outstanding individuals.

Normally there seems to be no room for more than two large political groups in Roumania crystallizing into opposite interests. This held true until the World War. The Liberals formed a sort of group of the Left, and the Conservatives one of the Right; there was no political middle class to speak of. The Liberals continued the traditions of Continental Liberalism. The Conservatives stood on the principle of the *status quo* and tried to prevent any radical reforms.

But the World War brought a profound political and economic change. The Conservatives disappeared with the land reform and because of the Germanophile tendencies of some of their members. On the other hand, the new provinces brought into the state various sections of the Roumanian people with widely different outlooks who found no satisfaction with the traditional political outlooks of pre-war days. The Liberals, with exhausted programs, swung to the Right under the attacks of Radicalism and Socialism and took the place vacated by the Conservatives. They had now to find a new program of reconstruction, eventually based on economic policy. Thus the two-party system was temporarily destroyed. Very rapidly, however, the millions of small and newly independent peasant proprietors found expression in a new National-Peasant Party, which developed a political creed corresponding to their new conditions. It took the place on the left wing of the Roumanian politics, held formerly, but now vacated, by the Liberals. Thus in a comparatively short time Roumanian politics completed a circle and returned again to what is virtually a two-party system.

With the return of this political system and in view of the changed political, economic, and social conditions of the country, it seems probable that in the future Roumania will tend to adopt fair constitutional methods of the Western type, based on free elections and popular opinion, as interpreted by the parliament and the Crown, subject of course to the raising of the level of political education of the masses.

One cannot, however, overlook the influence of the present electoral system. The electoral provision by which the party receiving more than forty per cent of the total votes is given fifty per cent of all the parliamentary mandates, and parties receiving less than two per cent of the total receive no mandates whatever, obviously has more disadvantages than advantages. It is true that the plan gives the government a strong working majority and so saves its program from delay; but that very situation prevents the formation of an effective opposition whose function of criticism and analysis is so indispensable to a parliamentary system. The government can too easily ride roughshod over all opposition. The National-Peasant Government entered office with a full recognition of this inequitable situation, for they had long suffered from it as a minority. Their intention was to substitute a real proportional representation system which would give more adequate expression to the political divisions of the country. They neglected to adopt the plan, however, and are now the victims of their own neglect.

The objections to the plan do not end with the weakening of parliamentary criticism but extend to the electoral process itself. In the first place, the character of the campaign is lowered by the inequities of the electoral system. The small parties, perceiving their hopeless position under the two per cent rule, either use extreme demagogical methods which add bitterness to an already discordant situation, or they conclude electoral agreements with other parties, usually the government, without any substantial unity in program. When these alliances are abandoned after the election, no clear meaning can be read into the public mandate. Secondly, the system encourages frequent and irresponsible changes of colors by party leaders who join the government groups to insure personal election. Parties are consequently unstable in character, and frequently "coalitions" are so mixed in character as to be incomprehensible to foreign observers and no doubt to many native ones as well. Personalities as substitutes for programs, one of the basic defects of Roumanian politics, are an inevitable accompaniment of the plan; lack of party discipline and the absence of clear-cut programs are further symptoms of its injurious effects. The electorate itself is thus habitually led to follow the glib but vague promises of political leaders.

When to these shortcomings there is added the tendency of the electorate to vote for the government, whose campaign efforts carry the seal and approval of a popular King, it is evident that Roumania has not yet worked out an electoral system which will effectively record the will of the electorate after a full and unimpaired discussion of concrete issues.

ORIGINS OF POLITICAL PARTIES

The origins of the Roumanian political parties can be dated from the eighteenth century, when the Greek influence began to make itself felt and the principalities had to struggle for the revival of their national entities. Certain alignments can be discerned among the *boiars,* who alone enjoyed political rights. The nationalistic factions, in order to oppose the Greek preponderance, rallied to the support of the neighboring powers and hence were called the "Austrian" Party, etc., according to the country upon which the faction relied. After 1798 these factions crystallized into a "National" Party under the influence of the French Revolution; it was dubbed the "French" Party by its opponents. Under the influence, on the one hand, of the French Revolution of 1848, and with the achievement of national independence, on the other, the political groups divided on the principle of internal reforms, giving the rise to the National-Liberal and Conservative parties. They were able to cooperate immediately before the accession of Prince Carol to the Throne and formed a coalition ministry at the introduction of the Constitution in 1866. Then they split again and soon their main programs were exhausted in hasty legislative actions. Very soon the principle of the leadership of personalities asserted itself. The parties began to be known according to the names of their leaders. Thus, for example, when a follower of Brătianu was asked to state the program of the Liberal Party, he replied: "We are a collectivity, of which M. Brătianu is the highest expression."[6] Hence the Liberals were often called "Collectivists."

THE NATIONAL-LIBERAL PARTY

The politics of pre-war Roumania during the war and for ten years after the war were dominated by the National-Liberal Party (Partidul Național Liberal). Its roots went back to the revolution-

[6] Great Britain, *Peace Handbooks,* No. 23, "Rumania," p. 64.

ary movement for independence of the "reds" in 1848, when Ion C. Brătianu and his brother Dumitru, C. A. Rosetti, the brothers Golescu, and Nicolae Bălcescu formed their revolutionary committee in Bucharest. They had a very small following of the intellectuals and small landed proprietors. Their creed was the creation of the independent Roumanian state. Between 1862 and 1866 Brătianu and Rosetti organized with their followers the National Party, which became in 1875 the National-Liberal Party. It did most of the ruling in Roumania. Under its auspices the national revival and the consolidation of the Roumanian state were zealously furthered. To its credit goes the first distribution of the land to the peasants in 1864; the establishment of the throne of a foreign dynasty in 1866, which put an end to the competition for this honor among the Roumanian families; and, finally, the victorious war of 1877, by which the independence of the country was established and Roumania became a kingdom. The Liberals created the economic framework of the country. The "Banca Națională," founded in 1880, as well as the "Banca Românească," founded in 1911, were in their hands and became the strongholds of their financial power and the undertakings of the country. The "Banca Agricolă," established by the Conservatives in 1894, had a difficult life and came finally, after the war, into the orbit of influences of the Liberal financial institutions.

As Roumania was predominantly an agricultural country, the Liberal Party could easily dominate the economic life of the state with their financial institutions enjoying the favors of the national bank. More independent groups were headed by the "Banca Marmarosch, Blank & Cie," founded in 1848 by Jews with foreign support; but to insure peace the Liberals were admitted to the administrative council of this bank. Foreign capital was needed and used—but frowned upon.

After 1907 the Liberals began to press for the introduction of universal manhood suffrage and an agrarian reform, which became the subjects of practical politics after the Second Balkan War but had to be postponed until 1917.

From the days of his surreptitious entry into his new kingdom, Prince Carol's sympathy was with Ion Brătianu, the great leader of the Liberals, whose family was to influence most actively the first hundred years of the historical development of modern Roumania. Ion C. Brătianu (1821–91), with King Carol I, was justly regarded as the founder of the modern Roumanian kingdom. He studied in Paris, and in 1848 he participated in the Roumanian rebellion, acting as prefect of police in the provisional government formed in that year. He was glad to escape to Paris after the arrival of the Russian and Turkish armies, but once there he continued his propaganda in favor of the union and autonomy of the Danubian principalities. His activity brought him a fine and imprisonment in a lunatic asylum for a short time. In 1856 Brătianu returned to his country and became one of the strongest Liberal leaders. He helped to depose Prince Cuza in 1866 and became very influential in the election of Prince Carol, whom he brought to Roumania. He held several ministerial positions afterward. In 1876 he formed a Liberal Cabinet, aided by C. A. Rosetti, which held its post for twelve years. The revision of the Constitution of 1883 estranged both leaders and after that time Brătianu was the sole leader of the Liberals. The extreme length of his tenure in office rendered him extremely unpopular in the country. He died on May 16, 1891.

Brătianu's associate, Constantin A. Rosetti (1816–85), was born in Bucharest, coming of an old *boiar* family of Italian origin. In his early youth not only was he a soldier in the national army, but his pen gained for him a considerable reputation, for he composed and published many Roumanian poems. As mayor of Bucharest in 1848 he contributed powerfully to the spread of the democratic movement and was forced to flee to France, where he was the companion of Michelet, Quinet, and other leading writers. With their help and that of the Brătianu brothers and Golescu, Rosetti managed to issue patriotic publications.[7] He became Minister of Education in 1866, was president of the Chamber of Deputies in 1877, and was appointed Minister of the Interior in 1881–82. During his last years he founded and edited the journal *Românul*.

The successor of Brătianu in the leadership of the Liberal Party was Dimitrie A. Sturdza, who started his career as private secretary to Prince Cuza but turned against him and joined Brătianu in his overthrow. In 1899 he was chosen to lead the Liberal Party. He became the most ardent defender of German policy for Roumania. Sturdza held the office of Prime Minister four times and represented the narrowest type of nationalism. During his régime the program of the Liberal Party was very near to that of the Old Conservatives.

---

[7] It is believed that he also enjoyed the support of William Gladstone, who became a Roumanian citizen by an act of the Roumanian legislature about 1861.

The younger members of the party, influenced partly by socialistic doctrines, were opposed to his conservative leadership. A schism seemed to be evident, but the unity of the party was renewed at the end of the nineteenth century when Ion I. C. Brătianu and Vintilă I. C. Brătianu, the sons of their great father, assumed the leadership. Under their influence new programs, especially of a social nature, were advanced.

Ion I. C. Brătianu (1864–1927), the older son of the late I. C. Brătianu, was educated in Paris as a civil engineer. In 1907 he was appointed Minister of the Interior of the Cabinet of Sturdza, whom he succeeded in 1909 as chief of the Liberal Party. His personality is intimately connected with the most famous and brilliant period of modern Roumania and his party. His pre-war foreign policy followed the desires of King Carol, despite the fact that he inherited the Francophile tendencies of his father. But he did not hesitate to stand energetically against the Germanophile desires of the King in the royal council, which met at the beginning of August 1914, and was able to have the country follow the policy of neutrality. After the death of Carol he convinced, with the aid of Queen Marie, the new King Ferdinand that the national interest of Roumania lay in the direction of the Allies. When the fortunes of the war turned against Roumania, Brătianu had to give up the leadership to General Averescu and to the leader of the Conservative Party, Marghiloman, who concluded the peace of May 7, 1917, which seemed to spell the doom of Roumanian aspirations. Notwithstanding the abuse of some of his countrymen, Brătinau stood firm in his opinion that the King should not ratify the "abominations" of the Bucharest treaty. The events justified his view, and in November 1918 Brătianu reassumed the reins of the government.

As the chief representative of his country at the Paris Peace Conference, Brătianu staunchly opposed the dominating attitude of the Allies. When he saw that the Allied leaders could not and would not understand the situation, he did not hesitate to occupy Budapest and stop the outrages of the bolshevized Magyars. In 1922 Brătianu witnessed the coronation of his sovereigns of the Greater Kingdom and in the succeeding year his government passed a new constitution. He died on November 24, 1927, being 63 years old. His death came very shortly after that of King Ferdinand. Both represented the transformation of the Old Kingdom into one of the most powerful and united states of that part of Europe. With him passed also the old and traditional conceptions of his party, and new spirit was soon to be imbued into the political life of Roumania.

King Ferdinand had trusted him implicitly and their relations had been friendly and confidential, even after Brătianu's position on the question of royal succession led him to take, unfortunately, a strong stand against the return of Prince Carol. During the periods when he was Prime Minister, and at one time when he was allied with the late Take Ionescu, he initiated and carried through many reforms, the more notable being the introduction of universal suffrage, the agrarian law which divided large estates, and measures for the amelioration of the conditions of the Jews. From 1922 until his death Brătianu, with his brother Vintilă, was practically the dictator of his country.

During the lifetime of Brătianu, the Liberal Party became the fundamentally conservative party of the new kingdom and clung to its financial, industrial, and commercial interests. It tried to strengthen its supremacy by imposing an economic program designed to strengthen the classes it represented, favoring high tariffs, trusts, and monopolies. It stood for nationalistic economic development, but sometimes its critics accused it of confusing the nation with its own partisans. To forestall the growing strength of the parties representing the peasant masses, the Liberals tightened their grip on the country, trying to keep the opposition weak and subordinate. They were able to do this for a while with the support of the King, who trusted Brătianu, the latter being convinced that it was his duty and his destiny to sustain his father's prestige.

The death of Ferdinand and Ion Brătianu weakened the Liberals to such an extent that Vintilă Brătianu could keep the Liberals in power only for a year.

Vintilă I. C. Brătianu, the second son of Ion C. Brătianu, was born in 1867 in Bucharest. He studied engineering in Paris and became an architect after his return to his country. When his older brother, Ion I. C. Brătianu, took over the political leadership of the Liberals, Vintilă joined the Liberals and helped his brother in reorganizing and restoring the party. Before the war he was mayor of Bucharest, and in 1916 he was appointed first Minister of War, and later Minister of Finance in all the Liberal cabinets, and introduced a number of financial and other economic reforms, pursuing until nearly the last moment a policy antagonistic to foreign capital. After the sudden death of his brother in 1927, Vintilă took over the leadership of the Liberal Party and became Prime Minister. Because of the uncertain economic and financial conditions of the country, he attempted to form a coalition government, his attempts always being frustrated by Iuliu Maniu. He had to resign on November 3, 1928, becoming the outstanding leader of the opposition. His opposition to the impending return of Carol became almost an obsession with him and in May 1930 he had a serious encounter with Prince Nicolae, a member of the regency council, over his intention to publish a pamphlet dealing with the personal affairs of the future king. When Carol was proclaimed King, Vintilă could not prevent a schism in his party. His nephew, Gheorghe I. Brătianu, declared in favor of the King. On July 9, 1930, Vintilă had to recognize the new political situation by having an audience with King Carol. He died suddenly soon afterward, on December 22, 1930.

Dr. Gheorghe I. Brătianu (1898–   ) has been professor of world history in the University of Iași since 1923. In 1927, 1929, and 1931 he was elected deputy and since June 1930 has continued to be head of a dissident Liberal faction, which seceded from the Liberal Party as a result of the party's opposition to the accession of King Carol.

The new attitude of the party came with the election of a very able and experienced statesman, I. G. Duca, to the leadership, in February 1931. In his speech at the conference of the Liberal Party Duca emphasized the fundamental points of the new Liberal program: complete loyalty to the Throne, and a determination to assist King Carol in carrying out his mission of consolidating a united Roumania. On the economic side Duca stood for a reduction of taxation, the heavy burden of which now made all economic development impossible. Satisfactory co-operation with foreign capital was especially affirmed by Duca. Nowhere in his address did Duca mention the traditional watchword of Vintilă Brătianu — "through ourselves." On the contrary, he insisted upon "a more active collaboration with foreign finance," and emphasized "the scrupulous respect of engagements contracted."

Dr. Ion G. Duca was born in 1879 at Bucharest. He studied law in Paris and commenced his career as a district judge (1903). He soon achieved a reputation as a political writer of ability. He has held several posts in past cabinets and achieved important successes in Roumanian foreign policy as Minister for Foreign Affairs from 1922 to 1925. He is one of the most agile and energetic leaders of his party, with tastes tending in a scholarly direction. He excels in logic and long debates.[7a]

During the absence of other Liberal chieftains, the leadership of the party went usually to one of the oldest members of the organization, Dr. Angelescu (1869–   ). Physician by profession and professor and director of the surgical clinic at the Faculty of Medicine in Bucharest, he has participated actively in politics only when the Liberals formed a government. From 1917 to 1918 he was Roumanian Minister to the United States. As Minister of Education in Brătianu's Cabinet of 1922–26 he reorganized the educational system, though he failed to provide the country with a satisfactory supply of trained teachers.

Another very strong candidate for two years for the leadership was Dr. Constantin Argetoianu (1871–), a very gifted though unstable politician, who at present is not in the fold of the Liberal Party. After studying law, medicine, and literature in Paris, he joined the diplomatic service in 1897. In 1914 he was elected senator and in 1918 joined Averescu's Cabinet as Minister of Justice. With Averescu and others he formed the People's League at the end of the war, which became the People's Party in 1920. Later he left it with a number of followers and joined the National-Democratic Party of Professor Iorga. Being again dissatisfied with the coalescence of this group with the Transylvanian *bloc* under Maniu, Argetoianu left it in 1925. In 1927 he joined Prince Ştirbey in his Cabinet and then transferred his allegiance to the Liberals on the eve of the death of Ion I. C. Brătianu, whom he left in 1930, and has continued to be active in politics as an independent. His personal wealth allows him to be opportunistic in his outlooks and convictions. He is well known as an excellent speaker who makes his speeches bitter with sarcasm. In the present Cabinet of Iorga, Argetoianu is both Minister of Finance and Minister of the Interior.

Among other important members of the Liberal Party can be

[7a] The photographs of Duca seem never to do him justice. His plain manners and simplicity of behavior make him very popular. In contrast to the luxuriousness of the homes of other politicians, the apartment of Duca in Bucharest is the simplest one observed by the author. The leadership of Duca had been acknowledged for some time and there was a strong undercurrent against Vintilă Brătianu's leadership before his death. The author had a distinct impression that Vintilă's control was based more on tradition than on the qualities of his leadership. At any rate, the author met him just before his death and could not fail to compare the pleasantness of Duca with the authoritative and superior attitude of Brătianu.

mentioned the following: Tancred Constantinescu, Chirculescu, N. Săveanu, Orleanu, Const. Brătianu, General Moşoiu, Tătărescu, Dr. Costinescu, A. Mavrodi, and the late Alex. Constantinescu and G. Mârzescu.

Fundamentally the party represents the Old Kingdom and has hardly any popular following in the new provinces. Its Transylvanian adherents are headed by General Moşoiu and Professor A. Lapedatu, who joined Averescu in 1926 together with Goldiş and Lupaş. In Bessarabia, Professor Inculeţ, a University assistant before the war and president of the Moldavian Republic (Bessarabia) from 1917 up to the union with Roumania in 1918, belongs to the Liberals together with the well-known Professor Ion Nistor of the University of Cernăuţi.

One of the most influential and conspicuous political personalities, standing somewhat outside of any regular political group but occasionally joining the Liberals, is Professor Nicolae Titulescu (1883–   ), now Roumanian Minister to the Court of St. James. He entered the political life of his country before the World War and was one of the Roumanian delegates to the Peace Conference and one of the signatories of the Treaty of Trianon. He has published numerous legal, financial, and political studies, and built his brilliant reputation, for the most part, by his debates on the optants' question before the League of Nations. Titulescu's influence is so far-reaching that he can join any cabinet at will. Before the war he belonged to the group of Take Ionescu. During the World War he participated in the Cabinet of Brătianu and Take Ionescu. In 1920 he went into the Averescu–Take Ionescu Government. When the latter died, Titulescu gave up his positive participation in internal politics and was appointed Roumanian Minister to London. His ability to defend his country in the international field is generally recognized and highly praised, and was proved by his election to the presidency of the League of Nations Assembly in 1930. Several times since his appointment to London he has been recalled to take charge of different ministries. He is considered a sort of "reserve" politician to be called upon to solve a serious political crisis.

Titulescu, however, proved himself unable to form a cabinet of "national unity" when charged to do so by King Carol in April 1931, after the fall of the Cabinet of Mironescu on April 4, 1931. His place was taken by Professor Iorga.

After the return of King Carol, the Liberal Party was uneasy and divided under the leadership of Vintilă Brătianu. But his death and the election of I. G. Duca as his successor opened a new chapter in the history of the National-Liberal Party, which doubtless will, in due time, return to office, especially if all the recent dissentients driven out of the party by Vintilă Brătianu's unbending policy can be speedily attracted back. Duca is an experienced statesman and has a sound reputation for moderation and conciliation.

The Conservative Party

The second largest group in pre-war Roumanian politics, standing on the extreme Right, was the Conservative Party, composed almost entirely of the large landowning class, the *boiars,* who made a weak and disunited organization; their voting strength in parliament rested almost entirely on their property qualifications. Politically the Conservatives were on the defensive and opposed especially the proposed agrarian reforms and the electoral laws. The rich and influential members of this political cluster all wanted to be the heads of the party and the government. Hence their discipline was poor. At the beginning of the century its main chiefs were: Titu Maiorescu, Petre Carp, Alexandru Marghiloman, and G. G. Cantacuzino. Some years before the World War, the party began dividing into two wings, viz., the Old and the Young Conservatives, who from time to time went their own way and then again joined together. The final split occurred in 1910. Take Ionescu formed then his Conservative-Democrats into a personal following. The views of the two factions seemed to be irreconcilable. The Progressive Conservatives favored the Germanophile policy after the outbreak of the World War and the Conservative-Democrats the Francophile.

The programs of the Liberals and Conservatives, or rather the Progressive Conservatives, had some noticeable differences. The Liberals always tried to imitate France as to centralization of administrative control and universal suffrage. The Conservatives avoided concrete reforms by claiming that reforms have to be introduced slowly and only as the educational standard of the populace is raised. Of course they opposed the Liberal plans for land reform; in general, the Conservatives favored the interests of agriculture and opposed the Liberal aim to industrialize the country by a protectionist policy.

The Conservative personalities of importance were Lascăr Catargiu, Gheorghe Cantacuzino, N. Filipescu, P. P. Carp, Theodor Rosetti, Titu Maiorescu, and C. C. Arion. It was Lascăr Catargiu under whom the Conservatives organized themselves in 1880 into a party. Its younger elements, led by Carp, the so-called "Young Conservatives" or "Junimiști," favored some social reforms for the peasants. The two wings of the Conservatives were sometimes called the "Cantacuziniști" (the old Conservatives led after the death of Catargiu by Cantacuzino), and the "Carpiști."

Lascăr Catargiu was born in Moldavia in 1823. The Conservatives supported his candidacy for the Throne in 1859 because of his views on agrarian reform. In 1871 Catargiu, for the first time in Roumanian history, formed a stable Conservative Cabinet. After holding ministerial offices in 1889 and in 1891, Catargiu again in 1891 formed a cabinet, which lasted to 1895 and effected useful financial reforms. His associate, Nicolae Filipescu (1862–1916), studied at Paris and Geneva, and joined the Conservative Cabinet of 1885. In 1910 he became the leader of the "Young Conservatives"; his feud with Take Ionescu resulted in the formation of the new Conservative-Democratic Party by Ionescu. While Minister of War in Carp's Cabinet of 1910, Filipescu reorganized the army, and his and Carp's agitation was responsible in a large measure for the participation of Roumania in the Second Balkan War. After the outbreak of the World War, Filipescu and his followers favored Roumania's intervention on the side of the Allies. His followers subsequently joined Take Ionescu's pro-Entente group.

Alexandru Marghiloman (1854–1925) studied law and political science in Paris. In 1914 he assumed the leadership of his party. Being convinced that economic reasons justified close relations between his country and the Central Powers, he soon favored the Germanophile policy and refused to join Brătianu in 1916. In March 1918 his government negotiated and signed a peace with the Central Powers which has never been ratified. The agrarian revolution and the unfortunate policy of the leader destroyed the Conservative Party, which failed to obtain even a single seat in the 1920 elections. The death of Marghiloman spelled the doom of this political organization, the remains of which fused with the other groups.

PARTIES OF IONESCU AND IORGA

Take Ionescu's activities were known internationally. Born in 1858, he studied, as did many other leaders of Roumania, in Paris.

His name became known through his spectacular career as a lawyer. In 1884, when twenty-six years of age, he was elected to parliament and later joined the Conservatives. In 1891 he became Minister of Education in Catargiu's Cabinet. In the new Conservative Governments in 1899–1901 and 1904 he headed the Finance Ministries. Foreseeing a need for agrarian reform, he favored a more liberal agrarian policy; but the negative attitude of his party made him leave the Conservatives in 1908, taking with him about one-third of the members as his followers, whom he organized in a new Conservative-Democratic Party. Under Ionescu's influence and through his wide program the internal policy of Roumania was now less a struggle of personalities and more, though not very markedly, the struggle of principles. In 1912, Take Ionescu joined Titu Maiorescu's Cabinet as Minister of the Interior. In 1913 he represented his country in the peace negotiations at Bucharest. When the World War broke out, Ionescu favored the intervention of his country on the side of the Allies. More and more he was becoming the interpreter of the national ideal as an orator and writer. In 1918 he went to Paris, where, taking the Czechoslovak National Council as his example, he founded the Roumanian National Council and attempted to organize Roumanian legions in France, Italy, and Serbia. His contacts with Beneš and other revolutionary leaders provided the foundation of the future Little Entente. After his return to Roumania in the spring of 1919 Ionescu began to reorganize his party, which, however, never had a large membership, the personality of its leader being really its *raison d'être*. In the 1920 elections Ionescu was elected by a weak majority in Bucharest; other members of his group were elected only in connection with Averescu's Party. A serious loss for Ionescu was the resignation of I. Cantacuzino, former minister, from his group. Ionescu joined Averescu's Cabinet in 1920. He died soon afterward, on June 21, 1922, in Rome, and most of his followers merged into the National-Peasant Party.

The fate of Ionescu's Party was characteristic of pre-war and post-war Roumanian political life. Until recently, none of the groups springing up from time to time with a view to furthering definite political ideals lasted long.

In 1910 Professor A. C. Cuza and Nicolae Iorga created the National-Democratic Party, asking for social reforms and the renovation of the public life of Roumania. The party has never gained a large following despite the drawing power of Dr. Iorga, who stands high in the esteem of every Roumanian.[8]

Dr. Nicolae Iorga was born in 1871 in Moldavia. His studious tastes amused his neighbors when he was only six years old. After studying in Paris, Berlin, and Leipzig, he was appointed professor of universal history in the University of Bucharest. Iorga's scholarly and highly valued academic work has produced enormous quantities of valuable material. As a result of his researches, Iorga published over 20,000 documents in the *Annals* of the Roumanian Academy,[9] of which he became one of the most prominent members. He is also associate professor at the Sorbonne, and is holder of many foreign distinctions. The thesis of Iorga's research was the conviction that there is no divided history of the Roumanian people. Its past is a record of a unified nation, separated by Magyar, Russian, and German domination. He has held also that history should include the study of literature and art, and has written a number of such studies. One of the greater services that Iorga performed for his country was the establishment of summer university courses at Vălenii-de-Munte, where even before the war numerous students of nationalistic type used to gather from all parts of the present Greater Roumania. Here was really laid one of the corner stones of present-day Roumania. It is significant also that the present King Carol owes his democratic education to Iorga, his tutor. Iorga's friendship with King Ferdinand is illustrated by the fact that he actively collaborated with Ferdinand in the latter's proclamation announcing his decision to institute land reform.[10]

[8] Professor Iorga is undoubtedly one of the most beloved and influential men of Roumania. His literary works make him not only an international figure but also known to every Roumanian nationalist. He is a man of long political experience and high academic distinction, for he is not only the head of his party but also the leading Roumanian historian and is rector of the University of Bucharest.

[9] We might cite as probably the outstanding the following works: *Geschichte des Rumänischen Volkes in Rahmen Seiner Staatsbildungen* (Gotha, 1905); *Geschichte des Osmanichen Reiches Nach den Quellen Dargestellt* (5 volumes, Gotha, 1908); *Histoire des Roumains et de leur civilisation* (Paris, 1920); *The Byzantine Empire* (London, 1907); *A History of Roumania* (translated by J. McCabe, London, 1925). Furthermore, Dr. Iorga has published a great number of smaller works, and numerous articles in English, Italian, and (mainly) French.

[10] D. Mitrany, *The Land and the Peasant in Rumania,* p. 100, quotes Professor Iorga as saying in 1925, when he rose in the Chamber of Deputies to protest against the suspension of an opposition deputy from Bessarabia, Ion Buzdugan, that "His Majesty will pardon me for saying it—in the writing of which [the proclamation of land reform] I am proud to have collaborated."

After the war the National-Democratic Party of Iorga in 1924 fused with the National Party of Transylvania. After the formation of the National-Peasant Party, Iorga broke away from the new party, declaring that he remained the sole leader of the National Party. Iorga is also the director of the *Neamul Românesc* (Roumanian Nation), the official organ of the National Roumanian Party.

The Parties of Lupu and Averescu

After the introduction of the universal suffrage in Greater Roumania, there grew up several new parties in addition to the two, or we may say, three, old parties. The Labor Party was created by Gheorghe Diamandy, Gr. Trancu-Iași, Gr. Iunian, and Dr. Lupu in Iași, but disappeared in a short time. Dr. N. Lupu (born 1873) started his career as a country physician and entered the political arena about 1905. His political career really began in 1907, when during the peasant revolt in the Falciu district he succeeded in pacifying the peasants. He served during the war as a propagandist in Europe and America. In 1919 he participated in the Cabinet of Vaida-Voevod as Minister of the Interior, representing together with Mihalache the Peasant Party, of which Lupu became one of the leaders, though he always was suspected of too strong socialistic leanings, his popularity with the workers of the cities being his main strength. His radicalism gave the Liberals an opportunity to dispose of this "Government of National Coalition." After that Lupu conducted in his journal *Aurora* a strong campaign against all his opponents. After the fusion of the National-Peasant Party, Lupu announced at a banquet, given to him by his followers, that he was leaving the new party because the new formation was in favor of the return of Prince Carol, and informed his hearers that he was renewing the "Old Țărănist" (Peasant) Party. He then became a member of the Cabinets of Știrbey and Brătianu.

Of greater importance was the founding of the "People's League" in April 1918 at Iași by General Averescu, fresh from his military victories. "Papa" Averescu's official pronouncements concerned simple aims: the improvement of political morals and a reaction against the old Roumanian parties. Enjoying immense popularity throughout the country and especially among the demobilized peasants, the "league" transformed itself into a "party," whose real organizer was Constantin Argetoianu. In Transylvania, Octavian Goga, poet and politician, and on bad terms with Maniu, declared himself for the general. In 1920 Averescu came to power but lacked the energy or political talent to maintain it. His followers represented no particular class and no vested interests and claimed to have sprung "from the sufferings of the war." Hence there was really no social reason for its existence except that the Liberals could use it as a political pawn. It had only an opportunist program and could not deal with the pressing problem of Roumania. Today its influence is in eclipse and the cementing power holding it together is the reputation of its leader.

General, now Marshal, Averescu was born on April 9, 1863, at Ismail (Bessarabia). His father, a Bessarabian Roumanian, was an officer in the Russian army, from which he retired to Iaşi, following different occupations in the Roumanian administration. His son studied at Bucharest and participated in the war of independence. He continued his studies at Turin, Italy, and from 1894 to 1895 was director of the High Military Academy at Bucharest. Then he was stationed as military *attaché* at Berlin for three years and earned renown through his writings on military subjects. Later he was sent by the King on several foreign missions, especially to Russia and Germany. His reorganization of the army proved its worth during the campaigns of 1913 and 1916–18. As Minister of War in the Government of Sturdza, he had the difficult task in March 1907 of suppressing the peasant revolt. In 1912 he was appointed chief of the army. The battle of Mărăşeşti made him a national hero and the King commissioned him for a short time to negotiate with the Germans. In March 1920 Averescu formed his second cabinet, with the professed aim of saving the country from internal and foreign dangers. In 1926 he was back in power for the third time. Among his adherents let us cite the following: P. P. Negulescu, Octavian Goga, General Coandă, Ion Mitilineu, Manoilescu, Garoflid, General Văleanu, I. Petrovici, Meissner, Goldiş, Lapedatu, Lupaş, Michail Sadoveanu, and Dr. Pilescu. The large majority of his supporters are bourgeois middle class, officials, intelligentsia, and former followers of Marghiloman. Some of them have changed their allegiance recently: Manoilescu and Petrovici went to the National-Peasant Party; Lapedatu and Lupaş to the Liberals; Garoflid heads a special agricultural group. Mitilineu was rather successful as Minister of Foreign Affairs, and tried with Averescu to effect a unification with the Peasant Party in order to form a great anti-Liberal *bloc,* though without success.

One of the leading members of the party is the poet, Octavian Goga, born in 1881 in Transylvania. He distinguished himself in his youth as the editor of the *Luceǎfarul* and by his unceasing efforts on behalf of the Roumanians of Transylvania. During the war he carried on extensive propaganda in favor of Roumania joining the Allies. He became Minister of Cults in 1922 and Minister of the Interior in 1926–27. As an eminent journalist and one of Roumania's foremost national poets, Goga is a member of the Roumanian Academy.

The "Partidul Poporului" (People's Party) has had a conservative program approaching closely that of the Liberal Party. Occasionally it gains the following of the peasant classes because of the naturally conservative nature of the Roumanian farmer. But the original enthusiasm worked up for Averescu is wearing off as the Marshal has failed to fulfill the hopes of his political program. Frequently he has been suspected of harboring secret contacts with the Liberals, and as many thought that the party has been nothing more than an appendage of the Liberal Party, numerous adherents have changed their allegiance and joined other leaders.

THE PEASANT PARTY

The creation of a peasant democracy coupled with universal suffrage led to the creation of the "Partidul Ţărănesc" (Peasant Party). It has grown from the same roots as the old Conservative Party, so to speak, for both have risen from the land of Roumania, with, however, opposed points of view—great landholder against peasant. It was founded immediately after the war by a group of village teachers and priests, together with a few progressive intellectuals from the towns. Its doctrine, however, had long been advocated by the Populist movement led by C. Stere, a movement which clustered around Iaşi's review, *Viaţa Românească.* The movement was, according to Dr. Mitrany, in a degree, a counterpart of the labor movement of Western Europe.

The organization was first put on sound foundations by Ion Mihalache, and several members appeared in the parliament in the post-war elections of October 1919, electing Mihalache to their leadership. Ion Mihalache, born on March 3, 1882, was a village teacher in the district of Muscel before the war and chairman of the local teachers' association; during the war he served as a lieutenant. After the war he was elected to lead the Peasant Party, as a figure well known among the village priests and teachers. He is a self-made man, an energetic and excellent speaker. He showed his ability by extending his party organization into the rest of the country. In the Cabinet of Vaida-Voevod he served as Minister of Agriculture, and today is one of the best-known leaders of the National-Peasant Party.

The second in command of the Ţărănist Party and its general secretary was Dr. Virgil Madgearu (1887–   ), professor at the Academy of High Commercial Studies, Bucharest. He was appointed Minister of Industry and Commerce in 1918 and later Minister of Finance. Madgearu wrote numerous treatises on economics and finance and was a serious critic of the financial system of Vintilă Brătianu; his interpellations in regard to financial affairs and his inquiries into political corruption made him well known. At his side stood Grigore Iunian, a well-educated man and a very clever lawyer.

In Bessarabia there existed also a Peasant Party (old Moldavian *bloc*), at the head of which stood Pantelimon Halippa, Constantin Stere, and Ion Inculeţ. Chafing under the strain of an excessive and incompetent centralism of Bucharest, they were attracted to Mihalache, and thus this rather radical group united with the Peasant Party. They were followed by the Socialists, who were opposing the mercantilistic practice of the Liberals. The Socialists are not very strong, for the greater number of industrial workers are peasants who own land and return to it whenever occasion or necessity requires.

The "invisible head," and the ideologist of the Peasant Party, was Professor Constantin Stere (1880–   ) of Bessarabia. As a former Socialist, he had been exiled to Siberia. After his escape to Iaşi, where he was appointed professor of constitutional law, he became the leader of peasant socialism in Roumania. Shortly before the war he joined the Liberals, and at their instigation went to Transylvania during the conflict and negotiated with the Germans. After the occupation of Bucharest he edited the Germanophile journal, *Lumina*. With the coming of the peace he was charged with treason and lost his chair; but for some mysterious reason he was not tried. After that he worked (behind the scenes) in the Bessarabian Peasant Party. He assisted in formulating the administrative reform law of 1930. Publicly the party was represented by Pantelimon Halippa (1883–   ), educated in Russian and Roumanian universities, who was one of the most prominent members of the "Sfatul Țării," which at Chișinău in 1918 voted for union with Roumania. This Peasant Party fused with the Peasant Party in the Old Kingdom in 1921. Dr. Lupu was also active for some time in the Peasant Party.

However, personal dissatisfaction and the unsatisfied ambitions of Stere give rise to occasional internal political complications. From the point of view of internal politics Bessarabia still remains a problem for Roumania. The responsibility for this state of affairs is to be placed equally upon the lack of political circumspection and inadequate economic policy of the former governments; partly also upon the peculiar mentality of the Bessarabian leaders. At times apprehensions of the immediate proximity of Soviet Russia led previous governments to put into effect police measures irritating to all the nationalities of this province. Bucharest public opinion asserts that the Russians, while they did not succeed in Russianizing the Bessarabian Roumanians, did not fail to imbue the masses with that strange non-realistic and semi-anarchic mentality which they consider peculiar to the wide masses of the Russian people. Bessarabian political leaders since the incorporation of Bessarabia have always ranked with the opposition. They sympathize especially with the Peasant Party. The parliamentary elections of 1928 showed clearly that the National-Peasant Party has not yet lost its leadership in this part of the country. At that time all Bessarabia cast her vote in its favor. But soon afterward the necessity of opposition made itself apparent among the Bessarabian leaders. From the moment when Stere recognized that he was ineligible for Maniu's Cabinet, owing to his previous political record, the long story of difficulties for the National-Peasant Government began.

The Țărănists were from the very beginning considered, with the exception of the Socialists, the most democratic party of the Left. It was accused of being anti-monarchistic and bolshevistic. For example, the opposition accused Stere of bolshevizing Bessarabia and notwithstanding many proofs to the contrary, public opinion let itself be carried away by these unfounded charges. But the creation of the Peasant Party is one of the most epochal events of post-war Roumania. Hitherto Roumania had not had any political parties based on class interests and idealistic and philosophic programs. This Peasant Party, with its social character, was a distinct novelty, introducing freshness into the old political façade of Roumanian political life. It really represented the backbone of the country—the peasant.

THE NATIONAL PARTY OF TRANSYLVANIA

While the new provinces were being incorporated into the Roumanian Kingdom, a new democratic spirit was sweeping over the western provinces. The Transylvanian branch of the Roumanians was undoubtedly on a higher cultural level than its eastern branch and was different from it also in its political psychology. The Roumanian of the Old Kingdom takes politics rather lightly and does not worry about the excesses of public life. The Transylvanian, on the other hand, has lived under the domination of the Hungarians and the Germans and under the influences of Western culture, and has learned to take politics more seriously.

The traditions of the National Party of Transylvania, which had originated in 1881, were now continued. At the moment of the unification with the Roumanian territory, at the head of the party stood Iuliu Maniu, Dr. Alexandru Vaida-Voevod, Dr. Ştefan Ciceo-Pop, and Mihail Popovici, the first three being Uniats, as are the majority of the Roumanians of Transylvania, and the last belonging to the Orthodox Church, which dominates the Old Kingdom.

Dr. Iuliu Maniu was born in 1873 in Transylvania. Maniu comes from a family with long legal associations. His studies in jurisprudence began at Cluj and were continued at Vienna and Budapest. He became an advocate at Blaj and also professor of jurisprudence in the theological academy there. When twenty-six years of age he joined the National Roumanian Party, inspired with the desire to improve the status of the oppressed Roumanian minority in Hungary. With the support of Vaida-Voevod and of Vlad, he induced the Transylvanian Roumanians to abandon their passive political policy in favor of an active opposition to the Magyar régime. Despite the bitter opposition of Count Stephen Tisza he was elected deputy and became the leader of the Roumanian opposition in the Hungarian parliament. In collaboration with the leaders of the Serb, Slovak, and Croat parties in the legislature he carried on a persistent struggle in behalf of the Hungarian minorities. As legal adviser to the Greek-Orthodox church in Transylvania, he was well liked for his modesty and sincerity and came to be considered the spiritual leader of all Hungarian Roumanians before the war.

Dr. Iuliu Maniu   Dr. Vaida-Voevod
Marshal Alexandru Averescu   Dr. G. Mironescu

In 1915 the German Emperor sent Herr Erzberger to Vienna on a special mission to endeavor to enlist Maniu's assistance for the Central Powers, but Maniu, speaking for the national committee, declined. Although under Hungarian law he was exempt from military obligations, the Magyar Government thereafter sent him to the Italian and Russian fronts. Emperor Karl called him to an audience, with other national leaders, before the break-up of the empire, and asked him again to pacify his followers. Maniu refused to compromise. In November 1918 Maniu as an artillery officer contributed largely to the successful effort of Czechoslovakia to assert her independence by giving an order at the critical moment to two Roumanian regiments, then at Prague, to lend their full support to the Czechoslovak revolutionary government. In Vienna he organized the revolt of the Hungarian regiments, composed of the Transylvanian Roumanians.

Shortly afterward, Maniu with the help of Vaida-Voevod and others prepared the national assembly at Alba-Iulia under the presidency of Dr. Ştefan Ciceo-Pop which proclaimed the union of Transylvania and the Banat with Roumania. Maniu was elected president of the "Consiliul Dirigent" (Directive Council), which took over administrative control throughout Transylvania. In 1919 Maniu was elected president of the National Party of Transylvania and held this office continuously until 1931, when he announced his resignation.

Maniu gives the impression of having worked hard and suffered much in his life. He is careful in what he says and does, but is nevertheless a debater of unusual ability, though he rarely speaks; he is consistent in his policy and entirely honest and sincere; he is stolid and imperturbable in times of crisis and has sound political judgment.

In June 1931 Maniu decided to retire from public life and handed in his resignation of the leadership of the National-Peasant Party. *The Near East and India* attributes his resignation fundamentally to the fact that the Nationalists and the Peasant sections began to break up after Maniu ceased to be Premier. In 1931 the differences within the party became more and more accentuated and led to the resignation of Maniu. Since then it has not been found possible for the National-Peasant Party to agree as to the choice of a new leader.

While Maniu became the first president of the subsequently formed National-Peasant Party, Ion Mihalache and Dr. Alexandru

Vaida-Voevod became its vice-presidents. The latter was also born in Transylvania, in 1872, studied medicine in Vienna and practiced his profession for many years at Karlový Vary, now in Czechoslovakia. He joined the National Party when twenty-eight years old and from 1906 to 1918 sat as a deputy in the Hungarian parliament. He was known for his temperamental speeches. During the collapse of the Habsburg monarchy Vaida-Voevod was voicing the claims of the Roumanian national committee in the Budapest parliament, and denied the right of Hungary to speak for his compatriots. After the revolution he was delegated to represent the Transylvanian Roumanians at the Peace Conference. In 1919 he became Prime Minister and Minister for Foreign Affairs and succeeded in concluding negotiations with the Allies for the recognition of the union of Bessarabia with Roumania. In the National-Peasant Government of 1928, Vaida-Voevod took the office of the Ministry of the Interior. He resigned with Maniu in 1930.

The first vice-president of the party was Dr. Ştefan Ciceo-Pop (1858–   ), who, in spite of his advanced age, became president of the chamber of deputies, elected in 1928. He had to suffer Magyar persecution when a Roumanian deputy at Budapest before the war. He was active in organizing the Roumanian national assembly of Alba-Iulia of 1918, over which he presided.

Several Transylvanians left the ranks of the party during the post-war years, including Vasile Goldiş, present president of the cultural society *Astra,* and the poet Octavian Goga. The former finally went over to the Liberals, though, at first, like Goga, he became an adherent of Averescu.

After the resignation of Maniu from the premiership in October 1930, though his resignation from the leadership of the National-Peasant Party came somewhat later, he was succeeded by Dr. Gheorghe G. Mironescu (1874–   ), professor of the philosophy of law in the University of Bucharest, several times deputy and senator since 1910, a Roumanian of the old school and of the Old Kingdom, a former follower of Take Ionescu. During the war Mironescu founded *La Roumanie,* a Roumanian newspaper, in Paris. He is a scholar and a cultivated man, an author and traveler who has made a prolonged study of international affairs. Mironescu is very wealthy and has a Western outlook. He became Minister for Foreign Affairs in the National-Peasant Government.

Other prominent workers are Sever Bocu, very popular in the

Banat; Sever Dan, former secretary of the National-Democratic Party, well-known lawyer and energetic party man; Dr. Ion Lugojanu, the right hand of Maniu, the real organizer of the party, who knows how to put Maniu's plans into effect; Voicu Niţescu; Pavel Brătoşanu; Mihail Popovici; Gr. Junian; Grigore Filipescu; St. Gheorgianu; and Aurel Vlad.

The Creation of the National-Peasant Party

With the rise of the new forces of the Roumanian politics there came a need to have both new parties unified in order to make them effective. Several factors prevented a quicker amalgamation of the two groups. There was a lack of homogeneity in the National Party, and its personnel could not collaborate effectively with the Peasant Party. The Liberals exerted all their influence against it, hoping to continue their system of opposition from some Conservative camp, like that of Averescu's People's Party—the Liberal method of ruling in season and out.

The negotiations of Maniu with the Ţărănists progressed haltingly. For a long time no results were evident. Then a striking incident gave it great impetus. A member of the Peasant Party in Bessarabia, Ţărănist Pan Halippa, was attacked and injured by governmental, that is, Liberal, agents on Good Friday, 1925. The refusal of the government to punish the guilty intensified the hostility of the opposition. The Nationalists and the Ţărănists immediately presented a so-called democratic opposition and bound themselves to work together for the overthrow of the Liberal Government. The announcement was made by Professor Iorga and created a real parliamentary sensation. However, a complete amalgamation could not be effected. Both parties were interested in the removal of the Liberals from power and the installation of a democratic parliamentary régime based on free elections; in strict legal administration of the state; in the removal of the state of siege, corruption, export duties on wheat; and in strong support of agriculture, freedom of commerce, and facilities for the participation of foreign capital in Roumanian development. Seemingly insurmountable differences appeared, however, during the negotiations over the division of portfolios in a possible future governmental coalition. Both parties, for example, wanted to control the Ministry of the Interior, which has always influenced the elections—the party man in charge of the ministry has always brought a parliamentary majority to his party.

Furthermore, there was a difference over the appointment of certain high officials.

Eventually the fusion came about on September 26, 1926, when the executive committee of the National and Ţărănist parties met at Bucharest and agreed to a fusion. The arrangement was ratified by the united congress of the parties held at Bucharest on October 10 of the same year. The official name adopted was "Naţional-Ţărănesc" (National-Peasant Party). Maniu was elected president; Mihalache and Vaida-Voevod, vice-presidents. Madgearu, an extremely well-informed man, became general secretary.

The fusion created an all-national party, with followers in the Old Kingdom as well as in the new provinces, viz., Transylvania, Bessarabia, and Bukovina. Thus the political life of Roumania was again limited, in general, to two major parties: (1) the Liberals, standing on the extreme Right; and (2) the National-Peasant Party, standing, if we except the Socialist parties, on the extreme Left, and basing its popularity on the masses of the agricultural population. Minor parties were now forced to struggle for their mere existence. Roumania now returned to the old two-party system, which, however, differed in its tendencies and was composed of new elements.

The next step was logically an active participation of the new National-Peasant Party in the government. In this direction they were opposed by the strongest political power in Roumania—the government of the Liberals.

While the Old Kingdom still revered the prestige of the Brătianus, in the provinces the name naturally did not carry the same weight. The Brătianus knew this and were determined to give their opponents no opportunity for popular contest. But the trend of the times was against them. The death of Ion Brătianu and of King Ferdinand foreshadowed the ascent to power of the new forces, which came within a year after Brătianu had gone to his grave.

DIFFERENCES AMONG THE LEADING PARTIES

There are some fundamental and underlying differences between the Liberals and the group of Maniu.[11] There is not very much dif-

[11] For an excellent discussion see: D. Mitrany, *The Land and the Peasant in Rumania,* pp. 553–60; "Politicus's," "Clear Field for the Peasant Party," and Professor C. Rădulescu-Motru's "Rumania's New Political Life," both in *Manchester Guardian,* November 28, 1929, pp. 15–20. The number contains numerous articles of value and should be consulted in any further investigation.

ference, however, in their outlook on foreign affairs. Both parties stand for the execution of the peace treaties and for alliances with the neighboring states, and particularly for the Little Entente. Both favor the League of Nations. In one of his messages, Maniu said:

As to foreign affairs, foreign policy ought not to be identified with any person or party. It is the policy of the country. Our Government will follow the policy of its predecessors. We shall maintain existing friendships and alliances and try to establish good relations with all our neighbors.

The fundamental difference is really the struggle between mercantilism and agrarianism. The only sentiment which both parties share is the institution of private property, though the peasant has a conception of it different from that of his opponent in the political field. The Liberals want to have the land distributed according to "ability"; the peasant desires to have it distributed equally.

The Liberal Party has the greatest political experience and enjoys the credit for the greatest advances of the kingdom in the pre-war days, for the country's entry into the war, and for its aggrandizement, and is indirectly responsible for the introduction of peasant proprietorship, universal suffrage, and the equality of the Jews. But with these reforms it exhausted the traditional Continental liberalism of the nineteenth century and with the disappearance of the Conservatives it found itself in the post-war years the defender of the existing order, represented by the concentrated wealth, the vested industrial, commercial, and, especially, banking interests. From the point of view of its opponents it could not break away from a tradition based on the prolonged domination, and failed to pacify the inhabitants of the new provinces who were determined to reform the administration of the entire kingdom according to the new principles propounded by them. Before the war the Liberals stood for agrarian reform and commercial and industrial development, in opposition to the feudal principles and vested interests of the Conservative Party; but in post-war Roumania they found that while their opponents were still the representatives of the landed interests, the "landed interests" were now small farmers and, as citizens of the new order enjoying universal suffrage, were fully aware of their political strength.

It cannot be said, however, that the provinces have contributed much in political ideology. In fact, more credit goes to them for the personnel they have produced. At their best we can distinguish differences of outlook in the various functions of the state. The Liberals are authoritarians, and their opponents emphasize the democratic application of the state functions. But both parties want the state to discharge all the functions.

For the Liberal the state represents the means of political domination, nearing the extreme of dictatorship. Professor C. Rădulescu-Motru points out that the Liberals have indeed considered the state as machinery for regulating productive activity, but these measures, bolstering up national industry, "have merely led to a disguised interference by the State on behalf of certain favored institutions or individuals." Following the lines of their political creed, the Liberals considered the organization of agriculture merely a political problem, which according to them had been largely solved. But they have not considered at length a number of technical problems with which the beneficiaries of the reform had to contend. The same outlook can be seen in their educational policy. For the Liberals the school is the means of producing future public officials and not future trained workmen.

The application of such attitudes was one of the major causes of the recent economic crisis of Roumania according to the interpretation of Rădulescu-Motru: "Oil and money are for the Liberals not economic factors to be placed at the service of national prosperity, but political instruments which statesmen must reserve for the ends of power." The conception of the National-Peasant Party, above all, makes the state the chief regulator of the nation's labors, though the activities of the individuals and of the collective associations should be freed from political tutelage as much as possible under the circumstances. In agriculture the state should intensify and rationalize the farming activity. Because the mass of the people are engaged in agriculture, the farmers should be the greatest beneficiaries of state functions. The power and influence of financiers, middlemen, traders, and others of this kind should be limited, and the intrenched position of the bureaucracy and the army should be closely watched. Hence administration of the country should be decentralized and the number of officials radically reduced. State ownership and control is approved, if necessary, for public good—but only if working for the good of the nation and not a privileged group of citizens. The workers and their labor organizations also deserve favored consideration from the point of view of democratic requirements. Theoretical education should be abandoned in favor of technical schools.

The Liberals look upon the National-Peasant Party as a typical demagogical organization, attempting to break the state with its inexperienced political practices and social and political radicalism.

On the whole, the program of the National-Peasant Party resembles that of the English Labor Party rather than that of the Socialist parties of the Continent. "In brief," says Dr. Mitrany, "the Peasant program represents economically and socially a select combination of the instinct of Liberalism with the ideal of Socialism; a combination that may become even in the industrial west the program of a progressive movement indifferent to doctrine but intent upon the early realization of a social justice, through applied evolution."[12]

Under the Brătianus the Liberal Party was quite nationalistic in its opposition to the influx of foreign capital; this stand, however, has been modified with the election of Duca to the leadership of the party. The National-Peasant Party, on the other hand, favors a platform advocating more friendly relations with foreign capital.

There is also some difference, though it does not belong strictly to the program of each camp, in relation to the problem of minorities. The Liberals are apt to adopt an uncompromising nationalistic policy in regard to the Roumanian minorities. Thus, for example, Brătianu resigned his office rather than accept the minorities treaties. The Liberal Governments have tried to weaken these disturbing groups. The National-Peasant Party, on the other hand, has members who have had experience with oppressive measures, especially of the Magyars, and now seek peaceful co-operation with the minorities scattered in the new kingdom. They want to forget the past and do not want to repeat the mistakes of Budapest. When Maniu attended the National Assembly at Alba-Iulia in December 1918, he proposed in the name of his party a wide cultural and administrative autonomy for the Transylvanian minorities. His views have been slightly modified but remain substantially the same. It was a leader of his party, Dr. Vaida-Voevod, who signed the minorities treaties in 1920, and his followers are willing to follow the execution of these obligations. An indirect result of the policy of the new régime

---

[12] D. Mitrany, *The Land and the Peasant in Rumania,* p. 560, quoted by permission of Carnegie Endowment for International Peace, publishers. See also Dr. Virgil Madgearu, *Rumania's New Economic Policy;* "A Change-over to Agrarianism," in the *Manchester Guardian,* November 28, 1929, p. 27; F. A. Ogg, "Rebuilding the Economic Life of Roumania," in *Current History,* 1930, XXXII, 725–31.

became evident recently. While previously the minorities were organizing themselves in nationalistic groups to defend their aims, they
are now split into class divisions. Thus, for example, the Magyars
have their party of large landowners, one of small farmers, and a
democratic group.

The Socialist and Minor Parties

The socialist parties have furnished a certain novelty in the political life of Roumania but have never been able to play a very
strong rôle. Rather they have been glad to survive. They cannot
become important in Roumanian rural society. The landless laborers and the insufficiently landed proprietors have been partially satisfied by the agrarian reform, and their energy is now absorbed by an
appetite for more land.

The socialist movement dates back to the '80's of the last century, when an able nationalist writer, Gheorghe Panu, led the Radical
Party of Iaşi. The brothers Nădejde founded a socialist group;
later they were joined by Dobrogeanu-Gherea, a brilliant essayist
who migrated from Russia. For a time both parties succeeded in
enlivening the political life of Moldavia with their periodicals, the
radical *Lupta* and the socialist *Contemporanul*. But after a short
span of existence the radicals, with the exception of Panu, joined
the Conservatives, where they had a very little influence, while the
other socialist intellectuals became the left wing of the Liberal Party.
In 1905 Christian Stantchoff Rakovsky, who in the post-war years
became the Soviet Ambassador to Paris, revived *România Munci-
toare* (Working Roumania), a socialistic journal. But a new Socialist Party of a more modern character originated in 1910, its
weak foundations being laid in large cities. Persecuted by the ruling
classes, it could not become very strong. Its deputies were impris-
oned in 1921 when they announced their intention to adhere to the
Third International. In the elections of 1920 the movement was
represented by eighteen deputies, who, however, followed a negative
policy, being divided into radical and moderate factions.[13] The attempt of the radicals to foment a general strike failed in 1920, and
the failure has reflected on the whole labor movement. Various anti-
socialist governmental measures followed. Frimu and Marinescu

---

[13] In 1917 ten advanced Liberal deputies seceded from their party under the
influence of the bolshevik revolution and formed the Labor Party under the
leadership of Dr. Cantacuzino, but had no definite organization.

succeeded in 1926 in bringing together all socialist groups existing separately in each Roumanian province. In the 1928 elections the Socialists had an electoral pact with the National-Peasant Party and obtained nine seats. In the 1931 elections the party won six mandates on their independent ticket. At the head of the party stand the general secretary of the party, Dr. L. Rădăceanu, Ilie Moscovici and Dr. Ghelerter of Bucharest, newspaperman I. Flueraş and I. Iumanca from Transylvania, in addition to Dr. Pistiner and former Senator G. Grigorovici. The leaders advocate the achievement of political democracy as the principal immediate aim. For them the achievement of democracy is the only possible basis for the social and economic advancement of the masses. Agreement with Maniu's party was looked upon as a matter of practical necessity,[14] and the political association came to an end once the elections were over. The two parties even worked independently in their campaign and in the elections. In fact, the Social-Democratic Party was opposed to the "bourgeois" policy of their allies, being discontented, above all, with the taxes falling on the earnings of labor and on the consumer. In another direction it criticized the absence of any reductions of expenditures on the army. It approved the passing of the eight-hour-day law and a law concerning labor agreements, but disagreed with the policy of enforcement. It demanded the setting up of labor boards and the provision of a modern social insurance. In the matter of the administrative reform the socialist leaders believed that it still left too much power to the state bureaucracy and that the minorities problem had not been handled adequately. The official view of the party was, in summary, as far as the National-Peasant Government was concerned, as follows:

The feeling is general among the workers that the government is proceeding with too little energy with the abolition of reactionary institutions, the purging of the state service, which is infested with "liberal" elements, and the building up of a bourgeois democracy. The workers consider that from time to time the government makes a feebler stand against the reaction than the relative strength of the parties would permit, and makes entirely unnecessary concessions to it, as, for instance, may be seen clearly in the quite purposeless persecution of the communists, who are of entirely negligible importance in Rumania.[15]

[14] See "The Struggle for Democracy," in *Manchester Guardian*, November 28, 1929, p. 22, written by Dr. Lothar Rădăceanu, secretary of the Social-Democratic Party of Roumania.

[15] Dr. L. Rădăceanu, *op. cit.*, p. 22.

A communistic party appeared in 1921 from the left wing of the Socialist Party, but its existence was officially dissolved on July 28, 1924,[16] and it is now known as the Workmen and Peasants' Group. The chief field for communistic propaganda is Bessarabia.

Among the minor parties are the Anti-Semitists. In 1922 Professor Cuza, old companion of Professor Iorga, founded the "League of National Defense," a small, but loud and rowdy, organization of the extreme nationalistic type. In the 1926 elections Cuza received about 5 per cent, in 1928 less than 2 per cent, and in 1931 nearly 4 per cent of the total vote. The main strength of this party is in Bukovina and northern Bessarabia.

The Parties of Roumanian Minorities

The new Roumanian state has within its borders about a quarter of the total population belonging to minority nationalities. The strongest politically are the Hungarians, who spent the first three post-war years in political passivity but then started to organize with energy. A Magyar League, which was to represent all Magyar interests, was formed. No Hungarian was to make any decision or to take any steps without consulting this "League," which was to have not only political but also economic and social interests. Former President of the House of Lords of Budapest, Baron S. Josika, became its chief. The Roumanian Government refused to allow the body, tending to become a state within the state, to pursue its aims, and invited the Transylvanian Magyars to organize themselves in a political party. Two were formed: the National Magyar and the Popular Magyar parties. The first represented the reactionary elements; the latter was democratic. Later, as has been mentioned, the Magyar minority split again into three groups: large landowners, small farmers, and "democrats."

The German Parliamentary Party[17] was founded in 1867, when by the so-called "Königsboden" the Germans lost their privileged position. The gathering of the Germans at Mediaş in January 1919 voted upon the union of the "Saxon nation" with the Roumanian kingdom, and referring to the proclamation of Alba-Iulia of December 1918 it asked for the granting of administrative autonomy

---

[16] A. J. Toynbee, *Survey of International Affairs, 1924,* p. 212.

[17] See F. Wertheimer, *Von Deutschen Parteien und Parteiführern im Ausland* (Berlin, 1927), pp. 166–90.

in return for a loyal policy. When it became evident that Roumania could not grant these extreme demands, the leaders of the Transylvanian Saxons conceived the idea of making one political *bloc* of all Roumanian Germans despite their religious differences,[18] which materialized in 1921 in the *Verband der Deutschen in Grossrumänien*. The president of the National German Party is Dr. Hans Otto Roth, who has tried to unify all Roumanian minorities in one political front, but without success. It has become common for the Germans as well as the Magyars to pledge their votes to the Roumanian party promising them most advantages, or to the party in power.

The Bulgarian Party represents the Bulgarian minority from Dobrogea, under the leadership of A. Brassanoff. Other minorities, the Ruthenians, Russians, Poles, and Slovaks, are not organized politically and co-operate with the regular Roumanian parties. The Serbs of the Banat decided during the Cabinet of Averescu of 1926 to form an independent party; from that time on its members have been adherents of various Roumanian parties, hoping that they could agitate for their demands; but they have had to depend mostly upon themselves. They have asked especially for some changes in the educational system and the creation of at least one Serbian high school.

The Jewish group is composed of various factions, one led by Dr. W. Filderman, which affiliated with the Liberals in 1928; another supported the Cabinet of Maniu; and a third, the Zionists, also favored the National-Peasant Party.

In summary it may be said that the pre-war as well as the post-war political life of Roumania was not very complicated. The two-party system of the pre-war days was renewed a few years after the creation of the new kingdom. Fundamentally, the psychology of the people is conservative and there exists a wide gap between the mass of the peasantry and the upper classes. The political infancy of the kingdom made it necessary to give the power of interpreting the political trends to the Crown. Before the war the political division belonged to the Conservatives and the Liberals. The disappearance of the landlords pushed the Liberals to the Right, which now protects the vested interests of business, finance, and economic institutions. The Transylvanian peasants under Maniu and peasants of

[18] The Germans of Transylvania are Protestants and those from the Banat, Bukovina, and Bessarabia are Catholics.

the Old Kingdom under Mihalache fused and formed the National-Peasant Party, which came to power in 1928 and represented the agricultural interests in contrast to those of mercantilism. Fundamentally the politics of Roumania are dominated more by strong personalities than by ideology and principles. The gradual democratization of public life gives assurance that the arbitrary methods of the past will eventually be succeeded by democratic methods. Several strong figures of Roumanian politics have passed recently from the political stage and new men of different outlook stand in the foreground ready to try new methods for the betterment of their country, methods which will be conditioned for some time to come by progress in raising the educational and economic standards of the Roumanian people.

CHAPTER VII

INTERNAL POLICY

GENERAL CHARACTERISTICS

So DRASTIC and sweeping was the transformation of Roumania from a semi-feudal state to a radically democratic experiment, in the short period of the war, that it is now generally recognized outside its borders that the home of the ancient Dacians was changed almost overnight from a land of baronial estates, resting on semi-feudal privileges, to a land in which the lowly peasant stood suddenly as the theoretical master of all he might survey. Roumania's leaders were not unaware of the difficulties inherent in such a revolutionary change. They perceived that although the peasant was now the possessor of both land and a vote he was hardly as yet an accomplished participant in the democratic process. As more than half of the peasant population could hardly read and write and had not reached an educational level sufficiently high to allow them to make intelligent use of their newly acquired political privileges, the politics of Roumania of the subsequent period reflected a cautious reaction against the sudden realization of theoretical democracy. It took some years of patient political education for the masses to learn how to use their political weapon, and we may safely assume that it was not until the National-Peasant Party came into power in 1928 that the mass of the Roumanian people was allowed to exercise its political right without hindrance.

Up to the World War Roumanian political life was dominated by the Crown and a few individuals. The old suffrage law of 1884 was based on taxable property and favored only certain classes. Then the war came and the peasant received his ticket for voting. It came so suddenly to him that he did not know what to do with it. His interest centered in the land, and that he had always been asking for. Now he received even more. He knew how to take care of his land, but the suffrage could easily become a very dangerous instrument in his hands and could be used by unscrupulous men in the heat of war and in the excitable days of the post-war period against the interest of the nation, the dynasty, and the country. The influence of the Russian Revolution and of demagogical elements in Roumania certainly had to be considered. Hence the internal policy of all Roumanian governments was influenced by the conviction that the new democratic privileges should be used with caution and their misuse made impossible.

That guardians sometimes misuse the privilege of guardianship is an age-old axiom of politics. In Roumania the final decision of politics had rested with the Crown. King Ferdinand and his advisers always kept in mind the fact that the Roumanian people had to get used to their constitutional privileges, and all their decisions were consequently conditioned by the fact that the general suffrage needed guidance and control. Democratic rights are often closely associated with tyranny, ignorance, apathy, smug self-satisfaction, intolerance, and bigotry. Democracies tend to follow passion and sentiment; racial antipathy, misunderstanding, excited feeling, impulse are all liable to threaten peace in democracy. It is only through education and broadening appreciation of the point of view of the members of democracy that these difficulties can be overcome and a sense of public responsibility developed. It is true that the oligarchies, which have to take charge of the educational processes before they can intrust the rule to the people, are subject to serious limitations. But that should not obscure the fact that democracy has not been such a popular thing since the war, and the post-war years have been bridged by dictatorships in many a country, well known to us. The problems of democracy have by no means been satisfactorily solved anywhere.

In Roumania the Crown and the ruling classes had a natural tendency to favor the government of the Right and to strengthen it as much as possible in order to avoid any marked surrender to the Left extremes. Often the parties that formed the cabinets did not assume power because of popular support; they were selected by the King on the basis indicated.

The Liberals, who have enjoyed most of the leadership of the state, had been the party of the Left before the war. When the Conservatives went to pieces after the war, the Liberal group was pushed to the Right and the place of the Conservatives was taken by new political formations. The Liberal Party, however, easily over-shadowed them in importance. Being well organized and having sufficient funds, it could keep itself in the privileged position. Its leader, Ion Brătianu, exercised the greatest influence.

Gradually, however, the same constellation of internal politics as had existed before the war took form. The rotation process of two parties, one always forming the government and the other the opposition, was resumed. In opposition to the governing Liberal group an anti-liberal *bloc* was soon formed, not very distinct from the first and lacking in unity at the beginning but slowly becoming crystallized into the formidable opposition of the National-Peasant camp of today.

One of the major political problems of post-war Roumania was the necessity of unifying a country with newly acquired provinces. Each of the five different parts of Greater Roumania had had its own individual development for centuries and had developed differences from the rest. The task of the post-war governments was to unify the state organism into a compact whole. Not only did the legal and administrative régime have to be reorganized, but an economic, social, and political transformation from diversity to unity had to take place. Another difficult problem was the question of agriculture. As agriculture is the foundation of the welfare of the Roumanian people, land reform and the expropriation of large properties was an insufficient program. The whole cultural, economic, social, and po-litical standards of the agricultural masses had to be raised, and a wide program of agricultural education, which would teach the peasant to use new methods, had to be planned. But, in addition, a higher cultural level had to be applied to the population as a whole, the whole educational system needing to be unified and reformed. In fact, the psychological damage from the war, which was neces-sarily reflected in the post-war years in Roumania, had to be repaired, and the Roumanian nation had to face post-war adjustments to the new conditions, which demanded a sudden turn from the years of fighting to the post-war years of upbuilding.

These staggering tasks were not isolated from economic diffi-culties of the first magnitude. The war destruction, the war exhaus-tion, the ruined railway system, and the depreciated currency required the attention of Roumanian statesmanship, in addition to the thousand and one other minor tasks of reconstruction. It could not be other than very difficult.

The Germanophile ministry of Marghiloman had to resign on October 24, 1918, and the new government was formed by the ministry of generals under General Coandă. But this cabinet was soon replaced on November 29 by the appointment of Ion Brătianu, who ruled on the basis of royal decrees. His difficulties with the Peace Conference led him to resign on September 27, 1919, and once more a cabinet of generals, this time under General Văitoianu, came in, sympathizing more or less with the Liberals.

The elections, held on November 8, 1919, were surprising. In the Old Kingdom, the Liberals won only 120 seats out of 247, and all the 321 mandates allotted to the provinces were distributed among the National Party of Transylvania, the Peasants of Bessarabia, and the Democrats of Bukovina. The latter were headed by Dr. Nistor and for the most part favored the Liberals. In the Old Kingdom Mihalache was returned with 60 deputies. Take Ionescu's Democratic Party and Averescu's People's League ostentatiously refrained from participation in the elections.

THE CABINET OF VAIDA-VOEVOD

(December 1919—March 1920)

The inexperienced and timid parliamentary majority produced the ministry of Dr. Vaida-Voevod, well-known as a defender of the Transylvanians in the Hungarian Parliament. The new currents brought in Dr. Lupu as Minister of the Interior, reputed for his radical tendencies. Dr. Vaida-Voevod succeeded in securing Allied recognition for the union of Bessarabia with the kingdom, and measures were elaborated for a definite solution of the agrarian question. The parliament agreed to intrust the drafting of the law of re-settlement to the Peasant Party, which included some of the keenest members of the ephemeral Iași Labor group, and the leader of which, Mihalache, was in charge of the Ministry of Agriculture. While Vaida-Voevod was abroad, he came into conflict with the Liberals, who disapproved of the Prime Minister's democratic reforms. Difficulties culminated when Mihalache introduced the resettlement scheme in the chamber; the cabinet was dismissed under opposition from the Liberals. Thus the government lasted only from December 2, 1919, to March 13, 1920.

The Cabinet of General Averescu

(March 1920—December 1921)

Though General Averescu had no parliamentary majority, he was commissioned by the King to form a government. Relying for support upon the Conservative and Liberal parties of the Old Kingdom, the new Premier adopted a policy looking to the centralization and economic reconstruction of Greater Roumania. To this end the number of deputies was reduced to 369 and the old chamber was dissolved on March 27. A further step toward centralization was the dissolution of the national councils of Transylvania, Bukovina, and Bessarabia, and the subdivision of the entire state into departments, with prefects nominated directly from Bucharest. The measure met with bitter criticism from Dr. Vaida-Voevod and Maniu.

The strength of Averescu lay in the alarm aroused at the court and among the upper classes by the bolshevistic agitation. The Premier had behind him the "League of the People," which contained many Conservatives and some "new men," and had for its program reforms of the abuses of the Liberals during the war. Now the Socialists also promised their support to the man of the moment. Averescu also concluded a pact with Take Ionescu.

The elections of May 12, 1920, reflected the hand that had conducted it. Out of 369 deputies elected, the People's Party won 209 seats, the Liberals only 17, and the Socialists 19. The Saxons of Transylvania returned 8 deputies. The Transylvanians were definitely estranged, charging discrimination because they had lost more seats in the general reduction in proportion to their population than the Old Kingdom.

The government took strong measures against the forces of the Left. In November 1920 the Premier caused the arrest of all Socialist and Syndicalist leaders who had indorsed the Third International.[1] All technical workers were called to the colors and put under military discipline.[2] Notwithstanding noisy demonstrations among the working classes, a new law against workingmen's unions was passed. But after that the number and importance of strikes

[1] The Communists, from whom the Social-Democrats had detached themselves under the leadership of the Bukovinian Grigorovici, were also disbanded.

[2] As an aftermath a bomb explosion in the Roumanian Senate killed, on December 9, Greceanu, Minister of Public Works, and Bishop Radu, and dangerously wounded several others.

diminished. In March 1921 Titulescu, in charge of the treasury department, tried to reduce to order the chaos of the treasury bonds, and introduced a bill heavily taxing new fortunes and capital in general. On the whole, however, the cabinet was unable to strengthen the economic life of the country.

In parliament the cabinet was stoutly opposed by the Peasant Party of Mihalache and Madgearu, the National-Democratic group of Professor Iorga, and the group under Dr. Lupu. This "National Opposition," in which the Peasant Party was very influential, tried to gain power and negotiated with the Transylvanian National Party. The Liberals stood aside, but because they had a majority of the ablest politicians behind them, also powerful newspapers as well as financial resources, their policy against Averescu, despite their small number, was really the most important one.

Meanwhile Averescu's Cabinet was torn by internal dissensions. Some of its members resigned, either not agreeing with the policies of their leader or disgusted with the attacks of the Liberals. Their posts were administered either by the Prime Minister or by the Minister of the Interior, Argetoianu. The voices asking for a reorganization of the cabinet were increasing in number. Popular opinion was antagonized by the new measures of taxation, and especially by the property tax of Titulescu. The famous declaration of the government regarding the constitutional prerogatives of the Crown weakened its position. Averescu had to make a special affirmation in parliament, at the instance of the King. The crisis came with the resignation of Take Ionescu from the Ministry of Foreign Affairs, and the Minister of Justice, Antonescu. The outstanding measure passed during the government's holding of office was the legalization of the distribution of the land to the peasants on the basis of the agrarian reform.

The Cabinet of Ion Brătianu

(January 1922—March 1926)

After Averescu, who submitted his resignation on December 17, 1921, Take Ionescu held the portfolio of Prime Minister until January 19, 1922, when the way was clear again for the return of the Liberals. Brătianu became Premier and remained in charge for four years. The Premier, in forming his cabinet, tried to conciliate the Transylvanian National Party under Maniu by offering it three portfolios in the government. Maniu refused.

The results of the March elections showed a decided shift to the Liberals. Where they had received only 17 mandates in the last election, they jumped now to 260. The Țărănists and the Transylvanian Nationalists won 62 seats, the group of Take Ionescu 8, the Germans 8, the Socialists and the Jewish *bloc* one mandate each. The party of Marghiloman failed to have even one deputy elected and Averescu's parliamentary representation was reduced to 11.

The results of the elections created serious unrest. The opposition groups determined to embarrass the Liberals by all available means. The Țărănists decided not to recognize the election and the same intentions were expressed by the groups of Professor Iorga and Take Ionescu, the latter of whom, however, died on June 21, 1922, leaving his followers disorganized. The executive committee of the Transylvanian Party gathered at Cluj in the second half of March 1922 and authorized Maniu to inform the King that the illegal means used by the Liberals in the elections and the denial of fair representation in parliament to Transylvania, Banat, and the Maramureş districts made it impossible for his party to recognize the Liberal Government as constitutional.

In spite of all this opposition, Brătianu formulated a wide program: the unification of Roumania, and the adoption of a new constitution which would include electoral and agrarian reforms.

The new constitution, promulgated on March 28, 1923, was bitterly contested by the opposition. The document was formulated without the aid or consent of the other parties, and was thus a partisan measure of the Liberals. Fundamentally, the other groups declared they were denouncing not so much the constitution itself as the Liberal Party and its practice, which, according to them, was illegal. All the attempts of Brătianu to come to an understanding with the Țărănists and the National Party of Transylvania failed because he was unwilling to concede the new and free elections which the opposition was demanding.

When the Liberal Government was ready to present the new constitution to the parliament, some opposition groups began to falter in their passive resistance, wondering whether or not it would be more advisable to enter the parliament and there prevent the passing of the fundamental document. Finally, at the beginning of 1923, the Țărănists began to participate in the parliamentary ses-

Vintilă Brătianu
Professor G. Brătianu

Dr. Constantin Angelescu
Ion I. C. Brătianu

sions. The National Party, strengthened by the remains of what was left of Take Ionescu's following, began to do the same, but the practice was given up later on. Meanwhile the excitement against the Liberal conception of the constitution spread from the parliamentary corridors into the streets. Mass meetings were held all over the country and everywhere the Liberal proposal was bitterly criticized. However, the opposition was unable to present a unified front and the Liberals decided to disregard it entirely. In the last moment the Bessarabian Țărănists under Inculeț and the Unionist Party of Bukovina headed by Dr. Nistor decided to support the government.

When the parliament gathered on March 26, 1923, for the purpose of passing the new fundamental law of the country, out of 369 deputies only 255 were present; 247 voted for the constitution, 8 against it, and the others retired before the voting commenced. The King was unsuccessful in his efforts to have the opposition participate in the election. The opposition insisted that it could participate only after the resignation of the Liberals. Meanwhile its deputies scattered throughout the country and began to agitate against the rule of the Brătianus.

After that the cabinet offered a series of special laws, outlined only briefly in the constitution. Vintilă Brătianu, brother of the Premier, was, as Minister of Finance, the chief inspirer of economic policy under the slogan *"prin noi înșine"* (by ourselves), resulting in the nationalization of various undertakings and the natural wealth of the country.

On October 15, 1922, the coronation of King Ferdinand and Queen Marie as rulers of Greater Roumania was celebrated. The coronation took place at Alba-Iulia, a small town in Transylvania, because it was there that Mihaiu the Brave, who for a short time united under his scepter the whole Roumanian-speaking people, had been crowned centuries before. The town was chosen because it symbolized to the Roumanians an ideal of national unity which had now become a fact. That political national unity was an ideal not yet completely realized was sharply demonstrated when the Transylvanians boycotted the coronation as a protest against the "illegal" election methods of the Liberal Party in the general elections of that year.

The rule of the Liberals was subjected to increasing criticism on other accounts. The failure to satisfy the peasants by a land division, the repeal of the more liberal declarations of the Bessarabian and Transylvanian assemblies of 1918, and the recognition of the Greek-Orthodox church as the dominant ecclesiastical body to the neglect of the Roman Catholics resulted in the strengthening of the opposition. The various minority organizations issued manifestoes denouncing the government and the laws enacted under it.

The reform of the electoral law in the spring of 1926 completed the constitutional plans of the Liberals. After their failure in the municipal elections in February, despite the government's questionable methods, a law was passed over the loud protests of the opposition, whereby the party gaining 40 per cent of the votes was to receive one-half of the mandates and was to participate also in the percentual division of the rest of the mandates. The party receiving less than two per cent of the votes was to have no representation.

The government also worked out an administrative reform, already approved in 1925, which divided the country into districts and "preturi." The educational system was changed and especially were the minority and religious schools remodelled at the beginning of the school year of 1923–24. By the end of 1925 the graduation language of all minority schools was to be Roumanian. A law for the unification of the church was passed, introducing the Transylvanian system of elective councils for each parish.

The first three months of 1926 were eventful for Roumania. At the end of December 1925 the heir to the throne, Prince Carol, left Roumania abruptly and renounced all his rights. It was no mystery that the Prince and Brătianu were at odds. A crown council met at Sinaia and the parliament ratified its decision, appointing on January 4, 1926, a provisional council of regency in view of the precarious state of the King's health. The National-Peasant Party after some hesitation abstained from voting.

Brătianu resigned under fire on March 27, 1926. The People's Party, the National Transylvanian Party, and the Peasant Party were pointing out that the attitude of Brătianu toward Prince Carol gravely damaged the interests of the country and of the dynasty. The five-year-old son of the Prince, Mihaiu, was proclaimed heir-apparent, and during his minority a regency, consisting of Prince Nicolae, Patriarch Miron Christea, and the first president of the court of cassation, Buzdugan, who was succeeded after his death by C. Sărăţeanu, was named to rule for him.

The illness of the King made the internal situation insecure. Voices were heard asking for a strong and trustworthy government.

The economic strain of the passive economic policy began to be felt, and the leu began to fall. The opposition blamed Brătianu's Government for an exaggerated tendency to help industry and for its refusal to allow the participation of foreign capital.

THE CABINET OF GENERAL AVERESCU

(March 1926—June 1927)

After much hesitation, the King asked General Averescu to form a cabinet, a fact which surprised the political observers, as the General had the support of a few deputies only and no supporters in the provinces. The personal basis of Roumanian politics was clearly shown in this case. The National Transylvanian Party and the Peasant Party were convinced that Brătianu had concluded a secret pact with Averescu, who continued the Liberal rule. The appointment resulted in many regroupings of the leaders. Goldiş and Lupaş joined Averescu. Goldiş's followers were mostly Greek Orthodox and their leader had been showing his dissatisfaction with the leadership of Maniu for two years, as the latter was followed mostly by the Transylvanian Greek Catholic uniats. It had been taken for granted that Goldiş would eventually transfer his allegiance, but this sudden turn to Averescu was somewhat of a surprise because it was known that Goldiş was in favor of a fusion with the Țărănists and was a very decided opponent of Averescu. But his wish to gain certain privileges and advancement was strong enough to change his views overnight.

The new government was in a difficult position. The leu was falling. Prices were rising. At one time the rise of prices was so great that the merchants were refusing to sell their goods. The King called his crown council in this critical situation and invited the leading financiers to attend. With their help the fall of the leu was temporarily halted.

The elections of May 25, 1926, were characteristic. The new electoral law—as worked out by the Liberals—was applied with success by the smallest party of the country. Averescu planned to gain in Transylvania through Goldiş's followers, but was disappointed in this respect. Then he put his hopes on the minorities and concluded an electoral agreement with them by promising them special privileges of an exaggerated nature.

The result of the election, owing to great pressure exercised at the polls, was astounding. Averescu secured 292 partisans out of 387. The Nationalists and the Peasants won 69 seats, the Liberals 16, and the Christian League (Anti-Semitists) 9. Brătianu failed to be elected in Bucharest, but as a senator "of right" had a seat in the senate. The Nationalists came out so strong that they gained new courage. And yet it was clear that the government existed largely on Liberal sufferance.

The program of Averescu promised a partial change of the hitherto unpopular economic policy of Vintilă Brătianu. New laws were to enable foreign capital to participate in the economic life of Roumania and more attention was to be paid to agriculture. But nothing was said about the financial stabilization of the leu. The economic situation steadily became worse. The harvest began to prove a comparative failure and taxation and high interest rates pressed heavily on the country. The Premier also initiated negotiations for a much-needed foreign loan, which, however, was cancelled by his successor, Brătianu.

In general, the only positive results of the short régime of Averescu were the conclusion of a treaty of friendship with Italy and the Italian ratification of the Bessarabian protocol, promised in Mussolini's letter to the Roumanian Premier on the occasion of the conclusion of the Treaty of September 12, 1926, which was effected on March 9, 1927. On June 10, 1926, a treaty of alliance and non-aggression was signed with France. An Italian loan was also successfully negotiated.

In October 1926 a very eventful political fact was accomplished. The National-Peasant Party was officially formed and its immediate program included measures for the encouragement of agriculture, the reorganization of the chambers of agriculture, credit facilities for co-operative societies, inducements to foreign capital to participate in Roumanian industries, and the raising of educational standards for peasants.

The internal situation in the early months of 1927 was seriously complicated by the severe illness of the King and the consequent question of the successor in case of death. At the crown council held in Sinaia on December 31, 1925, Mihalache indorsed Carol's renunciation; but Maniu, in the course of the debate in parliament on this question, was opposed to the setting up of a regency. Later his party refrained from voting on the succession and regency acts.

Early in February 1927 the National-Peasant Party requested the government to call a crown council meeting for the purpose of removing the barriers against the return of Carol as heir apparent to the Throne. But General Averescu stated in no uncertain terms that his government would not accede to the wishes of the National-Peasant Party and that the question of succession was closed. He furthermore ordered the suppression of all newspapers which advocated the return of Carol to Roumania. When the King reaffirmed his determination to uphold the dynastic settlement, the executive committee of the National-Peasant Party finally voted on April 4, 1927, not to reopen the dynastic issue.[3]

On the whole, Averescu held his position because of the confidence of the King and the Liberal Party. Public opinion was aggravated by his dictatorial leanings and by laws colored by his personal influence. The increasing independence of the Premier began to alarm the Liberals, particularly in view of the very precarious state of the King's health. Several of Averescu's measures displeased the Liberal leaders: the reduction of export taxes and railroad freight rates, the Italian loan, and the interference with the independent railroad administration by the creation of an Under-Secretary of State for railroads. Finally, the Liberals brought about Averescu's downfall on June 3, 1927.

THE CABINET OF PRINCE ŞTIRBEY

(June 1927)

Prince Barbu Ştirbey's ministry secured the support of the National-Peasant Party, and three members entered his cabinet at the request of the King, who desired the formation of a national coalition; the example of Maniu was followed by Brătianu. For the first time the two most important parties participated in a coalition cabinet, forming thus a sort of internal Locarno, which, however, was short-lived. The members of the government were conducting the elections with such energy and enthusiasm that each minister was attacking the others, and the government of "national unity" proved impossible. The Premier tried to calm his associates by a plan to have the Liberal Party and the National-Peasant Party nominate

---

[3] Foreign Policy Association, *Information Service*, Vol. II, No. 24, February 3, 1928, "Post-War Rumania," p. 383.

one set of candidates. Because the National-Peasant Party refused to stand by such agreement, Ştirbey's Government resigned, after a three weeks' term, on June 21.

THE CABINET OF ION BRĂTIANU

(June 1927—November 1927)

Ştirbey gave way on June 22 to Brătianu, who kept in his government nearly all the members of Ştirbey's group with the exception of the National-Peasant ministers. Titulescu, a politician of moderate views and of pronounced ability, and hitherto Minister to the Court of St. James, and permanent delegate of Roumania to the League of Nations, became Minister of Foreign Affairs. The cabinet carried also two members not formerly identified with the Liberal Party, Dr. Lupu and Argetoianu.

The elections of July 7, 1927, naturally went to the Liberals, who got the majority of 298 mandates out of 387.[4]

Averescu's Party secured only 1.84 per cent of the votes and thus not a single mandate. Dr. Lupu's Peasant Party, a split-off from the National-Peasant Party, was in the governmental coalition and came out with 22 mandates. The party of Iorga, Anti-Semitists and Socialists, received no representation in the parliament.

---

[4] The results of the elections of July 7, 1927 (figures supplied by the Roumanian Legation) were:

Lower Chamber		*Upper Chamber*	
Speaker: N. N. Săveanu		Speaker: C. I. Nicolaescu	
National Liberal	298*	National Liberal	158
National Peasant	49	National Peasant	15
Peasant	22	Hungarian group	1
Hungarian group	7	People's	1
German group	7		
Independents	1		
Jewish Union	1		
People's	1		
Total	386	Total	170†

* Including 10 Jewish deputies, who made a political agreement with the National-Liberal Party.

† Only elected members.

Before the excitement of the elections subsided, another event of serious consequence occurred. On July 20, 1927, King Ferdinand died. Dr. Seton-Watson calls Ferdinand "not a specially strong or able man, but a man of honour and of occasional vision."[5] He was sincerely mourned by his nation, which adores its royalty. Though of German blood, he was able to lead his people against the Germans. His reign was pregnant with political, social, and economic changes of the greatest importance. His name will always be associated with the formation of "România Mare," a dream of centuries which materialized against the greatest odds of the times and under his leadership. He gave his country general suffrage, and the peasant of Roumania must be thankful to his reign for changing the country from the feudalistic régime of big estates into an advanced stage of economic and political democracy.

According to the succession law, five-year-old Mihaiu became King of Roumania under the control of a regency which had been created by parliament a year and a half before.[6] But this fact did not settle the question of succession, brought up again with all its vigor. In October, Manoilescu, Under-Secretary for Finance in the late Averescu's Government, arrested on his return from Paris, was found to be bearing messages from Prince Carol to some political leaders of the country. Public feeling ran high in favor of the accused, who was acquitted. The incident divided the country into two sharply defined camps and aggravated passions on both sides. In November 1927 the executive committee of the National-Peasant Party passed a resolution instructing a committee to begin determined action against the government, using all legal parliamentary and extra-parliamentary means, and in case the government should persist in illegally misusing its power, to prepare and organize the resistance of citizens.[7]

However, on November 24 of the same year the great leader of the Liberals died. Ion I. C. Brătianu has for Roumania the same historical importance as Cavour, Bismarck, and Gambetta for their respective countries. His family played a great part in Roumanian history and he himself fulfilled what his father had begun. His influence switched the Kingdom of Roumania to the side of the Allies

---

[5] R. W. Seton-Watson, in *Slavonic Review*, 1930, IX, 485.

[6] Mihaiu, born on October 25, 1921, was proclaimed King on July 21, 1927.

[7] *Near East and India*, 1927, XXXII, 642.

in the World War and thus made possible the creation of Greater Roumania. He lived to see King Ferdinand crowned King of "România Mare" at Alba-Iulia. If his rule used extreme and semi-Oriental political measures, he had at least guided the country through the post-war vicissitudes and strengthened its national consolidation.

THE CABINET OF VINTILĂ BRĂTIANU

(November 1927—November 1928)

There was no political interlude following his death, because Vintilă Brătianu, Minister of Finance, a brother of the dead statesman, became the head of the reconstructed government, in which were included the representatives of Dr. Lupu's Peasant Party group.[8]

Appointed on November 24, 1927, the government of Vintilă Brătianu knew its weakness. The death of its great leader and the death of the King, who had been Brătianu's constant friend, left the Liberal Party without its main elements of strength. The creation of the regency brought a new and uncertain element into Roumanian politics. Vintilă Brătianu tried to strengthen his cabinet by forming a coalition ministry, and after the funeral of his brother he approached Maniu through Titulescu with an offer to the National-Peasant Party of fifty per cent of the portfolios and new elections in which the Liberals would accept fifty-five per cent of the mandates in the chamber. But Maniu decided not to yield on the question of the illegality of the last elections, and did not fail to make his views plain in the new session of the parliament, which gathered on December 7, 1927.

Throughout the spring and summer of 1928 Maniu's party held a number of stormy meetings, protesting to the regency against the state of political conditions and demanding that this body should keep itself free from the influence of the Liberals. The regency, it

---

[8] The cabinet was composed as follows: Prime Minister and Finance, Vintilă Brătianu; Foreign Affairs, Titulescu; Interior, I. G. Duca; Agriculture, C. Argetoianu; Public Instruction, Dr. C. Angelescu; Public Worship, A. Lapedatu; Justice, I. Nistor; Public Health and Social Welfare, I. Inculeț; Labor, Dr. N. Lupu; Communications, C. D. Dimitriu; War, General Angelescu; Industry and Commerce, L. Mrazec.

declared, should be a body above partisan issues if it were to have the confidence of the nation.

Maniu, however, could not unite all the opposition parties. Iorga announced that he would enter no ministry without being its Premier, and began to negotiate with Averescu. Rumors had it that a fusion of both parties would materialize, in which Dr. Lupu would participate. At the same time, Averescu began a strong campaign against Maniu through his trustee and former Minister of the Interior, Octavian Goga, denying the former all merits and political abilities.

Maniu retaliated by strengthening his stand against "all cabinets." All kinds of demonstrations were held by his party to make its demands effective. On March 18, 1928, an army of peasants, estimated at from 60,000 to 100,000, marched on Bucharest, and brought provisions with them, their leaders declaring that they would stay until the Liberal Government resigned. But the only tangible result was the withdrawal of the Peasants' representatives from parliament and the gradual drifting back home of the farmers. Another huge gathering was held in Alba-Iulia on May 6, 1928, which passed resolutions condemning the cabinet as "the enemy of the Roumanian people." The party was represented at the congress by 676 delegates from 71 districts. A declaration was issued appealing to the Allies and the League of Nations not to confuse the Roumanian people with "a government of usurpation." The situation remained acute all during the summer and in the early autumn, Maniu and his party refraining from participating in the parliament. The National-Peasant deputies formed their own "parliament" on July 26, 1928, on the same day that Vintilă Brătianu convoked the chamber in an extraordinary session to inform it of the results of his negotiations with foreign financial groups for a loan for the stabilization of the leu. The National-Peasant Parliament voted a resolution that the laws of the Liberal Chamber for any loan "had no obligatory force for the Roumanian nation."

Brătianu had also to deal with the increasingly troublesome optants' question, though he succeeded in concluding a treaty of non-aggression and arbitration with Greece at Geneva on March 22, 1928, and to effect a debt settlement with France at about the same time. But an outbreak of Roumanian students at Oradea Mare and Cluj redoubled the agitation of opposition.

The Premier was aware of his weakening position. In February

1928 it was stated that the Liberals would be willing to retire in favor of Maniu's group if only the latter would promise not to upset the main lines of policy adopted by them. Maniu again refused.

The immediate cause of the fall of Brătianu was the economic situation. The economic policy of the Liberals failed to bring about the promised result of national self-sufficiency. The realization of a loan from abroad was recognized as the only possible means of relieving the grave economic situation resulting from the failure of the maize crop. To secure it, Brătianu gradually sacrificed the main features of the financial policy which he had fastened on the country. Revalorization had been abandoned and preparations were made to stabilize the leu at an even lower rate than that at which it had stood when Vintilă Brătianu first became Minister of Finance. His final act of renunciation was the admission that the necessary funds for stabilization had to come from abroad. Negotiations were carried on with an international banking group through the summer of 1928 and had reached a point at which it became necessary to insure that there would be no danger of repudiation by the National-Peasant Party in the event of the loan being arranged. Brătianu also wished to have the assurance from the regency that in the case of the negotiations being successfully concluded he would be permitted to retain office, in order to enjoy the benefits of the loan. But Brătianu failed to persuade the regency to prolong his mandate indefinitely. Believing himself to be in a stronger position than he really was, Brătianu thereupon tendered his resignation on November 3, 1928, dramatically dropping the loan negotiations. It seems that Brătianu was as much taken by surprise as his opponents when the regency accepted the resignation with alacrity,[9] owing probably to its desire to celebrate the anniversary of the unification of the Old Kingdom with Transylvania on December 1 under a government in which the liberated province would be represented.

In the subsequent negotiations it was evident that there was a general willingness to form a coalition cabinet. But the fundamental difference between the Liberals and Maniu could not be bridged. Maniu made his condition of having new elections a *sine qua non*. The attempts of Titulescu, who returned from London, to come to an agreement were fruitless; Maniu did not want to allow the present administrative apparatus to take charge of the elections. Finally,

---

[9] *Near East and India*, 1928, XXXIV, 537.

after considerable political maneuvering on the part of the regency, Maniu on the evening of November 9, 1928, was given approval for the formation of his cabinet. The membership of the Ministry under the new government was announced and approved on the following day.

The passing of the Liberals and the coming into power of the new government was an epochal event for Roumania. For ten whole years Roumania had had a government of the Right, dominated by the Liberals whether or not they were a part of the government. While they made the Old Kingdom into Greater Roumania, their economic policy failed to make the country prosperous. They succeeded, either in their own name or under governments approved by them, as that of Averescu, especially, in saving the country from the influence of Magyar and Russian communism. The agrarian reform was carried out largely under their auspices and they gave a new constitution to the country which still is its fundamental document. They created a new educational system and many new schools, but rather overestimated their strength in the school program. The depreciation of the leu, due largely to the economic policy of Vintilă Brătianu, had grave effects on the economic life of the country. Brătianu depended too much on his conviction that the revalorization of the leu, viz., its return to the pre-war value, would come by small degrees and through domestic means. It took ten years of failure to convince him that the leu could not be saved in this way; and when he began to favor stabilization with the help of foreign capital, his political power was on the wane. His fall was caused largely by the refusal of foreign capital to help him on the basis of the guaranties of his cabinet. It remembered too well his previous policy of discouragement.

Politically, these ten years were seething with peaceful revolution. The peasant, who when he got his universal suffrage was mostly ignorant of the practicability of its use, now began to learn its possibilities and became more aware of his strength. When Ferdinand passed, the regency, not having so much personal influence as the late King, stood on constitutional principles and took an independent attitude on the political situation. When Brătianu resigned, the center of gravity of politics went from the Right to the Left, from the government of the Eastern shade, to the government conforming more to Western patterns, from the government interested in industry and mercantilism to the government whose interest lay in agriculture. One political observer considers it "the most peaceful revolution which has happened in recent years in any European state."

THE CABINET OF MANIU

(November 1928—October 1930)

Dr. I. Maniu became Premier, and two of his Transylvanian colleagues, Dr. Vaida-Voevod and Mihail Popovici, were appointed Minister of the Interior and Minister of Finance, respectively. Ion Mihalache, the leader of the Peasant Party in the Old Kingdom, took the Ministry of Agriculture, and Pan Halippa, the representative of Bessarabia in the cabinet, that of Minister of Public Works. General Cihoski, one of the ablest of the Roumanian high officers, became Minister of War. Professor Mironescu, who later succeeded Maniu as Prime Minister, went to the Foreign Ministry.[10]

The task of Maniu was formidable. The hitherto passive policy of his supporters had to be changed to a positive one. The tasks left to him by his predecessors were difficult ones. In a short time the cabinet had to introduce a new budget for 1929, to continue in the negotiations for a foreign loan, and to conclude them successfully as soon as possible. The public was impatient for improvement of the general situation. In general, Maniu's program stood for the monarchy, democracy, and social justice, and against fascism and communism; it favored political freedom and unhampered elections and the substitution of centralization of the central administration for decentralization. In the economic and financial field the government wanted to remove all the obstacles raised by the Liberals since 1923 against foreign capital, reduce custom duties on industrial products, and by that means raise the living standard of the country. Within a few weeks after its coming into power, the new administration abolished press censorship, abrogated the state of siege, dismissed 72 prefects along with a host of minor officials, reduced the gendarmerie by nearly 12,000, and dealt severely with anti-Semitic

---

[10] Other members of the cabinet were as follows: Virgil Madgearu, Minister of Industry and Commerce; Ion Răducanu, Minister of Labor; Sever Dan, Minister of Public Health and Social Welfare; Aurel Vlad, Minister of Culture; Nicolae Costăchescu, Minister of Public Instruction; Grigore Junian, Minister of Justice; General Nicolae Alevra, Minister of Communications; Sever Bocu, Minister for the Banat; Suciu Săvenau, Minister for Bukovina; and Voicu Nițescu, Minister for Transylvania.

riots. Martial law was abrogated throughout the provinces, except in a zone of seven miles along the Russian frontier. As regards the Dobrogea, an inquiry into the grievances of Bulgarians and Turks was instituted. In the following May the cabinet dismissed the whole of the temporary staff in the governmental offices and the Ministries of Health, Arts, and Public Works, merging these offices with those of Labor, Education, and Communications, respectively.

Despite the lack of preparations, Maniu called the elections for December 12, 1928, and received 78 per cent of the votes, a fact which nullified the usefulness of the electoral law of the Liberals.[11] His party won a similar victory in the senate elections of December 15.

The government pushed ahead its program of reforming the political, financial, and administrative systems of the country. Besides abolishing the three ministries named, it recalled seven ministers plenipotentiary and seventeen councillors and secretaries of legations, and reduced representation in the diplomatic service by one-half.[12] Of the many reforms which the government was engaged upon, the most important were embodied in the administrative reform bill, which was passed in July 1929. Its main object was to

---

[11] The revised figures of the composition of both chambers on the basis of the elections of December 12 and December 15, 1928, according to the figures supplied by the Roumanian Legation, Washington, D.C., are as follows:

Lower Chamber	Upper Chamber
Speaker: Şt. Ciceo-Pop	Speaker: Traian Bratu
National Peasant 324	National Peasant 160
Hungarian group 16	National Liberal 26
National Liberal 13	Hungarian group 6
Social Democratic 9	Jews 5
German group 9	Independents 2
Jewish groups 3*	
Minor parties 13	
Total 387	Total (elect.) ....199†

* There are also Jews among the Social-Democrats and Independents and also in the National-Peasant and National-Liberal parties.

† Besides elected members there are senators by right, whose number varies. It includes a clerical group—18 Orthodox prelates, 4 Greek Catholics, 1 Lutheran, 1 Reformed Church, and 1 Grand Rabbi. According to L. Boissier, B. Mirkine-Guetzévitch & J. Lafferière, *Annuaire Interparlementaire 1931* (Paris, Delagrave, 1931), pp. 513 ff., the Liberals received 12 Mandates, the National Peasants 315, the People's Party 4, and others 56.

[12] With the exception of Paris and London.

abolish the centralistic system of the Liberals in favor of local autonomy. The country was divided into seven directorates (provinces), a larger type of rural commune was created, and greater scope was given to local elective bodies. The formidable reorganization was founded on the principle which, on the whole, transformed the whole administrative system into an electoral one. The aim was to arrange the administration of the country according to its natural and historic divisions. The governors of the provinces were to exercise much of the authority hitherto concentrated in the Ministry of the Interior. The system of gendarmerie was thoroughly revised. Hitherto the solitary policeman in each village had been apt to become a local tyrant; the reform established fully equipped police stations at convenient centers, sufficiently staffed to provide prompt police assistance whenever required. The police corps were to be composed of ex-noncommissioned officers, re-engaged for the purpose. A special commission to investigate the problem of minorities was created. Definite efforts were made to check anti-Semitism. Government officials were demoted for failure to act in disorders, and court-martial of local gendarmeries was ordered when it was reported that anti-Jewish riots in the Ismail district had not been summarily checked.

The fiscal policy was changed, drastic economies were introduced in state expenditures, and heavy taxation—not very popular, of course—was imposed; for the first time provision was made for the efficient auditing of state accounts, and a complete break was made with methods that allowed the payment of taxes to be avoided for party interests and provided no effective accounting for government offices. Of outstanding importance were the laws adopted by parliament governing mining and the administration of state enterprises, which permitted foreign interests to secure leases on the same terms as those obtaining for Roumanian citizens. Following the stabilization of the leu in February 1929, a number of loans passed by the Liberals were revised, on the principle that there was to be no differentiation between foreign and Roumanian capital.

It was noticeable that the minorities groups, with the exception of the Magyar group, welcomed the Maniu's advent to power. The Roumanian public, and especially the lower classes, found the reforms of the National-Peasant Cabinet popular. But Vintilă Brătianu bitterly attacked the government on the ground that it was allowing foreign capital to gain control of the petroleum industry.

The conclusion, in February 1929, of the negotiations for a large external loan, was one of the most important events in Roumania's economic life. This loan made possible the legal stabilization of the currency, enabled the government to proceed with its extensive public-works program, including the long-needed rehabilitation and extension of the railroads and the building of railways, made it possible for the state to liquidate its indebtedness to the National Bank for treasury notes, and facilitated the balancing of the state budget and the redemption of the debts of the state railroad administration.[13] Charles Rist, assistant governor of the Bank of France, was appointed adviser to the National Bank of Roumania for three years. The proceeds of the loan were also used for loan funds for the buying of agricultural needs of the peasants.

In foreign affairs, Maniu continued the policy of the previous administration and co-operation with the Little Entente went on unhampered. The concordat with the Holy See, signed on May 10, 1927, was ratified. It gave official status to the Catholic religion in Roumania and provided for free religious instruction in Catholic schools and for the exchange of official representatives between Bucharest and the Vatican.

In September 1929 the deputies and senators of the Liberal Party withdrew from parliament as a protest against the administrative reform. Then a member of the regency, Buzdugan, died on October 7. The country was immediately faced with a serious constitutional crisis, owing to the desire of Queen Marie to be appointed to the regency council. But Maniu announced that the government had taken over the functions of the regency council pending the election of a successor to Buzdugan. For this action he was sharply criticized by the Liberals and by Averescu's followers, who maintained that the assumption of the royal prerogatives, while two regents were still alive, was practically the execution of a *coup d'état*. Maniu was unperturbed and proceeded to the election on October 9 of the brother-in-law of Popovici, his Minister of Finance, Constantin Sărăţeanu, to the vacancy on the regency council. The Liberals and General Averescu's Party withdrew from parliament as a protest.

A recent event of the greatest importance was the return of Prince Carol in June 1930. In order to make clear the background

---

[13] U.S. Department of Commerce, *Commerce Yearbook 1930,* II, 480–81.

Ateneul (Lecture Hall), Artistic Center of Bucharest

University of Bucharest

which made possible his return, we must go back to the main events and evolution of the National-Peasant régime.

The ascendancy to power of the National-Peasant Party was accepted by the people of Roumania as a sign of better times. A general impression prevailed that its administration would magically produce the prosperity of the pre-war years. The program of Maniu was so promising and democratic that these expectations did not seem to be exaggerated. It became evident very soon, however, that the picture of the economic conditions of the country painted by Maniu's group during the years of its opposition policies had been mild in comparison with the actual situation. The government of Maniu came in with the best intention of building new democratic and economic foundations for the state. But Brătianu's "splendid isolation" left a difficult heritage, and it seemed impossible to change the conditions overnight. Furthermore, the paternalism of the previous régime was to be replaced by the development of initiative and responsibility; but the years of the old régime could not be replaced by new virtues. For example, the bureaucracy, so long a part of the Liberal Party, was quite unwilling to transfer its allegiance to the new party in power.

Thus many good intentions had to remain good intentions. The democratic ideology of the government could not change the actual conditions by the magic of words and formulas. From the original program of the cabinet, the following points materialized: the state of siege was abolished, the administration of the country was decentralized, a normal and real budget was introduced, and laws directed against foreign capital were given up. But the public was not pleased with the raising of the tax rates; then came the agricultural crisis, not only of Roumania but of the world, making the economic situation even worse. The manifestations, demonstrations, and proclamations of the Liberals were undermining the public faith in the regency council. There was a general restlessness, and the hold of the Liberals on the financial and economic life of the country began to display its power. It was expected that the Liberals might return to power at any moment.

The insistence of Vintilă Brătianu on the legality of the exclusion of Prince Carol from the Throne still further endangered a situation already sufficiently precarious as a result of the serious economic crisis. At the beginning of the year 1930 the great Liberal congress, in spite of some dissensions in the ranks of the party, again con-

firmed Brătianu's position of leadership; he accused the government
of maintaining what he called "the equivocation of the constitutional
question."[14]

Suddenly Prince Carol made a dramatic return to Bucharest by
aëroplane on the night of June 6, 1930. He was welcomed by his
brother Nicolae, one of the regents, and during the night he was
visited by Maniu, General Condeescu, Minister of War, and General
Cihoski, Condeescu's predecessor.[15] When the first news leaked out in
the morning the public welcomed the Prince with enthusiasm and de-
votion. The council of regency resigned, and Maniu, who had taken
an oath of allegiance to the regency, followed its example. A ministry under Mironescu was formed and both houses of the parliament
were summoned to meet. Mironescu moved the repeal of the articles
of the statute of the royal house excluding Carol from the succession
and prohibiting his residence in Roumania. These provisions were
passed by the chamber and the senate on June 8. A private bill was
also passed conferring on ex-King Mihaiu the title of Prince of
Alba-Iulia. The two chambers then constituted themselves a national
assembly and similarly revoked the Exclusion Act of January 4,
1926. After this the national assembly proclaimed the Prince King
Carol II. Mironescu resigned on the same day, and on June 13 Carol
again appealed to Maniu to form a cabinet.

The attitude of Vintilă Brătianu on the whole question was at
first uncompromising. On June 9 the executive committee of the
Liberal Party issued a manifesto denouncing the proclamation of
Prince Carol. Gheorghe Brătianu, who favored Carol, was expelled
from the party. He, however, immediately started a new movement
within the fold of the Liberal Party, thus effecting a rupture in its
solidarity. Vintilă Brătianu soon recognized that he had been hasty,
and he accordingly accepted the situation by asking for an audience
with the King, who, willing to forget the past, granted it to the
Liberal chieftain. The subsequent notions of these two, however,
proved irreconcilable. Brătianu soon after that suddenly died.

On June 14 Maniu, in a speech to the chamber of deputies, explained that he himself had obtained permission from the regency
for Prince Carol to visit Roumania. A Bucharest correspondent,
writing on this point, offered an explanation of this policy in the
Near East and India:

---

[14] *Near East and India,* 1930, XXXVII, 651.   [15] *Ibid.,* p. 645.

A growing wave of popularity has led to the restoration of the former Prince Carol. The Maniu Government, being essentially constitutional, could not do otherwise than leave public opinion free to express itself, but it was also obliged to conform to the dynastic order that was established when it came into power. . . . . Hence . . . . the name of Prince Carol was never mentioned by the Ministers as that of a possible successor on the Regency Council. It is hardly right, therefore, to say that Dr. Maniu has brought back Prince Carol. He let him come, knowing of and encouraging the relations that existed between the members of his party and the father of the young King Michael; but he did no more than keep within legal bounds the manifestations of public opinion in favour of the return of him whom the nation persisted in regarding not only as its legitimate King, but also as the only authority capable of consolidating the prestige of the Dynasty and of satisfactorily conducting the affairs of the country. . . . . The King was not brought back by any party, nor by the Army, nor by a popular movement. He came back *propriu motu*. He made the journey with the help of some devoted friends. He put himself in the hands of his people. He was acclaimed by them, freely proclaimed by Parliament, elected by the nation, and was duly reintegrated in all his rights by the same Parliament. During the flight of Prince Carol over Roumanian territory and the few hours in which the decision of the Chambers was taken, the Maniu Government naturally made no attempt to restrict popular manifestations which expressed the will of the people.[16]

Carol emphasized his adherence to the democratic and constitutional régime in several interviews arranged to dispel illusions. At the same time, he expressed his wish to have an all-national coalition formed. This led to the publication of a revised program by the Liberals, the outstanding points of which were: opposition to any type of dictatorship; the belief that the party could rehabilitate the country economically (though no definite means were mentioned); the return of the National Bank to its normal function; the revision of the agrarian reform; and the abolition of the law for the new Dobrogea, which was intended to protect the Bulgarian settlers. The most important was the section dealing with foreign capital, which encouraged its co-operation. It was promised that the decentralized administrative reform would be reversed. The introduction to the program carried a manifesto, which read as follows:

The Liberal Party, which gained so many merits in the upbuilding of modern Roumania, has always been a true adherent of the monarchical régime and this monarchical outlook binds it even now to be the staunch supporter of the constitutionally established régime. Hence the Party will be the loyal servant of the bearer of the Crown, His Majesty King Carol II, whom it will help in his glorious task, begun by his predecessors.

[16] *Near East and India*, 1930, June 26, XXXVIII, 704.

With the exception of the changed views on foreign capital and the King, the Liberal program was disappointing to the Roumanian observers.

THE CABINET OF MIRONESCU

(October 1930—April 1931)

Premier Maniu resigned his post on October 6 after two years of power, declaring formally that his decision was based on poor health. He recommended that the King appoint Mihalache or Mironescu to the office. The former was probably too radical for the ruler, and Mironescu, Foreign Minister of the Maniu Government, was commissioned to form a cabinet, which was announced on October 10. The Premier also retained the portfolio of the Ministry of Foreign Affairs. Except for the disappearance of the Minister of the Interior, Dr. Alexandru Vaida-Voevod, and the addition of Dr. Emil Hatzeganu, Minister of Labor, the new cabinet was much the same as the old one.[17]

Mironescu's personal qualities qualified him for his post. His tactfulness, conciliatory views, and absolute independence in money matters (Mironescu is one of the richest men of Roumania), his cultural background, honesty, and good nature made him a good leader. With the exception of Vaida-Voevod, the second leader of the Transylvanian wing of the National-Peasant Party, the cabinet posts represented all the compact groups of the party.

The program of Mironescu was only the continuation of that which the Government of Maniu had intended to follow. In the main it had to bring in a budget reduced by about six milliards of lei, to negotiate an agricultural credit, to settle the problem of agricultural debts, and to conclude a foreign loan.

The feature of the opening of the Roumanian parliament on November 15, 1930, was the reappearance of the Liberals and the group led by Marshal Averescu. The way for their return had been

---

[17] The cabinet list was as follows: Premier and Foreign Minister, Gheorghe Mironescu; Minister of the Interior, Mihail Popovici; Minister of Justice, Grigore Junian; Minister of Agriculture, Virgil Madgearu; Minister of Railways, Voicu Niţescu; Minister of Education, Professor Costescu; Minister of Trade and Commerce, Manoilescu; Minister of Public Works, Hatzeganu; Minister of War, General Condeescu; Minister for Bessarabia, Pantelimon Halippa.

smoothed by King Carol's request. In his address from the Throne, the King urged the co-operation of all parties as the only means whereby Roumania could survive the economic crisis, and emphasized the special importance of Roumania's treaties with Yugoslavia and Czechoslovakia. The reorganization of the universities was promised and the minorities were assured treatment based on absolute justice and equality. An appeal was made for general support of a scheme of army expansion.

Vintilă Brătianu's retirement from public life did not last long, for he died on December 22, 1930, at 9:30 p.m. on his estate at Micăeşti of apoplexy. His death removed the outstanding member of the distinguished family which for seventy years had ruled Roumania. Gheorghe Brătianu, his nephew, not a regular politician, holds a professorship at Iaşi University. Another brother, Dinu, was far overshadowed by his brothers. I. G. Duca was elected to take the place of Vintilă Brătianu at the head of the Liberal Party.

The existence of Mironescu's Government was deemed precarious from the outset. At the beginning of his régime the Premier was faced with the necessity of dismissing thousands of government employees in order to cut expenses, and the long-protracted and unsuccessful negotiations were interpreted by the opposition as a crisis not only of the government but of the whole régime. Finally, on March 10, 1931, the long-negotiated loan agreement was signed in Paris. Under it Roumania received nominally $50,000,000.[18]

---

[18] Actually 1,325 million francs, of which the French share is 575 million. A group of French banks headed by the "Banque de Paris et des Pays Bas" took a major part of the loan, but other markets, including New York, Prague, and Amsterdam and the Kreuger group in Sweden, also participated. According to *Central European Observer*, March 20, 1931 (IX, 182), the yield of the loan, which represents the second part of the 1928 stabilization loan, was not more than about 1,060 million francs, as the issue price has been fixed at 86½. The loan bears interest at the rate of 7½ per cent, and matures in thirty years. Some 110 millions were to be devoted to the conversion of the loan raised with the International Telephone Company, while the remainder was to be allotted to numerous purposes, including capital and premises for the Mortgage Bank, and for the State Institution, the conversion of agricultural debts, road construction, railway re-equipment, and other productive investment representing a continuation of the stabilization program of 1929. Governor Burileanu of the National Bank of Roumania, who resisted the government's proposal touching the services of Roger Auboin, the French financial adviser, and without the consent of the board and the government took steps to frustrate the conclusion of the loan, had to be dismissed from his post. A former Under-Secretary for the Interior, Constantin Angelescu, took his place.

Meanwhile, economic conditions in Roumania, as in all agrarian states, were quite critical. The impossibility of selling at suitable prices the surplus of the last three years' crops led to the impoverishment of the country as a whole.

The Cabinet of Mironescu resigned on April 4, 1931. The resignation was due partly to the action of parliament, which refused to pass a bill of the Minister of Commerce, Manoilescu, and partly to that of King Carol, who declined to accept various proposals of Mironescu for the replacement of the Minister of Commerce.

Nicolae Titulescu, Roumanian Minister to London, received a telegraphic order to return to Bucharest to form a new cabinet. The task, however, was beyond him. The parties led by Gheorghe Brătianu, Dr. Nicolae Lupu, and Marshal Averescu refused to participate in a cabinet of national concentration, "although King Carol had pleaded with them until 5 o'clock this morning [April 16]."[19] Their refusal was ascribed to their conviction that by so doing "they would only involve themselves in an experiment doomed to fail, while by abstaining they could represent themselves after the failure as an alternative."[20] Titulescu was then charged by the King to form a cabinet of experts, whose mission was understood to be to conduct a general election. However, upon the failure of Titulescu to form a cabinet, Professor Nicolae Iorga took the oath of office.

THE CABINET OF IORGA

(April 1931—   )

Dr. Nicolae Iorga was appointed Prime Minister on April 18. He is also Minister of Education. His cabinet is composed of Dr. C. Argetoianu as Minister of Finance, Dr. I. Cantacuzino as Minister of Health and Labor, Mihail Manoilescu as Minister of Industry and Trade (subsequently appointed governor of the National Bank and replaced by Vasilescu-Karpen), Dr. Ion Camaraşescu as Minister of the Interior, Dimitrie Ghica as Minister of Foreign Affairs, N. Vâlcovici as Minister of Transport, Judge Constantin Hamangiu as Minister of Justice, Ionescu-Siseşti as Minister of Agriculture, and General C. Ştefănescu-Amza as Minister of War.

---

[19] *New York Times*, April 17, 1931.
[20] *Idem*.

Iorga's political program, as outlined in the press, proposed
a reduction in national expenditure to the strict minimum; a reduction in
salaries to parity with pre-war conditions; repeal of the law governing commercial bankruptcy and amendment of that exemption from seizure the personal property of bankrupts; abrogation of the Administrative Law, which
had proved an obstacle to the unification of internal administration in the
various provinces; abolition of super-taxes on gross revenue; enactment of
a Highway Law enlisting local help in the development of roads; encouragement of private initiative in commercial enterprise; harmonization of the
price of industrial products with those of agriculture; withdrawal of State
support to wasteful industries; enactment of a law making Cabinet Ministers
personally liable for public losses; institution of a rapid system of judicial
procedure; and adequate punishment of the misuse of public funds.[21]

In presenting himself before parliament, Iorga announced that
he planned the return to the Crown of the privileges it had been deprived of in the last few years, the transformation of parliament
from a battleground of party strife into a true representation of the
national will, the economic and cultural development of the peasantry, the replacement of the obsolete bureaucratic forms of government by local agencies, the reorganization of the schools in
keeping with present-day necessities, and the restoration of agriculture by thorough reorganization.

At a joint sitting of both houses held on April 30, 1931, the program of the new government was submitted to the members; subsequently Iorga announced that having been unable to secure the
support of the present parliament he had obtained the King's consent
to a dissolution.

The elections were held on June 1. All the groups which made the
electoral agreement with the National-Peasant Party in the 1928
elections naturally left it. The Germans, the Jews, the Ukrainians,
and the Social-Democratic Party freed themselves, as well as the
Bessarabian wing under Professor Stere, which formed itself into
the Peasant-Democratic Party. Still the National-Peasant Party
won first place among the opposition parties. All the leaders of this
group were returned to the parliament (their group being thirty
deputies strong) with the exception of Dr. Virgil Madgearu and
Dr. Vaida-Voevod, the latter having refused to become a candidate
—an expression of his protest against the elections, which he had
not considered free. Mihail Manoilescu was also returned—not as

[21] See Christine Galitzi, "Dr. Iorga's Political Program," in *Roumania,* 1931,
II, 7–9.

a member of this party but as its opponent. When he had been included in Iorga's Government, he had been expelled from his original fold.

The Government of Iorga, which conducted the elections, lacked the party apparatus of previous governments. A small foundation was provided by the party of Iorga which, however, was not sufficient. The prestige of the personalities composing the government could hardly win the contest without organization, though Argetoianu and Manoilescu are considered very strong. The government therefore decided to conclude electoral agreements of two kinds. Premier Iorga appealed first of all to the professional organizations to support the government in order to help new individuals to the leadership of the state on the basis of the representation of all classes of the nation in parliament. Finally, about eleven persons were selected from these organizations and placed on the governmental list of candidates, labeled the "National Union." To them was added the support of the so-called "Agrarian League" of Garoflid and the "Patriotic League" of Grigore Filipescu, director of the daily *Epoca* and president of the Roumanian Telephone Company since 1930. The government also appealed to the other parties to enter with it into an electoral agreement. Dr. Lupu and Gheorghe Brătianu announced their willingness, but the plan failed to materialize. An agreement was concluded with the Germans, the Ukrainians, and the Bulgars; the Germans received subsequently ten deputies and the Ukrainians two.

The most important understanding was that with the Liberals. The government appreciated the strength of the Liberal organization and its growing popularity in the nation. The Liberals, on the other hand, under the leadership of Duca, were anxious to show that they followed the King's desire for "national unity." They received seventy-five deputies. But Duca emphasized that the Liberal Party would follow its own policy in the parliament.

The governmental camp came out of the elections with 1,389,849 votes, viz., 49.68 per cent of the total. As the votes numbered more than 40 per cent of the total, the governmental *bloc* was proclaimed, according to Article 90 of the electoral law, the "majority part," which first of all received 50 per cent of all mandates, viz., 193. Then the remaining 194 mandates were divided proportionately among all the parties which had received more than 2 per cent of votes. The governmental group then was the recipient of 96 additional mandates, and has therefore the nominal support of 289 members out of a house of 387.[22]

The most important measures of the government were those planned by Argetoianu, ones which entailed severe economies, involving a reduction of budget expenditure from 38,000 million lei to 25,000 million, substantial reductions in the pay of the state employees, a reduction in the number of those employees, and reduced expenditure on productive investment; in addition, these plans involved the reduction of certain customs duties, excise, transport, and monopoly charges, rents, and the price of tobacco and a number of other commodities; furthermore, the plans provided for forcing down the cost of living, involving a change in the system of high protection and an attempt to lower wage levels, retail prices, and transport costs.

By way of summary, then, the internal policy of Roumania has been dominated in the larger part of the existence of the enlarged kingdom by the National-Liberal Party, whose chief leader, of unquestioned ability, was Ion Brătianu. Under his leadership Roumania was consolidated into a single national state and many reforms

---

[22] The details of the electoral results were reported by *L'Indépendance Roumaine*, June 7, June 12, 1931, as follows:

Lower House

PARTY	VOTES	PERCENTAGE OF THE TOTAL	MANDATES
National Union	1,389,849	49.68	289
National Peasant	433,761	15.68	30
Gheorghists	173,343	6.20	12
Averescu	141,229	5.05	10
Lupu	110,678	3.60	7
Cuza	113,850	4.07	8
League against Usury and Sterists	80,459	2.88	6
Socialists	95,953	3.39	6
Hungarians	126,858	4.53	10
Jews	64,175	2.29	4
Bloc of Work (Communists)	73,714	2.63	5*
	2,927,303		387

* According to the *New York Times*, June 18, 1931, the five Communist deputies were deprived of their mandates on June 17 and their seats were assigned to two Iorga men, one National-Peasant, one Socialist, and one member of Averescu's Party. "The pretext for the cancellation of the Communist mandates was that one of the Communist members, who figured on all the lists, was not a Roumanian, but a Hungarian subject." This report evidently fails to take into consideration the electoral law.

were effected. Economically, however, the Liberals failed to give their country the promised prosperity.

The opposition parties, standing on the Left, while the Liberals have been the party of the Right, were for several years unable to rally and unify their forces so that they could succeed the Liberals. However, the merging of the Peasant and the National parties provided the opportunity for their entrance into power in 1928, when the Liberals were weakened by the death of their leader, Ion Brătianu, as well as by the death of King Ferdinand. The return of King Carol in 1930 proved the need of a strong personality and of authority which would stand above the parties and which the regency could never sufficiently command because of its being composed of three members. After the retirement of Maniu at the end of 1930 the National-Peasant Party continued to hold the reins of the government under Mironescu, who, however, resigned in April 1931. Meanwhile the death of Vintilă Brătianu removed the obstacles to the change of the program of the Liberals, who finally accepted the new situation created by the return of Carol and by the developing needs of the country. On April 18, 1931, Professor Iorga formed his cabinet of "National Unity."

CHAPTER VIII

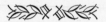

ROUMANIA AND HER NEIGHBORS

Fundamentals of Roumanian Foreign Policy

IF WE LOOK at the map of the European continent of 1918 and compare it with that of 1931, we immediately become aware of great changes which have come to Central and Southeastern Europe. In 1918 and 1919 Eastern Europe was in the throes of territorial redistribution. Millions of people were transferred in this region from one allegiance to another. In the Balkans proper, three great states emerged—Roumania, Yugoslavia, and Greece—besides a reduced Bulgaria and a small Albania.

While her defeated neighbors shrank in size, Roumania more than doubled her territory and her population. Thus the post-war period demanded that Roumania make her new possessions secure. The country realized the maximum of its territorial ambitions in the Balkans as well as in other directions. The ever-present menace of a Hungarian or a Russian *revanche* caused Roumanian statesmen to orient their foreign policy in favor of a guaranty of the *status quo* and a guaranty of security—a problem of international and of far-reaching importance. The most important political diplomatic steps of Roumania as well as of Europe during the past twelve years have been connected with this question, and its solution will be the major problem and the *directif* to Roumanian international politics for many years to come.

This fundamental of foreign policy was absolutely necessary from the point of view of internal policy. The devastations of the war and the havoc it had brought upon Roumania could not be repaired without a sense of security from without. Inasmuch as Roumania had allied herself with the Western Powers during the war, and as "România Mare" owes her existence to the peace treaties, Roumanian foreign ministers were the staunch defenders of the treaties and concluded a number of defensive alliances not only with France but also with other successors of the old order who have also been bent on defending the new settlement. The main objective of these alliances was, of course, the maintenance of the new frontiers and the new order established in that part of Europe by the peace treaties against subversive efforts on the part especially of Hungary and Russia. The instability of foreign relations, but their gradual improvement and moving toward the goal set by the Roumanian statesmen, has had its reactions on internal policy and partially explains the tendency toward a strong nationalistic policy on the part of Roumania, which, in a sense, can thus be understood and justified.

THE LITTLE ENTENTE

These general characteristics of foreign policy found their expression in the framework of the so-called Little Entente, an alliance of Roumania, Czechoslovakia, and Yugoslavia, which was originally founded by these three states on a negative principle, that of securing the benefits derived from the Treaty of Trianon and of countering the actions of Hungary tending to overturn the *status quo* in Central Europe. But the geographical situation of Roumania required that not only the Hungarian frontier but also the frontier toward Bulgaria and Russia should be guaranteed. As the two other members of the Little Entente have felt that in general the Bessarabian affair concerned only Roumania, Bucharest has been forced to find other support in this matter, as we shall see later. In the Balkans, Roumania and Yugoslavia easily control Bulgaria. Positively speaking, Roumania, as well as some of her neighbors, have wanted to crystallize the *status quo* policy into a Balkan pact or guaranty of nonaggression—a plan which has so far met with a lukewarm reception.

If we take for granted that the new Europe, and thus also Roumania, is far better politically and ethnically, notwithstanding defects, than pre-war Europe, we must take into account the activity of the Little Entente—a factor in international politics often misunderstood and misinterpreted. It is often forgotten, especially by hostile critics, that the original negative policy of this alliance is counterbalanced by a positive policy, founded on instances of cooperation before, during, and after the war, and tending now into channels of positive co-operation, which, in a way, is to restore the former structure of Austria-Hungary without the political subjection of the nationalities of the former empire to a Habsburg monarch.

The structure and the superstructure of the Little Entente is not composed of a unitary alliance, but of a triangular set of agreements among the three chief succession states of the Austro-Hungarian Empire, supplemented by other compacts. The foundation was laid by the Czechoslovak-Yugoslav Treaty of August 14, 1920; then followed the Czechoslovak-Roumanian Treaty of April 23, 1921; and then the Yugoslav-Roumanian Treaty of June 28, 1921. And these alliances have been extended and strengthened by a whole series of further understandings between each of the three and other states.

It is only fair to say, however, that the genesis of the Little Entente antedates the actual signing of the treaties. It lies deep in the roots of varied national movements against the methods by which the Austro-Hungarian Empire was fabricated and preserved.

In the pre-war days millions of the nationals belonging now to the members of the Little Entente were under the domination of the Germans and the Magyars who controlled the empire of the Habsburgs. On this account it was inevitable that they should have some sort of common political and national program. Thus the Roumanians of Transylvania had great sympathy with the Czechs and the Slovaks who were also oppressed by the empire.

The close community of such interests was fully revealed during the World War. The Yugoslavs, the Roumanians, and the Czechoslovaks fought together on the side of the Allies, and the Yugoslavs fought with the Czechoslovaks in the Dobrogea against Mackensen's army.

It was during the war period that the leaders of the Czechoslovaks and the Roumanians abroad began to form a definite plan for the future Little Entente.

When Roumania entered the war the Czechoslovaks made contacts with the Roumanians abroad and thus laid the foundations of a common policy, which they continued to pursue. Dr. Beneš states in his memoirs:[1] "From the first moment when they (Roumanians) entered the war we sought contact with them in Paris and London, and our relations became even closer from the time of the Roumanian military reverses." Masaryk, present president of Czechoslovakia, and the war-leader of the Czechoslovak liberation movement, paid an important visit to the Roumanian front in the autumn of 1917, and discussed the question of using the Czechoslovak troops

---

[1] Dr. Eduard Beneš, *My War Memoirs* (Boston and New York, 1928), p. 315.

from Russia there, while the Czechoslovak volunteers served side by side with the Roumanian soldiers in the Serbian division on the Dobrogea front.[2] Meanwhile Beneš continued his co-operation, mainly of a propagandist character, with the Roumanian representatives in Paris, Senator G. Drăghicescu, T. Viua, and Dr. Lupu. As early as October 1917 Ionescu and Titulescu agreed with Beneš that both countries should pursue a common policy after the war. After the Roumanian catastrophe, Florescu, a former minister, and Octavian Goga, who was subsequently a minister, "shared in the now highly developed activities of the oppressed nations of Austria-Hungary." Beneš has these warm words of appreciation for their co-operation in the subsequent period:

> When Rumania concluded peace with the Central Powers, the activities of their [Roumanian] representatives abroad by no means came to an end. On the contrary, they realized that their only hope of national liberation and unification lay in the victory for us all. They therefore became even more closely attached to our movement, and in the end they achieved victory.[3]

The principle of complete emancipation of the small nations of Central and Eastern Europe was given weight by international manifestations. For example, the Congress of the Oppressed Nationalities of Austria-Hungary was held in Kieff, Russia, in November 1917 and was attended by Czechoslovaks, Slovenes, Serbs, Croats, Roumanians, Poles, and Italians—representatives of all the non-German and non-Magyar races under the Dual Monarchy. Some months later a greater congress was held in Rome, and in 1918 one in Washington. On November 8, 1918, the Middle-European Union held a "liberty meeting" in New York, at Carnegie Hall, presided over by Dr. Nicholas Murray Butler of Columbia, where addresses were made by Masaryk, Hinković of Yugoslavia, and Captain Vasile Stoica of Roumania.

Meanwhile the idea of the Little Entente was discussed on several occasions by the statesmen of Roumania and their allies. Masaryk had seen the members of the Roumanian Government, including Take Ionescu, at Iași, in October 1917. However, the detailed working out of the plan came at the end of the war, and concurrently from

---

[2] Dr. Eduard Beneš, *My War Memoirs* (Boston and New York, 1928), p. 315.

[3] *Ibid.,* p. 316. The passages are quoted by permission of George Allen & Unwin, Ltd., publishers, and of Houghton Mifflin Company, who control the American rights.

several sources. The prime movers in the negotiations were Take Ionescu, Masaryk, Beneš, and Nicolas Pašić of Yugoslavia, with contributive efforts from British, American, French, Polish, and even Greek delegates to the Paris Peace Conference. Ionescu favored a common *bloc* of five states, which would settle all problems among themselves. He contemplated a closed understanding with the Yugoslavs, Poles, Czechoslovaks, and Greeks. All these five states were mutually to guarantee their territories and to have a common foreign policy. Ionescu believed that such a group could achieve a representation in the Supreme Council in Paris, at least for the questions concerning one of its members. Similarly it could be represented in the Council of the League. All the five states would have a common army organization and common defense plans.

Ionescu began to discuss his plan with Beneš, Venizelos, and Pašić at Paris and London early in the autumn of 1918. Then Masaryk and Ionescu met in the Hotel Maurice in December 1918. The Roumanian statesman spoke of "the necessity of enlarging our Entente till it stretches from the Baltic to the Agean Sea, thereby introducing Poland and Greece respectively." At Ionescu's request, Masaryk went to see Venizelos and they discussed the desirability of appearing before the conference with all questions agreed upon beforehand. Concurrently with Ionescu's idea, Masaryk put forward in his book, *The New Europe,* the demand that alongside of the big Entente should exist the Entente of the small states of Central Europe.

But the conceptions of Ionescu and Masaryk were harder of realization than the authors had imagined. At the Peace Conference only the Czechoslovak and Yugoslav delegations co-operated. The Roumanians and Yugoslavs disagreed on the Banat policy.[4] The Poles and Czechoslovaks could not settle the Těšín question; it was only during the negotiations regarding the Treaty of Trianon that common interests prevailed and prepared the way for a mutual policy by Roumania, Yugoslavia, and Czechoslovakia.

The international situation in the second half of the year 1919 was such as to make it evident that the mutual defense of the succession states against Hungary at home and abroad was of impor-

---

[4] Roumania and Yugoslavia settled their frontier differences on November 24, 1923, when certain modifications of the frontier were agreed to by the two governments. In March 1929 a joint commission met at Belgrade to settle the few questions still remaining between them.

tance and common to these three states. A new initiative came from the Czechoslovak Foreign Minister. Beneš offered to Pašić a defensive alliance against Hungary at Paris, in December 1918, and in the following January approached Bucharest with the same scheme. Other events hastened a decision in the matter. Hungary proved to be unreconciled to the new situation and started a bitter campaign against the Treaty of Trianon. Her final goal—the "resurrection" of Hungary—would mean the loss of Transylvania to Roumania. In addition, there was the danger of the return of the Habsburgs to the Hungarian throne. Karl the Last still considered himself the King of Hungary. Though he had abdicated, technically, according to the Hungarian law, his abdication was not entirely valid because it had not been signed by the Prime Minister and ratified by the National Assembly. In March 1920, after the Kapp "putch," there was danger of a monarchistic reaction in Germany, which might encourage events in Austria and Hungary in the same direction. Then a suggestion to the Supreme Council came from Hungary that some Magyar divisions should be used by France or by the Allies to protect Poland against the Soviets. It was understood that these troops were to occupy eastern Slovakia and Carpathian Russia.[5] Beneš left for Belgrade and on August 14, 1920, he and Ninčić, the acting Yugoslav Minister of Foreign Affairs, signed the first Treaty of the Little Entente. The preamble of the instrument stated that its main purpose was the maintenance of the Treaty of Trianon. In case of an unprovoked attack upon either state by Hungary, the two states were to assist one another in accordance with the terms of a military convention drawn up on August 1, 1921. Furthermore, neither party was to conclude an alliance with a third party without giving previous notice to the other.[6]

Ionescu, on the other hand, did not yet give up his plan to form an alliance of five states from Poland to Greece. He hoped to bring about a mode of conciliation between Czechoslovakia and Poland, still at odds on the Těšín division. However, he agreed that in case of an unprovoked attack by Hungary, the countries should assist one another pending the conclusion of a formal convention of a defensive nature.

[5] R. Machray, *The Little Entente*, pp. 122–23.

[6] The convention was to remain in force for two years and was to be registered with the League of Nations.

The first attempt of Karl in the spring of 1921 to regain his Hungarian throne brought the Roumanian Government to a final decision. The Treaty of April 23, 1921, signed by Roumania and Czechoslovakia, was identical with the Czechoslovak-Yugoslav alliance except that it contained an explicit provision that the two governments should pursue a concerted policy in regard to Hungary.[7]

A Yugoslav-Roumanian understanding, which could be embodied in a formal treaty, seemed for a time impossible, as both countries had been at odds over boundary delimitations in the Banat section.[8] But the intolerant and threatening activity of Hungary and the fear of a restoration of the Habsburgs outweighed frontier jealousies, and a treaty of defensive alliance was signed on June 7, 1921, on the model of the Czechoslovak-Yugoslav convention.[9] The main difference between this and the two preceding documents is that it provided for bilateral mutual protection in case of an unprovoked attack by Bulgaria, which is neighbor to both Roumania and Yugoslavia, as well as against Hungary.

The official reasons for the formation of the Little Entente were given by Beneš in a lengthy speech in the Czechoslovak parliament on September 1, 1920. His first reason was the unrest prevalent throughout Europe, which,

with the resultant feeling of insecurity, produces a certain nervousness, an irritation in the nations and states, and in the end a sense of fear and anxiety about the future. . . . . This is one of the reasons which have led us to try to bring about an atmosphere which would do away with this psychology, inspire the people with confidence, and produce order before long. We wanted to begin reconstruction, and to begin it in agreement with those who have identical interests and aims, and feelings similar to our own.

The second reason was the grave economic situation, and Beneš hoped that the Little Entente agreements would not "remain restricted to

[7] A supplementary military convention was signed on July 2, 1921, giving teeth to the political instrument.

[8] See H. W. V. Temperley, *A History of the Peace Conference at Paris,* IV, 207–12, 221–23, 229.

[9] All these three treaties can be conveniently found in the League of Nations pamphlet, Vol. VI, No. 2, "Post-War Political Alignments," published by the World Peace Foundation. They are also republished in R. Machray, *The Little Entente,* pp. 363 ff., and in *The Near East Year Book, 1927,* pp. 857 ff.

political questions alone" but would lead to rapid establishment of intimate economic relations. The third reason also related to certain objections against the new order.

From time to time we hear from different sides regrets that old Austria-Hungary has been destroyed. The various difficulties of the different national States are emphasized and held up as illustrations of the incorrectness of anti-Austrian policy during the War, and this serves as a plea for the various plans for a Danubian Federation, or at least of a Customs Union of the former Austro-Hungarian territories.

The *rapprochement* of the succession states was to give

a sufficient guarantee to Europe that we are able to maintain political order, build up necessary economic relations, and make possible a general European consolidation.

This last point is of special interest. The criticism of the behavior of the Central and Eastern European peoples has always been tinged with a note of contempt. Even today the Slavs and their neighbors in that part of Europe are considered by the Anglo-Saxons as slightly inferior, and "Balkanized Europe" was to them an expression of some contempt. In the words of one writer:

The entire region has now been "Balkanized," that is, broken up into a number of nominally "national" states, which are small, weak, jealous, afraid, economically dependent, a prey to intrigue, and pregnant with trouble of many descriptions, not to say wars. . . . . Hungary, fiery and unreconciled, bent on recovering its lost territories by any means whatsoever; . . . . Czechoslovakia, with its indefensible frontiers, fearful of Austro-Hungarian restoration, profoundly Slav in sentiment, yet forced by its economic and geographical situation to seek peace through the maintenance of neutrality; . . . . Roumania, a Latin nation in a sea of Slavs, gathered in a surly defensive, ready for any entente which promises self-preservation, but unwilling as yet to commit itself deeply to any direction; Yugoslavia, confident, valorous, warlike, dreaming of grandeur; . . . . Such are the elements out of which the federations or understandings, lacking which no genuine reconstruction will be possible, must be builded.[10]

This exaggerated characterization, written in the fever of postwar excitement and bitterness, represents the state of mind against which the members of the Little Entente had to prove their worth,

[10] P. S. Mowrer, *Balkanized Europe*, pp. 3, 248–49. Quoted by permission of E. P. Dutton & Co., Inc., publishers.

to "prove by work at home and abroad that the complaints made against them abroad were not justified."[11]

The work and objects of the Little Entente are identified with four stages of development: (1) A period of defense against Hungarian aggression, from the conclusion of the treaties in 1920–21 to the passing of the Habsburg danger. (2) A subsequent stage, initiated in 1922 at the Conference of Genoa, in which the purely defensive character of the Little Entente was subordinated to a twofold development—an active positive policy for the economic consolidation of Central Europe, and a vigorous effort to carry through the problem of security upon a general European basis as indicated by the Geneva protocol. The sharp outline of the alliance began to be lost and there was a tendency to merge the system into a wider system covering the Continent.[12] (3) A still later stage, inaugurated by the system of Locarno, the possible extension of which to Central and Eastern Europe was the principal aim of the Little Entente. It was a period vitalized by the effort, against numerous obstacles, to settle the outstanding questions between Hungary and her neighbors, which found its culmination in the signing of the Briand-Kellogg Pact and the reparations and optants' settlements at the beginning of 1930. (4) The present period, in which the Little Entente states are trying to put their economic relations on sound foundations on the basis of co-operation.

[11] Beneš again expressed these points in an article in *Foreign Affairs,* I, 67 ff.: "It has been our aim to show Europe that the Old Austria-Hungary is no longer necessary to Europe, and also that the idea of a Danubian Federation of whatever sort may be quietly and finally discarded because we ourselves form a group that can establish order and close co-operation without the creation of political and economic entities, possibly offensive to various states interested. We aim to show that in destroying the ancient Austro-Hungarian Monarchy the Allies did not commit an error, but rather laid a foundation for new groupings in Central Europe which will be more flexible in their relationships and which will be peaceful and help to maintain the equilibrium of Europe to a far greater degree than the old Monarchy or any possible federation." Quoted by permission.

[12] At that period France and Italy increased their interest in the Little Entente. Toward the close of 1923, France offered credits to Yugoslavia, Roumania, and Poland for the purchase in France of munitions and other military equipment. French credits voted to Roumania by the French Senate on December 17, 1923, were eventually refused by Roumania on January 2, 1924. But then the divergence of interest and policy in regard to Russia between Roumania and the other members of the Little Entente was brought into the open. Hence Roumania, who repulsed French overtures for an alliance in January 1924, made overtures herself after the breakdown of the Russo-Roumanian negotiations in April. See A. J. Toynbee, *Survey of International Affairs, 1924,* p. 441.

Within the term of its existence the Little Entente was necessarily drawn into the orbit of the Great Powers. France signed treaties of alliance with Czechoslovakia in 1924 and 1926;[13] with Roumania in 1926; and with Yugoslavia in 1927. Italy, quite determined to counterbalance the influence of France on the Little Entente, professed her friendship for Hungary in a treaty of April 5, 1927. Previously, Italy had been drawn into Central European affairs by her relations with Yugoslavia. The Yugoslav-Italian treaties of 1920 and 1921, however, failed to improve permanently the relations of the two countries, which have been always more or less strained. Cordial collaboration treaties were signed by Czechoslovakia in 1924 and by Roumania in 1926 with Italy, who also ratified the Bessarabian Treaty on March 8, 1927. However, an entire change in Italian diplomatic orientation came when Mussolini signed the Italian-Hungarian Treaty of Friendship, Conciliation, and Arbitration in 1927.

The subsequent events disturbed profoundly the relations of these states. As the control of the disarmament of Hungary was removed from inter-allied agencies on March 31, 1927, with the permission of the Little Entente, public opinion of these states became alarmed over the Rothermere campaign for the revision of the Treaty of Trianon[14] and by the discovery on January 1, 1928, of five carloads

[13] The treaty of September 14, 1926, guarantees the enforcement of the terms of the Locarno Pact. For convenient summaries of the treaties see N. L. Hill, "Post-War Treaties of Security and Mutual Guarantee"; *International Conciliation,* November 1928, No. 244; and Foreign Policy Association, *Information Service,* Vol. IV, No. 14, September 14, 1928, "The Little Entente."

[14] Lord Rothermere's campaign began with an article in *The Daily Mail* on June 21, 1927, entitled "Hungary and Its Place in the Sun." Lord Rothermere, who had appended his signature to the article, demanded a revision of the present status of Central Europe, that is to say: the restitution to Hungary of Transylvania, of Banat, and of Slovakia, or at least of some important regions of the provinces liberated by the Treaty of Trianon. See *Revue des Balkans,* No. 5, May 1929, "The Campaign against the Treaty of Trianon."

It is very interesting to note that Sir Philip Gibbs, whose writings always have been unfavorable to the view of the Little Entente, writes in his latest book, *Since Then* (New York, 1930, p. 103): "Hungary has kept the peace, but the fires of passion aroused by the Treaty of Trianon which drew their new frontiers are still smoldering, ready to break out into a flame of emotion or indignation at any reminder. It did so, in emotion, when Lord Rothermere, the great newspaper proprietor in England, championed their cause and denounced the Treaty. When his son made a tour through Hungary he was received as though he were a national hero, and flowers were strewn before him. A curious little episode since the war, strangely ironical! It was Lord Rothermere's brother and his paper, *The Daily Mail,* who raised the cry of 'They will cheat you yet—those

of machine guns, labeled "machine parts" at St. Gotthard, a frontier station between Austria and Hungary. The shipment was sent from Italy and evidently destined for Hungary. Because of the attitude that Italy took when the Council of the League of Nations discussed it, the whole matter was whitewashed.

It has become evident during the last few years that Mussolini is dissatisfied with the international situation. In order to strengthen Italy he would make himself and his country champion of the defeated powers, and would support their desire for revision of the peace treaties. Italy has been suffering from a serious ailment—a maladjustment of population. In a series of speeches beginning with his address of May 28, 1927, in the Chamber of Deputies, and continuing through the more irritating orations of last May (1931), Mussolini was opposing the maintenance of the political and economic *status quo* of Europe.

Fundamentally, his tactics are merely another form of an old diplomatic method—indirect pressure. The basic object of it is to induce France to make Italy substantial colonial and naval concessions. During the period Italy has concluded treaties of friendship and arbitration with four former enemies — Germany, Hungary, Turkey, and Austria. Furthermore, Princess Giovanna of Italy was married to King Boris of Bulgaria. Thus Italy aimed to break the ring of French influence in Europe. In his speech delivered on the eve of the eighth anniversary of the Fascist march on Rome, on October 27, 1930, Mussolini aligned his country with the policy followed by Hungary, viz., the revision of the peace treaties.[15]

But a new situation was created by the defeat of the Austro-

Huns!' when Lloyd George fought his khaki election and won it on hatred for Germany and her allies.

"It was Lord Rothermere's brother and his paper, *The Daily Mail*, who 'gingered' up Lloyd George when he wanted to be fair and even a little generous to the vanquished nations. They threatened to destroy him if he yielded anything of all those impossible demands for German reparations which amounted to more gold than existed in the world. 'They will cheat you yet—those Huns!' . . . . Strange that Lord Rothermere, of all men, should be a pleader for justice to Hungary." Quoted by permission of Harper & Brothers, publishers.

[15] "Even our policy of revision of the treaties—which is not new but was first advanced in 1928—aims at avoiding war. The revision of the peace treaties is not prevailing of Italian interest, but interests the whole of Europe and the whole world. Revision is not absurd or impossible, since the possibility of revision is contemplated in the covenant of the League of Nations. The only absurd thing is to expect treaties to remain absolutely immobile." (Reported by *New York Times,* November 2, 1930, Sec. 9, p. 2.)

German customs union. The revisionist *bloc* of substantial appearance in 1930 seemed to have melted into thin air in 1931. Central and Southern Europe's financial and economic difficulties were France's opportunity and the real factor in the whole situation. The bankers of France resumed the pre-war policy of making foreign loans to countries willing to submit to French political pressure.[16]

W. E. Rappard points out in his *Uniting Europe*[17] that since 1920 the Little Entente "has remained an active and important factor in the political situation of Central and Eastern Europe." According to this distinguished authority on international relations, three circumstances have strengthened it since then.

The first of these circumstances was the test to which the Little Entente was put when Karl the Last suddenly appeared in Hungary on March 27, 1921, and was forced to return to Switzerland. His escapade was repeated in October of the same year. Karl arrived by aëroplane, but the Hungarian Government captured him after protests by and at the request of the Budapest representatives of the Allied Powers and the Little Entente. Beneš asserted the authority of the Little Entente in the face of the Western Powers by declaring that he considered "the presence of the ex-King on Hungarian soil to be a *casus belli.*" The move led to the retirement of Karl and the acquiescence of the Great Powers, and strengthened the solidarity of the Little Entente.

In the second place, the defensive conventions, concluded originally for two years only, were renewed in 1922, and have now, since the Belgrade Conference of 1929, become practically permanent. A general, tripartite pact of conciliation and arbitration was signed in May of that year, a new departure, since the only bonds of the Entente heretofore had been bilateral treaties of alliance. At the same

---

[16] Notice that in March 1931 a French banking group, in co-operation with foreign bankers, loaned $42,000,000 to Roumania; in April French loans of $50,000,000 to Czechoslovakia and of $40,000,000 to Poland were announced; in May a loan of $42,000,000 to Yugoslavia was concluded; on August 14, Hungary borrowed $25,000,000. Some circles attribute the restoration of constitutional government in Yugoslavia, on September 2, 1931, to French pressure. The financial diplomacy of France must be analyzed in connection with the French plan for European reconstruction presented at Geneva on May 16, 1931. See Foreign Policy Association, *Foreign Policy Reports,* Vol. VII, No. 12, August 19, 1931, "European Efforts for Economic Collaboration," pp. 235 ff.; also R. L. Buell, "The Weight of France's Gold on the Scales of Diplomacy," in *New York Times,* September 13, 1931.

[17] New York, 1930, pp. 181–82.

time the general structure has been invigorated by commercial agreements.

The third circumstance in connection with the evolution of the Little Entente is that resulting from the various international understandings which each member of the group contracted with other powers. The treaties with Italy and France have been mentioned. Czechoslovakia has concluded political treaties with Poland, Austria, and Italy; Roumania with Poland and Italy; and Yugoslavia with Greece and Italy. The Hague agreements, which will be discussed presently, are of great importance, as they provide for the settlement of some outstanding difficulties between the Little Entente, acting in some cases as a unit, and the defeated states.

In order to arrive at a unified policy, the foreign ministers of the Little Entente have held periodic conferences, at which specific problems have been discussed. After the incorporation of the Little Entente, the three foreign ministers met at the marriage of King Alexander of Yugoslavia to Princess Marie of Roumania at Belgrade on June 8, 1922, and agreed to hold periodic meetings. The first conference met in Prague in August 1922, Poland participating. It was ascertained that local conflicts or differences among these states did not impair the fundamental identity of attitude toward the requirements of international politics. It was agreed also to advocate a financial and economic solution for Austria.

The second conference at Sinaia of July 1923 approved the Hungarian negotiations for a loan on the condition that the proceeds of the loan be used neither for new armaments nor for irredentist propaganda. It was decided that there were no objections to continuing normal relations with Bulgaria, in which a new government had been set up after the fall of Stambulisky in June 1923. The conference also closely scanned the program of the coming session of the Assembly of the League of Nations, especially as to the troublesome problem of minorities.

The Russian question and the reconstruction of Hungary were two principal matters discussed at the Belgrade conference of January 1924. An official *communiqué* of January 13 announced in the matter of relations with Russia that the Little Entente would "leave liberty of action to each of its members in order to allow them to take account of the circumstances of the moment and of their own special situation."

In July of the same year another conference was held in Prague, preceded by the most extraordinary rumors of the dissolution of the Little Entente owing to divergency of views respecting Russia. The discussions dealt with the question of inter-Allied debts and the agenda of the League relating to disarmament and agreements as to mutual guaranty.

The fifth meeting took place in May 1925 in Bucharest. The subjects under consideration were the bolshevistic activities in Bulgaria, the Geneva protocol, security, Soviet propaganda, the Hungarian problem in relation to the intensification of the irredentist movement, and the question of *Anschluss*. Beneš particularly expressed himself against any proposals of a Danubian federation.

It was evident by the end of 1925 that the financial reconstruction of Hungary was successful. Unfortunately, when the question of withdrawing the League of Nations control and when projects for the inclusion of Hungary in some kind of security pact as a sequel to the Locarno Pact came up, a plot for counterfeiting French currency was revealed. The forgeries and the resulting situation were among the topics discussed at a special conference, held in February 1926, at Timişoara (Roumania). It was hoped that the "sad affair" would not recur. The conference was arranged chiefly because of the importance attached to the meeting of the Council of the League of Nations in March 1926, when it was anticipated that Germany would join the League of Nations.

The seventh conference at Bled, Yugoslavia, in June 1926, was preceded by the signing of two protocols by Roumania with Czechoslovakia and Yugoslavia for the prolongation of the treaties for three years.[18] In regard to the question of the Bulgarian loan it was agreed that the Little Entente would demand the appointment of a Yugoslav delegate to the control commission which was to supervise the employment of the proceeds of the loan by Bulgaria. There appeared to be a general tendency toward a loosening of the bonds, though without the weakening of the friendship ties between the members of the Little Entente in this period. This seemed to be inevitable. The post-war difficulties were being liquidated, and each state entered into fresh relations with its neighboring states according to its immediate needs and interests.[19] The year ended with the conclusion of the Italo-Roumanian Treaty of September 16, 1926,

[18] The Yugoslav-Czechoslovak Treaty of August 31, 1922, had still a year to run.

[19] For an excellent account see A. J. Toynbee, *Survey of International Affairs, 1924*, pp. 440–56.

and the Italo-Albanian Treaty of November 27. The tension created by the latter dominated international relations of the following year. Toynbee remarks that "in 1927 Italy and France seemed to be assuming in Central Europe the rôles which Russia and Austria-Hungary had played there in a previous century." The Little Entente was particularly concerned with the problem of the Hungarian optants in Roumania and with the renewed campaign for the revision of the peace treaties. In April Mussolini came to an understanding with the Hungarians. Roumania, which a month before had been deeply gratified by the Italian ratification of the Bessarabian Treaty, did not welcome the Magyar-Italian agreement. A regular conference met in May 1927 at Jáchymov (Czechoslovakia) and emphasized the fact that any statement of lack of unity in the Entente was groundless.

The signature of the Briand-Kellogg Pact was hailed with gratification by the Bucharest conference of June 1928. As the conference was preceded by various pronouncements against the Trianon Treaty, the *résumés* of the ministers were strongly directed against any changes of territorial status. A special committee was set up to study the economic relations of the Little Entente in order to prepare concrete proposals. It was agreed to negotiate complete treaties of commerce, to create a joint chamber of commerce, and to improve rail and water communications and transit facilities. The practical result was a conference of delegates which met at Bucharest, in February 1929, and drew up a provisional plan of operations.

The tenth conference took place in Belgrade in May 1929. The economic problems stood at the front. A general, tripartite pact of conciliation and arbitration was signed and the Yugoslav-Roumanian Treaty renewed with a clause making renewals automatic in the future at the end of each five-year period.

The eleventh conference, which began on June 25 and ended on June 28, 1930, held at Štrbské Pleso in Czechoslovakia, codified in some important points the practices which had become customary during the last ten years. A permanent bureau of the press of the Little Entente was created which is to co-ordinate the activities of the three national committees. An additional agreement provided for an organization status of the Little Entente, as far as the calling of the conferences, their programs, the question of chairmanship, etc., were concerned. The statutes provided also for one delegate or one delegation to have the power to represent the remaining two in cer-

State Deposit Bank, Bucharest

Victory Street, Bucharest

tain cases. A Czechoslovak-Roumanian Commercial Treaty was signed. Mironescu and Beneš emphasized the possibility of co-operation with Hungary, which, after the Hague and Paris agreements, was in their belief not too difficult. In addition, the conference agreed upon a favorable stand toward Briand's Memorandum.[20]

The twelfth meeting of the Little Entente was held in Bucharest May 2–5, 1931, under the chairmanship of Ghica, Roumanian Minister of Foreign Affairs. In the *communiqué* issued to the press the problems under discussion were touched upon only in a general way. The foreign ministers discussed, in the presence of the Roumanian Ministers of Finance and Trade, the proposed Austro-German customs union, examining it from the juridic, political, and economic points of view. The necessity of a preferential system in favor of agricultural products was reaffirmed, and an agreement was reached on a common standpoint regarding the disarmament conference and the problems arising from the question of adjusting the Briand-Kellogg Pact and the Briand proposal to the Covenant of the League of Nations.

The chief aim of the policy of the Little Entente has been to check the outward thrust of Hungary's irredentism. The Hungarian view as to the revision of the peace treaties will probably prevent her co-operation with the Little Entente for some time to come. The extreme demands of the Hungarian Government, expressed by Premier Bethlen, proclaim that Hungary "wants, first, restoration of all her lost citizens of Hungarian nationality, and, second, a plebiscite among her former citizens of other nationalities to determine whether they should come back to her,"[21] a program which evidently cannot but find the most unsympathetic reaction from the Little Entente. Its realization would strike at the very basis of existence of the succession states.

Up to the present the Government of Hungary has carried on its propaganda of absolute irreconcilability to the new international order with undiminishing vigor. The Magyar irredentist watchword, "Nem, nem, soha" (No, no, never), is taught with religious conviction in all public schools in Hungary. In England certain parliamentarians, including Lord Sydenham of Combe and Sir Rob-

[20] *Central European Observer*, 1930, VIII, 173. The answers of the states composing the Little Entente to Briand's Memorandum can be found in *International Conciliation*, December 1930, No. 265.

[21] *New York Times*, November 17, 1930.

ert Gower, were successfully solicited. In 1929, for example, Sir Robert Donald published a picture-and-text book entitled *Hungary Illustrated* for the purpose of "confidently educating foreigners, especially ignorant politicians, on the virtue of the Hungarian people and the justice of her cause."

In general, the Treaty of Trianon is challenged in various ways —directly, by articles showing the alleged economic and social sufferings of the Hungarians; indirectly, by articles exploiting their ante-bellum happiness and the intriguing romances of individual Hungarians.

There is one interesting point which is emphasized in the Hungarian propaganda, and that is the idea of racial superiority. Hungary regards herself as racially pure and racially distinct from her neighbors, an argument as old as the Bible itself, with its story of the "chosen people." The Hungarians cannot claim originality for the argument. The first modern ideas of racial superiority started with the doctrine of Aryanism.[22] Great impetus to the belief was given by the publication of Comte de Gobineau's *The Inequality of the Human Races*. The notion is the thesis of Houston Stewart Chamberlain in his *The Foundations of the Nineteenth Century:* "Our whole civilization and culture of to-day is the work of one definite race of man, the Teutonic."[23]

Count Albert Apponyi claims the same honor for his race:

These [previous] considerations afford clear evidence of Hungary's fitness for the great mission she had to fulfil in the Eastern part of Central Europe, on the border-line of the West, in the field of armed conflict as well as in that of cultural efforts. She alone was qualified to fulfil this mission, by virtue of her political aptitudes, and that peculiar combination of originality and receptive capacity which characterizes her national genius.

He goes on to assert that the failure of the world to recognize the Hungarian "national genius" will endanger Western civilization:

Her [Hungarian] disintegration, the loss of great territories where Hungarian culture flourished (such as Transylvania and Upper Hungary) have weakened, not only the Hungarian nation, but also the defensive and expansive force of the West, in every respect: strategical, political and cultural. She no longer represents the Western spirit, issuing from its natural stronghold, supported by a sturdy phalanx, to extend its influence without material conquest; the ramparts of that stronghold are partially demolished, the phalanx has been weakened by the loss of some of its best troops. The

[22] R. L. Buell, *International Relations*, p. 74.   [23] *Ibid.*, p. 75.

Eastern spirit has assumed the part of aggressor and conqueror, which part, however, it cannot play by raising itself—that would take too much time—but only by oppressing the higher cultural forces. The result is terrifying.[24]

He then summarizes his views:

The Hungarian nation had and has a lofty world historic mission, determined by the achievements and tendencies of a thousand years, in the fulfilment of which it has been obstructed and weakened by the catastrophe of Trianon. This mission was, and still is the defence and the peaceful extension of the higher standards of Western life, by political and military, as well as cultural efforts, according to the requirements of the age. The Trianon mutilation has detached from the West territories it had already conquered, and thrown them back into semi-Oriental conditions, imperilling thereby existing Western culture in these territories, and slackening the progress of those who do not yet possess such culture, because they no longer feel the stimulus of its rival power. The mutilation of Hungary, the weakening of the Hungarian nation, is a loss of the great intellectual and moral interests of mankind, a loss without compensation.[25]

We can dispose of the point by quoting Dr. Buell:

When a nation acquires this attitude [of superiority], it comes to regard its character as a "soul" which has sprung out of racial origins, and as a result it gains a fatalistic confidence in a triumphal destiny. A nation thus regarding itself as a race usually feels superior to all other races. . . . . It substitutes instinct for intelligence and reason as its guide. . . . . However inconsistent the attitude may be, a nation intoxicated with racial theories is tempted to impose its racial "superiority" upon the remainder of the world. . . . . As a result of these doctrines of racialism, race prejudice is naturally intensified. . . . . On the other hand, racialism attacks the doctrine of internationalism, saying that co-operation with "inferior race" upon a basis of equality is quite impossible. On the other, it fervently supports the doctrine of imperialism, justifying the supremacy of a particular race over the remainder of the world because of its inherent physical or "racial" virtues. Furthermore, it subscribes to the theory of racial nationalism—namely, that the real basis of national life is not cultural but physical, and that all members of the same "race" should be united under a common flag.[26]

We can, therefore, conclude with Dr. Buell that

agitation based upon racial distinctions, whether in peace-time or in war, would intensify ill-feeling and bitterness, to a greater extent than that provoked purely by economic or nationalistic causes.[27]

[24] Count Albert Apponyi, E. Horváth, etc., *Justice for Hungary*, pp. 14–15.

[25] *Ibid.*, pp. 19–20. The passages are quoted by permission of Longmans, Green & Company (London), publishers.

[26] R. L. Buell, *International Relations*, pp. 73, 77–78.

[27] *Ibid.*, p. 94. The passages are quoted by permission of Henry Holt and Company, publishers. Notice that though recent writers have made it suffi-

There is another important element underlying the relations of Hungary to the Little Entente. It may be found in the explanation that while the Little Entente states have undergone a complete transformation in the matter of land tenure, and have, despite many divergencies in their social structures, become in their essence democracies, Hungary, on the other hand, as the solitary exception in the whole of Central and Eastern Europe, is more than ever before controlled by the great feudal landed families whose policies in prewar days contributed materially to the downfall of the Habsburg monarchy and who have evaded anything like drastic reform in the territory still remaining to it. The oligarchical domination of this caste is still supreme, their power lying in their control of the land. The land reforms of the Little Entente states changed the system by which the Magyar landlords formerly ruled the subject nationalities of the Hungarian kingdom. Therein lies most of their hostility to the Trianon Treaty. Thus the foreign policy of Hungary is distracting the attention of the Hungarian people from their own conditions, keeping them in constant agitation. A revision of the peace treaties, it is hoped by the ruling class, may return to it its confiscated property in the succession states.[28]

---

ciently evident that race, nationality, and nation are not identical (R. Muir, J. Oakesmith, L. Dominion, A. Keith, F. H. Hankins), for our purpose an outstanding fact historically is that wherever the conception of nationality arises, the conception of racial unity and solidarity arises with it and becomes a fundamental factor in the driving forces of national egotism. There are numerous publications on this point. C. J. H. Hayes characterizes it by pointing out in his *Essays on Nationalism* (New York, 1926, p. 230), that "some of it has scientific value, but a good deal of it, especially that part which has the greatest vogue among ardent nationalists, is chiefly rubbish." The best criticism can be found in F. H. Hankins, *The Racial Basis of Civilization* (New York, 1926), and his article "Race as a Factor in Political Theory" in C. E. Merriam and H. E. Barnes, *A History of Political Theories in Recent Times*. See also J. Rouček, *The Minority Principle as a Problem of Political Science* (Orbis, Prague, 1928), for a discussion and bibliography.

[28] Dr. Oscar Jászi, a Hungarian national of international renown, is relentless in propounding this view. For example, he writes in his article, "Dishonoring Kossuth," in *The Nation,* 1928, CXXVI, 331–32: "Hungary, mutilated by a cruel imperialistic peace and checked in her development by a rapacious oligarchy, never needed more the guidance of Kossuth than in her present dark period. . . . . But . . . . the most fundamental thought of Kossuth is not yet realized in Hungary. I mean the liberation of the bondsmen. For bondage has been eliminated only on paper, while the far greater part of the agricultural population is still kept in servitude because, in the absence of independent peasant property, they are compelled to toil for a starvation wage on the *latifundia* of the petty kings. . . . . Then why this disgusting farce? Why did Magyar feudalism need this comedy

Economic Program of the Little Entente

The Little Entente has promoted economic relations less successfully than political ones. Demands for closer economic co-operation
among the Little Entente states have been continually heard for
some years, but so far no very practical steps to this end have been
found possible. Although, at first glance, the highly developed industries of Czechoslovakia would seem to have their counterpart in the
agricultural character of Yugoslavia and Roumania, it must not be
forgotten that Czechoslovakia also is an agricultural country and
that Roumania and Yugoslavia present only a limited export field
for the manufactured goods of Czechoslovakia. Furthermore, the
two latter countries now possess new industries that promise satisfactory development in the future. The question of an economic
entente has not been simple, and its working out will, at best, be but
gradual. This is frankly acknowledged by Beneš in his article on
the Little Entente in the *Encyclopaedia Britannica:*

> The results of this economic co-operation have not of course been equally
> satisfactory in each of the States concerned, nor have they been enough in
> themselves to restore healthy conditions to those States whose economic,
> financial and currency difficulties left them with no alternative to calling in
> international financial help.[29]

Beneš here evidently refers to the effort of the Little Entente to
help in the reconstruction of Austria and Hungary. Some phases of
economic co-operation were displayed in the conferences of Genoa,
Porto Rosa, and Gratz, and in the increasing number of commercial
treaties. It is plain, however, that the leaders of the Little Entente
do not want to return to Vienna and Budapest their economic domination of the past. Their plan is to evolve an economic entente in
which all will share.[30]

---

with the monument of Kossuth? The reason is that its followers feel the soil
tremble under their feet, they are terrified by Kossuth's spirit, and they try to
falsify it by transforming Kossuth's spirit, the liberator of the peasants, the advocate of religious and racial equality, the father of the idea of a Danube Confederation, into a Kossuth conforming to *their* ideology. The people of Hungary,
muzzled by a bloody class rule, without a serious parliament, without a free press,
without a jury, under the yoke of a corrupt administration and judiciary, awaits
silently the return of Kossuth's spirit." Quoted by permission of *The Nation* and
the author.

[29] Thirteenth edition, XIV, 219–20.

[30] See *International Conciliation,* May 1929, No. 250, P. Slosson, "The Problem of Austro-German Union."

The difficulties standing in the way of the realization of such plans make the Little Entente weakest in its lack of economic solidarity. Economically they have very little in common, though their economic nationalism is considerably reduced in its intensity. The post-war difficulties required that each member of the Little Entente should create a new economic organization; thus each state has been confronted with the necessity of adjusting its economic life to new political conditions. Hence not much attention could be paid for a time to the demands of international economic co-operation. Each country desired to break away from the economic domination of Vienna and Budapest, and the ideas of self-sufficiency found ready acceptance in each state. Dr. Pasvolsky came to the conclusion in his excellent volume on *The Economic Nationalism of the Danubian States* that "the three victor states, although bound together politically by the Little Entente, still continued to be more or less isolated from each other economically."[31] However, a distinct improvement in their attitude came with the financial collapse of Austria and Hungary.

It is important to note that Austria is more important economically for Czechoslovakia than either Roumania or Yugoslavia.[32] Roumania has very little trade with Yugoslavia, and her exports to Czechoslovakia rank after those to Austria and Hungary. Czechoslovakia in 1927 exported to Roumania 14.24 per cent of the total Roumanian imports, while Czechoslovakia received only 2.85 per cent of the total Roumanian exports.[33] In 1929, the Roumanian export to Czechoslovakia represented only 2.75 per cent of her total, while Czechoslovak exports to Roumania rose to but 3.71 of her own aggregate. Yugoslav exports in 1926 to Czechoslovakia amounted to 12.01 per cent and to Roumania 10 per cent of the total exports of the country, while the imports to Yugoslavia in the same year amounted to 18.70 per cent from Czechoslovakia and 4.35 per cent from Roumania.[34] It is evident from the present economic situation that neither Roumania nor Yugoslavia will find larger markets for food exports to Czechoslovakia. Austria, despite

---

[31] Pp. 87–88.

[32] Pasvolsky, *op. cit.*, p. 285.

[33] Bureau d'Études de la Banque Marmorosch, Blank & Cie., *Les Forces économiques de la Roumanie en 1929*, p. 87.

[34] U.S. Department of Commerce, Trade Promotion Series, No. 61, K. S. Patton, *Kingdom of Serbs, Croats and Slovenes*, pp. 226, 229.

all efforts of the Little Entente to the contrary, still serves largely as the distributing center for the trade of Central and Eastern Europe.

The increasingly difficult economic situation of the last few years brought the economic co-operation of the members of the Little Entente into the sphere of practical politics. In a lengthy speech in the Czechoslovak parliament on April 23, 1931, Beneš stated very clearly what were the reasons against the *Anschluss;* on this occasion he said:

Let me say, at the outset, that the so-called economization of the Little Entente has been the subject of discussion in the Little Entente countries since the conference of that body at Jáchymov in 1927. The first resolution was passed there touching the necessity of mutual study of this question and the intensifying of economic relations among the States of the Little Entente. The first practical step, however, was only taken a year later, following the conference of the Little Entente at Bucharest in 1928. It was decided to set up a commission of study which was to meet at Bucharest in the Autumn of 1928. But some fears began to be felt in agricultural circles in Czechoslovakia about this committee. At that time the early difficulties in the agricultural crisis manifested themselves in Czechoslovakia, the meeting of the committee was postponed, and finally it did not take place at all in 1928. Attempts were again made in 1929, Yougoslavia and Rumania demanding further economic studies, and I was in complete agreement with them. The difficulties, however, of our internal political and economic situation did not permit us to draw up a fixed program for these discussions and negotiations. In considering these schemes we had always in view the improvement of communications by land and on the Danube, the establishment of export and import organizations, the arrangement of direct exchange of merchandise without the services of middlemen, etc. Consideration was also given to various forms of commercial and legal agreements. We were fully aware of the difficulties of any form of customs union from the standpoint of internal and external politics, and we never at any time entertain the idea of effectuating anything against other States or against their interests. In considering these matters we always loyally kept in view the preparation of the ground of economic co-operation with Hungary.[35]

The simultaneous announcement in Berlin and Vienna on March 21, 1931, that Germany and Austria had agreed to negotiate a customs union caught public opinion in Bucharest, Prague, and Belgrade unprepared. For Prague the plan was unrealizable and unacceptable. The answer of Bucharest was not so articulate. Into the attitude of

---

[35] Dr. Eduard Beneš, *The Austro-German Customs Union Project,* speech of the Czechoslovak Minister of Foreign Affairs delivered in the Chamber of Deputies, Prague, on April 23, 1931, Orbis, Prague, 1931.

Roumania there enters the question of doubtful gains to be derived from close co-operation with a country which may offer some prospects of solving Roumania's problems of agricultural surplus production. But the problem seems to have been solved; on September 3, 1931, Austria completely renounced her customs union protocol with Germany without awaiting the advisory opinion of the Permanent Court of International Justice of September 5, 1931, which held the proposed customs union to be incompatible with the protocol signed at Geneva on October 4, 1922. The action of Austria was considered in European financial quarters "a signal victory for French financial diplomacy."

THE HAGUE SETTLEMENTS

A very definite settlement of a series of economic and political disputes which have disturbed the relations of the succession states since the peace settlements occurred in connection with the new arrangements of the reparations and other obligations at The Hague and Paris. By it the Little Entente succeeded in settling its main difficulties with Hungary, with the exception of the Hungarian desire for a "revision" of the Treaty of Trianon. The ever-recurring question of the optants was liquidated. The difficult negotiations of the case had kept Roumanian foreign relations in the public eye and before the League of Nations since 1923 and had increased to a marked degree the ill-feeling between Bucharest and Budapest.

In 1917, the Roumanian parliament amended the constitution by passing a new article (originally Article 19 and now Article 18) of the new Roumanian constitution, which laid down the principles of land reform. A decree-law of December 16, 1918, put into application the principles thus enunciated. Compensation to the expropriated owners was to be granted in the form of agrarian state bonds, bearing five per cent interest and redeemable in fifty years.

At the time of the inauguration of the reform, the agrarian bonds represented fair compensation to the expropriated owners. But then the leu took a downward course, and the bonds depreciated proportionately. The resulting inadequacy of the compensation was one of the factors which dominated the dispute between Hungary and Roumania.

The Hungarian owners were protected by the Treaty of Trianon (Articles 61 and 63), providing that persons over eighteen, resident in former Hungarian territories, should automatically acquire na-

tionality of the state exercising sovereignty over the territory. At
the same time these Hungarians had the right to opt for Hungarian
citizenship and then had to transfer their residence to Hungarian
territory. But they were entitled "to retain their immovable property in the territory of the other state where they had their place of
residence before exercising their right to opt."[36] Furthermore, the
Treaty of Trianon provided that the property rights and interests
of Hungarians situated in Roumania should not be "subject to retention or liquidation," but were to be "restored to their owners freed
from any measure of any kind or from any other measure of transfer, compulsory administration or sequestration," notwithstanding
the confiscatory intent of Article 232.[37] Claims were to be submitted
to a mixed arbitral tribunal. In addition, Article 3 of the minorities
treaty confirms the privilege of the Hungarians of the annexed
provinces to opt for Hungarian nationality and reiterates that "persons who have exercised the above right to opt . . . . will be entitled
to retain their immovable property in Roumanian territory." Finally,
by Article 1 of the same treaty,

Roumania undertakes that the stipulations contained in Articles 2 to 8
of this chapter shall be recognized as fundamental laws, and that no law,
regulation or official action shall conflict or interfere with these stipulations,
nor shall any law, regulation or official action prevail over them.

The treaty came into force on July 26, 1921, and four days later
the Roumanian Government promulgated an agrarian law applicable
to Transylvania; thus the agrarian reform first applied to the Old
Kingdom was extended to the new province. The government proceeded immediately to the expropriation of landowners in this territory, including the Hungarian optants. The law was directed against
"absentees," and subsequent ordinances no longer exempted foreigners from the application of the original law. The compensation to
be paid to the dispossessed landowners was to be figured on the
basis of the value of the estates in 1913. But owing to the depreciation of the Roumanian currency, as intimated above, it was alleged
that the compensation represented only a fraction of the real value of
the expropriated property.

The case of the Hungarian optants was brought before the Council of the League of Nations in March 1923, and there became involved in a complex disputation over the powers and functions of

[36] Article 63, par. 4.   [37] Article 250.

the Council of the League. Practically all the European and some American authorities on international law were drawn into the dispute.[38]

Properly speaking it was not a problem of the minorities, since the optants chose to become Hungarian citizens. It was rather a dispute between Hungary, representing the optants, and Roumania, who refused to exempt them from the application of her agrarian laws. Fundamentally it was the familiar conflict between national sovereignty and international law as well as a conflict between treaty obligations and national legislation and between the juridical and the political method of handling an international dispute.

Hungary pressed her claim that in view of the exiguous compensation offered to the landowners and the drastic provisions regarding the property of so-called "absentees," "expropriation along these lines differed very slightly from confiscation pure and simple." On the other hand, the Roumanian Government declared that it could not agree to pay a special compensation to the Hungarian optants and "there cannot be therefore any question of creating for the landowners of Hungarian origin in the recently annexed territories a privileged situation, not only as to other aliens, but also as to a whole class of Roumanian landowners."

[38] *La Réforme agraire en Roumanie et les optants Hongrois de Transylvanie devant la Société des Nations,* Études rédigées par MM. Yves de la Brière, H. Capitant, etc. (Paris, 1928) ; A. Alvarez, etc., *Agrarian Reform in Roumania and the Case of the Optants in Transylvania before the League of Nations* (privately printed, 1927) ; A. Verdross, "Die Verbindlichkeit ihne Entcheidungen internationaler Schiedsgerichte über ihne Zuständigkeit, under besonderer Berucksichtigung des ungarisch-rumänischen Streitfalls über die Durchführung der Agrarreformen in Siebenbürgen," in *Zeitschrift für Öffentliches Recht,* April 1928 ; E. Bartin, A. Prudhomme & M. Picard, *La Réforme agraire Roumaine et les ressortissants Hongrois devant la Société des Nations* (Paris, 1927—Extrait de *Journal du Droit International*) ; V. Bercaru, *La Réforme agraire en Roumanie* (Paris, 1928) ; E. M. Borchard, *Opinion on the Roumanian-Hungarian Dispute* (1927, privately printed) ; F. Connert, "Zur Frage der Agrarreform in Siebenbürgen," in *Nation und Staat,* 1928, Vol. I, No. 4 ; M. Currey, *The Hungaro-Rumanian Dispute* (London, 1929) ; F. Deák, *The Hungarian-Roumanian Land Dispute* (New York, 1928) ; Mrs. E. Dugdale, *The Hungaro-Roumanian Dispute* (London, Association for International Understanding, 1928) ; N. Politis, "La Société des Nations et les Tribunaux Arbitraux Mixtes," in *Révue Bleue,* November 19, 1927 ; N. N. Petrascu, *Réforme agraire Roumaine et les réclamations Hongroises* (Paris, 1931) ; Zsombor de Szász, *The Minorities in Roumanian Transylvania* (London, 1927) ; Dr. W. Simons, "The Rumano-Hungarian Agrarian Conflict in the Light of Objective Law," in *Revue de Droit International,* 1928, VI, 43–45 ; A. Wahl, "La Question des optants Hongrois et le Conseil de la Société des Nations," in *Revue Politique et Parlementaire,* 1927, CXXXIII, 205–16 ; etc.

From December 1923 onward a number of the expropriated cases were submitted to the Mixed Hungarian-Roumanian Arbitral Tribunal and in February 1927 Roumania recalled her judge, refusing to accept a decision of the tribunal of January 10, 1927, which upheld the Hungarian view and ruled that

an expropriation without consent and by implication without compensation was a measure of liquidation under Article 250 and that it was necessary to examine each case independently on its merits to determine whether actually the expropriation or seizure in question constituted a "retention or liquidation."[39]

As the Council of the League of Nations was unable to settle the problem, embittered Roumanian-Hungarian relations threatened to disturb international peace, and Roumania appealed to the League under Article 11 of the Covenant. The vexed question was thus formally changed into a political dispute. Hungary, on the other hand, insisted on the legal rights of her nationals, while Roumania contended that the Treaty of Trianon "merely guaranteed to the Hungarian optants a right of property within the limits of the Roumanian law," and emphasized the social aspects of the problem.

It seems, however, that the law of expropriation was not devised for nationalist aims. Even Zsombor de Szász expresses the following opinion in his extremely anti-Roumanian publication, *The Minorities in Roumanian Transylvania:*

It would not be fair to say that the agrarian reform was aimed against the minorities exclusively; it was a general law introduced in different forms in every province of Roumania. But *as a result of the distribution of the land,* it hit first and foremost the Hungarians; and the difference in the provisions of the acts concerning the different provinces and the manner of their execution shows manifestly that it is used as a weapon against the minorities.[40]

Of Transylvania's rural population, 70 per cent were Roumanians. But among large owners the Roumanians were only three per cent, holding two per cent of the land in that category. Consequently the Transylvanian class division coincided with national division, and "any measure concerning the province was bound to affect one nationality more than another."[41] Even then, we may again cite de Szász, who quotes a Hungarian source to the effect that by 1925

[39] E. M. Borchard, *Opinion on the Rumanian-Hungarian Dispute,* p. 15.
[40] London, 1927, p. 156 (italics ours).
[41] D. Mitrany, "The Optants' Dispute," in *Roumania,* January 1929, pp. 47–52.

land had been distributed to 179,940 Roumanian peasants, or about 40 per cent, and to 66,968 of other nationalities, viz., nearly 50 per cent. Among the latter were 36,481 Magyars. Dr. Mitrany's careful examination of the problem disposes of the point as follows:

Hence, whatever the final figures, so much is clear that a much larger number of Magyars possess land in Transylvania now than did before the reform. The reform, therefore, has probably affected adversely the *quantity of land* in Magyar hands, because of the way in which land was previously distributed; but, for the same reason, it has favorably affected the *number* of *Magyars* who now own some land of their own. The real effect, therefore, of the agrarian reform has been in a large measure to dissolve the artificial and provoking national barriers which formerly separated the "haves" from the "have-nots" among Transylvanian landowners.[42]

The whole problem merged into the settlement of Eastern reparations and was liquidated by the Hague agreement of January 20, 1930.

While the settlement of the German reparation questions was the most important result of the two Hague conferences, held in the second half of 1929 and in January 1930, the liquidation of the so-called Eastern reparations was also of great economic and political significance.[43]

The protocol, approved at the plenary session of the first Hague conference held on August 31, 1929, provided for the appointment of a technical committee charged with the duty of preparing detailed recommendations in regard to "the final settlement of the reciprocal claims of the creditor governments in respect of ceded properties and liberation debts, and the final settlement of the liabilities of the debtor governments under the treaties of St. Germain, the Trianon and Neuilly." This committee met in Paris in September 1929, and continued its meetings in November, when it adjourned and met again at the second session of the Hague conference. After a series of complicated and often critical negotiations, the Hague reparation agreements were signed on January 20, 1930.[44]

[42] Mitrany, "The Optants' Dispute," in *Roumania,* January 1929, p. 50.

[43] Foreign Policy Association, *Information Service,* May 14, 1930, Vol. VI, No. 5, "The Reparation Settlement of 1930," pp. 95–99. Official documents are reprinted in *International Conciliation,* September 1930, No. 262, "The Final Settlement of the Reparations Problems Growing out of the World War."

[44] As the Hungarian accords signed at The Hague only outlined the cardinal principles, the final settlement was embodied in four conventions signed on April 28, 1930. It included the reparation agreement between Hungary and the creditor nations, the settlement of questions relating to the land reforms and the mixed arbitral tribunals, and the organization and powers of the special funds.

The three main sets of financial claims concerning the Little Entente were the Allied claims upon Czechoslovakia, Yugoslavia, Roumania, and Poland, the so-called "liberation" debt incurred by the Allies in liberating the people of these territories, the claims of the Hungarian Government upon the succession states for compensation because of losses incurred under the agrarian reforms by Hungarian nationals, and the problem of the pre-war foreign debts of Austria-Hungary.[45]

The settlement was facilitated by the renunciation of the Great Powers of all their shares in non-German reparation receipts in order to induce the Little Entente to reduce its reparation claims upon Austria, Hungary, and Bulgaria. Roumania, on the other hand, waived her claims upon Austria for compensation for deliveries made to the Central Power under the Treaty of Bucharest of May 7, 1918, and shall receive on account of reparations up to 1943 thirteen per cent of the Bulgarian and Hungarian payments. In addition, Bulgaria agreed to pay Roumania 110 million lei in two instalments, one three months after the ratification of the agreement and the other a year after the first payment. This sum was not included in the reparation payments. Roumania, on the other hand, agreed to return the sequestrated property of the Bulgarian citizens in Roumania to its owners.

According to the agreement with regard to the contributions to the cost of liberation, signed at St. Germain-en-Laye on September 10, 1919, Roumania was to pay 234,140,000 gold francs, as decided by the Reparation Commission on November 4, 1924. However, the Little Entente "had decided to regard the liberation debt as a paper agreement and apparently made no payments on it."[46] The Hague settlement disposed of the payments in favor of the Little Entente.

At first Hungary was unwilling to see any legal connection be-

[45] These foreign debts of the former empire were regulated and pro-rated among Austria, Hungary, Italy, Czechoslovakia, Poland, Roumania, and Yugoslavia by the Innsbruck Protocol of 1923 and the Prague Protocol of 1925. According to the *New York Times*, February 19, 1931, an agreement settling this controversy was signed on that day by representatives of the Allied and Eastern European governments, with the exception of Hungary. After the Hague agreement there had remained a part of this debt amounting to some 2,000,000,000 kronen still unsettled, and this question was regulated by the present agreement. Under its provisions Roumania agreed to pay the sum of 700,000,000 kronen in annuities extending over a period of twenty-five years to the allied creditors.

[46] Foreign Policy Association, *Information Service*, Vol. VI, No. 5, p. 96.

tween the optants' question and reparation payments. The Hague agreement settled the matter by a compromise without prejudice to the legal view of either side.[47]

Simultaneously with the reparation agreements, France and Italy made a very liberal settlement of the war debts of Roumania.[48]

According to Foreign Minister G. G. Mironescu, Roumania emerged from the settlements not only free of the forty billion lei claimed on various grounds by Hungary and of the forty-six billion lei of liberation and ceded property obligations but with an actual surplus over her eighty billion of war debts of about fifty-five billion lei.[49]

AGRARIAN CONFERENCES

The Hague conferences overshadowed for some time but did not touch the main problem of the Little Entente of today, the economic condition brought about by the agricultural crisis. The present

---

[47] A special fund, known as the "agrarian fund," amounting to a maximum of 240 million gold crowns was created and out of this fund all the agrarian claims of the Hungarian nationals will be met. Apart from these claims there were a number of other claims against Roumania, as well as against other succession states, on account of the seizure or liquidation of Hungarian property, viz., those of the Habsburg archdukes, the church properties, the local railway companies, and miscellaneous industrial claims. For the settlement of these claims a separate fund was created, described as "Fund B," amounting to a maximum of 100 million gold crowns to cover them. These two funds are made up by means of the following resources: payments or restoration of properties by the succession states under their national legislation; the shares of Belgium, France, the British Empire, Italy, Japan, and Portugal in the payments to be made by Hungary up to 1943, inclusive; and all the payments to be made by Hungary after 1943. France, Italy and Great Britain agreed, "in the interests of a general settlement," to contribute a maximum of 6,600,000 gold crowns a year, averaging about one-half of that amount.

[48] L'Europe Nouvelle, November 10, 1929, April 10, 1930.

[49] Thus the Odyssey of the optants, whose claims had passed through the council of ambassadors, the Peace Conference, the League Council, and the arbitration courts, was finally settled. As G. E. R. Gedye wrote in the New York Times of January 26, 1930, the righteous indignation of many Hungarians would have been less forceful had they realized that the whole agitation was to obtain greater wealth for a comparative handful of landlords who complained they had lost part of their vast properties. By the recent agreements, says Gedye, the people of Hungary are committed for an entire generation to contribute to the wealth of Count Karolyi, owner of 50,000 acres, Count Andrassy, owner of 34,000 acres, Count Zichy, owner of 19,000 acres, and others. Only 384 persons were concerned in the famous dispute, he adds, quoting the Budapest Nepszava, and of these forty-two were counts (among them, Bethlen, the chief Hungarian delegate at The Hague), and twelve were barons.

depression of the world, both industrial and agricultural, made the Little Entente states and especially Roumania feel keenly the pinch of hard times, owing to an overproduction of foodstuffs and raw materials.

To Roumania goes the credit for a new movement for economic co-operation in the form of a *bloc* of agricultural states in Central and Eastern Europe.[50] In a relatively short time a series of agricultural conferences were held in Central Europe in the second half of 1930. Dr. Virgil Madgearu took the initiative in the matter, being disappointed, in part, by "the atmosphere of deception produced by the lack of positive results from the economic activity of the League of Nations." Concurrently there appeared a Polish project. Both were fundamentally in accord, proposing national specialization in certain branches of agriculture, standardization of quality, and development of foreign markets. On the negative side, these statesmen were determined to protect their states against the rising tariff-walls in industrial Europe.

As the enthusiasm evidenced at the 1927 economic conference dwindled without practical results, Roumania became embittered. Her revised tariff of August 1, 1929, passed in accordance with the League's appeal for reduced customs' tariffs was not reciprocated by other states.

The first conference of Roumanian, Yugoslav, and Hungarian delegates met at Bucharest on July 22, 1930, and was of a purely provisional nature; nevertheless it caused a considerable though probably undue stir in the European press. Its significance lies in the fact that it was the first economic conference of European states, involving other than treaty negotiations, outside the pale of the League of Nations, at which the Little Entente had discussed mutual problems with Hungary. During the sittings of the conference Yugoslavia made a move which was not favorably received by Hungary. It was a proposal to form an economic union of the Little Entente along the lines of its political union. The meeting failed, however, to agree to create a centralized export monopoly. Otherwise, the conference drafted a joint answer to the questionnaire issued by the Geneva tariff truce conference, defining ways of

---

[50] For a good account of the movement for an agrarian *bloc,* see *Bulletin of International News* (The Royal Institute of International Affairs, London), Vol. VII, No. 10, November 6, 1930, "The European Agrarian Bloc," pp. 975–83.

Mountain Ranges in Transylvania

Balcic, on the Black Sea

marketing surpluses of agrarian products and augmenting the purchasing power of the agrarian population. A preference for European agrarian products was proposed, though it was a derogation of the most-favored-nation clause. Furthermore, suppression of all restrictions on agrarian trade, all bounties, and all transport obstacles was urged together with the creation of a state selling organization in each country, with a warehouse system, so that selling prices could be jointly maintained.

In the last days of July 1930 representatives from Roumania and Yugoslavia met at Sinaia, Roumania. A customs union was envisaged, and new commercial treaties on the basis of preferential contingents of exchanged products were planned. The creation of a joint institute for the marketing of cereals was also recommended.

The third link in the chain of these agricultural conferences was the meeting of the Ministers of Agriculture of Roumania, Czechoslovakia, Yugoslavia, Poland, Latvia, Estonia, Hungary, and Bulgaria at Warsaw from August 28 to August 30, 1930. The conference favored preferential treatment for the farm products of Europe. A permanent organization was set up, including secretariat, information bureau, and research staff. It was likewise resolved to hold regular periodic meetings of delegates and to stress the expediency of joint action on the part of the agricultural states on matters of common interest, particularly in the League of Nations.

Dr. Madgearu was very enthusiastic:

An actual entente cordial of agricultural States has been inaugurated. It was not hoary theories that were discussed, but real, concrete matters. The most-favored-nation clause is to-day no longer a vital force, and in its stead there is proposed a European preference clause. The deliberations were carried on to the exclusion of politics. The agricultural countries, irrespective of whether they are the friends or foes of yesterday, have come together; their work is a lesson for similar gatherings, and a lesson for national egotists. The Warsaw Conference can be regarded as a first step in the direction of a realization of Briand's pan-Europe.[51]

The decisions reached at Warsaw were transmitted to the League of Nations, but its discussions made it plain that no economic United States of Europe is possible without the industrial states of Europe proving their readiness to grant material concessions to the farming countries of Eastern Europe.

[51] *Central European Observer,* 1930, VIII, 297. Quoted by permission.

Following the League Assembly, another conference was summoned at Bucharest on October 18. The coherence of the agrarian states was much strengthened following the failure of the Assembly to accept Madgearu's proposals for a preferential system in Europe and by the results of the Soviet dumping system. The creation of state institutions to control all agrarian exports was urged, and exceptional measures were recommended. Where no preferential European import duty could be obtained, discriminatory duties on the imports from the particular country in question should be imposed. The quota system for industrial imports was not agreed to by Latvia, Estonia, and Czechoslovakia; but Roumania, Poland, Hungary, and Yugoslavia pledged to the quota system.

On November 10 another agricultural conference gathered at Belgrade. The delegates of Poland, Roumania, Hungary, Bulgaria, and Yugoslavia agreed to institute a basis for such collaboration as will eliminate harmful competition among the countries concerned. State institutions for the control of grain exports were to be established in each country in 1931, so that they can commence operations in July 1932 with the opening of the grain campaign.

The implications of these gatherings are pregnant with possibilities. The presence of the French Minister of Commerce at the second Bucharest Conference was also significant politically, as France seems to have enormous funds available and land mortgages are popular with the French investor.[52]

Of greater significance is the evident growth, within the League framework, of international co-operation in economic matters. During the last four or five years, the outstanding feature of international agriculture has been the demand of agriculturists that the League of Nations should actively concern itself with that problem. In November 1930 a special conference on agricultural credits was held in Warsaw with representatives present from Roumania, Bulgaria, Czechoslovakia, Estonia, Hungary, Latvia, Poland, and Yugoslavia, and at the end of the same month the second "conference with a view to concerted economic action" again discussed the matter in Geneva. On November 19 Manoilescu, Roumania's delegate, speaking also for Poland, Bulgaria, Hungary, and Yugoslavia, asked that preferential treatment on grain be granted those countries by

---

[52] In March 1931 the French loan to Roumania was signed, and negotiations for loans to Poland and Yugoslavia were also under way.

all the states where their products find a market. Only Germany was willing to negotiate under the conditions outlined and then only on the proviso of obtaining counter-concessions from the agrarian states, and the whole conference "had fallen short of expectations and not even the greatest optimist could call the results remarkable."[53] Then the stage of proceedings became quite confused in the following months. On December 15, 1930, a tariff war broke out between Czechoslovakia and Hungary—the latter a member of the agrarian *bloc,* the former a member of the European agrarian conferences. The evidence of agrarian demands and industrial nationalism became apparent. A series of new conferences was held and between November 1930 and January 1931 the agrarian movement became definitely linked to the Commission of Inquiry for European Union under the presidency of Briand, which at its second session, held at Geneva in January 1931, decided to study the world crisis and appointed three committees: one for the disposal of future harvest surpluses; one to collaborate with the financial committee of the League in the preparation of a scheme for the extension of agricultural credits; and one to study questions of organization and procedure. The third session of the European Commission, held at Geneva in May 1931, approved a scheme for the establishment of an international agricultural mortgage credit company.[54]

---

[53] *New York Times,* November 29, 1930.

[54] The whole complicated situation is connected with the various problems created by the preferential treatment, equivalent concessions, and the most-favored-nation clause. See Foreign Policy Association, *Foreign Policy Reports,* Vol. VII, No. 12, August 19, 1931, "European Efforts for Economic Collaboration," and references cited therein; also D. G. H., "The European Agrarian Movement," in *Bulletin of International News,* Vol. VII, No. 19, March 12, 1931, pp. 1183–90. This article should be read in conjunction with that entitled "The European Agrarian Bloc," *op. cit.,* and "The Movement Towards European Economic Coöperation," *ibid.,* Vol. VII, No. 23, May 7, 1931, pp. 1375–79. This author makes the following pertinent observations:

"A European agrarian movement which began as a *bloc* of economically identical interests has, in development, exhibited not only differences of interest, but has proved to be a symptom of world economic *malaise.* Perhaps M. Briand's thesis that the world *malaise* must be healed slowly and locally is right. But the European agrarian movement seems at present on the primrose path to speedy impotence. . . . . If Europe stakes her future on a 'back-yard nationalism' world recovery will come at the Greek kalends. If coöperation be preferred—coöperation between West, Centre, and East, the obvious economic divisions of the modern world—then economic reconstruction can begin where it ought to begin—at the foundations in the soil."

THE POSSIBILITY OF A BALKAN UNION

The geographical situation of Roumania intimately connects her interests with the region commonly spoken of as the Balkans.[55] The Roumanian expansion in this direction reached the point of saturation. Hence a sort of Balkan Locarno pact is quite agreeable to Bucharest.

The federalization of the Balkans is a very old and familiar program, but the forces working against it have always been stronger than those for it. When the liberation of Greece, Serbia, and Bulgaria became a fact in the nineteenth century, there were several occasions for Balkan co-operation. But the last occasion on which the nations of the Balkan peninsula actually succeeded in sinking their differences for the sake of co-operation toward achievement of a common aim was in 1912. In the First Balkan War, Montenegro, Serbia, Greece, and Bulgaria fought shoulder to shoulder against Turkey. But the brilliance of the successes divided the league and the Second Balkan War of 1913 made a permanent Balkan league impossible. New rivalries, jealousies, and hatreds flared up, only to find more fuel during the World War. The redistribution of the Balkan territory after the war left Bulgaria crushed and dissatisfied. Her dreams were rudely shattered. Other settlements by no means satisfied the victors. The minorities question, as always, has agitated each of the Balkan states. Bulgaria is never contented with the way Roumania treats her nationals in the Dobrogea. Macedonians complain of their treatment at the hands of the Yugoslav and Greek governments. Greece and Albania, and Albania and Yugoslavia also have their mutual irredentist problems. In fact, nobody seems to be free from irritation.

To make a long story short, we may take the conclusions of Dr. Mitrany for the basis of our present discussion. The picture he paints certainly gets at the nucleus of the problem:

> What general conditions must be given for a Locarno system to work in the Balkans? The historical incidents . . . . as well as present circumstances

---

[55] The Roumanians object to the assumption that their country is a part of the Balkans. As early as 1904, A. Sturdza read a lecture before the Roumanian Geographical Society showing that Roumania should not be included in the Balkan peninsula. The society accepted this view and a copy of the lecture was sent to all similar associations in Europe. See A. Sturdza, *La Roumanie n'appartient pas à la Péninsule Balkanique* (Bucharest, 1904), and N. Iorga, "Is Roumania a Balkan State?" in *Roumania*, 1930, VI, 14–16.

concur in pointing to the need of two main conditions. A general understanding must rest on some common interest, and this condition can easily
be satisfied, for the interest of putting an end to strife is general and potent
in the Balkans. The corollary is that democracy must be genuinely in power
in the various capitals; without it there is no stability in foreign policy and
hence no trust in international pacts of good-will. . . . . And the second
condition is that the outside world should really be willing to leave the Balkans to the Balkan peoples. One should always remember that the Eastern
question, which includes the Balkan question, never boiled over except when
some European fuel was added to the Balkan fire. It has always been as
much a European as a Balkan issue, and in conflict the Balkan States have
all too often been the spearheads of the rivalries and ambitions of the Great
Powers.[56]

Even this point of view gives us the impression of continual un-
certainty. If the first condition laid down by Dr. Mitrany should
be overcome, and it seems very reasonable that the domestic difficulties of the Balkan governments could be straightened out, the second
condition will remain a very distant ideal in view of the policy followed by the great powers in this region. Potential unfriendliness
seems always to be fomented by some interested Western power.

However, another idealistic movement gathered some momentum,
especially in 1925. A number of influential newspaper editors began
to advocate another plan for a Balkan pact, and similar movements
were started in Bulgaria and Bucharest. This, together with Beneš'
proposed Near-Eastern security pact, seemed to provide a link between the Central European governments and the Balkans. The
idea received recognition from Mitilineu, Foreign Minister of Roumania, who indorsed it in a speech before the Chamber of Deputies
on April 13, 1927.

In 1929 the matter outgrew the bounds of mere theoretical discussion. The necessity for "regional understanding" within a world
federation was discussed at the International Peace Congress held
in Athens in that year and a commission was appointed to consider
the two proposals of the Greek delegates, namely, the initiation of a
regular annual Balkan conference and the establishment of a Balkan
institute in Athens, under the auspices of the League of Nations.

Upon the recommendation of the Balkan commission, the Bureau
of International Peace took the initiative of inviting the various
Balkan governments to participate in the first Balkan conference,

[56] D. Mitrany, "The Possibility of a Balkan Locarno," *International Conciliation*, April 1927, No. 229. Quoted by permission.

which was held in Athens in October 1930, on an unofficial basis. The governments of all the Balkan states took an active interest in favor of holding it. The Greek parliament offered hospitality to all delegates. The remarks of Mironescu, Roumanian Minister of Foreign Affairs, preceding the conference, made a deep impression in Balkan circles in favor of a Balkan union.[57]

The delegates were chosen by national committees which included representatives of political parties, of municipalities, social agencies, the press, labor, professions, academic circles, and from agriculture, industry, and commerce.

The conference met beneath a specially designed flag of the United Balkans, showing stars on a multicolored ground. In addition to the 150 delegates in Athens, the resident diplomatic corps and representatives of the League of Nations were present. Despite the fact that the first session gathered just when the betrothal of the Bulgarian King to an Italian Princess was announced, coinciding with the reports of a visit of the Italian navy to Saloniki, the old animosities somewhat receded into the background. But during the first meeting the old problem of minorities was injected into the conference. Several bitter exchanges occurred between the Bulgarians and the Yugoslavs, as the latter insisted that Bulgarians did not exist in Yugoslav Macedonia and therefore there was no reason to discuss minorities. The Greek president of the conference, Papanastasiou, was forced to intervene to smooth things over.

Steps were taken for the foundation of an institute for intellectual co-operation in the Balkans with its seat in Constantinople. A resolution was adopted requesting the foreign ministers of the Balkan states to meet regularly every year to exchange opinions on the Balkan affairs and discuss means of solidarity among the Balkan peoples. The resolution also urged the Balkan states to study the proposed pact of Premier Papanastasiou of Greece, based on the following principles: first, outlawry of war; second, peaceful settlement of all disputes that arise among them; and, third, mutual assistance in case of violation of the obligation to abstain from war.[58]

[57] The *Herald Tribune*, October 5, 1930. See Foreign Policy Association, *Foreign Policy Reports*, Vol. VII, No. 1, March 18, 1931, "Recent Balkan Alignments."

[58] For the support given to the whole project by the Carnegie Endowment for International Peace, see its *Year Book, 1931* (Washington, D.C., 1931), pp. 95–96, 195. A second session was held at Saloniki in February 1931, comprising only

The importance of the meeting was evident from the international interest it created. Only the future can reveal the practical value of these idealistic plans.

ROUMANIA AND RUSSIA

The acquisition of Bessarabia by Roumania brought a very important factor into the diplomatic game of Europe and Roumania. The menace of an eventual war on the Hungarian and Russian fronts has been the main source of worry on the part of Roumanian diplomacy. In fact, Roumanian interest lies more in her eastern frontier than on the western borderland. The Roumanian statesmen have not considered Hungary so real a danger as the Soviet Government. None of the Little Entente states has recognized the Soviets as a *de jure* state, although Czechoslovakia signed a trade treaty with Moscow on June 5, 1922, which accords *de facto* recognition. But to this day the Soviets dispute the legality of the annexation of Bessarabia by Roumania in 1919.

The Treaty of October 28, 1920, between the principal Allied Powers—the British Empire, France, Italy, and Japan—and Rou-

---

delegates of the managing committees of the six nations that prepared the agenda for the next meeting in Istanbul in October 1931. According to the *Herald Tribune,* September 6, 1931, the Bulgarian delegation decided to make the question of discussion of minorities a condition to participate in any future Balkan confederation and the problem has been included in the Istanbul agenda.

Very little was realized of the resolutions voted in 1930. In that period of one year lay many commercial wars, misunderstandings, the problems of emigration, debts, and reparation payments, in addition to the minority questions, the custom tariff problems, and even the problem of railway connections. The second conference, again composed of unofficial delegates, began its work on October 20, 1931. It reached its crucial point when the discussion centered on the question whether economic or political problems involving minorities should be taken up first. This somewhat heated discussion was sidetracked by the formation of a special committee which was to elaborate the non-aggression pact with particular reference to the rights of minorities. Parallel with this fundamental problem a series of practical questions, mostly of an economic nature, were taken up, and real progress was made in the discussions of the project of a Balkan postal union, the establishment of a common office for controlling and co-ordinating the production of tobacco, the foundation of a Balkan cereal union, and the establishment of a Balkan Chamber of Commerce. Important questions of transport and law were discussed. The Balkan-pact resolution was passed; its final clause confirms the principle of the outlawry of war as a means of international policy and puts the principle of arbitration in its place. In addition, the resolution recommended that the individual states conclude two-party arbitration treaties.

mania, authorized the transfer of the province to Roumania.[59] The validity of the document was conditioned upon the subsequent ratification. Hence Roumanian diplomacy has endeavored to secure the ratification of the treaty, Russian recognition of the *status quo,* and the building up of a system of defensive alliances against eventual attempts of the Soviets to recover the territory.

The first country to ratify the document was Great Britain on April 14, 1922; France followed the example on June 7, 1924,[60] and the Italian Government delayed ratification until March 19, 1927.

The efforts of Bucharest to build a system of defensive alliances in the Russian direction have not found a ready encouragement from the other two members of the Little Entente, who are not directly concerned with this problem. Roumania has never succeeded in forming a united front against its Soviet enemy in these quarters. Even though the conclusion of the German-Russian Treaty of Neutrality of April 26, 1926, roused Yugoslav and especially Czechoslovak suspicions, their policy continued to be based on the principle that the Russian problem concerned each of the members of the Little Entente individually.[61]

Roumania, however, found an ally in another direction. Poland, as well as Roumania, had annexed Russian territory and was determined to keep it intact. But Poland was in a more advantageous situation. The Peace Treaty of Riga of March 18, 1921, recognized the Polish acquisitions of the Russian territory. No analogous renunciation has been made in the case of Bessarabia. Hence the Polish-Roumanian Treaty of Alliance of March 3, 1921,[62] which

---

[59] Though the document was not signed by Russia, it provided that all questions concerning its details and raised by Russia should be submitted to the arbitration of the Council of the League of Nations, whose authority Russia has consistently refused to recognize.

[60] England and France would agree to the ratification only after Roumania had agreed to pay their nationals in Bessarabia, expropriated by the agrarian law, practically the full value of their land. See C. U. Clark, *Bessarabia,* pp. 227–28.

[61] Foreign Policy Association, *Information Service,* Vol. III, No. 24, February 3, 1928, "Post-War Rumania," pp. 385–86.

[62] The Polish Government specifically recognized the agreements made by Roumania with other states for the maintenance of the Trianon and Neuilly treaties, while the Roumanian Government recognized the agreements concluded between Poland and France, the most important of them being Franco-Polish agreements of February 19, 1921, which provided for defensive action in common against unprovoked attack on the territories or legitimate interests of France and Poland.

was renewed on March 26, 1926,[63] and on January 15, 1931, constituted a triumph for Roumanian diplomacy.

It must be noted that this convention went still further than the Little Entente treaties. Not only have both the countries undertaken "to assist each other in the event of being attacked without provocation" on their present Eastern frontiers, but they have so completely identified their respective destinies that in case of a defensive war against the Soviets they have agreed "not to negotiate nor to conclude an armistice or a peace without the participation of the other State." Neither party was to be at liberty to make an alliance with a third party without previous agreement with the other, but "alliances aiming at the maintenance of the Treaties" already signed in common by Poland and Roumania were exempted from this condition. Evidently both parties bore in mind the possibility of connecting their treaty with other treaties in a new system, which might even include Russia. Toynbee remarks that the treaty "might be regarded in one sense as making a transition stage between the old idea of group alliances and the new conception of a regional guarantee pact on the lines of Locarno."[64]

Next to the Polish alliance the strongest guaranty of the Bessarabian territory is the French-Roumanian Treaty of "peace, understanding and friendship" of June 10, 1926. Though the treaty offers no military assistance against Russia, France is bound indirectly to help Roumania through the Polish alliance.

---

[63] This Treaty of Guarantee, in imitation of the Locarno treaties, was a regional agreement in conformity with the Covenant of the League, as is seen especially in the second article: "In the event of Poland or Roumania, contrary to the undertakings imposed by Articles XII, XIII, and XV of the Covenant of the League of Nations, being attacked without provocation, Poland and reciprocally Roumania, acting in application of Article XVI of the Covenant of the League of Nations, undertake immediately to lend each other aid and assistance. In the event of the Council of the League of Nations, when dealing with a question brought before it in accordance with the provisions of the Covenant of the League of Nations, being unable to secure the acceptance of its report by all its members other than the Representatives of the parties to the dispute, and in the event of Poland or Roumania being attacked without provocation, Poland or reciprocally Roumania, acting in application of Article XV, paragraph 7, of the Covenant of the League of Nations, will immediately lend each other aid and assistance. Should a dispute of the kind provided for in Article XVII of the Covenant of the League of Nations arise, and Poland and Roumania be attacked without provocation, Poland and reciprocally Roumania undertake immediately to lend each other aid and assistance."

[64] A. J. Toynbee, *Survey of International Affairs, 1926,* pp. 147 ff.

While Russia had tried several times to conclude a pact of non-aggression with the borderland states and Poland,[65] the influence of the negotiations between France and the United States with regard to a treaty for the renunciation of war led Russia to envisage a special protocol whereby the states participating in the Pact of Paris (Briand-Kellogg Pact) would give immediate applicability to the principles of it and thus also reinforce the Soviet security system. On December 29, 1928, the Soviet Government proposed that Poland and Lithuania join in an anticipatory protocol, putting the Paris Pact into immediate effect among themselves without waiting for the ratifications of it by all the countries adhering to it. Poland suggested in her reply of January 10, 1929, that the problem would have to be dealt with also by Roumania, Estonia, and Latvia. Litvinoff at once agreed to the proposal, and on February 9, 1929, Russia, Estonia, Latvia, Poland, and Roumania signed the Exclusion of War Pact at Moscow.[66]

It is necessary to notice, however, that though the pact may be taken as another guaranty of peace, this does not imply, according to the Soviets, that the Russian Government had renounced its claim to Bessarabia. It may be taken for granted that Russia will use only "pacific means" to advance her claims. The Roumanian Government indicates that its country is not threatened with acute danger from Russia.[67]

ROUMANIA AND BULGARIA

Bulgaro-Roumanian relations have been marked by the results of the Second Balkan War. The attitude of the Kingdom of Bulgaria, however, has not been so hostile as that of Hungary or of Russia. Bucharest has protested occasionally with Yugoslavia and Greece against the activities of the *comitadji* bands on the frontiers, but the Roumanian Government has never had to exert much pressure to close these incidents. After the fall of Stambulisky's Govern-

[65] *International Conciliation,* September 1929, No. 252, M. W. Graham, "The Soviet Security System."

[66] Lithuania was not on good terms with Poland and refused to sign.

[67] This is suggested in a letter of Carol A. Davila, Roumanian Minister to the United States, to the *New York Times,* February 23, 1931, in which he states in regard to recent Soviet assertions that "Soviet Russia has no warlike intention toward Roumania on account of Bessarabia," and that "this I already knew when I myself signed the Litvinoff protocol at Moscow on February 11, 1929, outlawing war." See also Carol A. Davila, "Roumania and Russia," in *Roumania,* 1930, VI, 7–10.

ment in 1923, the Tsankoff's Government announced that it would scrupulously execute the obligations of the peace treaties. The bolshevistic danger and propaganda led Roumania to co-operate to some extent with Bulgaria against this common danger. The leanings of Stambulisky's régime toward Russia and Bolshevism produced somewhat strained relations, but the régime of Tsankoff met with the whole-hearted approval of Bucharest. On the other hand, the problem of the Bulgarian minority in the Dobrogea stands in the way of a complete understanding between the two countries.[68]

ROUMANIA AND GERMANY

Recently Germany and Roumania also have put their relations on a more friendly footing. The occupation of Roumania by the Central Powers inflicted wounds which cannot be healed easily. The post-war relations became complicated by the difficulties of the reparations and other financial settlements. Until recently a number of financial questions have been outstanding between Bucharest and

[68] Lands had been taken from Bulgarian farmers in the Dobrogea who had no Turkish title-deeds and given to Roumanian Macedonians who had been imported into the region. In 1929 the Roumanian Government created the office of commissioner of colonization to supervise and reorganize the work of settlement throughout the country. The majority of the Dobrogea colonists have settled in the districts of Caliacra and Durostor, near the Bulgarian frontier. Among them are about 2,300 refugees from Macedonia; in 1929 the treasury and the Central Co-operative Bank advanced them a sum of 140,000,000 lei, to finance the erection of 2,000 one-family houses in Southern Dobrogea. The law of July 1930 for the reorganization of the Dobrogea, passed by the National-Peasant Government, was welcomed in Sofia as a partial attempt of Bucharest to regulate this situation in favor of the Bulgarian minority. But a further petition was sent to the League of Nations in January 1931 asking for the redress of the Bulgarian grievances. The Roumanians, it may be said, claim that, leaving aside irredentist elements who are in league with nationalist organizations in Bulgaria and actively connive at *comitadji* raids, etc., the billeting in the Bulgarian homes is purely temporary till the colonists have had time to build their own dwelling. The Roumanian Government claimed ownership under the agrarian land reform laws, particularly the older law applying to the Dobrogea since 1878, of certain lands up till then the property of the Ottoman State, but which had been given in usage to Bulgarian peasants. These lands were used to colonize Roumanian peasants from other overcrowded districts. See D. Mitrany, *The Land and the Peasant in Rumania,* pp. 179–80, 212–13, who feels that "a somewhat irrational scheme of colonization has been made worse by its erratic application," and that "psychological factors have deepened the feeling among the minorities that they were being deprived of some of their land because of national prejudice." See also Foreign Policy Association, *Foreign Policy Reports,* Vol. 7, No. 1, March 18, 1931, "Recent Balkan Alignments"; A. Tibal, "Bulgares et Roumains," in *L'Esprit international,* 1928, II, 380–93.

Berlin. These included the Roumanian debt held by Germany before the war, the notes issued by Germany during the occupation in payment of supplies, the German property in Roumania which had been seized after the victory, and various minor items.

The prolonged and perplexing diplomatic negotiations on these points changed the attitude of both powers. The various claims and counter-claims were seen month by month in a new perspective. There were very important economic considerations to be dealt with. Before the war about two-fifths of the entire Roumanian imports came from Germany, who also provided the capital, machinery, and engineers for the Roumanian petroleum industry.[69] Post-war Germany was soon aware of her trade possibilities with Roumania. The very fact that Germany paid her reparations to Roumania in goods rather than in cash meant that Roumanians were accustomed to German products. Germany is again playing a very important part in providing capital for Roumanian enterprises either directly or as agent for other countries. The "Societatea Bancară Română," founded in 1929 by the Dresdner Bank, represents German banks as well as the banks of London and Amsterdam.

The desire to resume normal economic relations with Roumania determined the political attitude of Berlin. Roumania received several offers after 1921 to settle the outstanding problems. At the beginning of 1927 more serious negotiations began. By July 1928 Vintilă Brătianu saw that Roumania could not solve her pressing financial problems without foreign capital. When he could not succeed in getting a loan in Paris and London, he was practically forced to go to Berlin. Thus the German position was strengthened and Roumania adopted a more conciliatory attitude. But both governments based their demands on different principles, and hence an agreement was rather difficult. The Roumanian representatives claimed that the Versailles Treaty had absolved their country from any obligations in regard to the pre-war debts. The Germans, on the other hand, held to the principle that the Dawes plan freed them from any obligations to make restitution to Roumania for the paper money put into circulation during the occupation of Roumania in 1917–18. The protracted negotiations ended on November 19, 1928. Germany agreed to pay 75,500,000 marks in four yearly instalments,

[69] For an excellent summary see H. Feis, *Europe the World's Banker, 1870–1914,* chapter iii, "German Foreign Investment," and chapter xii, "The Financing of the Balkan States."

in settlement of all the financial matters outstanding between the two countries. These included claims regarding the "Banca Generală" and the notes issued by the German army of occupation and those put forward as regards various Reichsbank deposits. Roumania agreed to liberate the German sequestrated property and renounced appeal to Article 18 of the Versailles Treaty, which gave her the right to indemnify herself from the goods of Germans lying within her jurisdiction.

Subsequently, after a series of vicissitudes, the German-Roumanian commercial treaty negotiations were concluded in Berlin on June 22, 1931, with the initialing of a draft agreement. By the treaty, preferential treatment was accorded only to agricultural produce, not to industrial goods, and it was claimed that it followed strictly the principles recommended in Geneva for international negotiations with the Southern and Eastern European states and that no attempt had been made to evade the most-favored-nation obligations.

The Danube Controversy

Recently the Danube controversy was amicably liquidated. The question of the Danube has always been troublesome. Europe began to be more interested in the river in the nineteenth century as its importance increased with the Black Sea corn lands production. The Treaty of Paris of March 30, 1856, provided for international control of the Danube. Provision was made for a temporary commission, with Great Britain, Austria, France, Prussia, Russia, Sardinia, and Turkey represented on it. Its duties were to be taken over after two years by a riverine commission, but the jealousy of the Great Powers constrained them to renew their own jurisdiction after its term had expired and the permanent commission has never come into existence.

The European commission (representing England, France, Italy, and Roumania) was kept in existence, and the Treaty of Berlin of 1878 made it a permanent international entity entirely independent of the territorial authority.[70] Roumania was admitted as a member

[70] The task of the commission was to look after the improvement of navigation and administration. An inspector general was in direct charge of the work of the commission at Galați, and major disputes may be submitted since 1922 to the advisory and technical committee on inland navigation of the League of Nations, but its findings have no binding power unless sustained by a World Court decision. The commission finances its operations through levying tonnage duties.

and the jurisdiction of the body was extended to Galaţi, and in 1883 to Brăila, a move which Roumania has ever since protested.

By Articles 346–53 of the Versailles Treaty the European commission was reinstated in the section below Galaţi, while provision was made for the control of the section above that point by an international commission under a definite statute to be concluded at a later date. Thus Germany, Austria, Roumania, Bulgaria, Hungary, Belgium, France, Great Britain, Greece, Italy, Yugoslavia, and Czechoslovakia met in Paris and on July 23, 1921, signed "the Definite Statute of the Danube."

But Roumania had contested the jurisdiction of the European commission over the channel from Galaţi to Brăila, and maintained that, in view of her consistent refusal to recognize that the pre-war authority of the European commission extends beyond Galaţi, only technical and not jurisdictional functions could be performed by the commission. In 1924 Great Britain called the attention of the League of Nations to the dispute, and the question was submitted to the World Court in December 1926. Fundamentally, Roumania wanted the suppression of the European commission and the extension of the authority of the international commission to the entire river.[71] The World Court decision of December 1927 stated that the powers of the European commission extended over the whole of the maritime Danube.

The subsequent negotiations were concluded at Geneva in March 1929.[72] The conciliatory attitude of Maniu's Government helped in the matter. The commission retained its control of the river from Brăila to the Black Sea, but all juridical rights in respect to that section of the Danube were vested in Roumania, while Great Britain, France, and Italy waived their right to keep guardships in Roumanian waters. All infractions of the navigation regulations or of the regulations concerning the Danubian ports are brought up before national courts, and, on appeal, to a mixed court. All employees of the commission are amenable to the discipline of their hierarchical chiefs, without consideration of nationality; all offenses committed within the commission's jurisdiction are tried by Roumanian courts,

[71] See League of Nations, *Report on Danube Navigation,* C. 444(a), M. 164(a), 1925, pp. 24–27; G. A. Blackburn, "International Control of the River Danube," in *Current History,* 1930, XXXII, 1154 ff.

[72] *Near East and India,* 1929, XXXV, 417.

and only in cases of appeal is reference allowed to a mixed court, on which sit foreign representatives.

OTHER COUNTRIES

The United States has friendly, though indifferent, political relations with Roumania.[73] Greece concluded a treaty of non-aggression, conciliation, and arbitration with Roumania on March 23, 1928;[74] on August 12, 1931, a commercial convention was signed, an agreement regarding Greek Church schools in Roumania, and a third regarding the indemnities payable to the owners of Greek trawlers requisitioned during the war. There has been a certain lack of cordial relations between Roumania and Turkey, largely owing to the difference in their respective attitudes toward Russia.[75] Other nations, like Switzerland, Sweden, Poland, and others, have treaties of arbitration and conciliation with Bucharest.[76] The improvement in the general outlook is manifested by various commercial treaties in force or in progress of negotiation.

Roumania adhered to the Briand-Kellogg Pact on September 4, 1928, and on October 8, 1930, the Roumanian Government signed the optional clause of the Statute of the Permanent Court of International Justice with certain reservations.

To recapitulate, the immediate concern of Roumania after the war was the preservation of the *status quo*. Hungary as well as Russia has been determined to undermine the situation created by the peace treaties, as far as Roumania has been concerned. The

[73] In 1924 Roumania protested against the immigration law of the United States of that year, though the protest was only perfunctory. On July 12, 1931, the Roumanian Government dispatched a reply to the United States stating that it was prepared to adhere to the Hoover plan and expressing the hope that the sacrifices involved would not endanger its new policy of financial reconstruction.

[74] The treaty has not much importance. The Kutso-Vlach question, so prominent in Macedonia at the beginning of the century, no longer exists. The so-called Aromâni of Thessaly and Macedonia do not use the word Kutso-Vlach or "lame Vlach," but call themselves Rumâni; their neighbors call them Vlakh, Kutso-Vlaks or Tsintsar; this last word originates from the word *tsintsi* (five) which these nationals use instead of *cinci* in Roumanian. According to S. Panaretoff, *Near Eastern Affairs and Conditions* (New York, 1922, p. 26), they number about 160,000, being scattered mostly around Mount Pindus in Thessaly and throughout the other half of Macedonia.

[75] See Foreign Policy Association, *Foreign Policy Reports,* Vol. VII, No. 1, March 18, 1931, "Recent Balkan Alignments," p. 15.

[76] See M. Habicht, *Post-War Treaties for the Pacific Settlement of International Disputes* (Cambridge, Mass.), pp. 373 ff., 172 ff., 713 ff.

creation of the Little Entente and the conclusion of treaties with other powers induced a sense of security for Roumania. While very successful on the diplomatic side, the Little Entente seems to be rather weak on the economic side. The necessity of improving the sale of agricultural products abroad led Roumania to participate in a series of international conferences, which so far have not materialized in any concrete results. The idea of a Balkan Union has been revived. On the whole, the post-war period of Roumanian foreign relations has been moving steadily toward a consolidation of foreign relations, and the Hague agreements of 1930 are a corner stone of amicable settlements in which the troublesome dispute over the optants' case was liquidated along with other problems. The problem of Hungarian, Bulgarian, and other minorities will somewhat color future developments, but the situation is undergoing a process of gradual improvement.

CHAPTER IX

THE PROBLEM OF MINORITIES

The Difficulties of Dealing with the Problem

WHEN Roumania emerged from the World War with additions of large territories inhabited by Roumanians, one of the problems of her history was solved. But another one was created. Before 1918 about one-half of the Roumanians lived in their independent kingdom, forming a homogeneous mass. After that year certain foreign elements appeared as definite patches on the ethnographic map of the kingdom. The problem of unity of the nation, a dream of the past centuries, could not be solved without creating the inevitable problem of minorities, a problem which today is the burning one of all Europe. We are flooded with literature and arguments of the opposing groups, and each side presents its side so passionately that one wonders if the whole controversy is not itself taking on the religious aspect which has characterized the missionary and crusading movements of the past.

Professor Charles Hodges of New York University, writing an introduction to my volume on the international problem of minorities,[1] said:

Nothing has been more provocative of international ill-will than problems of inter-racial relations. To-day, we see constant references to the future "conflict of color," "the struggle between the White and the Yellow Races," and similar battle-cries of racial supremacy. Important though the racial differences between the Occident and the Orient may be, the peoples of the world might also give greater consideration to problems closer home. These may not have the dramatic interest that heralded clashes of color possess; but they come closer to precipitating actual trouble. The most challenging aspects of these racial, religious and linguistic groups, which constitute "minorities" in the midst of more numerous and dominating populations, had much to do with underlying hatreds and machinations that furnished the back-

[1] J. S. Rouček, *The Working of the Minorities System under the League of Nations*, Orbis Publishing Co., Prague, 1929.

ground of the Great War. They remain—tragic though it seems at the end of the first peace decade—a continued source of trouble. Though frontiers have changed, their alteration far too often has resulted only in the accentuation of the general problem which confronts the Old World. . . . . The need of dealing with [the problem of minorities] is overwhelmingly pressing. The development of greater knowledge of the world importance of the question becomes of prime importance to international goodwill.[2]

What is most tragic for the student of the minorities difficulties is his inability to secure the impartial facts which would serve as the foundation of examination. Each arguing party of course considers its argument as the purest expression of the truth and nothing but the truth.[3]

The whole difficulty seems to lie in the fact that the matter of interpretation is so difficult. The authorities differ considerably even in the definition of the word "minority" and how the interpretations should be applied to the census-taking procedures.[4] Without any further discussion of the point, we may proceed to deal with our problem on the basis of the assumption that the minorities are the inhabitants of the state who differ from the majority of the state by language, race, or religion.[5] All these three concepts are of course subjects of quite divergent interpretations.[6] For our purposes the fact remains that though nation and race cannot be identified,[7] in popular discussions the concept of nationality and of racial unity is intermingled. As speech is a fundamental element in creating con-

[2] J. S. Rouček, *op. cit.,* p. 11.

[3] Thus, for example, the Czechoslovak census figures of last year brought forth the usual amount of recriminations. G. E. R. Gedye made the following observations in his dispatch to the *New York Times,* February 8, 1931 : "The decennial numbering of the various people of Central Europe, just concluded, revealed no diminution of pre-war racial jealousies, nationalist intrigues and manipulations. The census was often resented, much as it was in biblical times, and its methods were little better than those Herod sometimes employed. Chauvinism, often displayed, made the peasant eager to emulate the example of the Holy Family and flee before the census-taker."

[4] See, for example, Dr. I. Teodorescu and N. Istrate, "Méthode pour la connaissance de minorités ethniques" (Extrait de "Les Annales économiques et statistiques," Ateliers Graphiques Socec & Co., S.A., Bucharest, 1928) ; Cornélius-Alexandre Rudesco, *Étude sur la question des minorités de race, de langue et de religion,* pp. 21–24; J. Foucques-Duparc, *La Protection des minorités de race, de langue et de religion,* p. 16.

[5] J. S. Rouček, *op. cit.,* pp. 56–57.

[6] For a summary of various authorities see the author's booklet, *The Minority Principle as a Problem of Political Science,* pp. 21 ff.

[7] F. H. Hankins, *The Racial Basis of Civilization* (New York, 1926), p. 11.

sciousness of kind, language is a matter of prime importance to determine a minority group. And though the attempt to erect national unity upon the sole basis of religious unity has always failed, religion still plays a great part in creating stereotyped nationalities, notably in Eastern Europe.

Though the Roumanian minorities are not so numerous as those in other European states, the presence of them in the territory of Roumania is a subject of frequent and bitter discussions even in the American press. Mr. Walter Littlefield, a member of the staff of the *New York Times,* puts this phenomenon into the following words:

> Just now it seems the fashion to wash Roumania's soiled linen in foreign tubs. That of other countries has endured similar ablutions and has emerged more or less clean, more or less intact. Almost all the things complained of by the censors of Roumania, always omitting those of the Budapest propagandists, exist more or less in all the countries expanded by the Peace Treaties of Paris.[8]

A great number of literary and political volumes and newspaper and magazine articles published in this country in absolute good faith are in reality nothing but propaganda. It would be a thankless task to prepare a bibliography of these works. Many of them are, however, mentioned in our bibliography, and we shall here consider three or four of the most extreme ones.

Reverend Louis C. Cornish compiled in collaboration with the Anglo-American commission which visited Transylvania a volume entitled *The Religious Minorities in Transylvania.*[9] The good faith of the authors and the compiler is evident from the pages of the volume, but serious defects have been pointed out by another author in the field, H. M. Tichner, who declares in her little volume, *Roumania and Her Religious Minorities,*[10] that, for example, no member of the commission—as far as the critic is aware—could speak any of the minority languages and that the commission declined offers of official interpreters as well as interpreters of the minorities. "And yet the commission does not state what interpreters it used nor what measures it took to assure itself of their impartiality."[11]

[8] W. Littlefield, "The Ethnic and Religious Minorities of Roumania," in *Roumania,* January 1929, pp. 56–66.

[9] The Beacon Press, Boston, 1925.

[10] London, A. M. Philpot Ltd. (no date of publication stated).

[11] H. M. Lichner, *Roumania and Her Religious Minorities,* p. 11.

What Mr. Littlefield calls "the most formidable and, at the same time, most specious arraignment of the liquidation of the minority problem" is a very interesting volume published by the American Committee on the Rights of Religious Minorities, called *Roumania Ten Years After*.[12] Here also an impartial observer immediately discovers several superficialities in the findings of the commission.[13]

A great stir was created by the publication of Zsombor de Szász's *The Minorities in Roumanian Transylvania*.[14] Again, a damaging amount of evidence was collected by this critic, but Professor Sylvius Dragomir of the University of Cluj pointed out the weakness of the publication in his volume entitled *The Ethnical Minorities in Transylvania*.[15] And so the discussion probably will go on to the burdening of authors' postmen.

THE MINORITIES GROUPS OF ROUMANIA

According to the figures of 1912, the Old Kingdom of Roumania counted 7,200,000 inhabitants, of whom more than 92 per cent were Roumanians and about 8 per cent were of different nationalities.

This proportion was, of course, greatly changed with the formation of the greater Kingdom of Roumania. The mixture of the added population defied separation and it was humanly impossible to make the frontier coincide everywhere with the ethnographical boundaries. Consequently, after 1918, Greater Roumania contained nearly 13,000,000 Roumanians in addition to minorities, who brought up the figure to more than 17,000,000. We may safely estimate that from 69 to 71 per cent of the inhabitants belonged to the ruling nation and the rest to the minority groups.

According to the official figures[16] the national structure of Roumania appeared in 1920 as follows:

---

[12] Boston, The Beacon Press, 1928.

[13] W. Littlefield, *op. cit.*, says, for example, regarding this point: "This is particularly obvious in the case of the anti-Semitic propaganda of Professor Cuza (for no mention is made of his having been retired from his chair at the University of Iaşi or of his obnoxious organizations being placed under the ban of the press and religious laws), and particularly obvious in the gratuitous condemnation of the closing of certain schools and churches in Transylvania, ignoring the fact that the places proscribed had become a menace to peace and order as the hotbeds of Budapest political and Roman Catholic propaganda."

[14] London, The Richard Press, 1927.   [15] Geneva, Sonor Printing Co., 1927.

[16] Quoted by C. G. Rommenhoeller, *La Grande-Roumanie*, p. 70. I. Bowman, *The New World* (4th ed., 1928), p. 362, gives lower figures for the minorities in

	New Roumania	Old Kingdom	Total	Percentage
Roumanians	5,005,000	6,800,000	11,805,000	69.9
Hungarians	1,518,000	50,000	1,568,000	9.3
Ukrainians	792,000	.....	792,000	4.7
Germans	690,000	35,000	725,000	4.3
Jews	600,000	300,000	900,000	5.3
Bulgars	140,000	150,000	290,000	1.7
Gypsies	60,000	225,000	285,000	1.7
Russians	59,000	40,000	99,000	0.6
Poles	37,000	.....	37,000	0.2
Turks	.....	170,000	170,000	1.0
Various	196,000	30,000	226,000	1.3
	9,097,000	7,800,000	16,897,000	100.0

For the sake of other opinions, we may take the figures of a well-known authority, Th. Ruyssen:[17]

Majority		Ukrainians	1,100,000
Roumanians 11,576,000		Ruthenes	793,800
		Jews	770,000
		Bulgars	251,000
Minorities		Serbs	62,300
Magyars 1,659,500		Turks and Tartars	230,000
Germans 804,000		Various	579,000

On December 29, 1930, a census was taken for the first time since the union of the provinces with Roumania. The final returns have not yet been issued, but preliminary calculations show the following figures.[18]

Roumania. Detailed figures showing the proportion of the minorities population of today to that of the native Roumanian are not as yet available. The official estimates of 1923 gave the following distribution according to origin of the population then numbering 16,736,283:

Group	Percentage	Group	Percentage
Roumanians 74.0		Russians and Ruthenians.. 3.3	
Hungarians and Szeklers. 8.4		Bulgarians 1.5	
Jews 5.0		Turks and Tartars....... 1.0	
Germans 4.3		All others 2.5	

[17] *Encyclopaedia Britannica* (13th ed.), II, 931–33.

[18] It must be noticed that the figures are now somewhat changed, especially in view of the fact that the population of Roumania increases very rapidly. In 1928, the excess of births over deaths, in both rural districts and the cities, per thousand

	OLD KINGDOM	NEW PROVINCES	TOTAL	PERCENTAGE
Roumanians	8,109,412	5,511,893	13,621,305	75.72
Hungarians	.....	1,387,719	1,387,719	7.67
Germans	30,000	692,000	722,000	4.00
Jews	308,085	676,128	984,213	5.20
Ruthenians	.....	550,000	550,000	3.05
Bulgars	184,000	116,000	300,000	1.70
Turks-Tartars	171,000	59,000	230,000	1.33
Others (Russians, Poles, Serbs, etc.)	.....	230,000	230,000	1.33
Total	.....	.....	18,025,237	100.00

The Roumanians are scattered throughout the country in equal proportions. For the most part they are engaged in agriculture and stock raising. Isaiah Bowman remarks that "the Roumanians . . . . have had a greater national and cultural solidarity than any other Balkan people except the Greeks."[19] Their distinct Roumanian speech is based on Low Latin. The Slav invaders left a large number of words of Slav origin. Charles Upson Clark characterizes it "a fresh and virile tongue," which "smacks of the open Macedonian mountain and the glens of the Carpathians."[20] Nearly all Roumanians are adherents of the Greek Orthodox church.

The most numerous minority group in Roumania are the Hungarians. Their stronghold is Transylvania, and especially the frontier districts of Satu-Mare, Bihor, and Arad. Their population is composed of four groups, their relative strength being as follows:

of population, was 15.6. According to the *Annuaire statistique de la Roumanie 1929*, pp. 16 ff., the increment of the population was as follows:

	1921	1922	1924	1926
Transylvania	57,664	55,618	47,224	40,013
Bukovina	9,424	8,022	10,258	9,199
Bessarabia	48,472	44,504	46,474	37,320
Old Kingdom	132,742	129,346	135,709	148,452

The excess of births over deaths, per thousand population, in 1928 were as follows:

	COUNTRY	CITIES	AVERAGE
Old Kingdom	+22.3	+7.3	+18.9
Transylvania	+11.3	+3.1	+11.3
Bukovina	+15.3	+4.5	+12.8
Bessarabia	+20.1	+7.2	+18.2
Banat	+ 2.1	−2.7	+ 2.3
Average	+18.1	+5.6	+15.6

[19] I. Bowman, *op. cit.*, p. 363.

[20] See his chapter on "The Roumanian Language," in *Greater Roumania*, pp. 343–50.

(1) Szekler group, about 50 per cent; (2) Hungarians of the towns, about 30 per cent; (3) Hungarians of the border departments, about 20 per cent; and (4) Hungarians scattered in Transylvanian villages, about 10 per cent.[21] According to the Hungarian census of 1910, the Roumanians had a population of 1,472,021 in Transylvania, the Hungarians and Szeklers numbered 918,217, the Saxons 234,085, while the rest of the 2,678,367 total was divided among Gypsies, Bulgarians, Armenians, Ruthenians, Greeks, Jews, Czechs and Slovaks, and others. The Roumanian statistics of 1925, compiled by Dr. Teodorescu, give the entire population of Transylvania as 5,487,966, of which the principal elements are the following:[22]

	NUMBER	PERCENTAGE
Roumanians	3,232,806	58.90
Hungarians and Szeklers	1,357,442	24.00
Germans and other Teutons	557,683	10.00
Jews	203,191	3.71
Gypsies, Ruthenians, etc.	136,844	2.50

The most numerous of the Magyars are the Szeklers, living in the departments of Odorhei, Ciuc, Trei-Scaune, Tărnava-Mică, and Mureş. They dwell in compact masses. They settled here, after the establishment of the Hungarian state more than one thousand years ago, to defend the eastern frontiers. They can hardly be considered expatriated. Their geographical situation enables them to form islands of ethnical exclusiveness which form an almost compact block in the southeastern corner of Transylvania. We must also notice that "Szekler" or "Czekler" is the German version of the Hungarian name, and is actually a misspelling. The original and correct term is "Székely."

The Hungarians of the towns form a considerable group. As for their origin, there is a distinction between the *oppida privilegia* which

[21] S. Dragomir, *op. cit.,* p. 40. The following summary of the location of the minorities groups of Roumania is based on the works quoted hereafter, and mainly on C. G. Rommenhoeller, *op. cit.,* N. Iorga, "La Politique des minorités dans la nouvelle Roumanie," in *Le Monde Slave,* 1926, III, 22–36; S. Dragomir, *The Ethnical Minorities in Transylvania,* pp. 18 ff.; M. E. de Martonne, "La Répartition et le rôle des minorités nationales en Roumanie," in Dotation Carnegie pour la paix internationale, *Bulletin No. 2, 1929,* pp. 61–86; Dr. Georg H. J. Erler, *Das Recht der Nationalen Minderheiten* (Aschendorffsche Verlagsbuchhandlung, Münster in Westfalen, 1931), pp. 240 ff. See especially the bibliography on each minority provided by this last-named author.

[22] Cited by W. Littlefield, "The Ethnic and Religious Minorities of Roumania," *Roumania,* January 1929, p. 58.

developed under the direct protectorate of the county or landowner and as such were Hungarian in character, and the so-called *liberae et regiae civitates,* cities under the protectorate of the King in which the town-constitutive elements were largely German. The German character of many towns, except in the specific German zones, like the *Universitas Saxonum,* gradually vanished after the Turkish wars when the Hungarian influx into towns greatly increased. In the border departments of Transylvania the Magyars do not form a homogeneous ethnographic strip along the border but are divided into a number of villages, where they form small islands in a Roumanian sea. All the Hungarians are very industrious but politically unreliable; the expropriated Hungarian landowners particularly, who previously held great estates in Transylvania, have until very recently kept up violent agitation.

In the eighteenth century and during part of the nineteenth century many of the Transylvanian towns had a German character. Subsequently they lost this character as a result of the Magyar national drives against the non-Magyar inhabitants. Germans now are chiefly artisans, merchants, and members of the liberal professions. In the Dobrogea, where they established themselves in the '60's, they are exclusively agriculturists. Though they preserve their German customs and ways of living, they are loyal citizens of Roumania.

In general, the Germans of Roumania are composed of five historic and geographical groups: (1) the Saxons of Transylvania; (2) the Germans of Bukovina; (3) the Souabians of the Banat; (4) the Germans of Bessarabia and the Dobrogea; and (5) the Germans of the Old Kingdom.[23]

---

[23] See Dr. K. Bell, editor, *Banat (Das Deutschtum im Ausland)*; *Siebenbürgen (Das Deutschtum im Ausland)* (Dresden, 1930); G. Engelmann, *Das Deutschtum in Rumänien—Siebenbürgen* (Gotha, 1928); F. H. Reimesch, *Das Deutschtum in Grossrumänien;* T. Grentrup, *Das Deutschtum an der Mitleren Donau in Rumänien und Jugoslavien;* F. Müller-Langenthal, *Die Siebenbürger Sachsen und Ihr Land* (Stuttgart, 1922, 4th ed.); O. Boelitz, *Aus Grenz- und Auslands-deutschtum* (München & Berlin, 1926), pp. 77 ff.; A. von Balogh, *Der Internationale Schutz der Minderheiten,* pp. 176 ff.; G. D. Teutsch and F. Teutsch, *Geschichte der Siebenbürger Sachsen Für das Sachsische Volk* (4th ed., Hermannstadt, 1925), Vol. IV; F. Teutsch, *Kirche und Schule der Siebenbürger Sachsen in Vergangenheit und Gegenwart* (2d ed., Hermannstadt, 1923); G. Müller, *Die Sachsische Nationsuniversität in Siebenbürgen* (Hermannstadt, 1928); R. F. Kaindl, *Geschichte der Deutschen in den Karpathenländer* (Gotha, 1907, 2 vols.), II, 3 ff.; B. Kleinschmidt, *Ausland Deutschtum und Kirche* (Deutschtum und Ausland, herausgegeben von Georg Schreiber, Heft 19/22, Münster, 1930, 2 vols.).

The Saxons form the largest part of the German population in Roumania. The Hungarian King Geisa (1141–62) brought them into the country to colonize Transylvania. Dr. Oscar Jászi quotes in his *The Dissolution of the Habsburg Monarchy* a poem which reputes the Saxons to be none other than the descendants of the children who were piped out of Hamelin by the Pied Piper:

> In Transylvania there's a tribe
> Of Alic people who ascribe
> Their outlandish ways and dress
> On which their neighbours lay such stress
> To their fathers and mothers having risen
> Out of some subterraneous prison;
> Into which they were trepanned
> Long ago in a mighty band
> Out of Hamelin town in Brunswick land;
> But how and why they don't understand.

The Saxons have been able to keep their cultural and economic superiority to the present day, forming islands and islets within the triangle Bistriţa-Braşov-Oraştia. They are about 230,000 strong.

Compact masses of the Germans could also be found in the Banat, somewhat later than in Transylvania. They were nearly exterminated in the wars between the Hungarians and the Turks. After the victories of Prince Eugene, the Austrian Government began to resettle the country with the settlers called the Souabians. The names of the towns readily signify their German origins—Wesskirchen, Weschetz, Mercydorf, etc. Their strength of about 300,000 is centered in the Banat, Arad, and Satu-Mare. They emigrated here mostly during the eighteenth century and never succeeded in collecting themselves into a united ethnical group, being scattered over too large an area. They could not withstand successfully the denationalizing policy of the Magyars. In Bukovina there are about 70,000 Germans.

During the nineteenth century, a number of flourishing colonies appeared in Bessarabia, devoted to the agricultural pursuits. Their localities carry German names pertaining to Biblical origins—Jakobstal, Friedental, Rosenfeld, Hoffnungstal, Karlsfeld, Danielsfeld, Gottlieb, Friedensfeld, etc. The most important center of the German minority does not carry a German name. It is called Tarutino and is located, as are the places named above, in the district Cetatea-Albă.

The Germans of Bessarabia are estimated at 113,000. They were favored by the Russian régime. Their settlements are known for their prosperity.

A part of the Germans who emigrated to Bessarabia continued their march southward. In 1842 some 6,000 of them immigrated into Roumania and founded Jakobsontal near Brăila. Some of them felt dissatisfied and went to the Dobrogea, establishing themselves at Tulcea and Babadag and in the district of Constanţa. In 1878, together with the whole district, their colonies went to Roumania.[24]

The problem of the Jews in Roumania is one of the most delicate and also one of the noisiest ones that the country has to face. The remarkable ability of the Jew to get hold of the business life of the country and his practice of banking makes him, it is claimed, the most unpopular figure in some nationalistic classes of Roumania of today. He is fundamentally an economic and social problem. Thus, as fundamentally the immigrant alien in America is not an Anglo-Saxon problem, so the Jewish problem of Roumania does not concern the problem of race and religion.

The official figures of the Jews themselves give us the figure of 900,000.[25] According to this, the Jewish population forms about 5.5 per cent of the total population, a small number in comparison with the importance that it assumes.

The Jews have been settled in the Roumanian provinces since the early Christian centuries.[26] They migrated for the most part into Moldavia, in two big waves after the Polish partitions (1772–95) and after the Treaty of Adrianople. During the eighteenth century especially a large Jewish population filtered in, continually augmented by refugees from Austria, Poland, and Russia. Many Jews took up their residence in Roumania during and after the World War. In 1856 the first Judeo-German journal appeared at Iaşi. In 1895 the *Israelitul Român,* in Roumanian and French, appeared at Bucharest. Other journals, with more or less ephemeral existence, followed, written in Judeo-German, in German, in Roumanian and German, and in Russian and Hebrew. Together with other

[24] The names Saxons and Souabians do not signify that these Germans came originally from German districts thus named. In fact they came from all parts of Germany.

[25] *The American Jewish Year Book, 5690* (1929–30), XXXI, 313.

[26] See Dr. E. Schwarzfeld, "The Jews of Roumania," in *The American Jewish Year Book, 5662* (1901–1902), pp. 25–87.

foreigners, chiefly Greeks and Armenians, they soon absorbed most of the trade of the principalities. They are found chiefly in towns in the northern part of the kingdom. Most of them speak a bastard German, the idiom of the Galician and Polish Jews.

The anti-Semitist Roumanians maintain that the Jews remain foreigners, refusing to participate in the national life or even to learn the Roumanian language. They are also accused of taking advantage of the lack of thrift of the peasants and, in general, exploiting them. In addition the extremists assert that they support one another in acquiring a monopoly of commerce and industry.

The Jews reply that they were ostracized in the matter of naturalization and that the inferior conditions of the peasants are caused by the old-time political influences; also that Jewish control of industry and commerce is due to the Roumanian's own preference for state service and the professions and also to the former special laws which prohibited them from entering other professions.

In general, there are two classes of Jews in Roumania. Many of the Eastern Jews still retain their Semitic customs, language, manners, and character. Another group of them, descending from the Spanish Jews, who arrived in Roumania in 1494, have been completely assimilated and play an important part in the economic development of the country.

Besides the Magyars, Germans, and Jews, the Slavs, composed of Serbs, Ruthenes, Russians, Poles, and about 50,000 Czechoslovaks, add their number to the minorities. More than 50,000 Serbs live in the Banat, mixed with the Roumanians and the Souabians. They came to this territory as fugitives from the Balkans in the seventeenth and eighteenth centuries. They live in amicable relations with the Roumanians and all Serbians speak Roumanian. There are also several Serbian villages in Wallachia, for example, the village Brebeni, in the district Obate.

The Ruthenes have their origin in Ukrainia, and call themselves also Small Russians. They speak a Russian dialect. Principally they can be found in northern Bukovina, Bessarabia, and several colonies along the Dniester. In the mountains of Bukovina and Maramureş, they are known as Huţules. There are at least 500,000 Ruthenians in Roumania.

It is estimated that the Old Kingdom has about 40,000 and new Roumania 59,000 Russians, making the total 99,000. They live dispersed in southern Bessarabia, in the north of the Dobrogea, at the mouth of the Danube, and in some villages of Moldavia. They are also numerous at Iaşi. They live in amicable contact with the Roumanians, being members of the same church and willing to help their brethren—refugees from Russia.

The Poles dotted Bukovina, Transylvania, and Bessarabia with their city inhabitants. They are estimated at from 37,000 to 50,000 and occupy themselves with agriculture, trade, and the liberal professions. They also are friendly to the Roumanian state.

The Czechoslovaks in Roumania have seven Czech and eight Slovak schools, located mostly in the Banat and Transylvania, taught by teachers sent there from Czechoslovakia with the permission of the Roumanian Government. The first Czech immigrants were called to the Banat in 1823 by the military administration. Most of them are farmers, woodsmen, and miners. They are considered good neighbors and culturally more developed than the other nationalities of the districts. Nearly all of them are Catholic. Up to 1919, the Slovaks formed a compact mass in the Banat, and after the World War, at first, wanted to become a part of Yugoslavia. On July 19, 1919, they voted that the Slovak districts should be added as an independent unit to Greater Roumania. They are farmers and the Magyar oppression left them on a rather low cultural level. There are colonies of Czechoslovaks in Bucharest, Craiova, Galaţi, Orşova, Reşita, Anina, Timişoara, Arad, Cluj, Sibiu, Cernăuţi, and Chişinău, the most important of them being the Bucharest settlement of about 3,000. During and after the World War they received the support of the United States Minister to Roumania, Charles J. Vopička, an American citizen of Czech origin. Many of them have executive positions in industrial and banking institutions; their undertakings receive support from a branch of the Credit Bank of Prague at Bucharest.

The Armenians, to the number of 12,000, have been nearly assimilated by the Roumanians. Most of them are merchants, fabricants, artisans, and also functionaries and advocates. They try in marriage to conserve the purity of their race, being also anxious not to lose their fortunes by marriages with other nationalities. Their language is nearly forgotten among them and they are distinguishable from the Roumanians only from the religious point of view.

The Greeks, like the Armenians, are found mostly in towns, and supplement the Jews in controlling the minor aspects of Roumanian economic life (retail business, peddling, usury, etc.). Most of them reside in the Danubian ports and on the Black Sea. Their number is relatively small. They have their own schools and churches, like other minorities. Historical memories do not make them very popular with the Roumanians. But the descendants of the former ruling classes can be found in the political life, though of course they are entirely Roumanianized (Cantacuzino, Mavrocordat, etc.).

The Gypsies are found throughout the country. They may be divided into the sedentary and the nomadic groups. Some of them are known as musicians and resent being considered Gypsies. The nomads still use the original language they brought with them from Asia when they arrived in Roumania during the barbaric invasions. They pick up their precarious living by fortune-telling, horse-trading, and roguery. Altogether the Gypsies number about 285,000.

The Turks and Tartars are found only in the Dobrogea and Bessarabia. The Tartars number a little more than 200,000. They take no interest in politics and are mostly herdsmen and shepherds. In the more cultivatable areas they are peasants. The Turks are about one-half as numerous as the Tartars. Most of them are merchants, coffee-house keepers, and agriculturists; some of them engage in trading buffaloes. It is estimated that 80,000 of them are Christians, though still speaking the Turkish language.

The Bulgars are not looked upon with favor. The sentiment more than likely has a political basis. During the Bulgarian occupation of the Dobrogea, the Bulgarian districts declared themselves for union with Bulgaria. This has never been forgotten by Roumania. But the Bulgarian minority has complained less than the other minorities. The most important complaint relates to the introduction of colonists into the Dobrogea under the agrarian reform laws, and the billeting of these colonists in Bulgarian homes. Another complaint concerns the so-called Dobrogea Law, under which the tenure of property was changed; and in the change, it is claimed by the Bulgars, many Bulgars who had held *émiri* property lost one-third of their holdings without receiving any compensation.[27]

Altogether some 290,000 Bulgars live in the Dobrogea, most of them distributed over the Quadrilateral (viz., that part of the Dobrogea acquired by Roumania in 1913), and the districts of Constanţa and Tulcea, and in southern Bessarabia, the districts of Ismail

[27] For the Roumanian position on this problem, see p. 177, note 68.

and Cetatea-Albă. Several villages in Muntenia were absorbed into Greater Roumania. What is interesting is that some of these communities are Roman Catholic, as Cioplea village near Bucharest.

Here is a table showing the number of members of the principal denominations in Greater Roumania, according to the last official statistics (1931), and the state subventions in lei of each denomination, according to the budget of 1931:

DENOMINATION	MEMBERSHIP	SUBVENTION
Greek Orthodox	13,027,305	592,917,671
Greek Catholic	1,320,000	102,856,501
Roman Catholic	1,196,357	52,493,732
Calvinist	717,162	52,811,767
Lutheran	392,200	17,637,696
Unitarian	72,000	9,054,284
Jewish	984,213	10,125,000
Islamic	156,000	11,523,808
Others (Gregorians, Baptists, etc.)	160,000	....
Total	18,025,237	849,420,459

Before the war, religious prejudices scarcely existed at all, for the Greek Orthodox church was rather tolerant. After the war Roumania, following the reunion of the new provinces, fell heir at the same time to a rather important religious problem. A considerable number of the Roman Catholics and Greek Uniats of Transylvania, who recognize the spiritual authority of the Pope of Rome, led the Pope to appoint an apostolic nuncio to Bucharest. The majority of the population of the country professes the Greek Orthodox religion, but there is a considerable number of Protestants in Transylvania. Roumanian emigrants from America, who have returned, profess the Baptist, the Methodist, or the Adventist faith. They are spiritually-minded people and their labor is making proselytes, notably in the country among the peasants.

The Greek Orthodox church and the Greek Catholic church are the two national churches recognized in the constitution. The Orthodox church of Roumania is an autocephalous branch of the Orthodox Eastern (Greek) church. It established its independence from the Ecumenical Patriarch of Constantinople in 1864 and gained recognition in 1885. In 1872 laws were passed establishing a holy synod as the supreme authority in all ecclesiastical matters. Since 1893 the state has taken over the entire support of all members of the Orthodox church. On November 1, 1925, the first Patriarch of Roumania, Miron Cristea, was enthroned in Bucharest, with the consent of the Ecumenical Patriarch. The metropolitans and the bishops are elected by the Senate and Assembly of Deputies sitting together as an electoral college, which includes the metropolitans and bishops already elected. Metropolitans are selected from among the diocesan bishops, and the diocesan bishops from among the bishops in partibus. The latter are appointed by the Minister of Cults and Arts from lists prepared by the synod.

The clergy of the Roumanian Orthodox church are paid by the state. Religions recognized by the state receive a subvention from the state. Those with less than 50,000 followers are regarded as religious associations, and are dependent entirely on their own resources.

INTERNATIONAL PROVISIONS CONCERNING ROUMANIA

The problem of minorities is both internal and international. Oppression of minorities by the governments under which they live results in irredentist activities, supported by the states related to the oppressed by race, nationality, and religion, and leads to international complications of the bitterest kind. Again, the support of the dissatisfied group within a state by another state may embitter the endangered state. The problem is very old and has received international recognition in past centuries.[28]

In order that the minorities, which as a matter of necessity or for some other reason had to be included in the new boundaries, might not become a new cause for future international conflicts, the Paris Peace Conference demanded from Roumania, as from some other states, the signature of the minority treaty, which in turn constitutes an international obligation.[28a] It was signed on December 9, 1919, and has in general provisions similar to all other minorities treaties,

---

[28] The literature on the subject is growing daily. The reader is referred especially to the following publications: Foreign Policy Association, *Information Service,* Vol. II, No. 9, July 3, 1926, "Protection of Minorities in Europe"; *International Conciliation,* September 1925, No. 222, "The Problem of Minorities"; André Mandelstam, "La Protection des minorités" in Académie de Droit International, *Recueil des cours 1923,* Tome I, pp. 362–401; etc.

[28a] The Roumanian treaty and other international acts concerning the problem of minorities are conveniently gathered in Dr. H. Kraus' *Das Recht der Minderheiten.*

Interior of Peasant Home, Soroca District

Gypsy Children of Dobrogea

with the special provisions rendered necessary by the special conditions of Roumania.

To summarize, all inhabitants of Roumania are guaranteed absolute and unlimited protection of life and liberty, without distinction of birth, nationality, language, race, or religion, and are entitled to the free exercise, whether public or private, of any creed, religion, or belief whose practices are not inconsistent with public order or public morals. Roumanian nationality is granted to all those habitually resident within the territory forming a part of Roumania, subject to exceptions provided for in the peace treaties. The persons in question have the right to opt for another nationality, but in case they exercise this right they must move to the state for which they have opted. All Roumanian citizens are assured of equal civil and political rights, irrespective of their race, religion, or language. Minorities have the right to establish and manage their own charitable, religious, social, and educational institutions, in which they may freely use their own language and exercise their religion; in the towns and districts where there is "a considerable proportion of Roumanian nationals of other than Roumanian speech" their children have the right to receive instruction through the medium of their own language in the primary schools. Furthermore, these minorities are assured a fair share in the application of public funds for educational, religious, or charitable purposes.

With the exception of the last two provisions, Roumania made the stipulations of the minorities treaty part of the fundamental law of the land.

The treaty also provided for the supervision of the minorities clauses by the League of Nations, and for submission of disputes arising under them to the Permanent Court of International Justice. Special clauses obliged Roumania to recognize Jewish inhabitants of Roumania who did not possess another nationality as Roumanian nationals *ipso facto* and without special formalities. Furthermore, the communities of the Saxons and Szeklers in Transylvania were afforded local autonomy in regard to scholastic and religious matters, subject to the control of the Roumanian state.

The subsequent interpretation of the minority treaty is of great importance to all the parties concerned. In the first place, there is nothing in the treaty which could be construed as making the minorities special new subjects of international law, a wish especially propounded by the Hungarian representatives to the League of

Nations.[29] A contrary conception cannot be entertained without jeopardizing the protection guaranteed the minorities, on the one hand, and the integrity of the state guaranteeing them, on the other. It is clearly specified that the minorities are not afforded autonomy as special state units, for the simple reason that the term "protection" cannot apply to the minorities any more than it does to the majorities. And what is apportioned by the state for minority benefit may also be apportioned for majority benefit, in the descending order of state, municipality, commune, etc. Minorities cannot form budgets any more than majorities can. The minorities treaties are intended to promote the consolidation of Roumania and not primarily to perpetuate for all time alien communities within her borders.

As to the relations of the minorities with the League so far developed, there are two conceptions: one headed by General Smuts, who regards the status of minorities as similar to that of the inhabitants of the mandates; and the other led by Briand, who believes that the ultimate aim of the minorities treaties is to produce a homogeneous nation. Hence, according to the former, as he wrote in October 1928:

> The League has failed to secure the rights of racial minorities which were committed to its sacred charge. We have here probably the most serious menace to the future peace of Europe. The League has failed here to its grave discredit and injury.

According to Briand, however, in a speech at the Assembly of the League in September of the same year:

> This delicate problem must not lead to shattering of governments and to endangering the work of the League of Nations. The minority question must not develop itself into a new element of uncertainty. Peace must be the guiding idea. Even if equitable minority demands were submitted, the League of Nations might be compelled to silence them if they were of such a nature as to endanger peace.

Probably the most compromising attitude is taken by Dr. Eduard Beneš of Czechoslovakia:

[29] See, for example, the suggestion of Count Apponyi in the sixth Assembly contemplating the institution of an entire procedure, with a hearing of evidence on both sides, as between the interested state and the representative of the minority concerned, the method and the rules to be followed being similar to those of the procedure in use for disputes between private persons in the ordinary court, in the League of Nations, *Official Journal*, 7th Year, No. 2 (February 1926), pp. 294–95. For further discussion, see J. S. Rouček, *The Working of the Minorities System under the League of Nations*, pp. 71–75.

In practical terms [the wording of the minorities treaties] means that the States possessing minorities must treat them with justice and wisdom. The development of Europe, the World War, the philosophy and outlook of the present day, demand that the respect for national liberty should be a real and genuine thing. On the other hand, however, because the minority problem is not one which applies only to a few States, but is of world-wide political significance, the minorities themselves must realize that what is known as the minority policy must not be carried to extremes; it must be moderate, and it should be generally pursued only within reasonable grounds. Otherwise it would lead to results entirely opposed to those intended.

As to the minority complaint, this must be in a form carefully defined.[30] If it conforms to the required formula, it is then submitted by the League Secretariat to the defendant state. If the state objects, the question as to eligibility is settled by the president of the Council. If there is no objection, the petition is placed on the agenda of the Council and the state concerned is allowed a sufficient time in which to make answer to it. These answers, together with the petition, are then communicated to the Council and examined by the president and two disinterested members. Thus each petition, so to speak, invokes a minorities committee of three, any member of which may bring the whole question before the Council and, failing decision either in committee or in Council, to the World Court, whose decision is final.

At the session of the Council held at Madrid in July 1929 a resolution was adopted introducing a number of practical improvements in procedure. The measures dealt with the composition and meetings of the committee of three, and with publicity of documents. In the future, the membership of the committee can be increased to five in cases of exceptional difficulty, and its meetings may be held, when necessary, independently of the sessions of the Council. Petitioners are henceforth to be informed of the result of each examination of a petition by its minorities committee and, if the government concerned consents, the results are to be made public. Furthermore, the Secretariat publishes each year statistics of the number of petitions received, those found non-receivable, and the action taken on those

---

[30] See J. S. Rouček, "Procedure in Minorities Complaints," in *American Journal of International Law*, July 1929, XXIII, 538–51; League of Nations Official No.: C. 8. M.S. 1931. I. *Protection of Linguistic, Racial or Religious Minorities by the League of Nations* (Geneva, March 1931); Secretariat of the League of Nations, *Ten Years of World Co-operation* (Geneva, 1929), p. 369.

found receivable, also the number of committees appointed, and the number of meetings held by them.[31]

The conflict between the provisions of the minorities treaty and domestic legislation has given rise to many baffling problems. The most serious one, viz., that of the Roumanian optants in Transylvania, is dealt with above in the chapter on "Roumania and Her Neighbors," pp. 158–64.

On the whole, the system of international protection of minorities presents many difficulties and is the subject of continual discussion and criticism by the members of the League, by various writers, and by the minorities themselves. We must bear in mind, however, that the system cannot be criticized so much for the fundamental principles underlying it, as for its practical execution and enforcement.

Roumanian Minorities Policy

The extreme liberal tendencies of the resolution of Alba-Iulia, passed by the National Assembly of the Transylvanian Roumanians on December 1, 1918, which proclaimed the union of Transylvania with the mother country, could hardly receive any formal recognition in the Constitution of 1923, as they concerned only a part of the kingdom and could not determine legally the future policy of the entire Roumanian state. The provisions are, however, interesting to note. They provided for:

(1) complete national liberty for all the cohabiting peoples of Transylvania. Each people to educate, govern and judge itself in its own language through the medium of persons from its own midst. Every people to have the right of legislative representation and of taking part in the administration of the country in proportion to the number of individuals of whom it is composed. (2) Equality and complete autonomous religious liberty for every denomination in the state.

The Constitution of 1923, as discussed in another chapter, emphasizes the unitary character of Greater Roumania, and the National-Peasant Party agreed with the Liberal Party in regarding the kingdom as a unitary and national state. It refuses to grant the minorities the political, administrative, and judicial autonomy implicit in the 1918 resolutions, though its general policy toward the minorities is more liberal than the one favored by the Liberals.

[31] For a typical example as to how a complaint of a Roumanian minority is dealt with by the League of Nations, see League of Nations, *Official Journal*, 7th Year, No. 2 (February 1926), pp. 148–53; J. S. Rouček, *op. cit.*, pp. 111–13; C. A. Rudesco, *op. cit.*, pp. 143–47.

The constitutional provisions agree fundamentally with the intentions of the minorities treaties. "Roumanians, without distinction of ethnic origin, language or religion, enjoy freedom of conscience, freedom of education, freedom of the press, freedom of meeting, freedom of association, and all freedom and rights established by law"; and "difference of religious belief and confession, of ethnic origin and language, does not constitute in Roumania an impediment to the obtaining of civil and political rights and their exercise." Every citizen is equal before the law. All faiths enjoy equal liberty and protection; liberty of conscience is absolute. Meetings are allowed and all Roumanians have the right to form associations, though "the right of free association does not imply in itself the right of creating juridical persons."[32]

The American Committee on the Rights of Religious Minorities does not criticize the constitution itself so much as its application, which of course involves the delicate problems of discretion and opinion which can be settled only by a court of law. Its report says in part: "The new Constitution of Roumania, however valid and admirable it may be in most respects, is so used that in many respects its provisions fall short in their application." But a similar criticism could be applied to any country and primarily to the United States. No document can immediately alter the concepts which are the results of centuries of conflicts. Hence it is interesting to note that the commission admits in its conclusions that "there has never been in Roumania what has come to be technically known as a 'pogrom'; that is, a massacre inspired and sanctioned by the state."

But that is the consideration of the extreme. What is more important to take into consideration is the psychology of the minorities and majorities, reacting to the process of integration and assimilation, which determines, after all, the behavior of each group and its individuals. Possibly the greatest weakness of the system of international protection of minorities lies in the fact that it is based entirely on legal considerations, with little attention to the political, historical, economic, and social factors. When the peace treaties speak, for example, of "race," they evidently assume that there are differences originating in race-differences, if not in the inequality of races. This, however, is still to be proved. Race-differences are a factor of the situation wherever two or more races are in contact;

[32] All these rights are subject to laws passed in accordance with the constitutional provisions.

but it must also be evident that the members of two or more racial groups sometimes intermingle on terms of greatest friendliness. Thus we blind ourselves to the existence of variable causes which alone account for the variable consequences that appear in the presence of racial constants. They are, however, the result of cultural, economic, social, political, and intellectual conditions in various parts of the world. Thus, for example, race-prejudice in America has followed the frontier when the Indian interfered with the exploitation of the country, just as the Roumanian prejudice against the Jew follows the practice of usury.

If the causes of the relations of minorities with the majorities in any country lie quite beyond the reach of any simple explanation, the manifestation of this behavior is perhaps capable of an analysis which from the sociological and psychological point of view will render the whole situation somewhat more comprehensible.

Within every state there can be found some diversities of blood, language, and religion. These inhabitants, differing from the mass of its people in race, language, nationality, or religion, constitute a minority. If in the case of Central and Southeastern Europe the racial factor seems to be the most fundamental mark of distinction, such a group is commonly referred to as an ethnic minority. Thus, in discussing the problem of minorities, the term is taken to apply to groups of persons who differ in race, language, nationality, or religion from the majority of the inhabitants of the country. But ethnic differences indeed form one of the greatest sources of weakness in a state, because one or another of the groups may wish the disruption of the state in order to secure complete independence. Hence effective unity and ethnic differences are difficult to combine, as any external or psychological dissimilarity between peoples is always a hindrance to friendly co-operation. The state, therefore, tries to overcome the difficulties by the process of assimilation. But assimilation is always accompanied by emotional disturbances and is accordingly a tortuous process. The emotional reaction of the group, viz., of the minority, and the persistence of traditional and nationalistic ways tend to resist assimilation. But the state is bound to follow such a policy, because the most important of the fundamental rights of the state is that of existence, which involves the right of self-preservation, based upon an instinct controlling in the last resort all living organisms.

One of the easiest methods of assimilation is the one dealing with succeeding generations brought up from the start under the new conditions and environment. Consequently the clashes resulting from the state dominating its minorities center around the school, the church, and publications. Education becomes the chief instrument of conformity and naturalization; it is opposed by the resistance of nationalistic and religious emotions.

The result is that the most important motive which governs the relations of minorities and majorities and the attitude of minorities toward the state is the fear motive. Minorities naturally react to the attempts of the state to amalgamate and fuse its population. The fear is widespread that the state tends to suppress not only national aspirations but also national cultures of its minorities, which ascribe more aggressive intents and motives to their state than the state possesses, and fail to understand that the normal thing for any country is to promote its own national culture and preserve its national experience. The consequent condition is a supersaturation of mutual misgiving, mistrust, and suspicion. The state, first of all, has the apprehension of doom, is afraid of losing its identity as a nation-state, and fears possible internal disruptions. The minority, reacting to this stimulus, undertakes to worry about the life and honor of its clan and commences to resort to emotional appeals in order to repulse and resist the onslaughts or to prepare for a possible attack. Under the stress of fear, which is the parent of hate and of anger, both being always handmaids to other impulses, the minority is angry when it sees a threat to its interests, and is prompted to seek outside aid. It feels that its present protection is not equal to the danger it is in. The whole complicated situation in which an oppressed group exists manifests itself in a whole set of particular actions called nationalistic behavior. Seeking outside aid will take the form of pleading to the tribunal of public opinion, attempting to get other people to take an interest in their fate, and petitioning for aid, relief, and patronage.[33] In addition, when a minority assumes that there is little or no possibility of ever converting itself into a majority, there is the peril of a rebellious and mutinous attitude on the part of such minorities. And then minori-

[33] M. S. Handman, "The Sentiment of Nationalism," in *Political Science Quarterly*, 1921, XXXVI, 104–21, and especially p. 105; W. B. Pillsbury, *The Psychology of Nationality and Internationalism* (New York, 1919), chapter iii, "Hate as a Social Force," pp. 63–89; G. E. Partridge, *The Psychology of Nations* (New York, 1919), pp. 41 ff.; C. J. H. Hayes, *Essays on Nationalism* (New York, 1926).

ties are apt to be arrogant, feeling virtuous, noble, and righteous in their wicked and depraved environment; they may feel superior and unequalled, looking upon the majority as a rabble. Majorities likewise, it is true, are not always humble, and react occasionally by passing measures inflicting the most severe disabilities on the minority.

The implication of inferiority on the part of the minority, as well as its reverse process, is insulting, and thus aggressive feelings are aroused.[34] Hate plays an important part here. The minority has the notion that it is the victim of all sorts of intrigues and persecution and the "delusion of persecution" and the "delusion of grandeur" commonly go together. Both are strengthened by the remembrance of a long series of retaliations and a long history of struggles. Both delusions are bound to become chronic, though often groundless. But the perpetual moods of hatred, bitterness, and grudges become dangerous forces, ready to explode whenever any discords and misunderstandings arise. The leaders usually take care to recall the memory of archaic grievances as a pretense for actuating fresh ones. The very factor of the existence of a group,

[34] The Hungarians and their minorities are especially apt to harp on this point of superiority. The reader should consult *Justice for Hungary* (Longmans, Green & Co., London, 1928), referred to already in the chapter on foreign relations of Roumania. Some of the excerpts illustrate the point: "The Eastern spirit [Roumania] has assumed the part of aggressor and conqueror, which part, however, it cannot play by raising itself . . . . but only by oppressing the higher cultural forces [the Hungarians]. The result is terrifying" (p. 15). "In spite of the cultural inferiority demonstrated above, the Roumanians of Transylvania are on a higher level than those of the former Kingdom. . . . . Thus the extension of Roumanian rule to the territories alienated from Hungary will obviously and necessarily result in a catastrophic decline of the standard of government, and, owing to the natural desire of the ruling race for speedy equalization, in oppression, if not destruction, of the higher culture" (p. 19); etc. In 1929, there appeared in Budapest a publication entitled *Hungary Illustrated,* edited by Sir Robert Donald, a former editor of the *Daily Chronicle* and managing director of the United Newspapers Ltd., who also published a book, *The Tragedy of Trianon.* We quote his statements: "Few races are gifted with the capacity to govern their fellow men. The Magyar and English peoples share this capacity among other characteristics" (p. 13). He then quotes Count Keyserling and continues: "They are . . . . 'born rulers,' and through all their vicissitudes have 'nevertheless remained a pure ruling race!' The Magyars are also the most aristocratic race of the Continent. . . . . The Magyars, like the English people, have an inborn capacity for government. . . . . The Magyars are the only race fit to rule in Central and Eastern Europe" (p. 14). The reader can draw his own conclusions. Sir Donald evidently considers even the foreign observers rather inferior, for he concludes: "Let Hungary go on confidently educating foreigners, especially ignorant politicians, on the virtues of her people and the justice of her cause. . . . ."

assembled and organized for offensive and defensive purposes, creates a strong contrariety between the feeling of individual persons of the cluster toward one another and that directed toward strangers. Within the group there is friendly co-operation and good faith, which appreciate exaggerated estimation of the group's accomplishments and luxuriate in keeping the memory alive that one is a member of it; these mental processes become strengthened by cognitive rivalry with other groups. The members of the group consider the good identical with what benefits their own group. Then it must follow that the bad becomes identified with what fails to benefit the group, even if it should happen to be useful to everybody concerned. And if the other group is wrong there can be no compromise with it, for truth must not and cannot enter into any compromise with error. The attention of the group is called continually to the "principle" of the matter and especially to its brilliant and illustrious days of yore, because the group, or any crowd for that matter, always insists on being flattered, being jealous of its dignity and honor.

The ruling group presents reactions analogous to those of the minority. The first group reacts to the possibility of danger, the second to that of insecurity.

Much water will have to flow under the bridges before the psychology of these minorities groups will be changed. The archaic system of defense involved in maintaining an attitude of distrust and misunderstanding and fear cannot be dispelled very quickly. It seems to be evident, however, that this spirit is slowly disappearing in Roumania.

The whole problem of minorities is very often misunderstood in the United States; the "melting-pot" functions so well and so naturally here. But there is one important difference between America and Europe in this respect. The minorities in America are there by their own free will. Their presence presupposes a disposition on their part to conform to the laws they find there. But the cases of the minorities manipulated by the Peace Conference are different. The peace treaties placed them and their territory under an alien régime without their volition. Often they were against it. That is why the "melting-pot" over there functions badly.

The decrees of May 22, 1919, and August 12, 1919, provided a solution for the question of the nationality of Jews in Roumania. The decree-law of December 29, 1918, granted civil rights to all persons, irrespective of their religion. But until the advent of Maniu to power no specific minority policy was followed by the Roumanian governments. In fact, such a policy is very difficult. All the minorities of Roumania vary in social and cultural conditions. While the Germans of Transylvania, the Saxons, had enjoyed autonomy for centuries, other minorities, like the Turks, have hardly produced any national organization of their own. Some minorities have existed in Roumania for centuries. Others became minorities only after the war. Altogether any unified and consolidated policy is bound to dissatisfy some minority groups.

The government coalitions have usually bargained with the representatives of the minorities before the elections. In this connection we must note, in regard to the electoral law of March 28, 1926, that Article 91 gives a special privilege to the minorities parties. If such a minority party receives an absolute majority of votes in an electoral district, it receives a number of mandates proportionate to the percentage of votes, even if it fails to obtain 2 per cent of the votes polled throughout the country. From the rest of the mandates, one-half is given to the majority party as such, and the other half is divided percentually among the majority and the minorities parties. In this figuring all votes for the majority party are included in the total number of votes for this allotment; in regard to the minorities parties the number of votes in this allotment is counted only from those districts where they had not received mandates on the basis of the privilege mentioned above.

In practice these provisions are sometimes advantageous to the minorities parties. As most of the Roumanian minorities live in more or less compact masses in certain districts of the state, they can form an absolute majority in their own districts. Of course the matter becomes actually of practical importance only if they can get 2 per cent of all votes in the whole state. Thus the Magyar Party benefited by these provisions in the December 12, 1928, elections, receiving sixteen mandates; otherwise (without these stipulations) the party would have received but twelve mandates. But it must also be realized that even the minorities parties are divided in their political allegiance and hence usually do not form compact political voting bodies.

The political struggle of minorities has concerned the church, the school, and publications. A Roumanian authority estimates that of the 1,263 publications (709 newspapers and 554 periodicals) in

Roumania, other than books, 947 are in Roumanian, 179 in Magyar, and 95 in German.[35] Of the total number of 709 daily and weekly papers, 505 are published in Roumanian, 7 in French, 112 in Hungarian, 72 in German, 5 in Russian, 2 in Bulgarian, and 8 in Yiddish. The 554 periodicals published in Roumania are classified as follows: 433 in Roumanian, 11 in French, 69 in Hungarian, and 30 in German.

For the preservation of the language and culture of the minorities, the atmosphere is provided by the schools. For this purpose the status of the minorities has been fixed by the following laws: the primary and normal education laws of 1924; the law on private education of 1925; the secondary education law of 1928, which was amended in 1929; and, finally, the cults law of 1928.

The minorities maintain 1,525 primary minorities schools in Roumania. The private schools are supported by contributions of the budgets of the communes and countries, by state grants from the budget of the Ministry of Education, and by a tax of 30 lei per person collected from the membership of various cults. The minorities further support 51 secondary schools, 11 commercial schools, 13 normal schools, 2 professional schools, and 57 colleges.

In 1925 a law was passed by the Roumanian parliament regulating definitely the situation of the denominational and private schools in Roumania. Private schools, founded, conducted, and maintained by confessions, communities, or private individuals, must have on an average at least 10 children per class; elementary schools may have a minimum of 20 for one school. These schools are divided into kindergartens, elementary schools, and secondary schools. Higher institutions of learning cannot be founded by private initiative. Kindergartens and elementary schools must follow the state program. The language taught in private schools is determined by those who maintain the schools. But it is required that the Roumanian language, Roumanian history, and Roumanian geography be taught in all schools, beginning with the third elementary class.[36]

[35] The figures were provided by Mr. Filotti, director of the press bureau of the presidium of ministries. See also Emanoil Bucuta, "National Unity—at a Price," in *Manchester Guardian,* November 28, 1929, p. 21.

[36] The text of the law can be found in P. Rühlmann, *Das Schulrecht der Minterheiten in Europa,* pp. 472–534; see also T. Grentrup, *Die Kirchliche Rechtslage der Deutschen Minderheiten Katholischer Konfession in Europa* (Berlin, Deutsche Rundschau, 1929), pp. 278–330. Foreign critics point out that Article 27 of the private school act deprives the private schools of their previous public

In addition, the state maintains special minorities schools in every commune having a majority of a minority population; where there is only a smaller proportion of the minority population, the state schools have special minorities sections. Thus the state maintains 335 primary schools for the minorities, in addition to 283 with sections for minorities.

The recognized cults of Roumania are as follows: Roumanian, Greek, Russian, Serbian, and Bulgarian Orthodox; Roumanian Graeco-Catholic (United Church); Roman Catholic; Graeco-Ruthenian and Armenian; Reformed (Calvinist); Lutheran; Unitarian; Armeno-Gregorian; Mosaic; and Mohammedan. The churches have been left to various denominations, with their old self-governing organizations. The Roman Catholic church was strengthened by the concordat, ratified on July 7, 1929, and the agreement of August 15, 1930. The religious conditions in general are regulated by the law of April 22, 1928. Equal protection and liberty is guaranteed to all cults. All religious denominations enjoy a wide autonomy. They establish, conduct, and control cultural and charitable institutions and may maintain special institutes for training their clergy. Altogether there are four Roumanian-Catholic-Magyar institutes with about 190 students, one Magyar-Unitarian theological institute with over 25 students, a Reformed Church theological institute with about 155 students, and a Mohammedan seminary with 130 students. The ecclesiastical organizations have juridical personality, and when they reach a certain size they send a representative to parliament. In case of need, the state contributes to the maintenance of the personnel and the institutions of a denomination.

The National-Peasant Government practiced a liberal policy

status and thus the act itself serves the unitary educational policy by transforming the former denominational schools into private schools. It must not be forgotten, however, that the government must apply itself to making Roumania a homogeneous nation. The Magyar minority objected very strongly "to the decree issued by the former Minister of Education Angelescu, which established several so-called 'cultural zones,' where the Roumanian teachers, picked and trained especially to this (nationally-chauvinistic) purpose, had to carry on a more intensive activity both within and outside the schools." (*A Nation Sentenced to Death,* edited by Dr. István Milotay, Budapest, 1929, p. 45.) See also American Committee on the Rights of Religious Minorities, *Roumania Ten Years After,* pp. 60–61, and a detailed refutation of the Magyar allegations by S. Dragomir, *The Ethnical Minorities in Transylvania,* pp. 84–94. For the whole case, see League of Nations, *Official Journal,* 13th year, No. 1 (January 1932), pp. 157–82. See also Appendix below.

toward the minorities. A co-operative law gave the minorities freedom to organize their co-operative system. The policy of endowing the minorities began with placing at their service a first grant of 25 million lei.[37] A special commission of parliament was appointed to study the minority problems in the various European states.

The American Jewish Year Book of 1929–30 makes the following statement: "Dr. Maniu's Government declared its intention to maintain order, and to put into effect the provisions of the Roumanian Constitution guaranteeing equality to all citizens regardless of creed. Insofar as maintaining order is concerned, the Government showed that its pledges were sincere."[38]

The subsequent report of the American Jewish Committee again referred to their dissatisfaction with the conditions under Maniu. The report of Morris D. Waldman, secretary of the committee, who has recently studied the minorities problem in Roumania, is a very interesting mixture of stereotyped accusations and occasional appreciation of the real situation.[39] The other side of the problem is presented by the official Roumanian authorities. It is admitted by the Jewish leaders that their periodical protests "were invariably met by denials of the accuracy of the press reports and by repeated utterances that the Government of Roumania was fully alive to its obligations and was sincerely desirous of protecting the rights of all of its minorities."

From the standpoint of impartial consideration of the minorities problem, it might be well to quote further from the report of Mr. Waldman, who sees the Roumanian situation occasionally in an impartial light:

It might not be imagined from these occurrences of the past year that the government as a whole consciously encouraged anti-Semitic propaganda and the excesses. Nor should it be thought that the Roumanian people as a whole have been in sympathy with them. On the contrary the general Roumanian press had continuously decried them and urged the government to take severe measures against them. The trouble was that the government regarded them for a long time as merely sporadic and unimportant occurrences and was averse to strong measures because, in contradistinction to the more despotic preceding government, it was averse to doing anything which might appear as subversive of the freedom of speech and assembly.

[37] See an article by a Deputy for the German Minority, Rudolph Brandsch, "M. Maniu and the Minorities," in *Manchester Guardian,* November 28, 1929, p. 20.

[38] *5690,* XXXI, 51.

[39] The American Jewish Committee, *Twenty-Fourth Annual Report* (New York, 1931), pp. 91 ff., here quoted by permission.

Evidently Mr. Waldman does not deny the good faith of the government:

The Government as a whole is not only not the instigator of excesses, but recognizing the embarrassment and danger to the country's prestige, would be glad to consign Cuza and his associates to oblivion. . . . . Protests on the part of our Committee and other similar organizations have not been without some effect, especially during the administration of the present government, whose great desire for foreign financial help makes it especially sensitive to the world's opinion.

The report also points out that "the task of securing the desired amelioration is complicated by the internal differences which obtain among the Jews themselves." One group follows the nationalist policy, and the others are anti-nationalists, and the dilemma arises from the vacillating policy of the minorities, affiliating now with the parties of the majority and now with the other minorities. "The situation is complicated, moreover, by personal rivalries and antipathies which frequently degenerate into amazingly bitter rancor and abuse."

It might be well to state the extreme demands of the Jewish minority group in Roumania as summarized in the committee's report:

Full citizenship has not yet been accorded to all of the Jewish population. A satisfactory community organization law has not yet been enacted. Adequate support of Jewish communities and schools has not been forthcoming. Nor has complete justice been done with regard to Jewish teachers and the curricula in the schools. Discrimination in the field of financial credits has not yet been removed.

But it is significant that Mr. Waldman declares in his conclusion:

I carried away the impression that Roumania, though suffering a serious economic setback together with the rest of the world, is earnestly endeavouring to set its house in order and enjoys the prospect of becoming one of the most prosperous, if not best governed, countries of Europe. The Jews of the world desire to see it prosperous because the prosperity of all of its elements including the Jewish population is predicated on the general prosperity of the country. . . . . Roumania's one million Jews, constituting a little over five per cent of the population, can readily be absorbed into the economic life of the country without disadvantage to the non-Jewish population; on the contrary, to their great advantage.

But do the Jews of Roumania want to be absorbed?

The National-Peasant Government planned to settle the minorities problem by a special minorities law. A commission for its drafting was created and much material was collected at home and abroad by Deputy Popp and by a bureau attached to the presidency of the council of ministers, headed by Z. Paclişeanu, for the study of the problem. Probably the economic and financial difficulties postponed the passing of the law. The Government of Iorga made this bureau a part of the newly created State Under-Secretariat for the Minorities, attached to the presidency of the council of ministers, at whose head was appointed Deputy Dr. Rudolf Brandsch, one of the outstanding representatives of the German minority in Roumania. Z. Paclişeanu was appointed secretary-general of this new department, and Professor Arpád Bittay, a Magyar from Alba-Iulia, became its technical adviser for the Magyar questions. Dr. Brandsch announced that the main functions of his office would be as follows: (1) the study of the minorities problems, especially as they are presented in the foreign press, the examination of minorities publications, and the check-up on the activity of various special minorities organizations; (2) the following of the ways and means by which the minorities problems are being practically solved abroad; (3) the control of the news about the conditions of the Roumanian minorities abroad; (4) the study of the character and ways of living of nationalist minorities in Roumania; (5) and, finally, the study of the situation of the Roumanian minorities abroad from the cultural, social, economic, and political points of view. The results of these studies are to be published once a month. The under-secretariat is to function as an advisory organ of the government for the solution of the minorities problems and especially as an organ between the minorities and the government. All official decrees are to be examined by this department, whose advisory body will include representatives of minorities and recognized authorities on the minorities problems.[40]

[40] It was reported in the autumn of 1931 that plans were afoot to modify the provisions for private schools in favor of the minorities and that the law for the acquisition of citizenship was to be changed. As far as the appointment of Dr. Brandsch was concerned, the German minority of course favors co-operation with Iorga's Government, though objections were heard that Dr. Brandsch was appointed without any consultation with the German minority. However, personal objections were overcome when the leader of the German Party, Dr. H. O. Roth, was received in an audience by the King and when Dr. Roth succeeded on June 6, 1931, in making an electoral agreement with the party of the "National Unity" whereby the Germans were given eleven mandates in the House of Deputies and two seats in the Senate. The Magyars under Count Bethlen objected to Brandsch, whom they consider hostile to the joint Magyar-German opposition *bloc* and

In addition, the Government of Iorga created chairs for the minorities in their respective languages in the universities of Bucharest, Cernăuți, Cluj, and Iași.

In conclusion it may be said that one of the most serious problems of post-war Europe is the problem of minorities. Along with a number of other states, Roumania had to sign the minorities treaty, which guarantees certain rights to the minorities. The practical application of the treaty will always be a subject of discussions and interpretations. A tolerant attitude of certain minorities toward their new state is greatly needed in order to improve the mutual relations and to dispose of occasional or chronic bad feelings. The same applies to the state. The psychology of the whole matter tends toward exaggerated nationalistic behavior. The minorities groups have the right of appeal to the League of Nations. The minorities were not made juridical persons in the eyes of international law, though they are given the privilege of benefiting by its procedure and decisions. The state is still the foundation of international life today and before we can admit the minority as a juridical person, we must substitute for the foundation of international law, the state, some other political form. · The protection of minorities seems, however, to be a merely temporary means of tiding over the difficult period until citizens of the same state but of different race, religion, or language have grown accustomed to each other's peculiarities and no longer find in them a cause of offense and a reason for hostility. The minorities must recognize that the majority in the state will strenuously oppose groups which are a constant source of unreasonable irritation, complaints, and demands for special privileges.

The popular plan of solving the problem by frontier changes will not become subject-matter of politics for some time to come. No Roumanian government would dare to hand her population back to Hungary, just as no Italian government would ever assent to an international discussion about her minorities. The immediate possibilities lie in the field of the *status quo* and the willingness of both the state and the minorities to be tolerant. But, in general, the minorities question is certainly less strained than hitherto, and will gradually work itself out on equitable lines, satisfactory to both sides.

adherent to German-Roumanian co-operation. It was also claimed that the Magyars should head the under-secretariat, because they are the strongest minorities party numerically.

PART III

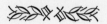

THE CONSTITUTIONAL AND ADMINISTRATIVE SYSTEM OF ROUMANIA

CHAPTER X

CONSTITUTION AND ADMINISTRATION

THE IMPORTANCE OF THE CONSTITUTIONAL DOCUMENT

A PEOPLE'S way of life is profoundly affected by the form and nature of the government under which it lives. With the advancement of a civilization life becomes more and more complex, and man's dependence upon government to maintain equilibrium among continually changing and often bewildering forces becomes more and more pronounced. This is as true of the corner of Europe which is Roumania as it is of other parts of the Western world, perhaps truer there.

The experiment of the Kingdom of Roumania in the art of government possesses that interest which Lord Bryce described:

> Every creation of a new scheme of Government is a precious addition to the political resources of mankind. It represents a survey and scrutiny of the constitutional experience of the past. It embodies an experiment full of instruction for the future.

If we are to understand something of the realities of Roumanian life, we must understand the constitutional development of Roumania; we must learn about her experiment in constitutional forms, her activities in politics.

The creation of the Roumanian Government was a step in the evolution of that country toward political independence; it now carries on the national independent life of the kingdom; and the future prosperity and welfare of the Roumanian people will be largely determined by Roumanian political practices.

The practical politics of Roumania are interesting also from another point of view. The difficulties in the way of building up self-governing institutions there have proved very great indeed. The experiment, a very sudden one, of creating a constitutional monarchy out of the ruins of the despotic Turkish Empire was surely a

highly speculative endeavor. If it has not proved altogether successful according to the views of some observers, it must be remembered
that the price paid has been worth while in terms of the general
situation of today. For, after all, the gradual influence of Western
liberalism on the corner of Europe where Roumania is located has
become constitutionalized, on the basis of nationalism. The striving
for and the belief in national democracy is the most satisfactory
ground on which the whole experiment can be evaluated and appreciated. The work is not completed. We find ourselves today in the
process of the transition. Momentous political development is going
on under our very eyes. To understand it we shall now delve into
its texture, composition, and functioning.

The Constitution of 1866

While the growth of economic capitalism in Western Europe was
followed by the formation of liberal institutions, the Roumanian
constitutional document was adopted under the influence of Western
practice and cleared the way, in its turn, for possible economic reforms—as has been pointed out by Dr. Mitrany. In the heat of
excitement and enthusiasm two of the more radical leaders produced
within twenty-four hours a modified translation of the Belgian Constitution, whereupon the special Constituent Assembly made its own
draft and passed it unanimously on July 12, 1866. It resembled the
Constitution of Belgium more than any other model. With three
modifications, it served Roumania until 1923.

The first modification followed the acceptance of the Treaty of
Berlin in 1878. Article 43 of this treaty proclaimed the independence
of Roumania under certain conditions (Art. 44), and Article 7 of
the Roumanian Constitution was changed to conform to it, giving a
new status to foreign and especially to Jewish inhabitants. The second revision was provoked by the changes made in the form of the
state. The law of March 26, 1884, elevated the country into a kingdom and an enlargement of the basis of the electoral system for
the lower chamber from the existing four-class franchise into a
three-class franchise was carried through.[1] Other modifications, of
secondary importance, concerned the liberty of the press, the recon-
stitution of the Council of the State in regard to disputed administra-

[1] The electoral law was proclaimed on June 21, 1884, and remained in force
for a long time, with important modifications in 1903, 1904, 1906, and 1907.

tive matters, the creation of sub-secretaries, etc. Fundamentally, the influence of the landlords was modified and the middle class given more influence. A third revision was on the way because of the vigorous campaign of the Liberal Party of Brătianu, but was interrupted by the outbreak of the war. Finally, in 1917, the principles of expropriation of private property and universal suffrage were adopted and agrarian reform was made possible.

The Constitution of 1866 was theoretically very liberal. Article 35 (now 39) spoke of the power of the King as being "entrusted" to him, and Article 96 (now 91) declared that "the King has no other powers than those which the Constitution gives him." But the ruler had an absolute and unconditional veto on all legislation. The right of the initiative rested with either the lower house or the senate. The executive power was intrusted to the ruler and his ministers, the latter alone being responsible for the acts of the government. Nine executive departments were created. The bills concerning the strength of the army and the budget had to be first submitted to the house of representatives. The ruler also convened, adjourned, and dissolved the parliament. The inviolability of the domicile and the liberty of the press and of assembly were recognized, while distinction of class and privilege was prohibited. Individual liberty and property were guaranteed. But only Roumanian citizens could acquire property. Military service was made compulsory. Capital punishment existed only for military offenses in time of war. Religious liberty was proclaimed, and "as for the Israelites, a special law is to regulate their gradual admission to citizenship."

The system of electoral colleges nullified effectively any other democratic features of the document. The legislative department was composed of a chamber of deputies of 189 members, elected for four years, and a senate of 120 members, elected for eight years. All citizens of full age and paying taxes were electors and were divided into three colleges: For the chamber of deputies, electors who had a yearly income of at least 1,200 lei per annum from real estate voted in the first college. Those having their domicile or residence in an urban community and paying direct taxes to the state of 20 lei or upwards annually, or being persons engaged in the liberal professions, retired officers, or state pensioners, or who had been through the primary course of education voted in the second college. All other electors voted in the third college; those who had an income of 300 lei or paid a rental of 1,000 lei yearly and could read and write and came from rural lands voted directly, as did also the village priests and schoolmasters. The rest voted indirectly. For each election every 50 indirect electors chose a delegate, and the delegates voted along with the direct electors of the colleges. The first college elected 77 deputies, the second 72, the third only 40.

For the senate there were only two colleges, elected by the large landowners and by the towns. The first college consisted of those electors having property yielding annually at least 80 lei; the second, of those persons whose income from property was from 32 lei to 80 lei per autumn. Of the 110 elected senators, 60 were chosen by the first college and 50 by the second college. The senate had equal powers with the lower house; it could veto any bill and overthrow any government.

For the purposes of local government old Roumania was divided into 17 departments in Wallachia, 13 in Moldavia, and 4 in the Dobrogea, each governed by a prefect nominated by the Minister of the Interior and appointed by the King. The administration was highly centralized and resembled the French system of "arrondissements." The prefects were aided by sub-prefects, each of whom was responsible for maintaining order in a certain number of rural communes.

There were urban and rural boroughs, the administration of which was in the hands of a council and of a "primar" (mayor), elected among its members. The election of the mayor had to be sanctioned by the King, who also had the right to dissolve the departmental councils elected by the inhabitants of the department and divided into three electoral colleges, as in the election of the deputies. It authorized the budget of the department, created, maintained, and improved the departmental organizations, supervised the public works of the department, etc. In the intervals between its sessions the council was represented by three of its members, who formed a departmental commission, who deliberated with the prefect on the measures to be taken for the administration of the department. On certain questions the prefect was obliged to consult them.[2]

Such villages and hamlets as were not seats of municipal councils had village councils, which occupied themselves with the immediate needs of the village and sent a delegate to the municipal council of the larger area. Each Roumanian subject had to be registered in

[2] In July 1918 a scheme of reform of local government was brought in under which Wallachia and Moldavia were divided into 12 instead of 30 departments.

some commune. The municipal councils were elected for a period of four years. The electors in the urban communes were divided into two colleges and in the rural communes formed a single college. Each commune enjoyed autonomy, though an indefinite proviso existed to the effect that the central government must not interfere with it except in the interest of public order and the general good. Practically, the Bucharest government exercised considerable power over the communes. All the more important decisions of the municipal council had to be approved by the general council of the department, by the Minister of the Interior, by the King, or by the Legislature. The importance of the system, however, lay in the fact that the municipal councils formed independent centers of public opinion.

Each commune had its mayor, who represented both the commune and the central government. He presided over the municipal council and executed its decisions and was responsible for public order and for the enforcement of the laws of the country. A secretary of the commune, nominated by the central authority, had charge of the mayor's office and signed all communal documents.

In 1918 the reform program divided the departments into districts ("plăşi"), each under a "pretor," and initiated a greater local autonomy.

The presence of a considerable proportion of alien population in Dobrogea necessitated somewhat different organization there. The general council had twelve members, their names having been submitted by the prefect and nominated by the Ministry of the Interior, and all its decisions had to be approved by the prefect. The municipal councils were also under strict control of the prefect and the Ministry of the Interior.

The Constitution of 1923

The political changes of the World War demanded a profound revision of the old constitution. The old document did not respond to the needs of the new Roumanian state. The newly acquired provinces needed to be incorporated under a uniform legal and political system. Further, the old property qualifications for the senate and chamber of deputies could no longer withstand the gospel of democracy; and, lastly, some of the most influential Roumanian political leaders did not approve of foreign exploitation of the country's mineral resources, especially oil.

The new constitution, promulgated on March 28, 1923,[3] was worked out by the Liberals without the co-operation of other parties. It was voted upon by 257 deputies out of 369, 247 voting for acceptance, 8 against, and 2 being absent. In the senate the vote of March 27 was 137 against 2, with 2 abstentions, out of the total of 194 senators.

The new document did not include everything that the government originally proposed that it should. For instance, the increase of the power of the state officials was not included in the final text. But the international and unsettled internal situation had had a marked influence on its formation.

Roumania is a hereditary constitutional monarchy under the Hohenzollern-Sigmaringen dynasty, in direct legitimate line from King Carol I, the succession passing from male to male in order of primogeniture, to the exclusion of females and their descendants.

A curious aspect of the constitution is to be seen in the official version, which reports the King as declaring when approving the clauses of the document: "I confirm it with my Royal and Constitutional sanctions,"[4] as though it were derived of his grace. The preamble to the text says: "We approve and sanction what follows."[5] And yet Article 33 declares: "All powers of the State emanate from the Nation."[6] But these powers cannot be exercised directly and the means of "delegation" is "according to the principles and regulations laid down in the present Constitution."

The necessary bases of the state, viewed concretely, are its territory and its people. The Roumanian kingdom is declared a national, united, and indivisible state; its territory cannot be alienated, and its boundaries cannot be modified without the passing of a proper law. Historical memories are reflected in the provision which prohibits the colonization of Roumania by people of an alien race. The Roumanian language is the official language of the state. The colors of the Roumanian flag are red, yellow, and blue, arranged vertically.

---

[3] The text can be found in Joseph Delpech and Julien Laferrière, *Les Constitutions modernes*, II, 354 ff.; B. Mirkine-Guetzevitch, *Les Constitutions de l'Europe Nouvelle*, pp. 277 ff.; Roumania, Ministère des Affaires Etrangères, *Constitution* (Bucharest, 1923). *The Near East Year Book, 1927*, pp. 424–39, contains an English translation as does *Current History*, 1923, XVIII, 1017–24, made by Professor A. I. Andrews.

[4] ". . . . je la confirme par ma sanction Royale et Constitutionnelle."

[5] "Nous approuvons et sanctionnons ce qui suit."

[6] "Tous les pouvoirs de l'État émanent de la Nation."

The important problem of administration in the Old Kingdom as different from that of the newly added provinces was staunchly debated by the representatives of the provinces. The principle of centralization was incorporated into the constitution. All laws existing in different parts of the country were to be revised in order to put them in harmony with the constitution, and until then they remained in force. All laws, decrees, rules, and other acts, however, contrary to the new constitution became invalid.[7]

The diversity of the subdivisions of the country was ended. Article 4 of the new constitution divided the state into districts (departments) and communes, on the model of the French political structure, and through them the will of the state is executed.[8] No other economic, political, historical, or cultural divisions of the territory are recognized. Each resident of the country, without distinction of sex or nationality, must appertain to a commune and must declare any change of his domicile. Strangers can establish themselves in a commune only after complying with certain formalities.

The second part of the constitution deals with the rights of Roumanians. There is no special section dealing with the minorities, as, for example, in the case of the Czechoslovak constitution. The Roumanians without distinction as to racial origin, language, or religion enjoy liberty of conscience, instruction, meeting, association, and the press. "Censorship or any other preventive measure against the appearance, sale or distribution of any publication whatsoever may not be established." Derelictions of the press are tried by jury except in the following cases, which are tried by ordinary courts according to the common law: (1) crimes committed against the sovereign of the country, members of the royal family, heads of foreign states and their representatives; (2) direct instigations to murder and rebellion if they have not been already followed up with their execution; (3) and slanders, abuse, defamations directed against private individuals or public officials of whatever character, attacking their life or their personal honor. The last provision seems to be of an especially conservative character in view of the fact that the executive branch of the government can thus muzzle all accusations directed against its officials.

These rights can be enjoyed only by the Roumanians, all of

[7] Article 137.

[8] The form was provided by the administrative law of June 13, 1925, published in *Monitorul oficial* on June 14, 1925.

whom are equal before the law and are under obligation to contribute without distinction of racial origin, of language, or of religion to the taxes and public charges. Aliens enjoy the protection "given by the law to persons and property in general," and are admitted to public offices only in exceptional cases.

The first victory was won by the Roumanian women when woman suffrage was included in the constitution in Article 6. But this was no more than a recognition of the principle, and no date was set for the actual enfranchisement. Even today their vote is limited to municipal elections. This vote is extended to women of twenty-one years who have met the required educational test, namely, a four years' course at the lycée, but every mother of three children, irrespective of education, is entitled to vote, and every war widow.[9]

The process of naturalization is difficult. It is accorded individually by the Council of Ministers after certain requirements have been fulfilled and investigated by a commission composed of the Prime Minister and the presidents of the Court of Appeal. Naturalization cannot be made retroactive, and the wife and minor children also profit by the process, though not the adult children. No privileges, immunities, or class monopolies are recognized and titles of nobility remain inadmissible.

Individual liberty is guaranteed and no one may be prosecuted and searched except in accordance with the forms provided by law. Persons can be arrested only by virtue of judicial decrees, and such decrees must be communicated to them within twenty-four hours if arrested in cases of *flagrante delicto*.

The right of domicile is inviolable and the law proscribed a visitation. Punishment must be based on law, but the penalty of confiscation of property must not be created. The penalty of death, abolished by the old constitution, cannot be re-established except by the military codes in time of war.

The right of property is guaranteed. The old constitution allowed the expropriation of the land only for the making of roads, of works of defense, and for reasons of public health. In 1917 the

---

[9] The first general municipal elections in Roumania with women participating were held under the National-Peasant Government. Article 108 provides that "members of District Councils and of Communal Councils are elected by Roumanian citizens, by universal, equal, direct, secret, compulsory vote, and with representation of minorities according to forms provided by law. To these councils may be added, by law, members ex officio and members chosen by co-optation. Among the members thus co-opted may likewise be women of legal age."

principle of wholesale expropriation of the large estates against compensation was passed and a limit of landholding fixed. Article 131 confirms the series of laws executing it.[10] To check any further radical proposals, Article 17 makes a stipulation that any other laws of this kind must be voted by a two-thirds majority, and limits expropriation to cases of public utility, public health, extension of communications, national defense, and, where in the direct interests of the state, the army, public administration, and culture. The courts decide on indemnity in case of appeals.

The ancient fear of foreign domination appears in Article 18 allowing only Roumanians to acquire rural landed property. Foreigners retain the right to the value of such landed property only.

Foreign interest centered in the nationalization provisions for the subsoil and its effect on the prospect of oil companies. The provision here is somewhat vague in its application. It is not really "socialization," for the government has no intention of running the mines as a state service; nor is it "nationalization" in a political sense, because in Roumania land cannot and could not be owned by foreigners. It approximates state socialism, however, and we shall quote it in view of its importance:

Mineral deposits as well as the wealth of whatever nature in the sub-soil are the property of the State. Excepted are masses of rocks suitable for building material and deposits of peat, if not in conflict with the rights acquired by the State by virtue of previous laws. A special law on mines shall determine rules and conditions for the valuation of this property, shall fix rent due to the proprietor of the surface land and shall indicate at the same time the extent and manner of his participation in the exploitation of such mineral wealth. Account shall be taken of acquired rights in so far as they correspond to putting a valuation on the sub-soil, and according to these privileges, which shall be made in a special law. Mining concessions for exploitation already instituted or given, conforming to the laws today in force, shall be respected during the period for which they were granted, and the existing mining exploitations shall be made for the proprietors only for the time when they shall work them. No perpetual concessions may be made.

The concessions and exploitations could, at that time, be allowed the maximum duration of fifty years.[11]

The public domain is composed of channels of communication,

[10] The laws for the agrarian reform in: Oltenia, Muntenia, Moldavia, and the Dobrogea (the Old Kingdom) of July 17, 1921; Bessarabia, March 13, 1921; Transylvania, the Banat, Crișana, Maramureș, July 30, 1921; Bukovina, July 30, 1921.

[11] From 1923 to 1973, that is, from the date of the promulgation of the constitution.

atmospheric space, and navigable or floatable streams and waters producing water power and those which can be utilized in the public interest. These also can be expropriated for the purpose of public utility, as well as forests in certain cases.

While liberty of conscience is absolute, the relations of the state with the Christian Orthodox and the Greek Catholic church make the first the dominant church in Roumania and give the second first rank over any other form. They are financed by the state. Civil acts take precedence of religious sanctions, despite the importance attributed to organized religion in Roumania.

Education is free.[12] Primary education is obligatory.

The courts of justice may make exceptions in the case of the guaranteed secrecy of written correspondence, telegrams, and telephone conversations.

The vague statement that "Roumanians without distinction as to racial origin, language or religion have the right to meet together peaceably and without arms as long as they conform to the laws which regulate the exercise of this right, in order to discuss every sort of question," may be effectively nullified by the provision enabling the police power to regulate "meetings, processions and demonstrations on the streets and public squares." A reference is made to the possible establishing of corporate bodies of minorities, which are prohibited, though the minorities may form associations. Another prohibition in the same direction provides that "none but constituted authorities have the right to address petitions in the collective name."

A practical application of Article 31 providing that "no prior authorization is needed for the bringing of suits by the injured parties against public officials for acts of their administration" is of little value. Recourse must be had to the penal code, which says that an executive agent is not responsible for an abuse of authority committed by order, but that responsibility rests altogether with the superior authority which may have issued the order.[13] Consequently, the minister in charge would have to be prosecuted in political cases and impeached by a two-thirds majority of the parliament.[14]

---

[12] There is of course the customary provision in regard to the free exercise of religion and education "unless their exercise affects public order, good morals or the laws of State organization."

[13] See D. Mitrany, "The New Roumanian Constitution," in *Journal of Comparative Legislation and International Law*, 1924, p. 117.   [14] Article 98.

The only check, then, is the principle of ministerial responsibility. Another effective nullification of civil and political rights can be materialized from Article 128, which allows that "in case of danger to the State, there may be constituted by law a state of siege, general or partial." As the government has always controlled the parliament, it can easily secure the passage of a law creating the state of siege. The interpretation of "in case of danger to the State" can evidently be stretched pretty far.

One of the most important duties of the male Roumanian citizen, without any distinction whatsoever, is universal military service in force for every male Roumanian from the ages of 21 to 50.[15] Out of this period two years are spent in the army (or three years in the navy), 18 (17) years in the reserve, and nine years in the militia. Upon completing 19 years of age young men are at the disposal of the war office and are liable to be called for preparatory training.

Like other constitutions of recent years, the Roumanian Constitution divides the powers of the state into legislative, executive, and judicial.

The legislative power is exercised collectively by the King and the parliament, divided into the senate and the chamber of deputies. Every law needs the approval of these three branches of the legislative power, and each of them has the power of initiation. However, the laws relating to the budget or to state revenues and expenditures or to the armed forces must be voted first by the lower house. All laws are promulgated by the Ministry of Justice.

Bills are voted upon article by article and are passed by an absolute majority in each house. An equality of votes rejects the proposition.

The rules concerning the membership of both houses resemble,

---

[15] For detailed figures and data, see the League of Nations Publications, *Armaments Year Book*. The following categories of Roumanians are debarred from military service: (1) persons who have been sentenced for crime; (2) persons who have been sentenced by a court of law to more than two years' imprisonment; (3) persons who, as the result of a sentence, have forfeited the right to bear arms or serve in the Army. There are of course certain exemptions: young men who are disabled or physically unfit are exempt; postponement of service may be obtained for a period not exceeding two years, on account of under-developed physique; young men completing their education may, on application, obtain postponement up to 27 years of age. Only sons, legitimate or adopted, or oldest sons who are the sole support of poor families, are provisionally exempted and placed in the militia. Young men between 18 and 21 may enlist as volunteers for a period of not less than three years.

on the whole, those found in all other European parliaments. Each member of the chambers has the right to address interpellations to the ministers, to which they must respond. Members of legislative bodies are elected for four years.

In 1917 the Iași Parliament adopted "universal, direct, equal, secret and compulsory franchise with proportional representation." Article 64 now replaces "proportional" by "minority" representation. The elections of 387 deputies take place by lists from electoral constituencies in proportion to population. The following qualifications are necessary for an eligible deputy: Roumanian citizenship; the right to exercise civil and political rights; minimum age twenty-five years; a domicile in Roumania.

The senate composition and powers are of the most conservative character. While the new democracies after the war, e.g., Finland, Estonia, Latvia, Lithuania, Yugoslavia, Turkey, and Bulgaria, experiment in the unicameral methods, and others, e.g., Czechoslovakia, Germany, Austria, and Poland, subordinate the upper house to the lower chamber, Roumania not only allows equal legislative powers to the senate but its membership does not always reflect the popular will and provides an unrepresentative basis of membership.

The senate is composed of elected senators and senators by right (*de drept*). Of the senators, 113 are elected by constituencies and 91 by colleges, as follows: (1) 113 senators are elected by direct obligatory vote of citizens above forty years of age from electoral districts and counties returning at least two senators in this category. (2) Seventy-three are elected by a college made up of members elected by the urban and rural municipal councils, by the county councils, and by the chambers of agriculture, commerce, and industry; the members of these chambers gather in separate colleges, and elect one of their members as senator for each of the categories named above and for each electoral division. (3) Four senators are elected for each university (Bucharest, Iași, Cluj, Cernăuți) by the votes of professors. (4) The chambers of commerce of Bucharest, Iași, Galați, and Cluj each elect one senator. The agricultural chambers of Bucharest, Iași, Galați, and Cluj also elect one senator for each of these electoral districts.

Among life senators are included: the heir apparent, when eighteen years of age, who, however, has only a deliberative voice until he is twenty-five years of age; the Patriarch; five Orthodox and Graeco-Catholic metropolitans; seventeen diocesan bishops of the

Orthodox and Graeco-Catholic churches; the High Mufti of the Mohammedan faith; the Chief Rabbi of the Mosaic faith; and the president of the Roumanian Academy.

In addition, there are numerous *ex-officio* senators: former prime ministers of four years in office; former cabinet ministers who have held office in one or more governments for a total of at least six years; former presidents of the legislative assemblies of eight sessions' standing; former deputies and senators who have been in ten parliaments of any length; former first presidents of the High Court of Cassation and Justice of five years' standing; retired generals and generals of reserve who have commanded an army in the face of the enemy during the World War for at least three months or who have been either chiefs of the general staff or inspector-generals of the army in peace time for at least four years; the former presidents of the National Assemblies of Chişinău, Cernăuţi, and Alba-Iulia; and the first president of the first parliament of Greater Roumania.

This composition of the senate effectively excludes the new peasant electorate. Dr. Mitrany calls it "a formidable gathering of professional vested interests."

The same qualifications as those for the deputies are required for the senators, with the exception of the age limit, which is raised to 40.

A legislative novelty and an unusual feature of the legislative procedure is the legislative council, which aids in a consultative way in framing and co-ordinating laws emanating from either the government or the parliament. It also draws up general rules for the application of the laws. With the exception of budgetary credits all bills must be submitted to the legislative council, which must give its opinion within a certain time.[16] It is an adjunct of the Ministry of Justice. Among its numerous duties are that of examining codes, laws, decrees, and ordinances and their application and that of drawing the attention of the executive and legislative bodies to the need of their modification or abrogation. Its membership is permanent and is nominated by the Minister of Justice, except that temporary members are appointed for occasional collaboration and as *rapporteurs* to conduct research. The council is divided into three

[16] I. C. Filotti and G. Vrabiesco, "Le Conseil législatif de Roumanie," in *Revue des Sciences Politiques*, 1929, LII, 481–98.

sections: the first has its competence in the domain of public and general, constitutional, and administrative law; the second, in the field of private, civil, and commercial law, the code of procedure, private international law, and the uniformization of the codes; while the third has under its jurisdiction social, economic, and financial problems. The bureau is administered by a general secretary.

The executive power is vested in the King and the ministers. The King reaches his majority at the age of 18 years and takes the following oath: "I swear to observe the Constitution and the laws of the Roumanian people, to maintain their national rights and the integrity of their territory."[17] His person is inviolable and each of his acts must be countersigned by a minister, who thus assumes responsibility for the signed act. During the interregnum period the constitutional powers of the King are exercised by the ministers in the name of the Roumanian people.

The list of powers of the King is very long, surpassing by far those of the Belgian King. He appoints and dismisses his ministers. As the elections have been held until now by the Cabinet appointed by the King and have been won by the same government, the King can regulate and control the trend of parliamentary action. He can veto or sanction any law and has the right of amnesty with the exception of criminal cases against ministers. He appoints and confirms to public offices, though a special law is needed for the creation of any new office. All necessary regulations for the execution of the laws are made by him, but he cannot suspend or modify them nor authorize exemptions from them. He is the head of the armed forces and confers military ranks. He confers decorations and has the right to coin money. He concludes foreign conventions, which, in order to have full authority, are to be submitted to parliament.

The parliament gathers on October 15 of each year without convocation, unless it has been convoked by the King in advance; he opens each session by a message. He has the right to close the session, convoke an extraordinary session, and dissolve both chambers, simultaneously or separately. In the case of dissolution, the convocation of the electors must take place within two months and that of the chamber in three months. Prorogation of the chambers

---

[17] Article 79 makes a provision in case of the vacancy of the Throne. Article 83 created a regency council. This became inoperative in view of the fact that King Carol II took the place of his minor son in June 1930.

may not exceed one month and cannot be renewed in the same session without the consent of the chambers.

Thus there is no little rhetoric in the paragraph of the constitution which reads as follows: "The King has only those powers granted to him by the Constitution."

The ministers exercise the executive power in the name of the King. Collectively they compose the Council of Ministers, presided over by the president of the Council of Ministers, who is intrusted by the King to form his Government. The members of the royal family cannot become members of the Cabinet.

The ministers who are not members of the parliament may take part in the debates, but cannot vote. One minister at least must be present at each session of the chambers, and the presence of ministers at its deliberations can be demanded by either of the chambers.

The King and the chambers can impeach the ministers by a two-thirds majority vote of the members present and can arraign them before the High Court of Cassation, which tries them in full bench.[18] Indictments are drawn up for commission to the High Court of Cassation, composed of five members, which decides as to prosecution.

A doctrine of administrative jurisdiction is little known in England and the United States and in countries generally where English legal institutions have been introduced. The English and American doctrine is that all legal controversies must be decided by the ordinary judicial courts. Just as in France, Germany, and a goodly number of other continental European countries, there exists in the Roumanian constitution a provision creating the right of any party injured by a decree or by an order signed or countersigned by a minister, which violates a precise reading of the constitution or of any law, to sue for money damages for the prejudice caused.

The judicial system of Roumania is headed by the High Court of Cassation and Justice. It alone has the right, all sections united, to judge the constitutionality of laws and to declare inapplicable those which are contrary to the constitution; the decision is limited to the suit at litigation. The Roumanian Constitution of 1866 made no provision for the settlement of a conflict between the constitution and an ordinary law. This gave rise to various differences of opinion

---

[18] Except as to the exercise of civil action by the injured party, and except in criminal acts and offenses committed outside of the exercise of the ministerial functions.

as to whether or not the courts could deny the application of a law which contradicted the constitution.[19] By the Constitution of 1923 the question has been definitely settled. Notice, however, that in the case of Roumania the Court of Cassation cannot render a decision upon request of the government in a hypothetical case. Furthermore, the interpretation of the laws with the force of authority is made solely by the legislative power,[20] and the judicial power has not the authority of reviewing the acts of the government nor those of a command of a military character.[21]

Judges are irremovable. Commissions and extraordinary tribunals cannot be especially created. Jury trial is guaranteed in all criminal cases and for political offenses, with the exceptions noted above.

The Chamber of Deputies each year votes the budget and settles the accounts. If the budget is not voted at the proper time, the government has the right to provide for the public services according to the budget of the preceding year, but can do so for only one year. The receipts and expenditures of the state are controlled by the Court of Accounts, which reports regularly to the Chamber of Deputies. No special privileges or exemptions as to taxation are allowed; pensions and gratuities must be granted by a law.

The matter of armed forces has already been partly described. The contingents for the army are voted each year by the parliament. A Supreme Council of National Defense is created for the organization of the national defense. Foreign troops cannot be employed by the state, and a special law must be passed to allow entrance to or crossing of the Roumanian territory by foreign armed forces.

The process of revision and amendment is truly a cumbersome affair in Roumania. A proposal may emanate from the King or either of the houses. The two chambers then meet and separately decide, by absolute majority, whether or not such amendment is

[19] See J. W. Garner, *Political Science and Government* (New York, 1928), p. 763 and note 1. Professor Garner points out that "under the former constitution of Roumania the courts without express constitutional authority asserted and exercised the right to pronounce upon the question of unconstitutionality and to refuse to apply acts of the legislature which were found to be in violation of the constitution," and draws attention to a decision of the Court of Cassation of March 16, 1912, discussed in the *Revue du Droit Public,* 1913, pp. 153, 365.

[20] Article 36.

[21] Article 107.

necessary. If they agree that it is, a mixed commission is chosen from among their members, and this body proposes the actual text. The text is read in each chamber twice and with an interval of fifteen days; then both chambers meet, and, two-thirds of the total membership being present, they decide by a two-thirds majority on the final form of revision. Upon this the chambers are dissolved and elections take place. The new chambers, in agreement with the King, proceed to review the points submitted for revision. For this constitutional work the chambers need a quorum of two-thirds, and acceptance of proposals requires a two-thirds majority.

CRITICISM AND SUMMARY

The Roumanian Constitution of 1923 was needed in order to adjust the fundamental document of the country to the enlarged territory, and may be considered virtually new. The most fundamental changes were the incorporation of the acquired provinces under a uniform legal and political system and the establishment of universal suffrage and agrarian reforms with relative finality. The new document consists of 138 articles and is based in general upon European models.

The constitution is a curious mixture of most democratic and extremely conservative provisions. While the composition of the senate may be called reactionary because it fails to express and correspond to the popular will of the electorate at a given moment, the incorporation of "universal, equal, direct, secret, compulsory vote," with representation of minorities, equals the most advanced provisions of any democratic document. The length of the constitution is noticeable; yet a great number of principles are left to be defined and elaborated by subsequent laws, making the fundamental law very flexible in political exigencies. Such is its flexibility that it may be interpreted as either the friend or the enemy of popular government, and even the legislation which grew out of it prior to the advent of the National-Peasant Party, particularly the electoral law, was calculated to perpetuate a strongly centralized administration from which, indeed, the masses might receive benefits but only such as would enhance those of the government. Now, much of this legislation, notably the electoral law, has been turned against those who brought it into being.

Furthermore, strict control over foreign relations is omitted and the practice here corresponds to that of Great Britain, where this power is exclusively in the hands of the executive, parliament having some share only where legislation may be necessary to perfect the treaty or carry it into effect.

In contrast to the old document, the new constitution gained much "at the expense of former elusive idealism." Its centralizing tendency was severely criticized by the politicians of the new provinces. It entirely disregarded regional interests and the principles of various national pacts of the Union, although they had been recognized by the King as constitutional acts. Considered from the standpoint of concentration and distribution of power and the relation between the central and local authorities, the Roumanian Constitution of 1923 provided for a unitary system, the administrative sections being based largely upon French models. For convenience of administration, Roumania was in fact subdivided into districts, cantons, and communes, with their spheres of autonomy and restricted powers, but their power is delegated to them by the central government and may be freely enlarged and contracted by it. However, the reform of the National-Peasant Party tended to correct the system in favor of decentralization.

One of the most serious problems of the adjustment of territories left to Roumania is the problem of minorities. How are the rights of these minorities groups to be secured? What can political constitutionalism do for them in Roumania? While the peace treaties guaranteed the rights of the minorities, they left to the constitution-makers the provision of methods whereby the guaranties would be implemented. The device coming nearest to helping a solution was the system of minority representation. While other constitutions, like that of Czechoslovakia, granted their rights integrally in a special section of the constitution, the Roumanian constitution established the principle of equality of "Roumanians, without distinction as to racial origin, language, or religion," who vote on the basis of "minority representation," a system which in one way or another has been adopted in nearly all the newly adopted constitutions. J. W. Garner concludes that "it may now be said that in some form or degree the system is in force in every European country."[22] How-

---

[22] J. W. Garner, *Political Science and Government,* p. 652 (see also pp. 648–55); W. W. Willoughby and L. Rogers, *An Introduction to the Problem of Government* (New York, 1927), pp. 173–77; C. F. Strong, *Modern Political Constitutions* (New York, 1930), pp. 178–86; M. W. Graham, *New Governments of Central*

ever, the system is still too definitely in its experimental stage to warrant a definite judgment.

The relation of the executive power to the legislative organs has been always a difficult problem in constitutional systems. The separation-of-powers principle is one of the foremost tenets of modern governments, and is carried in some states about as far as possible, especially in the United States. While the makers of the Roumanian constitution followed theoretically the same precept, actually the executive branches of the Roumanian Government, that is, the King and the ministers, have controlled the work of legislation to a remarkable degree, doing so by extra-constitutional devices.

The senate of Roumania exhibits only two points of inequality in respect to the lower chamber. As in the United States, France, England, and several Latin-American countries, financial legislation must be first voted by the lower chamber, as well as the provisions for the armed forces of the country.

The power of the King is expressed in terms similar to that of the King of Belgium, where the Crown plays a more important part than in England; but practically it comes near to the powers of the former Spanish King and resembles closely the strength of the German Emperor before the war in reference to the imperial cabinet.

The practice of judicial review of the constitutionality of laws in such states as the United States, Germany, Austria, Czechoslovakia, Norway, Greece, and others was incorporated in the Roumanian constitution; administrative courts of the type created in France and Germany, a system little known in the United States and England, are also functioning in Roumania.

The novelty of the legislative council has some resemblance to the German economic council, which, like its Roumanian prototype, examines all drafts of social and economic laws, though the Roumanian counterpart has wider powers and basis of action. It is not unlike the Grand Council of Fascismo in Italy.

The amendment process of the Roumanian constitution theoretically stands at the other end of the line from the system used by Great Britain, France, and Italy and is nearly as inflexible as that of the United States. Practically, the Roumanian constitution can be classified from the standpoint of its application as a written, flexible

Europe (New York, 1926), and *New Governments of Eastern Europe* (New York, 1927); and others cited by these authorities.

Chişinău, Bessarabia

Oradea-Mare, Transylvania

constitution, creating a constitutional monarchy based on democratic principles, with a unitary form of government and a cabinet system responsible to the Crown and the legislature.[23]

THE ADMINISTRATIVE MACHINERY

The administrative machinery of France served as the model for the governmental structure of Roumania.[24] The executive power is exercised directly and in the name of the King by the ministers, presided over by the Prime Minister. The number of the ministries was reduced by Maniu's Government. The previous cabinets had the following posts: Interior; Foreign Affairs; Finance; War; Industry and Commerce; Agriculture and Public Domains; Communications; Justice; Public Works; Public Instruction; Religion and Arts; Public Health, Labor and Social Insurance; and special Ministries for Bessarabia, Bukovina, Transylvania, and Minorities.

Each ministry is composed of a number of bureaus under the direction of a *chef-de-bureau*. They study the facts and inform the minister, prepare decisions and decrees, and direct technical and accounting questions. Several bureaus are grouped under a director, who executes the orders of the minister and signs the documents. Above them is a general secretary who decides all the questions not reserved to either the minister or the director and signs the documents in the name of the minister if so authorized by a notice in the official journal.

Ministers are also advised by counsellors and commissions who assist the minister in special questions. Thus, for instance, there exists the Supreme Council of National Defense as the permanent authority for insuring the organization of national defense. Article 100 of the constitution creates the under-secretaries of state who may take part in the debates of the legislative assemblies on the responsibility of their ministers.

The home police is under the Ministry of the Interior, which has a gendarmerie corps, recruited from the regular army, at its dis-

[23] The constitution of Roumania is being continually supplemented and implemented by new laws, like the administrative law of June 13, 1925, the mining laws of July 4, 1924, and March 4, 1929, etc., which are cited throughout this volume.

[24] The following summary is taken mainly from C. G. Rommenhoeller, *La Grande-Roumanie,* pp. 30 ff., and R. Boila, "Die Verfassung und Verwaltung Rumäniens Seit dem Weltkriege," in *Jahrbuch des Öffentlichen Rechts der Gegenwart,* 1930, XVIII, 324–54.

posal. These forces are distributed throughout the country, their duty being to maintain public order. While receiving their instructions in the first instance from the Ministry of the Interior and being directly subordinate to it, they collaborate with the executive authorities and are responsible for carrying out the orders of the War Office in localities in which there is no military garrison. The Ministry of Finance has at its disposal a corps of frontier guards.

The position of civil servants was not regulated before 1923 in a uniform way.[25] Certain officials, such as civil engineers, teachers, and doctors, were free in a varying degree from removal. The law of June 19, 1923, was passed within the shadow of a general strike of civil servants and settled the legal situation in so far as recruitment, promotion, and retirement are concerned.[26] Public officials must pass an entrance examination one year after assuming the duties of office.[27] There are two classes of "stability" civil servants. Those in one group can be transferred in the interest of the service by higher authorities with the approval of the commission on appointments and promotion; others are immune from removal and cannot be transferred without their consent even by way of promotion.

Under the administrative law of June 13, 1925, which organized and unified the administration of the country, the territory was divided into 72 districts (*judeţele*) and the districts into communes. For purposes of effective administration, the districts were subdivided into "preturi" (cantons).

Summarizing, then, the authorities representing the state in the country are: (1) the prefects in the districts; (2) the sub-prefects as substitutes; (3) the "pretors" in the cantons; (4) the notaries in the rural communes; and (5) the police as the executive arm.

A prefect is appointed by a royal decree on the nomination of the Minister of the Interior. He must be over 30 years of age and must have a graduate diploma from a higher institution of learning recog-

---

[25] See P. Negulesco, "The Roumanian Civil Service," in L. D. White, editor, *The Civil Service in the Modern State*, pp. 341–60.

[26] The necessity of drawing up a general law for the public service was recognized by Article 131 of the Constitution of July 1, 1866, but was not enacted until June 19, 1923, under the aegis of the new Constitution of 1923, though that constitution contains no provision on this subject.

[27] So far the government of Roumania has not organized a system of professional training for public officials, but in October 1928 the institute of administrative sciences was founded.

nized by the state; while holding his appointment he cannot perform other public functions or follow other professions.

As the representative of the central power in the district, he communicates with all the ministries. He also executes all the decisions of the subordinate representative bodies and with them supervises the administration of the districts and communes, with the exception of the urban communes. He is chief of the police of the district. In general, nearly everything happening in his jurisdiction comes under his observation. Twice a year he summons a conference, which discusses the local problems, and at the end of the year he sends a report to the Minister of the Interior and publishes a report, detailing the financial, economic, cultural, and administrative situation of the district and the communes.

In each district there is formed the council of the prefecture, presided over by the prefect, and composed of the administrative personalities of the district and the representatives of the Ministry of Industry, Commerce, and Work, which meets once a month or oftener. Its duty is to harmonize different administrative services of the district and to abolish the difficulties resulting from the application of laws and ordinances. When an accord is impossible, the prefect reports to the ministry concerned.

The sub-prefect is nominated by a royal decree. He assists the prefect and takes his place in his absence, and is also in charge of the judiciary police.

District and communal councils are elected by universal, equal, direct, secret, compulsory vote, in which women of legal age share. Minorities also are represented. Three-fifths of the members are elected and two-fifths are nominated according to a special law. The size of the membership depends on the population of the commune.

The mayor and from two to nine members of the communal council form a permanent representative body, which takes care of the budget, the setting up of the electoral lists, inspections of the communal institutions, etc. The mayor executes the decisions of the council, is the chief of the municipal police, presides over the sessions, and represents the commune in general.

The notary is an agent of the central authority, the chief of the administrative police in the village communes, and an officer of the judiciary police; he receives complaints about the infractions of the laws, and represents the mayor in general, except in the marriage ceremony. Large communes have secretaries for the notary.

In municipalities the notary participates in the sessions of the municipal councils, but does not vote.

District councils are composed, like municipal councils, of elected and nominated members, and meet on October 1 and March 1 of each year, more frequently if necessary. The sessions last from 10 to 15 days in the presence of the prefect. The members are not paid for their services.

This body forms five commissions (administration, finances, and control; public works; economic; public instruction and religion; sanitation). The *rapporteurs* of these commissions form the permanent representative body of the district under the presidency of the prefect. It has various functions, like those of surveying the administration of the district, controlling the communes, approving the decisions of the municipal councils, and hearing appeals. It is a consultative organ of the prefect, and can be suspended or dismissed just like the permanent representatives of the communes.

All these representative bodies are elected by the Roumanian citizens over twenty-one years of age who fulfill the legal requirements and have their domicile in the district or the commune. For election to these offices the requirements are the same, in addition to those of a minimum age of twenty-five and the ability to read and write. Election cannot be refused. The elections take place every eight years; one-third of the members of the council retire every four years.

The canton is in charge of the pretor, appointed and having the same duties, in general, as the prefect, who can delegate to him some of his powers. Every two months he assembles the mayor, the notaries, and other special employees for discussions of questions of general interest, and reports to the prefect.

The Reorganization of the Governmental Structure by the National-Peasant Government

With the coming into power of the National-Peasant Party in 1928, both central and local administration underwent a reconstituting which, as described by Professor R. A. Egger of Princeton, "for comprehensiveness and thoroughness, is unprecedented in recent reform movements."[28]

---

[28] R. A. Egger, "Administrative Reorganization in Roumania," in *National Municipal Review*, 1930, XIX, 724–25; see also D. Mitrany, "Democracy in the

The number of ministries was reduced to ten. Only the following have been retained: Interior, Foreign Affairs, Finance, Justice, Education and Cults, War, Agriculture and Domains, Industry and Commerce, Public Works and Labor, Health and Social Welfare. The ministries were subdivided into directorates, services, sections, and offices. By defining the powers and the responsibilities of functionaries the administrative procedure was simplified.[29] Duplication of functions and functionaries was to be eliminated. So far Roumania has been employing in its government approximately three per cent of the country's population.[30] All administrative commissions were abrogated and their functions reconsigned to the appropriate ministries.

The presidency of the Council of Ministries was created to coordinate the work of all other ministerial offices. The ministries were reorganized in their internal structure and divided into directorates, the directorates into services, the services into sections, and the sections into bureaus. A permanent disciplinary commission, attached to the presidency of the council, was to control the administration force.

The radical reorganization of local government was called by Dr. Mitrany "perhaps the most important act of the new Roumanian Government."[31] The creation of the rural commune by the law of 1925, governed by the representatives of villages, seemed to be artificial and unsuited for the purposes of local administration under the new National-Peasant Government. A new law for the reorganization of local administration was promulgated on August 3, 1929, based on the principles of decentralization and local autonomy.

The kingdom is now divided into seven provincial directorates

Villages," in *Manchester Guardian*, November 28, 1929, p. 17; J. S. Rouček, "Reorganization of the Governmental Structure in Roumania," in *American Political Science Review*, 1931, XXV, 700–703; *Roumania*, 1930, IV, 51–52; *ibid.*, October, 1929, p. 75; *Near East and India*, 1929, XXXVI, 100; and R. Boila, "Die Verfassung und Verwaltung Rumäniens Seit dem Weltkriege," in *Jahrbuch des Öffentlichen Rechts der Gegenwart*, 1930, XVIII, 346 ff.

[29] The reform does not extend to minor officials or those not exercising considerable discretionary authority.

[30] R. A. Egger, *op. cit.*, gives other figures for several countries: Bulgaria, 2.2; Switzerland, 1.7; Poland, 1.5; Holland, 1.1; Italy, 0.53; Prussia, 0.42; Japan, 0.16.

[31] D. Mitrany, "Democracy in the Villages," in *Manchester Guardian*, November 28, 1929, p. 17.

for administrative purposes, viz., Muntenia, Moldavia, Oltenia, Transylvania, Bukovina, the Banat, and Bessarabia. Each region is headed by an administrative director representing the government, who has the rank of under-secretary of state. These directors severally reside at Bucharest, Cernăuţi, Chişinău, Cluj, Craiova, Iaşi, and Timişoara.

Each directorate comprises seven departments corresponding to the Ministries of the Interior, Finance, Education and Cults, Agriculture and Public Domains, Public Works and Communications, Industry and Commerce, and Labor, Health and Social Welfare. The departmental heads are set up by these ministries but are subordinated to the directors. Together with the elected delegations of the county councils and municipalities, they all form an administrative council, called the local ministerial directorate, which guides and co-ordinates the whole administrative activity of the territory. Thus the executive organs from the central government are closely intertwined with the local elected bodies arising from the village.

Fundamentally, the smallest administrative unit recognized by law is the commune. Groups of communes form counties. The rural commune is considered an association of villages, but each village has its own administrative machinery. Each village is free to decide whether or not it wants a council or to discuss the affairs of the village in an informal assembly. The villages are represented through their mayors or their deputies in the communal council and its permanent delegation.

There are urban communes (towns and municipalities) and rural communes, 14,744 in all, divided into 16 municipalities, 154 urban communes, 116 sub-urban, 4,802 rural (having village councils), and 9,387 small administrative units. The rural commune is administered by a communal council with a delegation as the executive body, the mayor being the president of the communal council. The village mayors act as deputies of the communal mayor. The urban commune is administered by a deliberative communal council. Here the councillors are either elected or *ex officio*. The mayors of the urban communes must be elected from among the elected councillors. Municipalities do not form an integral part of the county in which they are situated but are granted county status. The communes are divided into sectors for administrative purposes.

Above the commune is the "judeţe" (county). Several communes form a county. The country is divided into 72 counties, administered by county councils, composed of the *ex officio* members and those elected by universal and secret vote in the same way as the communal council. The executive body of the county council is a permanent delegation of four members of the council. The chairman of this delegation is the administrative head of the county, while the prefect is only the government's representative of the head of the county, whose powers are those of general oversight and surveillance. The prefect also controls the county police. Administratively, the counties, like the communes and sectors, enjoy full juridical status.

Corresponding with the areas of the seven ministerial directorates are seven regions of administration, or districts. The council of the general association of departments, as the regions are designated, is the regional legislature, and is composed of the representatives of county councils and municipalities. It deals with those problems which are of common interest and importance throughout the region. The administration proper is headed by the president, two vice-presidents and a secretary, with additional personnel as needed. The functions of the region are unlimited and it is, in the eyes of the law, a juridic person. At the headquarters of each directorate is a local revision committee (the one in Bucharest being known as the central revision committee), which reviews, revises, and controls the acts and decisions of the local bodies. The other organs exercising the administrative control are the prefects, the ministerial directors, and the Ministry of the Interior. The whole system began to function as of January 1 (3), 1930.[31a]

The law was violently opposed by the Liberals. It was argued that the measure was unconstitutional in view of Article 1 of the constitution, which proclaims the kingdom "a national State, united and indivisible." Professor Egger points out that "except for the absence of functional definition and limitation, the law is not appreciably dissimilar in its basic idea to the recently proposed Regional District Act of New Jersey."[32]

[31a] The Government of Iorga abrogated this Administrative Reform Act of 1929, which is to be replaced by a new law with more centralistic tendencies but easier of application, especially because of economic reasons.

[32] The City of Bucharest is divided for administrative purposes into four sectors, each having a council headed by a mayor; delegates of the four councils form the municipal council of the city.

The Judiciary

Roumania bears in its legal system the distinct traces of Roman law as well as Slavic influences. These basic ingredients have subsequently been molded by the historical development. The next important advance was made in the period of Russian protectorate over Roumania from 1828 to 1856. Petty courts were then established and magistrates were made irremovable. The present legal system began to take form during the time of the union of the principalities in 1859. The Code Napoleon and the French Penal Code were adapted to Roumanian conditions.

The present judicial system was unified in 1925. The magistrates' courts and the tribunals (district courts) are the courts of the first instance, and the courts of appeal those of the second instance. The whole system is headed by the High Court of Cassation and Justice, which insures uniformity in the interpretation of laws. It is not a supreme court of appeal in the usual sense, because its function is limited to the cassation or annulment of the decisions of the lower courts, which have wrongly interpreted the law.

The judicial system of Roumania is composed of the following courts: 512 "judecătorii" (magistrates' courts), one being located in every town and in certain of the large villages; 72 district courts, one located in the capital of each county;[33] 12 courts of appeal, one or more each in Bucharest, Craiova, Iași, Galați, Constanța, Chișinău, and Cernăuți.

The judges are appointed by the Ministry of Justice. They must possess the degree of "licenciate-at-law,"[34] and must pass an examination after a certain period. They are irremovable.

The magistrates' courts, composed of a judge and a deputy-judge, have jurisdiction in civil and commercial controversies where the amount involved is less than 50,000 lei, and in criminal cases where the offense is a minor one, with the right of appeal to the district court. In the villages the magistrate has the powers of a public prosecutor.

Next come district courts, consisting of one or several sections, each section having a president, two judges, and a deputy-judge. They hear appeals from the decisions of the magistrates' courts, and have original jurisdiction in all commercial and civil matters

---

[33] There is also a county court in Caransebeș, though it is not a county capital.

[34] Foreign degrees are recognized for this purpose.

where the sum involved is more than 50,000 lei; in serious penal cases,[35] with the right of appeal to the court of appeal; and in cases not specifically reserved by law for special courts, as assizes, surrogate, etc.

A court with twelve jurors, composed of citizens over twenty-five years of age, in full enjoyment of all civic rights, tries offenses under common law,[36] political and criminal offenses, and cases of libel and slander.[37] Each trial is presided over by a president selected from the court of appeal, assisted by two judges from the local district court. A majority of votes decides the verdict of the jury, and none of the decisions may be appealed, except to the High Court of Cassation.

Then there are courts of appeal. Their sessions must be held in the presence of at least three judges. Each court of appeal has its own assistant attorney-general and junior public prosecutors.[38] No juries are used by the courts of appeal in any of its sections. The work is confined almost entirely to the hearing of appeals from the courts below and more particularly to the hearing of arguments on points of law. In most instances the decision of a court of appeal is final.

The High Court of Cassation and Justice sits in Bucharest and has a bench of forty-nine judges, including a chief president, three divisional presidents, and forty-five councillors. The divisional presidents and councillors are permanently assigned each to one of the three divisions. The chief president presides over the entire court in joint-division, over cases when the councillors differ in their opinions, and in any other divisions when necessary. In cases of civil law the High Court of Cassation functions as such. All suits against cabinet ministers or other high dignitaries are tried before the High Court of Justice, except when the offense is a crime or misdemeanor outside the exercise of ministerial functions. The court judges all suits on the facts in evidence and as a court of cassation it takes note of sentences pronounced in all other courts,

---

[35] With the exception of offenses under common law, electoral offenses, and cases of libel and slander.

[36] Minors are tried by the district court.

[37] In case the person libelled is of public consequence.

[38] Those with several sections have a chief prosecutor and junior prosecutors with deputies. In Roumania, prosecutors, attorneys, bailiffs, and other court functionaries, as in France, are regarded as members of the judiciary.

with a view to insuring that they are in accordance with the laws and with the forms of procedure. It cannot change the verdict of a lower court, but must either confirm the decision or refer the case back for a new trial to a juridical unit of the same rank. If this new court pronounces the same verdict, opposing the opinion of the High Court of Cassation, the verdict by the high court in plenary session is final.

The High Court of Cassation in plenary session is the only court competent to pass upon the constitutionality of laws. A section of the High Court of Cassation deals with litigation between the state and its officials or private people.

The High Court of Cassation performs its task in three divisions. The first division deals with all general questions, and especially with those relating to property. The second division has jurisdiction in criminal cases. The third division hears appeals against decisions concerning cases of the High Court of Accounts, public utility expropriations, pensions, and fiscal and administrative disputes and laws.[39]

Mention ought to be made of four Mohammedan (Cadiate) courts in the Dobrogea, in addition to the military courts, which decide on the basis of the military code, and religious courts.

---

[39] With the exception of cases concerning matters pertaining to chancery and governmental acts.

PART IV

ECONOMIC ROUMANIA

CHAPTER XI

ECONOMIC GEOGRAPHY

THE LACK OF ECONOMIC DEVELOPMENT

ROUMANIA is an economic paradox, a fact which strikes the traveler the moment he crosses the boundary of the country even for the first time. Take Ionescu described his country well when he said that "Roumania is a poor land, though rich with natural wealth." Picturesque scenery and quaint customs vie with each other. The wheat and corn fields of the plains remind the tourist of Kansas and Iowa. The costumes of the workers of the fields are a continual joy to eyes wearied by the ready-made clothing of the Western world.

In contrast with these idyllic scenes there are the busy and smutty oil-fields, where American tractors and machinery are operated by experts of various nations and not infrequently by Americans. From the mountains, the beautiful Carpathian Mountains, which might literally be called the backbone of the country, comes Roumania's wealth of timber. On the Danube River, which forms the southern boundary of the country for three hundred miles, we find such busy centers as Brăila and Galați, active lumber- and grain-shipping ports during the months when the Danube is free of ice. And on the Black Sea is located Constanța, the modern year-round port with its docks where may be seen ships flying the flags of all maritime nations of the world.

In spite of the fact, however, that Roumania is extremely rich in natural resources, economically the country is practically unknown. Fundamentally, these resources have as yet been only very slightly developed. Education, favorable legislation, and foreign capital will some day develop Roumania to her fullest economic capacity. But adequate means of transportation and rapid communication facilities still are very important problems confronting the Roumanian people.

In fact Roumania is a country of the future. Her resources are enormous, as we shall presently see, and are awaiting capital to develop them. Until very recently the people of Roumania could pay but little attention to the natural wealth of their land. Most of their energies were consumed in the hot fires of political strife. Whatever was produced in this period of clamor and frustration was immediately absorbed by the unlimited demands of the foreign domination for taxes and tribute. But the nineteenth and twentieth centuries brought with them the realization of the national ideal, and present-day Roumania has turned perforce to a greater concern with economics than, as heretofore, with politics and nationalistic aspirations. Effective stabilization of the political life will be logically followed by economic expansion, the intensity of which will no doubt surprise many casual observers.

The present period of the economic life of Roumania is a period of transition. The post-war political readjustments needed duplication in the economic sphere. This process has not been by any means completed. The difficulties confronting Roumania now are due in part to this process, as well as to the internal and foreign situation. Primarily, however, we must take into consideration the universal slump in trade.

The first step toward the extrication of the country from its economic difficulties was taken in 1922 with the consolidation of Roumania's debts. The period of transition continued throughout 1924 and 1925, the principal difficulties being poor communications and the instability of the currency, as well as exorbitant rates of interest charged on loans. The situation improved in 1926, but the harvest of 1927 was much below that of 1926. The year 1928 was one of economic, financial, and trade difficulties, for the harvest had failed. The outlook was brightened by the materialization of a loan by the beginning of 1929, and there loomed a prospect of the railroads and other communications being set in order. The value of the leu was put on a gold basis, and a definite budget could now be drawn up. The subsequent good harvest, however, was followed by the usual fall in prices. This problem dominated 1930 and 1931, though the harvest of 1930 was again good. The fall of commodity prices, commencing in the late autumn of 1929, has continued into 1931 and has upset all calculations, despite abundance everywhere. The present difficult situation is due to the fact that the corresponding prices of manufactured goods are not adjusted to the changed conditions; the index number of the cost of living is still maintained at its high level, as the retail prices of commodities have not been greatly affected. Another serious problem is that of taxation.[1]

But, whatever is the cause of the present difficult situation, "Roumania's importance, because of its economic potentialities, is vast, and in proportion as its resources are developed its economic importance will increase"—as we are assured by the United States Department of Commerce.[2]

AGRICULTURE

Roumania began her existence as a predominantly agricultural country. Indeed, Roumania is even now a leading agricultural nation in Europe. The principal occupations of the people, as well as the greater part of the products of Roumania, are agricultural. For two thousand years the peasant of Roumania tilled the soil—though not always his own soil. The psychology of the Roumanian people explains much of his political activity, being based fundamentally on his attachment to the soil. The traditions of the farmer have never produced a very effective Roumanian business man or trader; hence this side of economic life is left, perhaps unfortunately, largely to the foreigner.

The agricultural character of Roumania, though the country is extremely well-wooded, is evident from the following table from N. L. Foster's and D. B. Rostovsky's *The Roumanian Handbook* (p. 224):

	Bessarabia	Bukovina	Transylvania	Old Kingdom	Greater Roumania
Area by provinces:					
Hectares	4,179,250	1,106,230	10,318,510	13,885,210	29,489,200
Percentage of country's total area...	13%	3.7%	35.3%	48%	100%
Arable land:					
Hectares	2,862,308	321,720	3,143,551	6,683,410	13,010,989
Percentage of provincial area	68.4%	29.1%	31%	49%	44%

[1] For an excellent analysis of the whole economic situation of Roumania, see R. J. E. Humphreys, Commercial Secretary to His Majesty's Legation at Bucharest, "Economic Conditions in Roumania," Great Britain, *Trade Reports,* London, 1931.

[2] U.S. Department of Commerce, Bureau of Foreign and Domestic Commerce, Special Agents Series, No. 222, *Rumania: An Economic Handbook* (Washington, 1924), p. 1.

	Bessarabia	Bukovina	Transylvania	Old Kingdom	Greater Roumania
Meadows and natural pastures:					
Hectares	448,309	171,723	2,034,685	1,399,758	4,054,475
Percentage of provincial area	10.7%	15.5%	20%	10%	14%
Orchards and vineyards:					
Hectares	148,245	7,400	187,758	270,211	613,614
Percentage of provincial area	3.5%	0.6%	1.87%	1.9%	2.1%
Forests:					
Hectares	233,095	491,040	3,568,768	2,931,168	7,224,071
Percentage of provincial area	5.3%	45%	35%	20%	24%
Buildings, roads, water, quarries, mines, and uncultivated lands:					
Hectares	487,293	114,347	1,383,748	2,600,663	4,586,051
Percentage of provincial area......	11.6%	10.3%	13%	18%	16%

The importance of Roumanian agricultural production did not begin until the nineteenth century. Up to about 1830 the agricultural products of Roumania outfitted the armies and supported the domination of the Turk. With the signing of the Treaty of Adrianople, however, trade rapidly expanded and the Danube river boats were loaded high with outward-bound cargoes of Roumanian grain. Before the war, Old Roumania ranked sixth among the wheat-exporting countries of the world. In the 1923–27 period the country ranked seventh in the world production of wheat (after the United States, Russia, Canada, British Indies, Argentina, and Australia).[3] Of the total exports cereals and derivatives represent over 46 per cent of the total value, live stock and animal products 13.5 per cent, timber 16.5 per cent, and petrol and its derivatives about 19 per cent. Thus over three-fourths of Roumania's total exports consist of agricultural and forestry products. Out of the total population, about 80 per cent are farmers. In 1929, however, cereals were displaced by

[3] XIVme Congrès International d'Agriculture, Bucarest, 7, 8 et 10 Juin, 1929, *La Roumanie agricole*, p. 431; U.S. Department of Commerce, *Commerce Yearbook 1930*, II, 623. There are several reasons why the post-war wheat crops have been restricted; the unsettled conditions, the frequently changed policies of exports, the lack of transportation, and the land reform, as well as the general effects of the World War, may be mentioned. The same causes and the serious decrease of live stock have restricted the post-war corn crops.

oil at the head of Roumania's exports, as a result of poor harvests and unfavorable conditions of the world market. The Roumanian peasant, on the whole, is in a very difficult situation today, owing to a number of causes, including the frequent failure of the harvest in the post-war years, the low prices obtainable for cereals especially in 1929, 1930, and 1931, the heavy taxation, and the high interest charged on loans. But the economic conditions of Roumania and the prosperity of trade depend largely upon the agricultural production, or rather, on the prosperity of the peasant population. Consequently ways and means have to be found of increasing the cereal production per hectare in order to save the farmer from losses if prices do not increase very soon. The lack of irrigation and of grain elevators also affects Roumanian agriculture. It must be remembered, however, that despite the good total harvests of 1929 and 1930 the economic life of Roumania was detrimentally affected by the fall in world prices—a circumstance which Roumania alone cannot help.

The distribution of the territory of Roumania according to the utilization of the land is as follows, in hectares:[4]

	1926	1927	1928
Arable land	12,276,807	12,448,272	12,751,636
1. Cereals	10,405,047	10,540,356	10,910,496
2. Artificially sown grasses and other fodder crops	605,503	656,558	640,846
3. Other crops and bare fallow	1,266,257	1,251,358	1,200,294
Permanent meadows and pasture	4,156,155	4,064,675	4,054,475
Trees, shrubs, and bushes	556,127	613,657	613,657
Woods and forests	7,248,987	7,248,987	7,224,071
Marsh, heath, uncultivated productive land and unproductive area	5,251,124	5,113,609	4,845,361
Total area	29,489,200	29,489,200	29,489,200[5]

In the spring of 1930, of the total area of farm lands, 85.8 per cent was devoted to cereals, as against 86.2 per cent in 1929, and an average of 85.3 per cent in the period 1925–29. The area de-

---

[4] International Institute of Agriculture, *International Yearbook of Agricultural Statistics, 1926–27,* pp. 64–65; *1928–29,* pp. 64–65 (Rome, 1927–29).

[5] Percentage in relation to the total area (1928): Arable land, 43.2; permanent grass and pasture, 13.7; wood and forests, 24.5; other land, 18.6. The area under cereals in 1928 was 10,911,000 hectares, and its percentage in relation to the arable land was 85.6 per cent and to the total area 37 per cent. According to *Roumania,*

voted to maize was the largest (4,426,689 hectares, or 34.4 per cent of the total farm land), followed by wheat (3,055,904 hectares, or 23.7 per cent), barley (1,975,191 hectares, or 15.3 per cent), oats (1,087,057 hectares, or 8.4 per cent), and rye (391,616 hectares, or 3.5 per cent). In comparison with 1922, wheat and rye areas showed increases (2.6 per cent and 1.1 per cent, respectively), while the others showed decreases ranging from 7.7 per cent for maize to 3.8 per cent for barley.[6]

The soil and the climate make for a considerable variety of forms of production. In the great plains the soil is exceptionally productive and is capable of yielding large crops year after year without manuring. In the hill region on both sides of the Carpathians, on the other hand, the soils are usually poor and call for much hard work. The great extremes in temperature and in rainfall are not altogether favorable to agricultural production. Sometimes excessive rainfalls are followed by long periods of drought. The least-favored part of the Roumanian plain from the view of rainfall is, however, the best place for cereal cultivation. There we meet with the famous "black earth" (*cernozium*) which produces a fine quality of cereal products.

The new provinces of Roumania, Transylvania and Bukovina, carry on intensive agriculture and cattle-breeding, and Bessarabia, besides having a definitely agricultural character, has an extensive and well-developed fruit-growing industry. Notwithstanding these additions, Roumania's agriculture still lingers in the almost exclu-

---

1931, VII, 57, the classification of the land in 1930, as compared with the average for 1925–29, was as follows:

	1930		1925–29	
	Hectares	Percentage	Hectares	Percentage
Farm land—				
1. Cereals	11,035,771	37.42	10,710,010	36.32
2. Clover, millet, etc.	658,110	2.23	624,524	2.12
3. Lentils, beans, cabbage, carrots, onions, potatoes	416,429	1.41	425,531	1.44
4. Hemp, flax, sunflower, tobacco, mustard, cotton, colza, etc.	399,532	1.35	390,704	1.32
5. Fallow lands	347,296	1.18	400,644	1.36
Pasture lands*	4,054,475	13.75	4,129,747	14.00
Tree nurseries*	613,614	2.08	588,461	2.00
Forests*	7,224,071	24.50	7,237,563	24.54
Unproductive land	4,739,902	16.08	4,982,016	16.90
Total	29,489,200	100.00	29,489,200	100.00

* No survey of the lands under these divisions was made during 1930; the figures given are those of 1927.

[6] *Roumania,* 1931, VII, 57.

sively cereal stage, cereal crops covering about 86 per cent of the arable land.

Maize and wheat are the most important cereals cultivated in Roumania. Both form important articles of export.[7] The districts contributing most are Old Roumania and Transylvania, with Bessarabia having the third place. The amount produced per acre varies a great deal. The average for all Roumania is about twelve and one-half bushels of wheat per acre.

Maize is the staple food of the peasant and provides also an excellent fodder for his cattle. Wheat was the crop of the large landowners, but is also planted by small holders, especially in the Danubian plains and in the lower-lying parts of Transylvania. Generally speaking, the area under wheat has been reduced, while maize, oats, and barley are more extensively cultivated. There is also a decrease in the return per hectare for all the crops. The land reform brought about an augmentation in the production of industrial crops and grasses and of other crops, which are profitably grown on a small scale and accommodate themselves better to a rural economy founded largely on the keeping of animals. In addition, price restrictions, export duties, and other extraneous factors played their part in causing the area under wheat to be diminished.[8] Arable land

[7] Prior to 1914 Roumania's diversified imports were largely balanced by exports of wheat. No less than 50 per cent of the wheat, 33 per cent of the corn, 34 per cent of the barley, 70 per cent of the oats, and 63 per cent of the rye production in the Old Kingdom were exported in 1913 (*Rumania: An Economic Handbook*, p. 96). In the period 1923–27, the cereals formed 41.6 per cent in weight, and 51.6 per cent in value of exports, according to *La Roumanie agricole*, pp. 434–35. *Commerce Yearbook 1930*, II, 468, provides the following figures:

Commodity	Quantity in Bushels (1927)	Value 1927	Value 1929
Wheat	7,836,000	$12,382,000	$ 336,000
Rye	2,646,000	3,104,000	477,000
Barley	32,477,000	31,315,000	33,945,000
Oats	6,153,000	3,346,000	958,000
Corn	69,565,000	57,746,000	11,191,000

[8] The matter is thoroughly analyzed in the standard book of D. Mitrany, *The Land and the Peasant in Rumania.* In the following table an attempt has been made to compare the 1928 figures of area and production in Roumania with those of the pre-war years covering the same area (International Institute of Agriculture, *International Yearbook of Agricultural Statistics, 1928–29*, p. 567):

Product	Area in Hectares 1928	Pre-war Average	Production in Quintals 1928	Pre-war Average
Wheat	3,206,470	3,716,314	31,449,370	45,738,618
Rye	295,704	493,615	2,916,877	5,239,936
Barley	1,749,212	1,416,772	15,110,386	14,567,407
Oats	1,116,450	890,058	9,804,376	15,043,045
Maize	4,455,492	3,913,162	27,563,720	59,115,919

lost some of its importance within the new frontiers. The production of artificial grazings and fodder crops is steadily growing, while that of cereal crops is decreasing. The new habit of eating bread is likely to consume any future increases in the wheat harvests.[9]

The exports, renewed in 1920, differ considerably in quantity and in kind from the pre-war exports. There was a decrease in corn exports caused by the fall in Roumania's own production and by a redistribution of the world's production and trade. With regard to the export of maize, Roumania holds third position, after the United States and Argentina, and takes fifth place among the producers of wheat. In general, Roumania has held her position among the producing countries as far as maize, oats, and barley are concerned, but has relinquished her place in the case of wheat, dropping from fifth to tenth in the wheat table, and retaining second place in the export of barley, fourth place in the export of oats, and third place in the export of maize.[10]

Another serious problem is the standardization of the quality of wheat for foreign exports in order to gain a steady position in international markets.[11] However, the standardization of cereals, which was embodied in a text of law already passed by parliament, is to be introduced forthwith.

It may be assumed, however, that the production of the Roumanian peasant can be radically increased by proper training and more adequate equipment. The great and lasting fertility of the soil is a real asset; furthermore, the country has some 4,000,000 hectares of land which could be irrigated. The government is planning to regain new soil for agriculture by the abolition of parts of vineyards. Rich soil can be obtained from the swamps on the Danube. The low banks of the river are not sufficient to prevent spring inundations, which leave there lakes and swamps, their only usefulness being for primitive fishing. From the Iron Gates to the Black Sea about 1,900,000 hectares of the best soil could be gained by the ele-

---

[9] Mitrany, *op. cit.*, p. 299. This authority blames this decrease on the governmental policy, the money crisis, and the consequent high rates of interest, and concludes that "Wheat growers were unable to obtain from the official prices even their investments." Because maize plays only a negligible part in the food of the urban population, the government did not discourage its cultivation.

[10] *La Roumanie agricole*, pp. 431–32; *Commerce Yearbook 1930*, II, 623–30.

[11] About one-half of the wheat harvest is of very good quality; about one-third is of good quality, and the rest is mediocre.

vation of the Danube banks, and it is estimated that about 250,000 families could settle there.

The whole agrarian policy of Roumania, discussed elsewhere, tending toward the increase and improvement of production is even more urgent because concurrently with the increase of the population of the peasantry the needs of the peasant multiply and the consumption of the agricultural products is automatically rising. Furthermore, the estates left after the agrarian reform call for reorganization of their working methods. The general result of the land reform is as follows:[12]

| | Before Reform | | After Reform | |
	Hectares	Percentage	Hectares	Percentage
Small owners	12,025,814	59.77	18,033,911	89.56
Large owners	8,108,847	40.23	2,100,750	10.44

In 1930 the total area planted with vegetables was 416,492 hectares. Beans, potatoes, melons, cabbages, onions, peas, and lentils are the principal vegetables grown. Considerable quantities of beans are exported. The potato is used and grown comparatively little, and is limited to Bukovina; it is used mostly for food and fodder, smaller quantities being employed in the preparation of alcohol and starch. The total area devoted to industrial crops is 399,532 hectares. A large proportion of this area is covered by the sunflower, cultivated most extensively in northern Bessarabia and northeastern Transylvania; its seeds are used for making cooking oil and oil cakes, the latter being mainly exported. Most of the rapeseed raised is exported. The Old Kingdom produces half the total production of sugar beet, which is being grown to an increasing extent. Hemp is partly exported, but mostly is used by the peasants for making oil and yarn. Flax is grown mainly for its fiber. There are 34,427 hectares covered by tobacco. Northern Bessarabia, Muntenia, and Transylvania produce about 80 per cent of the total yield of tobacco of the country, but better tobacco is imported from Macedonia.

VINEYARDS

The new provinces gave importance to the products of vineyards, located in the valley of the Mureş, Transylvania, in the north of Moldavia, in Bessarabia, on the Olt, and in northwestern Banat,

[12] D. Mitrany, op. cit., p. 221; Bureau d'Etudes de la Banque Marmorosch, Blank & Cie., Bucharest, Les Forces économiques de la Roumanie en 1929, p. 6.

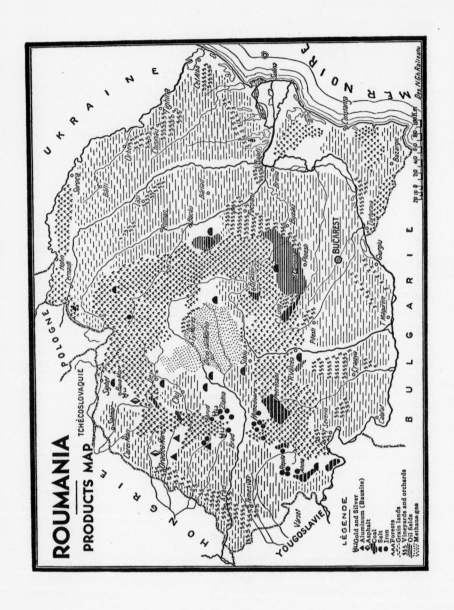

ROUMANIA

PRODUCTS MAP

LÉGENDE.

Au Gold and Silver
▲ Aluminium (Bauxite)
◆ Asphalt
▮ Coal
◗ Salt
● Iron
⋀⋀⋀ Forests
SSS Grain lands
555 Vineyards and orchards
●●● Oil fields
∷∷∷ Methane gas

Des. N.Gh.Raiceanu

MER NOIRE

UKRAINE

POLOGNE

TCHÉCOSLOVAQUIE

HONGRIE

YOUGOSLAVIE

BULGARIE

BUCAREST

20 0 20 40 60 80 100 Km

covering 239,825 hectares of the surface, compared to the pre-war area of 71,476 hectares.[13] Roumania follows France, Italy, and Spain in leading European production from vineyards. But the industry lacks standardized types, and the exports, especially those to Poland and Germany, are not as large as they could be. About 5 per cent of the total number of vines are of first-rate quality, 45 per cent are good table vines, and 50 per cent are of mediocre quality. The government is attempting to help the vineyard owners by high taxes on alcohol made from wheat and potatoes.

FRUITS

A somewhat similar situation exists in the fruit-growing industry. The pre-war production was approximately equal to the consumption of the country. Only plums showed surpluses, but because of the difficulties encountered when exported they were made into alcohol. Now, thanks to Bessarabia, which formerly stocked Russia, the country has a surplus of all varieties of tree fruits, of which only nuts have found a market in Germany. The intended exports to Poland have not materialized for lack of speedy transportation facilities. Industrial utilization of fruit is now being developed, though the city population of Roumania is accustomed to consume California canned fruits. Plums, cherries, and walnuts are particularly good. Shelled and unshelled walnuts, apples, prunes, pears, and dried cherries are exported. The fruit trees are estimated to number 74,167,916. In 1913 walnuts ranked nineteenth in value of articles exported; in 1921, exports of walnuts to the United States alone totaled 1,928 tons, exceeding in both quantity and value all other exports to the United States for that year.[14] But the production of fruit in Roumania is still undeveloped. The chief fruit is the plum. A law was recently passed for the organization and standardization of fruit exports.

LIVE STOCK

The raising of live stock gives grave concern to the Ministry of Agriculture and all agricultural workers. In all, some 14 per cent of the total area of the country is devoted to pasture land. Live stock

[13] *Les Forces économiques de la Roumanie en 1929,* pp. 19–20.

[14] *Rumania: An Economic Handbook,* p. 100. In 1927 Roumania exported $955,000 worth of walnuts.

is an essential part of the farm economy. The war losses had a serious effect on the number of the animals, and the recovering of these losses is important to the economic and social welfare of Roumania.[15]

The post-war increase has been very slow, owing partly to the popularity of motor-vehicles.[16]

Between 1919 and 1929 the totals of the most important classes of live stock were:[17]

Year	Horses	Mules	Oxen	Buffaloes
1919	1,379,916	2,805	4,633,999	
1920	1,485,200	11,719	4,729,766	145,858
1921	1,686,728	12,842	5,520,914	200,256
1922	1,802,051	12,989	5,745,534	186,676
1923	1,828,129	14,359	5,553,871	185,280
1924	1,845,208	12,622	5,398,704	184,755
1925	1,814,804	12,213	5,049,078	169,872
1926	1,877,285	12,652	4,798,384	193,286
1927	1,939,438	14,100	4,552,166	192,268
1928	1,944,700	12,539	4,435,697	189,641
1929	1,958,509	12,590	4,334,441	186,606

Year	Sheep	Goats	Pigs	Total
1919	7,790,633	354,775	2,289,458	16,451,586
1920	8,689,996	499,922	2,513,610	18,076,071
1921	11,119,047	573,900	3,150,578	22,264,265
1922	12,320,569	551,712	3,146,806	23,766,337
1923	12,480,967	584,647	2,924,603	23,571,856
1924	13,611,902	531,236	3,133,144	24,717,571
1925	12,950,212	493,583	3,087,869	23,577,631
1926	13,581,869	476,760	3,167,722	24,107,958
1927	12,941,051	418,616	3,075,782	23,133,421
1928	12,800,576	386,045	2,831,524	22,600,722
1929	12,406,428	372,807	2,412,498	21,683,879

Horses from Moldavia have always been famous; indeed, there is an old Turkish proverb, which says: "Nothing better could be wished for than a Persian peasant and a Moldavian horse." However, the usefulness of the horse is decreasing. The typical horse

[15] According to *Rumania: An Economic Handbook*, p. 99, a comparison of live stock for 1920 with the census taken before the war losses (in 1916 for the Old Kingdom and Bessarabia, in 1910 for Bukovina, and in 1911 for Transylvania) shows losses, due primarily to the war, for the Old Kingdom of 13 to 40 per cent, for Transylvania even higher as regards horses and hogs, for Bessarabia of 7 to 19 per cent, and for Bukovina of 15 to 56 per cent.

[16] At the end of 1929 Roumania had 30,728 automobiles.

[17] *Roumania*, 1931, VII, 58. These statistics coincide with those given in *International Yearbook of Agricultural Statistics, 1925–26*, pp. 62–63; *1928–29*, pp. 64–65.

of Roumania is small, hairy, very persevering, but weak. The ox is also used for field work, and the construction even of Roumanian carriages reflects his presence.

The number of animals exported in 1929 and their value is given in the table below:

	Head	Value (Lei)
Cattle	92,516	1,256,058,000
Sheep	9,170	6,246,000
Pigs	112,823	566,924,000

Live stock is exported chiefly to Czechoslovakia and Austria, and smaller quantities of cattle are shipped to Italy and of sheep to Greece. The government is making serious efforts to increase the foreign market possibilities, especially in Austria and Italy. The cattle industry did not assume importance for Roumania until after the war. The tariff war with Austria-Hungary between 1886 and 1891 ruined this industry in the Old Kingdom. On the other hand, the Transylvanian cattle business was well developed and had good markets in large Austro-Hungarian cities, which have become inaccessible for the most part since the war. The consumption of beef at home is small. The home consumption of mutton and swine, on the other hand, is much larger. The growing number of swine is especially noticeable. The raising of sheep has few prospects for the future and is receding in importance in the economic life of the country. The sheep are of a special breed, variable in size and yielding an inferior quality of wool—ţurcană or tărsană. Their milk is of a pleasant taste but is not copious. A large number of fowls, ducks, geese, and turkeys are reared by the housewives, but only well-to-do peasants can afford to reserve them for their own use. Usually they are marketed.[18]

FISH

The sea, the Danube, other rivers, and numerous lakes and ponds are of great importance to Roumania not only because of their value to the transportation system but also for their abundance of food fish. Owing to the uneconomical exploitation of the fishing grounds and the damage caused by steam navigation, the industry declined in 1893. In 1895 strict supervision was introduced. Up to 1895 the

[18] According to *Les Forces économiques de la Roumanie en 1929*, p. 15, it is estimated that Roumania has 32,500,000 fowls, 4,200,000 geese, 6,730,000 ducks, 1,700,000 turkeys, 80,000 peahens, and 620,000 pigeons.

state rented its water reserves to individuals. A new law was introduced then, making the reserves a state monopoly. At the present time the state owns 1,902,250 hectares of water reserves, and individuals 74,450 hectares. There are also 1,200 natural and 12 artificial ponds, covering 49,800 hectares.[19] The fisheries are controlled by an autonomous institute (known as *P.A.R.I.D.*), established in 1929.

On the whole, primitive methods are used and the income accruing to the state does not correspond to the abundance of the fish. There is now a tendency to leave the industry to co-operative associations which pay a certain percentage or rent to the state. The greatest difficulty in regard to the internal trade is the lack of special wagons for the transportation of fish. The chief fish is the carp, which attains remarkable size. Other species are sturgeon, tench, mackerel, silurid, sterlet, mullet, pike, and perch. In the mountain streams trout and salmon are of common occurrence; the rivers in the region of the hills contain barbel and other fish. Roumanian sturgeon caviar, which is sold as Russian caviar abroad, finds a ready market. It is coarse-grained but is often preferred to the small-grained Russian. In 1926 the caviar produced by the state fisheries amounted to nearly 110,000 pounds. Oyster culture is encouraged and there are oyster beds in the Danube delta and on the Dobrogea coast. Large quantities of smoked mullet are exported to the East.

FORESTS

After agriculture and the oil industry, the most important element in Roumania's wealth is forest products. The Carpathians and the foothills are luxuriantly covered with timber, which is systematically exploited. But this systematic exploitation was replaced during the German occupation of 1916–18 by a heavy and harmful depletion of the reserves to meet German war needs.

But the provinces increased the total forest area two and a half times, and after the war Roumania found herself with a much larger

---

[19] *Les Forces économiques de la Roumanie en 1929, p.* 20. According to *The Near East Year Book, 1927,* p. 250, the revenues and expenditures of state fisheries between 1920 and 1924 were (in thousands of lei):

	Gross Revenue	Expenses	Net Revenue
1920	25,864	6,652	19,211
1921	32,449	8,746	23,703
1922	25,555	9,333	26,224
1923	83,008	14,503	68,506
1924	97,125	21,762	75,363

output of timber available for export. The forests cover an area of 6,524,753 hectares, or, including glades and clearings, 7,248,985 hectares; this makes 25 per cent of the territory of Roumania and about an acre per head of the population.

While the Old Kingdom has only 20 per cent of its surface wooded, Transylvania can boast 35 per cent and Bukovina 45 per cent; Bessarabia has only 5.3 per cent of its surface covered by forests. The forests and woods are concentrated in and near the Carpathian Mountains; there are almost none in Bessarabia, in the Danubian plains, and in the center of Transylvania. In 1922 the state owned 28.4 per cent of the forests, the communes 11.6 per cent, institutions and religious bodies 19.2 per cent, and private owners 40.8 per cent. The ownership has partly changed since 1922, owing to agrarian legislation which turned over to individual peasants about 976,000 hectares of state and other forest and to villages about 625,000 hectares. The wood-products industry accounts for one-fourth of the total value of the industrial production. In the absence of adequate Roumanian capital, the companies exploiting the Roumanian forests are mainly financed by Swiss, Italian, Czechoslovak, and German capital. The exploitation is especially enterprising in Moldavia, where logs are floated down the streams to sawmills at Piatra or down the whole course of the Siret to Galați. Before the war, wood was mainly exported to Turkey, Greece, and Egypt, and to a similar extent to the north coast of Africa. But the volume of export has grown rapidly since 1920, and from 1922 to 1927 averaged 2,271,000 tons, the bulk comprising planks. Hungary takes about 60 per cent, the Levant 14 per cent, the Balkans 10 per cent, and other countries 16 per cent.

In 1930 there were 501 sawmills and wood-working plants, employing more than 44,000 workmen, not including pulp and paper factories with over 60,000 employees. In 1927, in addition to 78 large corporations, 473 peasants' co-operative associations with 57,000 members were engaged in lumbering. The state sells timber to these co-operatives at reduced prices, and the National Bank lends them capital at low rates.

Silver fir, Norway spruce, oak, and beech are the principal woods. Norway spruce is in great demand in the European markets, just as are pitch pine and common oak. Beech is largely used within the country for building, for railroad sleepers, and for fuel.

Sawmills are scattered throughout the country, the largest being located at Cluj, Cernăuți, Târgu-Mureș, Piatra-Neamț and Reghinul-Săsesc. In 1927 the Roumanian wood-working industry was employing 41,470 employees. The production of the timber industry leaves a considerable surplus for export. In 1928, the value of wood exports was 4,653,000,000 lei. The government has taken active measures in recent years for reforestation, especially of the areas which were devastated during the war, and it is also undertaking the more thorough training of a personnel to supervise lumbering operations.

OIL

Before the war the Old Kingdom, aside from salt and oil, had hardly any minerals which would come under consideration in her economic life. Coal and iron ores were especially lacking. Transylvania and Bukovina have added varied deposits of ores—gold, silver, copper, iron, zinc, lead, antimony, manganese, aluminium, chromium, mercury, bismuth, molybdenum, and arsenic—besides oil and the highly valuable natural gas. The most important of these is oil, which together with cereals and timber, makes up the chief source of Roumanian wealth.

Roumania shares with America the distinction of being one of the first two countries in which rock oil was extracted. Her production of crude petroleum in 1913 was exceeded only by those of the United States, Russia, and Mexico. Roumania now occupies second place (after Russia) as a European producer of petroleum and seventh place in importance among the oil-producing countries of the globe.[20] Stated in these terms, however, the relative importance of Roumania in world production is exaggerated, for Roumania's share of the world output was only 2.9 per cent in 1910, 3.6 per cent in 1913, 1.2 per cent in 1919, and 1.2 per cent in 1922,[21] and 2.4 per cent in 1929.[22]

The existence of oil-bearing strata in the country had been known for hundreds of years, but no attempts to exploit them had been made until about the middle of the nineteenth century. It was in

---

[20] *Commerce Yearbook 1930,* II, 648. The production, in thousands of barrels of forty-two United States gallons, has been steadily increasing: 1900, 1,629; 1913, 13,555; 1921, 8,368; 1925, 16,650; 1926, 23,314; 1927, 26,368; 1928, 30,773; 1929, 34,930.

[21] *Rumania: An Economic Handbook,* p. 106.

[22] M. Pizanty, *Petroleum in Roumania* (Bucharest, 1930), p. 4.

1883 that a French company established the first oil wells in the Bacău district, after which other French, British, and native enterprises began to interest themselves in Roumanian petroleum resources. It was only natural that in the early period of the country's oil history the work was not organized and lacked proper scientific research. In 1890 there were some 45 petroleum enterprises, representing a total capital of about 77 million lei. It was during this period that the first mining laws of the country were passed. The law of 1895 recognized the principle that the subsoil pertained as a matter of course to the respective landowners. As no attempt whatever was made to attract national capital, the major part of the state domain and many private oil-bearing areas were given over to foreign interests. Among the first companies were the Steaua Română (1895), Berea (British), Gura-Ocniței and Băicoi (Dutch), Telega (at first British, then German), Buștenari (Roumanian, then German), and Câmpina-Moreni (Austro-German). The German financiers were the main backers of these enterprises, with the participation of capital from other countries. The construction of pipe lines, refineries, tanks, and other equipment implied increasing investments, and in 1913, their total value was estimated at $77,200,000, representing German, British, Netherland, American, and Franco-Belgian interests.[23] Roumanian capital participated in the industry before the war to the extent of only about one per cent of the total.

Beginning in 1904, the Roumanian petroleum industry may be said to have established itself on a more modern basis. A tendency toward the amalgamation of small enterprises into large units became continuous. The Consolidation Act of 1904, amended in 1913, helped the consolidation, because difficulties had been encountered in obtaining possession of the lands, and the present act entitled the leaseholders to exploit their plots even if it were proved that the lessor was not the rightful owner. The régime of free transference of property and the exploitation of the subsoil helped the industry to make big strides. The development of the production was interrupted during the war and reached its lowest ebb in 1917, when the oil wells were blown up in order to prevent them from falling into the hands of the invaders.

The Constitution of 1923 established the principle of the na-

---

[23] U.S. Department of Commerce, Bureau of Foreign and Domestic Commerce, *Commerce Reports,* 1930, September 15, No. 37, p. 677.

tionalization of the subsoil (Article 19), and this rule was elaborated
by the mining law of 1924. The law aimed to supplant the different
laws and decree-laws governing the new provinces and establish a
new mining régime for the whole country. The most important aim
was to secure for the state a permanent control over the exploitation,
manufacture, and trade of the industry. An aggressive nationalistic
mining policy was inaugurated through the creation of a type of
Roumanian mining company with registered shares, with 60 per
cent Roumanian capital, and with complete Roumanian direction.
The result was not very advantageous to Roumania. Roumanian oil
companies founded on the basis of the new mining régime suffered
as a result of the provision for the registration of shares because they
could find no reserves of Roumanian capital, and foreign capital
refused to participate under such conditions. The production of
these companies declined from 36 per cent of the total production
of the country to 24.5 per cent in 1928. However, the new Government of Maniu modified this law on March 28, 1929. The amendment does not affect the basic principle of the law, that is, the
nationalization of the subsoil, nor does it affect the state's rights
according to the old law. The new provisions are especially designed
to appease foreign capital and give it full opportunity and equality.
Foreign and domestic capital are put on an equal basis and complete
freedom is given to capitalists in appointing their managing staff;
as regards other workers, 75 per cent of the personnel must be Roumanian.

By the close of 1930 it was estimated that the petroleum investments of Roumanian and foreign capital[24] in Roumania were as
follows (in thousand lei) :[25]

Nationality	Num-ber	Capital 1930	Reserves 1930	Investments 1930	Profits 1929	Losses 1929
American ..	1	635,474,200	....	....	....	....
British	17	10,838,750	565,386	11,384,437	581,979	216,642
French	14	412,922,405	38,318,021	268,596,795	17,672,008	2,934,446
Belgian	10	521,400,000	119,412,448	183,949,232	50,994,316	2,717,431
Dutch	2	19,000,000	6,340,384	25,794,840	1,016,104	71,776
Italian	1	140,000,000	....	....	....	....
Roumanian	113	19,050,254	4,195,433	22,942,135	917,987	303,788

[24] It is impossible to secure accurate figures. When the author asked for information from the New Jersey Standard Oil Company, New York, the company,
"for the best interest of the company," refused to give it.

[25] *Roumania,* 1931, VII, 59.

It might be interesting to notice that with the exception of the Standard Oil Company of New Jersey, which as far back as 1904 founded the "Româno-Americană" Company, with paid capital of 1,250,000,000 lei, entirely owned by it,[26] for the exploitation, refining, and transportation of petroleum products, no American capital has been invested in Roumania on a large scale.[27]

Consul J. R. Childs[28] values the capital of the British concerns at $41,225,000; Netherlands capital, interested in Roumanian petroleum in conjunction with British, at about $7,638,000; French capital at $717,400, and Franco-Belgian capital at approximately $34,104,000. Italian capital first obtained an interest in Roumanian oil in 1926 with an investment of $2,104,000.[29]

The following table shows the most important Roumanian petroleum companies, the year when each was established, its invested capital, and the groups which finance it:[30]

	Founded	Paid Capital (lei)	
Astra Română.........	1910	2,034,000,000	Belongs to the Geconsolid. Holland Petr. Co., which is controlled by the "Royal Dutch" group.
Româno-Americană	1904	1,250,000,000	All shares are held by the "Standard Oil of New Jersey."

[26] *New York World,* July 13, 1924, estimates the Standard Oil Company's investments in Roumania at 70 million dollars. R. W. Dunn estimates in his book, *American Foreign Investments,* p. 155, that the total American investments in Roumania may be 85 million dollars, with additional large loans to the Roumanian railroads, the Roumanian government, the city of Bucharest, and the Industrial Mortgage Bank of Roumania.

[27] G. Boncescu, "Rumania and Foreign Investments," in *International Communications Review* (International Telephone and Telegraph Corporation), 1930, VI, 19.

[28] *Commerce Reports,* 1930, September 15, p. 677.

[29] As a result of the war the control of the Deutsche Bank and the Disconto Gesellschaft of the Steaua Română Company passed into the hands of British, French, and Roumanian groups, and the German interests in the Concordia, Vega, and Creditul Petrolifer, controlled by the Deutsche Erdöl Aktien-Gesellschaft, into Belgian hands. According to M. Pizanty, *Petroleum in Roumania,* p. 75, the participation of various capital in the country's production in percentages of the total is as follows: British capital, 20 per cent; Anglo-Dutch capital, 20.2 per cent; Franco-Belgian capital, 23 per cent; Roumanian capital, 20 per cent; Roumanian capital participating with foreign companies, 77.7 per cent; American capital, 6.6 per cent; Italian capital, 1.7 per cent; other capital, 0.8 per cent.

[30] Pizanty, *op. cit.,* p. 77.

	Founded	Paid Capital (lei)	
Steaua Română.........	1896	1,000,000,000	Steaua Română (British) branch of the Steaua Română, Française, group of Roumanian banks, private Roumanian shareholders, and the state.
Sospiro	1920	700,000,000	The group "Sospiro Ltd."
Creditul Minier.........	1920	605,000,000	Roumanian banks and shareholders and relations with French capital through the "Credit Minier Fr.-Roum."
I.R.D.P. (Industria Română de Petrol Societate anonimă română)..	1920	600,000,000	25 per cent of the shares belong to the French group "S.I.P.E.R." constituted into Roumanian banks and shareholders.
Româno-Africană	1927	600,000,000	Belongs to the "Service Petroleum Ltd." concern.
Petrol-Block	1918	569,210,275	French capital by the "Petrol Block Français" and Roumanian financiers.
Concordia	1907	500,000,000	Most of the shares belong to the "Compagnie Financière Belge des Pétroles" (Petrofina) and, in a smaller proportion, to Roumanian capital and state.
Româno-Belgiană de Petrol	1908	400,000,000	Franco-Belgian capital.
Colombia	1905	380,000,000	French capital financed by "Omnium International des Pétroles" concern.
Unirea	1921	300,000,000	The British group "Phoenix Oil and Transport Co."
Prahova	1920	255,000,000	Most of the shares are owned by the Italian group "A.G.I.P."
Redevența	1918	225,948,700	A group of Roumanian shareholders and banks.
Foraj-Lemoine	1923	220,000,000	The group "Lemoine Lièges" and the "Société Française Lemoine."
Sondajul	1922	200,000,000	The bank "Marmorosch, Blank & Comp." and Roumanian shareholders.
Sirius	1925	200,000,000	Most of the shares are held by the "Compagnie Financière Belge des Pétroles," a Dutch group, and in a smaller proportion by Roumanian shareholders and banks.

Hereunder are shown the most important British companies working directly or participating in various Roumanian oil enterprises:

	Founded	Paid Capital (Pounds)	
Phoenix Oil and Transport Co. Ltd.........	1920	3,776,552	Controls the group of enterprises "Unirea" and "Orion" as well as the following six companies with exploitations in Roumania: "Roum. Cons. Oil Ltd.," capital, £1,432,192; "Trajan Roum. Oil Co. Ltd.," £200,000; "Chiciura Oil-Fields of Roumania," £151,514; "Anglo-Roumanian Oil Co.," £150,000; "Stavropoleo-Moreni Oil Prop.," £134,254; "Beciu (Roum.) Oil Fields Ltd.," £100,000.
Steaua Română (British) Ltd.	1920	2,025,000	Holds 25 per cent of the share capital of "Steaua Română."
Service Petroleum Co. Ltd.	1927	1,000,000	Holds all the shares of the "Româno-Africană" Co.
Hamilton's Oil Concordia Ltd.	1920	366,089	Holds all the shares of the "Sondrum" Company.

Among the companies with French capital with interests in Roumania can be mentioned:

	Founded	Paid Capital (Francs)	
Steaua Française	1920	115,000,000	Participates in the "Steaua Română" Co.
Soc. Ind. des Pétr. Roum. (S.I.P.E.R.)	1925	70,000,000	Holds 25 per cent of the shares of "I.R.D.P." Co.
Omnium International de Pétroles	1911	60,000,000	Holds most of the shares of "Colombia" Company.
Soc. "Française Lemoine"	1923	47,000,000	Participates in the "Foraj-Lemoine" Co.
Crédit Minier Fr.-Roumain	1927	35,000,000	Interested in the "Creditul Minier" Co.

Reșița Iron Works

Lumber Industry in Bukovina

The most important Belgian companies interested in the Roumanian oil industry are:

	Founded	Paid Capital (Francs)	
Compagnie Financière Belge des Pétroles	1920	300,000,000	Most of the shares of the companies "Concordia," "Sirius," and "Vegas."
Forapetrol	1927	100,000,000	Holds the shares of the "Foraky" and "Foraky Românească" companies.
Nafta, Anvers..........	1906	40,000,000	Related to the group financing the "Concordia-Sirius-Vega."

The leading companies with capital in Dutch florins with interests in Roumania are:

	Founded	Paid Capital (Florins)	
Gecons. Holland Petr. Co.	1907	18,200,000	Controls the "Astra Română" Company.
Arnhemsche Petr. Maat..	1897	800,000	Owns exploitations in Roumania.

The "Azienda Generală Italiană Petroli" Company is interested in the "Prahova" and "Petrolul Bucureşti" companies with 140,000,000 Italian lires.

So far, 8,120 acres of the oil-bearing lands have been exploited and have produced in the 68 years (1858–1924) 31,390,000 tons of oil.[31] The total extent of oil-bearing area is estimated at 120,000 hectares; areas under concession amount to 47,613 hectares; but the exploited areas amount only to 3,644 hectares.[32] No exploration has as yet been undertaken with a view to a general survey of the subsoil.

Oil is found in the whole region of the Carpathian foothills on the Old Roumanian side from the district of Suceava in the north to the valley of the Dâmbovița in the south, a distance of nearly two hundred miles. The greatest amount in pre-war times came from the Prahova field, of which Ploeşti is the center. Other principal producing areas are grouped around Dâmbovița, Bacău, Buzău, Vâlcea, and Maramureş. The principal fields are Băicoi, Moreni and

[31] The Near East Year Book, 1927, p. 359.
[32] Les Forces économiques de la Roumanie en 1930, p. 34.

Câmpina, Buştenari, and Ţintea. New fields have been worked in recent years under the concessions from the state, and fresh concessions given out under the mining law of 1929 should bring important further progress in the next few years.

About 97 per cent of the total Roumanian crude oil passes through various processes of refining. The treatment of crude oil and its derivatives is assured by 30 refineries of great capacity and an equal number of smaller refineries. Most of the crude oil is treated in the refineries situated in the neighborhood of the oil-fields, viz., in the Prahova district. The annual capacity of the Roumanian refineries may be estimated as:[33]

	Capacity—Tons		Capacity—Tons
Distilling	6,756,000	Lubricating oils....	419,000
Refining	1,895,000	Cracking plants....	500,000
Rectification	1,460,000		

The daily cracking capacity of the installations owned by various enterprises is as follows: Astra Română, 100 tank cars; Steaua Română, 48; and Colombia, 22. The largest installation is located at Câmpina, which is also the largest refinery in Europe, and belongs to the Steaua Română Company.

The main production centers and refineries are connected by pipe lines with each other and with the centers of distribution and export. The length of the state pipe line amounts to 760 kilometers (472 miles). The railways possess about 10,262 tank cars for the transportation of oil products, of which 7,894 belong to oil companies and the rest to the Roumanian state.[34]

In 1929 the technical personnel consisted of 23,732 Roumanians and 244 foreigners, and the administrative personnel of 27,916 Roumanians and 292 foreigners.

The internal consumption of oil products is small compared with the country's area and population—1,207,441 tons in 1929—owing to abundance of other fuels, like coal, methane, and wood, and the use of water power, as well as to the insufficient railway network. But in 1929 internal consumption increased by 11 per cent over the preceding year. The steady increase of oil exports, on the other hand, is of great importance to Roumania. Thus exports of oil in 1925 increased by 81 per cent as compared with the year 1924, and

[33] Pizanty, *Petroleum in Roumania,* p. 44.

[34] *Ibid.,* p. 61.

by 89 per cent in 1926 as compared with the year 1925,[35] despite the competition of American and Russian trusts in the world markets. However, the country is favored by its geographical position and the transportation facilities of the Danube and the Black Sea. The annual exports of various oil products fluctuated from 1,056,009 tons in 1913 to 436,018 tons in 1924 and to 2,822,900 in 1929.[36] The value of these exports in 1913 was 131,441,000 gold lei, 2,755,-566,000 paper lei in 1924, and 9,532,326,000 paper lei in 1929.[37] Out of the various states importing Roumanian oil products, Italy participated to the extent of 20.36 per cent in 1929, and was followed by Great Britain (10.63 per cent), Egypt (10.16 per cent), France (8.48 per cent), and Germany (7.54 per cent).

Crude oil production increased uninterruptedly after 1904 until the outbreak of the World War. The record figure of production was reached before the war in 1913, when the production realized an increase of 255 per cent within a period of ten years.[38] After the war restrictions a regular annual increase reappeared, beginning in 1924, and leaving the following record:[39]

Year	Production (Tons)	Increase of Production Compared with 1919 (Percentage)	Value (Lei)	Increase of Value Compared with 1919 (Percentage)
1919	920,488	......	142,675,640	....
1920	1,034,138	12.35	517,069,000	.262
1921	1,163,315	26.38	1,163,315,000	.715
1922	1,365,830	48.38	2,322,211,000	1.527
1923	1,515,658	64.65	4,168,059,500	2.821
1924	1,851,303	101.12	4,813,387,800	3.273
1925	2,316,504	151.66	5,791,260,000	3.959
1926	3,241,329	252.13	8,103,322,500	5.579
1927	4,268,541	363.72	7,833,000,000	5.390
1928	3,661,360	297.76	6,590,448,000	4.519
1929	4,827,278	424.42	7,482,280,900	5.144

[35] *Ibid.*, p. 67.

[36] *Ibid.*, pp. 71–73. *Commerce Yearbook 1930*, II, 483, gives the following figures of petroleum production (in thousands of barrels): 1913, 14,555; 1923, 10,867; 1925, 16,650; 1926, 23,314; 1927, 26,368; and 1928, 30,773. In 1929 the production of petroleum was 34,930,000 barrels.

[37] The ratio between the increase of exports and the respective value in lei is not proportional because of the fluctuations of the Roumanian currency, which was stabilized in 1929.

[38] *Commerce Reports*, 1930, September 15, No. 37, p. 678.

[39] Pizanty, *op. cit.*, p. 17. The considerable increase in value of production is due to the monetary depreciation of the leu.

The same authority provides us the ratio between the quantities of crude oil treated in refineries and the bulk production during the recent years, as compared with the year 1913:

Year	Production (Tons)	Treated in Refineries (Tons)	Percentage
1913	1,885,619	1,787,245	94.8
1922	1,365,830	1,212,823	88.9
1923	1,515,658	1,337,222	88.2
1924	1,851,303	1,644,144	88.9
1925	2,316,504	2,151,149	92.7
1926	3,241,329	3,089,777	95.3
1927	3,661,360	3,533,346	96.1
1928	4,268,541	4,132,271	96.8
1929	4,827,278	4,756,000	98.5

The exact production of all refineries by categories of products was as follows:

	1927		1929	
	Tons	Percentage	Tons	Percentage
Light Motor spirit	380,240	10.77 ⎫	596,048	12.50
Medium Motor spirit	50,643	1.43 ⎭		
Heavy Motor spirit	206,496	5.85	269,141	5.64
White spirit	71,316	2.02	63,235	1.32
Kerosene	679,776	19.23	912,309	19.14
Gas oil	289,295	8.19	522,226	10.94
Lubricating oils	85,935	2.43	104,959	2.25
Paraffin	3,514	0.10	6,971	0.15
Residuum	1,402,921	39.70	1,879,105	39.44
Total	3,170,136	89.72	4,353,994	91.38
Fuel oil in refineries	257,102	7.28	323,040	6.78
Total	3,427,238	97.00	4,677,034	98.16
Manufacturing losses	106,108	3.00	87,966	1.84
Total crude oil treated	3,533,346	100.00	4,765,000	100.00

In 1929 Roumania produced 2.4 per cent of the total world production. Compared with 1928, the production of crude oil in 1929 in Roumania increased nearly 14 per cent, drillings more than 20 per cent, and refining operations about 20 per cent.[40] The situation, however, was not entirely satisfactory. The crisis of the oil industry continued throughout 1929, 1930, and 1931 and was attributed to world overproduction and to competition at home. Improvements

[40] *Commerce Yearbook 1930*, II, 483.

in drilling methods and the discovery of the very prolific meotic sands on the southern flank of the Moreni salt dome led to a very intensive drilling activity. The Moreni meotic wells, giving a steady daily production of from 15 to 45 tank cars have increased the production of Roumania much beyond the possibility of handling its production. The pumping and storage capacity, though ample in 1929, proved utterly inadequate in 1930.[41] By June 1930 most companies had to limit radically their operations, and prices of crude oil collapsed. In order to relieve the situation the Astra-Română and the Româno-Americană companies proposed reducing the daily production. About 98.7 per cent of the other companies agreed to the proposition. But when the Steaua Română concluded big contracts abroad, especially in Spain, the agreement collapsed. This resulted in an expansion of oil output and a pronounced slump in prices in 1930 and in 1931. Unfortunately for the Roumanian oil industry the setback in prices during this period was about 45 per cent, whereas the drop in foreign (American) prices did not exceed 36 per cent. However, the industry presents a very alluring field for foreign investment.

METHANE GAS

Partly connected with the exploitation of oil is that of methane gas, which appears concurrently with oil deposits and is used for the driving of machines in the petroleum fields, and also occurs in enormous quantities in the Mediaş-Turda district of Transylvania, which basin supplies 58 per cent of the total amount of gas used, the remainder being furnished by oil-field gases. Transylvania gas is one of the richest methane gases of the world, containing from 97 to 99.25 per cent methane, and its constant composition increases its industrial value. The most important wells are situated at Sărmăşel, Saroş, and Bazna. The main industrial centers of Transylvania are connected with the gas wells by means of pipe lines, and gas is used for heat and light in homes and by industry as a cheap substitute for coal. The concern of the future is how to recover gas which escapes, mostly into the air. Oil-field gases flow at Moreni, Ceptura, Aricești, and Boldești; in the Dâmboviţa district, at Ochiuri and Gura Ocniţei; in the Buzău district at Arbanaşi; and in the Bacău district

---

[41] See "Roumania's Critical Production Condition," *World Petroleum*, January 1931, pp. 38–40.

at Mărgineşti and Solonţi. The prospect of better collection and utilization is very promising. The supply of gas led to the establishment of new factories in the area served, and the construction of pipe lines to other districts is under consideration. The cost of securing the gas is one-tenth that of securing coal, and its transportation is easier.

The table below shows the quantities of natural gas used for industrial and other purposes from 1927 to 1930. More than two-thirds of the estimated available supply (about 5,110 million cubic meters in 1930) is at present allowed to escape.

District	1930 1000 cu. m.	1930 % of total	1929 1000 cu. m.	1929 % of total	1928 1000 cu. m.	1928 % of total	1927 1000 cu. m.	1927 % of total
Prahova	1,067,809	75	415,980	52	260,652	42	119,381	27
Dâmboviţa	159,707	11	125,793	15	75,452	12	60,129	13
Buzău	535	...	1,000	...	1,748	...	3,759	1
Bacău	5,629	1	4,959	1	3,095	1	3,456	1
Transylvania ...	192,708	13	258,867	32	272,076	45	252,312	58
Total	1,426,388	100	806,599	100	613,023	100	439,037	100

By a royal decree of August 19, 1930, the methane gas industry became a state monopoly.

MINERALS

In addition to petroleum, the mineral wealth of Roumania includes coal, iron, gold, salt, copper, and manganese. The Old Kingdom lacks coal and iron; but the new boundaries include the coal mines and, thanks to the output at the Lupeni and Petroşani fields in Hunedoara department of Transylvania, the Roumanian state railways are freed from the necessity of importing it from abroad. Most of the Roumanian coal is lignite, inferior "brown-coal"; the main seam is located in the Petroşani basin near the southern end of the Carpathian Mountains. Mixed with residues, it is used for fuel also in factories. Deposits exist in the departments of Mehedinţi, Muscel, Dâmboviţa, Bacău, Râmnicu-Sărat, Buzău, Putna, Gorj, and Prahova. Anthracite is found in the environment of Caraş and Severin in Bukovina and also in the Gorj department in Oltenia. The home consumption is approximately covered by the home production and only the better kinds of coal have to be imported for industrial purposes (metal-making) from England, Czechoslovakia, and Belgium. Coke is used principally by the smelters of the Reşiţa works and the state works at Hunedoara. The coke production increased from 2,116,221 tons in 1922 to 3,027,240 tons in 1928. The Transylvanian mines, producing more than three-fourths of the total production, have been helped in their development by high protective tariffs.

The iron ores are nearly all located in the mountainous districts of Transylvania and the Banat. The chief deposits are located in the district of Ghelar, southwestern Transylvania; ferrous ores are found in the northern part of the Banat and lodes in the region of Bihor and eastern Transylvania. In comparison with other states the deposits of Roumania are small—estimated at about 23,000,000 tons.[42] In 1928 the total output was 83,860 tons. Both the state and the private metallurgical works are increasing their activities and modernizing their installations. Two of these nine works may be termed mechano-metallurgical. As members of the European cartels, they are guaranteed certain prices.

The Old Kingdom has been noted for its salt deposits, and salt is second in importance among the mineral resources of Roumania. The salt as mined is known for its purity, containing 99 per cent of sodium chloride. Salt mining is a government monopoly. The most important deposits occur in the districts of Prahova, Bacău, Vâlcea (Old Kingdom); Sibiu, Alba, Turda, Odorhei and Someş (Transylvania); Suceava (Bukovina); and in the Maramureş. The reserves are estimated at about four milliards of cubic meters, or 8,777 million tons. Over half of the production is consumed at home, and the greatest part of the exports are directed to the countries situated below the Danube, Bulgaria and Yugoslavia; small amounts at times are sent to Egypt, Senegal, and the Congo. In 1929 the total production reached the figure of 318,802 tons. The export figures, however, are small, principally because the Transylvanian mines lost their former markets in the Austro-Hungarian Empire. Increased output could easily supply the whole of Europe for many years to come.

Gold and silver are normally found in association; the richest gold fields are in central and northern Transylvania—the Western Mountains and the region of Baia-Mare, Brad, Săcărâmb, and Zlatna. Next to Russia this district is believed to possess the great-

[42] *Rumania: An Economic Handbook,* p. 114.

est store of gold in Europe. In the Old Kingdom the mines of less importance are located principally in Oltenia in the department of Vâlcea. In 1928, 58,161 ounces (troy) were produced, a very small output despite the richness of the mines.[43]

Silver is invariably found in conjunction with gold, and is mined in the state mines of Baia Sprie and Capnic, in Transylvania. Both metals are separated in the metal in the metallo-chemical works of Firiza-de-Jos, Strâmbu, and Zlatna. The production of 1929 was 73,271 ounces (troy), compared to the 1927 production of 140,691 ounces.[44]

The other minerals, produced in small quantities, deserve only brief mention here. Copper is found only in association with other metals, and because of the relatively high cost of its extraction little is produced. Zinc is found in general in deposits in the form of blende, in lead, copper, and silver veins. In the Maramureş regions ores containing 20 to 25 per cent of zinc are found. Other minor mineral resources are those of aluminum (bauxite), antimony, asbestos, asphalt, cement, chromium, graphite, manganese, pyrites, sodium compounds, and sulphur. There are very great deposits of mercury in the Western Mountains of Transylvania and of mica in the region of Valea Lotrului, at Voineasa.

In general, the mining industry of Roumania was employing in 1928, with the exception of the petroleum industry, 445 technical, 2,134 administrative, and 47,366 ordinary workers, a total of 49,945 employees.[45] At the beginning of 1929, 76 joint stock companies were interested in the mining industry with a capital of 2,780,311,437 lei. The value of mineral and metal production of the country is shown in the following table:[46]

Year	Total Value ($1,000)*	Principal Products	Value, 1928 ($1,000)*
1921	28,592	Petroleum	44,076
1925	44,415	Lignite, including coal	16,871
1926	56,292	Salt	4,562
1927	64,119	Natural gas	2,074
1928	72,156	Pig iron	1,591

* Conversion at average exchange rates for years 1921, 1927, at the new rate for 1928.

[43] *Commerce Yearbook 1930,* II, 482.
[44] *Idem.*
[45] *Les Forces économiques de la Roumanie en 1929,* p. 62.
[46] *Commerce Yearbook 1930,* II, 482–83.

The production of the mines is estimated as follows:[47]

Product	Unit	1913	1923	1925	1927	1928
Lignite	1,000 metric tons	13,555	2,229	2,615	2,850	2,630
Coal	1,000 metric tons	453	292	314	373	398
Natural gas (con-sumption)	million cu. ft.	...	10,139	13,060	15,504	21,649
Salt	1,000 lbs.	738,914	675,957	728,393	723,177	755,691
Iron ore	metric tons	465,000	99,293	107,384	97,138	83,869
Gold	troy oz.	...	43,146	40,028	64,494	58,161
Silver	troy oz.	...	75,265	76,583	140,691	73,271
Copper	lbs.	...	156,114	292,464	474,992	296,800

With the exception of the petroleum and salt industries Roumania is behind other states in exploitation of her natural wealth. The large natural resources and the large deposits of a variety of metals need, however, foreign capital to develop them within their potentialities. It may be taken for granted that the increased production of the future will increase the buying power of Roumania and thus make it also an attractive market.

INDUSTRY

Before the World War the industry of Roumania was based primarily upon agriculture. Since the war Roumania has become also an industrial country. Transylvania, Bukovina, and the Banat were more industrialized than the Old Kingdom and hence many industrialists, though of non-Roumanian origin, are engaged in the increasing national manufacturing activity. New large areas and new blocks of industrial population were joined with the enlarged state. The coal and iron, textile, sugar, chemical, and other industries of Transylvania and Bukovina, and the numerous iron and steel works of the Banat were added to the petroleum industry of Old Roumania. The war of course caused tremendous damage to the economic life of Roumania, and her post-war development was hampered by the nationalistic policy of the government in addition to the evils of currency inflation followed by an attempt at deflation. On the other hand, shortly after the war these industrial enterprises launched extensive schemes of reconstruction and development, encouraged by high protective tariffs and in part by the results of the agrarian reform, which induced many former large landowners to undertake industrial enterprises.

[47] *Ibid.*, p. 483. The 1913 figures relate to post-war territory, with the exception of salt.

Post-war Roumania ceased to be an entirely agricultural country and seems now in the transition stage from the agrarian to the industrial state of development. However, some authorities deny this assertion and point out that in comparison to the number of the inhabitants engaged in agriculture and the value of the agricultural production, the industrialization of the country is entirely subordinated to the agricultural needs. The point is well expressed by Dr. Virgil Madgearu in his recent publication, *Rumania's New Economic Policy.*[48]

United Rumania is primarily an agrarian country, in spite of the fact that in Transylvania and Banat industries of considerable proportions exist. Four-fifths of the population of the country is engaged in agriculture, and, since the great reform which expropriated the large landowners, 85 per cent of the arable land of the country has been in the hands of small farmers. It is to be expected that under such physical and social conditions agriculture should have precedence in the active preoccupations of the Government. Any increase in the productivity of the countryside increases the national income, the consumption and taxable capacity of the population, and lightens the burden of the large mass of the common people.

For ten years this political axiom had been neglected in favor of the chimera of a forced industrialization with economic self-sufficiency in view. . . . .

We cannot formulate an adequate picture of the comparison between the pre-war and post-war years for lack of statistics. It is certain, however, that while Roumania was recuperating from the effects of the war a strong industrialization policy was pursued until recently, and an attempt was made to make the country independent of the imports of foreign industrial products. In order to achieve this chimerical ideal, the economic forces of the land were strained in the industrial direction. Thus the condition of the industry of the post-war years is different from that of today. This statement covers not merely the Old Kingdom but also the new provinces, as, for example, Transylvania, where the number of factories grew from 1,101 in 1919 to 1,573 in 1927.[49]

[48] London, 1930, pp. v–vi. Quoted by permission of P. S. King & Son, London, publishers.

[49] *Les Forces économiques de la Roumanie en 1929,* p. 81. The statistics of *Rumania: An Economic Handbook,* p. 123, give 2,747 as the total number of Roumanian industrial plants in 1919; the previous authority gives the total number 4,094 for 1927. Hence in the course of eight years, 1,347 new establishments were formed.

However, the rapid development of industry had also its dark side. A great majority of the factories were created without the necessary capital, and most of them were administered in not too rational a way. They could exist only with the help of high tariffs. Now the government would like to reduce the rates of the tariffs and thus also the prices of the products, but is in doubt what industries should be given up and how to prevent the already existing unemployment. Besides, the whole industrial system is closely connected with the Roumanian banks. Any sudden change in the industrial policy would automatically aggravate the financial crisis. All these circumstances must be considered by the government when introducing a tariff, and the protection of the industrial system cannot be radically changed.

At the beginning of the World War the Old Kingdom had 1,114 factories; on January 1, 1929, the Kingdom presented the following industrial picture:[50]

Industries	Number of Factories	Invested Capital (Millions of Lei)	Horse-power	Fuel Consumption (Millions of Lei)	Value of Raw Material (Millions of Lei)
Metallurgical	453	7,564	78,302	704	3,916
Timber	832	4,217	72,038	105	2,905
Paper and Printing Trades	126	1,804	31,396	162	1,019
Chemicals	378	6,546	62,890	438	5,713
Textiles	511	5,023	34,964	246	5,186
Victualling	1,147	11,335	125,266	603	11,876
Tanneries	269	1,641	13,237	65	2,019
Pottery and China	38	117	727	73	190
Electrical	14	89	63	5	87
Building Material	294	2,563	42,122	336	261

[50] *Annuaire statistique de la Roumanie 1929*, pp. 186–187; *Les Forces économiques de la Roumanie en 1930*, p. 81. *Commerce Yearbook 1930*, II, 483, contains the following table:

Branch of Industry	Wage Earners (Thousands) 1922	1927	1928	Horsepower (Thousands) 1922	1927	1928	Value of Products (Thousands of Dollars) 1922	1927	1928
All industries*	147	214	207	..	463	473	.....	356,750	365,791
Electrotechnical } Metallurgical }	33	41	41	64	79	83	18,776	53,224	52,077
Wood	44	41	40	60	72	72	22,485	29,920	31,486
Chemicals	10*	18	20	..	63	65	.....	69,175	68,080
Food products	20	35	30	83	125	130	42,431	105,348	111,632
Textiles	14	37	37	17	35	39	20,705	52,167	52,351
Leather	8	10	9	10	13	15	10,044	19,426	18,288
Other industries	18	32	30	64	76	69	7,467	27,890	31,876

* Including petroleum refining in 1922, but not in other years.

Interior of a Salt Mine

Moreni Oil Fields

Industries	Value of Manufactured Goods (Millions of Lei)				
	1924	1925	1926	1927	1928
Metallurgical	4,862	6,025	7,057	8,576	8,496
Timber	5,064	5,232	5,843	4,952	5,248
Paper and Printing Trades	1,333	1,459	1,774	2,387	2,484
Chemicals	10,095	10,846	11,148	11,449	11,340
Textiles	4,878	5,644	6,656	8,684	8,725
Victualling	14,428	10,239	14,959	17,436	18,605
Tanneries	2,599	2,544	2,967	3,149	3,048
Pottery and China...	422	489	572	669	717
Electrical	82	103	115	233	184
Building Material....	976	874	1,594	1,561	1,661

Native industry supplied on the average 56 per cent of the home demand for manufactured goods, though we must take into consideration the high tariffs. All branches of industrial production exist in Roumania. In respect to the value of the products the most important industry is that of foodstuffs, and that without reckoning the produce of farmers' mills. The value of this industry's output is one-third of the total output of Roumanian industry. However, the great mills of Transylvania and the Banat have not been able to expand fully because of the former export duties. Flour mills are to be found all over Roumania. Besides raw foodstuffs, a number of food products, such as oils, cheese, pastes (macaroni), flour, glucose, and preserves also are manufactured. Distilleries use maize, potatoes, barley, and wheat as their chief materials. The more important centers are at Oradea Mare, Arad, and Bucharest.

The various chemical industries take second place in the value of their products. Fertilizers, glue, etc., are produced in sufficient quantities to meet domestic demands. The state factories at Zlatna, Firiza-de-Jos and the Valea Călugărească produce sulphuric acid. The most important chemical factory is that at Diciosânmartin, Transylvania, which manufactures carbide, cyanamid, ammonia, caustic soda, nitrogen, and oxygen. About 60 per cent of the chemical products came from this province, and only the production of soap and candles is centered in the Old Kingdom—at Galaţi, Brăila, Bucharest, Braşov, Craiova, Bârlad, Iaşi, Chişinău, and Timişoara.

The textile industry occupies third place in the schedule of national productive assets. It may eventually reach second place. In percentage of total consumption it ranks ninth, with about twenty-nine per cent, in the list, again naturally headed by foodstuffs, with ninety-seven per cent. But the total consumption of textiles, both domestic and imported, has an annual value of over $115,000,000, or nearly three times that of foodstuffs. This seemingly paradoxical situation is accounted for by the fact that the textiles still head the list of imports with a value of over $80,000,000, or over seventy per cent of the total consumed, while the value of foodstuffs imported is under $2,000,000, or little more than two per cent. Before the World War the articles made from wool in thirteen factories with 700 mechanical looms were of poor quality. At present Roumania manufactures fabrics of a high quality in 103 establishments with over 3,000 mechanical looms and is able to satisfy eighty per cent of the quantity required at home. Most of the worsted yarns used for the manufacture of fine fabrics are imported. Next in importance in material is cotton. Then come silk, jute, flax, and hemp. The finer grades of natural silk, both unmixed and in combination with wool, have to be imported. Cotton yarn is produced in Roumania by only two factories, one in Arad and the other in Bucharest. The greatest textile establishments are located in the Old Kingdom, while Transylvania has a number of small establishments around Brașov and Cenadie. The main consumer of home-made goods is the army. Silk-growing is encouraged by a law of 1924, and the industry covering both natural and artificial silk fabrics has indicated a promising future. The chief centers are in the Banat (Caraș-Severin, Timiș, and Arad districts). The total number of mulberry trees is estimated to be 300,000, planted along the highways.[51] The World War brought large losses to this industry in Bessarabia. Tighina, Cahul, Ismail, and Cetatea-Albă are the chief centers. The market for woolen hat forms is favorable, and the production of the hat form factories steadily exceeds the home consumption.

The metallurgical industry consisted mainly of small workshops before the war, which limited their work mostly to the repairing of agricultural machines and machinery needed for the petroleum industry. Raw materials had to be imported from Germany and Austria-Hungary, as well as from England and Belgium. In this respect Roumania was absolutely dependent on foreign deliveries, and this was felt most keenly after the outbreak of the war. Now, thanks to Transylvania and the Banat, Roumanian metal industries

[51] *The Near East Year Book, 1927,* p. 357.

are more independent, because the greater part of the raw materials is of native origin. However, home products can keep their home market only with the help provided by high tariffs. Because the industry is considered necessary for the defense of the country no government dares to reduce the tariff rates as the needs of the consumers would seem to require. Metallurgical works are centered in Reşiţa and Chişinău. The state iron works are at Hunedoara, Zlatna, Cugir, and Firiza-de-Jos. Metal and machinery works connected with the oil industry are located at Ploeşti.

The timber industry suffered great losses during the war. However, it employs the greatest number of workers, 41,400, or about 20 per cent of the total, and as far as the number of the establishments is concerned, this industry takes second place (after foodstuffs). The forest lands of Transylvania and of Bukovina increased the number of sawmills, which exist elsewhere throughout the country. Among the largest can be mentioned those at Cernăuţi, Cluj, Mânăstirea-Caşin, Reghinul-Săsesc, Nehoiu, Vatra-Moldoviţei, Târgu-Mureş, and Râmnicu-Vâlcea. The immense forests containing timber of the very best quality could easily compete with similar products from other countries if a commercial organization commensurate with the great economic possibilities could be built up.

The hide and leather industries were already well developed in the latter half of the nineteenth century in the Old Kingdom. Transylvania dates the beginning of these industries from the twelfth century. They declined at the end of the nineteenth century as a result of Austrian competition and preferential tariffs. The incorporation of the territory into Greater Roumania revived them again. Raw hides are mostly of native origin. The bulk of them are ox and buffalo, goat and kid, sheep and lamb skins. Tanneries are distributed throughout the country, the more important centers being Bucharest, Bacău, Iaşi, and Mediaş. The boot and shoe factories in Transylvania and the Banat, and chiefly at Bucharest, supply about 90 per cent of the demand for shoes. Gloves and belting have to be imported.

The paper and kindred industries played a rather important part in pre-war Roumania and have continued to do so in the new state. The factories at Petrifalău, Zărneşti, and Arad kept their place second to those at Buşteni, Câmpulung, and Piatra-Neamţ. With the exception of the finest paper, all home consumption is supplied by the domestic goods.

Building materials are entirely of native origin. Brick and tile factories numbering 189 can be found throughout the country. Among those producing the best work are those at Bucharest, Cluj, Oradea-Mare, Câmpina, and Ploeşti. The most important is the manufacture of cement, and the chief factories are located at Brăila, Cernavodă, and Turda. Lime is mostly produced at Câmpulung. The ceramic industry, consisting of 38 factories, produces earthenware, terra-cotta stoves, heat insulating material, and porcelain.

Electrical equipment is largely imported. The glass industry is nearly all located in Transylvania, and consists of 39 factories (Turda, Mediaş, Diciosânmartin). Glue and fertilizers are produced at Timişoara, Sfântul-Gheorghe (Transylvania), Chişinău, Rohozna, and Rădăuţi (Bukovina). There are 47 breweries, located at Bucharest, Timişoara, Cernăuţi, Turda, Braşov, Cluj, and other places.

The government aids the process of rationalization by having established in the Ministry of Industry a department of industrial rationalization. The lack of adequate transportation and of economic organization is being overcome. The growing population and the depression of the markets for the agricultural products show that Roumania will eventually have to plan expansion of her industrial activity on the basis of sensible tariff protection and with the help of foreign capital.

The situation at present, however, is not satisfactory. In 1930 and 1931 certain representative industries of Roumania were working greatly below capacity as a result of the agricultural crisis, which reduced the national income by thirty per cent and seriously curtailed the purchasing power of the country. This is evident from the following table (published by the *Argus,* Roumanian daily of commerce and industry, of April 5, 1931) showing the theoretical production capacity of the various industries, the maximum output attained in the post-war period, and the actual output in 1930 in tons and percentage of capacity:

Industry	Theoretical Capacity (Tons)	Highest Yearly Output (Tons)	1930 Output (Tons)	Percentage of Capacity
Steel—				
Cast iron	260,000	73,935	68,716	26.4
Pig iron	210,000	152,000	151,000	72.0
Laminated iron	300,000	174,706	147,231	49.0
Sheet iron	60,000	44,882	44,882	74.0
Nails and wire	79,910	39,038	26,200	32.8

Industry	Theoretical Capacity (Tons)	Highest Yearly Output (Tons)	1930 Output (Tons)	Percentage of Capacity
Textiles—				
Wool	10,000	6,720	3,300	68.0
Cotton	14,500	8,918	9,500	66.0
Knitted	6,000	1,758	1,500	25.0
Paper—				
Paper	73,560	46,807	40,875	65.0
Cardboard	5,310	3,585	3,536	46.0
Construction—				
Lumber	2,990,615	1,446,000	873,111	29.0
Brick	1,965,000	1,782,000	545,950	27.0
Cement	66,900	....	27,359	41.0
Glass	60,800	42,640	26,500	43.0
Vegetable oils	54,000	24,000	24,000	44.0
Soap	34,000	....	8,500	25.0

Furthermore, since the fall of the Liberal Government, the interests of the industries, though by no means lost sight of, have had to yield somewhat to those of agriculture. There are complaints that the height of the taxes has increased the general depression and that the export taxes have lessened the competing ability of Roumanian industries in foreign markets, especially as regards the oil industry. The instruction of the National Bank to the provincial banks not to increase small industrial credits has only complicated the problem. Roumanian industry will have to adjust itself to the changed economic conditions, resulting from the stabilization of the currency, namely, lower prices. But industries connected with the natural resources seem to have their future assured in view of their steady development.

LABOR

As far as labor is concerned, about 214,000 people are engaged in the industries. The lumber industry has the largest number of workmen and the proportion of unskilled labor here is large. The largest proportion of female workers is to be found in the textile industry. In general, the labor supply in Roumania is cheap and abundant; yet little unemployment exists. Before the war there was hardly any working class and even with the annexation of Transylvania, the Banat, and Bukovina the labor problem did not become serious.[52] The skilled workers of the provinces supply the needs of industry in the less developed parts of Roumania. The efficiency of

[52] U.S. Labor Statistics Bureau, *Monthly Review*, 1929, XXVIII, 487.

the unskilled labor is not high. Foreign specialists, skilled labor, and technicians are imported. The lower wages offset relatively the lower quality of work. The maximum hourly wage of skilled workers is 17 cents, 8 cents for factory laborers.[53] In Bucharest the maximum wage of carpenters and of metallurgical skilled workmen is 31 cents per hour, while the minimum wage of unskilled workmen is 12 cents per hour. About one-half of the industrial workers have their wages and working conditions established by collective bargaining.[54]

The Old Kingdom paid some attention to labor legislation. But only since the establishment of the Ministry of Labor in 1920 have attempts been made to co-ordinate labor legislation. The first act, passed in 1920, created the obligatory settlement of labor disputes.[55] Trade unions and similar associations were legalized in 1921. Labor exchanges were established in the same year and numbered 39 in 1930. A law of 1925 authorized Sunday rest and a rest of 24 hours on eleven national holidays. In 1927, 31 regional inspectors of labor were appointed. A law of 1928 further modified the law of 1907 for the protection of women and children; no child under 14 may be employed in commercial and industrial establishments. A maximum eight-hour day or 48 hours a week is compulsory. Night work for women is not allowed.

Strikes and lockouts are not serious. The only general strike in Roumania, in 1920, was a failure. On April 8, 1928, a law was passed for the protection of woman and child workers. The normal hours of actual work was fixed at eight in the day or 48 in the week. In addition, the juridical status was granted in 1928 to collective labor agreements. So far Roumania has ratified sixteen draft conventions and twelve proposals adopted by the International Labour Conferences.

Until 1927 no official assistance was given to the unemployed, though free employment bureaus were organized in 1921. As early

[53] U.S. Labor Statistics Bureau, *Monthly Review,* 1929, XXVIII, p. 489.

[54] According to the statistics of the Ministry of Labor, 148 collective agreements affecting 41,505 workmen were made in 1927, and 133 agreements affecting 46,288 workmen continued over from the preceding years.

[55] Article 21 of the Constitution of 1923 laid down a number of important principles. All the factors of production are to enjoy equal protection before the law; the state is empowered to legislate in any matter concerning the relationship between these various factors in order to prevent economic and social strife; the freedom of labor is guaranteed; and legislation insuring workers against sickness, accident, and other risks was to be passed.

as 1925 a law was passed protecting domestic labor against the importation of foreign skilled labor.[56] Trade unions pay out relief to their unemployed members, which in 1930 amounted to approximately $60,000. Small sums for relief have been supplied by municipalities since 1927. In 1928 the state also provided a limited support. In 1931 five per cent of the petroleum tax (amounting to about $15,000 a month) was allocated to unemployment relief.

INTERNAL TRANSPORTATION AND COMMUNICATIONS

The first railroad in Roumania was built in 1869 by an Austrian concern and connected Bucharest with Giurgiu, its Danubian port, a distance of 74 miles. Subsequent lines were gradually bought up by the state; in 1888 the government controlled the whole system. However, railway development was slow and in 1916 Roumania owned about 2,500 miles.[57] The war disorganized the whole system. The war ravages reduced the rolling stock, and the new system lacked co-ordination because the newly acquired lines in Transylvania were directed toward Budapest, Vienna, and the Adriatic, and those of Bessarabia toward Moscow and Odessa. The government endeavored to remedy the situation out of its own resources, and the greater portion of the reparations received from Germany has been used for this purpose. Work has commenced on four connecting lines in Transylvania, Bukovina, and Bessarabia. All railroads are state-managed, and most are state-owned. In 1929 Roumania had 6,915 miles of railroads.[58]

The increasing demand for service on the railroads and the deterioration of the stock, due primarily to war conditions, are evident from the following table:[59]

Item	1923	1928	1929
Length of line, miles	7,322	6,913	6,915
Locomotives, number	4,536	2,189	2,179
Passenger cars, number	6,273	2,671	3,661
Freight cars, number	90,244	52,343	55,022
Passengers carried, thousands	46,545	39,518	37,199
Passenger-miles, millions	1,988	1,736	1,794
Freight carried, 1,000 metric tons	13,268	17,039	21,557
Ton-miles, millions	1,545	1,973	2,370

[56] This law has been modified and made more strict.
[57] *Rumania: An Economic Handbook*, p. 58.
[58] *Commerce Yearbook 1930*, II, 484.
[59] *Idem.*

Item	1923	1928	1929
Gross receipts, million lei	3,095	11,344	10,926
Passenger service, million lei	1,248	3,729	3,567
Freight service, million lei	1,847	7,044	7,218
Gross receipts, equivalent $1,000	15,290	69,541	65,118

In proportion to the area of the country and the size of its population, Roumania is considerably worse off than any other Central European country in respect to railways. A large part of the proceeds of the stabilization loan concluded in February 1929 was allocated to a general reconstruction of the railways, including relaying some 870 miles of trackage, double-tracking 214 miles, and improving or adding to bridges, stations, telephone and telegraph system, rolling stock, and safety devices. Despite the administrative and accounting reforms the system is still operating at a loss, the excess of expenses over receipts being 1,003 million lei in 1929 and 945 million lei in 1930, though Roumanian freight charges are higher than those of most other European countries.

A further effort toward improving the management of the railway lines has been put forward by the Government of Iorga. Since 1929 the railways have been under a so-called "autonomous régime," but under the new one they will be directly in charge of the Ministry of Public Works and Communications. A board of management and administrative council is to be appointed, which is to pass the budget of the railways, allot contracts, and in case of a deficit can borrow from the treasury up to 20 per cent of the amount of the previous year's net earnings. The railway budget will be part and parcel of the state budget. In addition, to build up the system, the government has under way a program of improvement and expansion involving the expenditure of 21,600 million lei (about $130,000,000).

The increasing use of the automobile makes it necessary to maintain and to develop the entire system of Roumanian highways. In 1929 Roumania possessed 65,920 miles of roads, of which 7,133 are national roads, 7,200 are departmental roads, 19,674 are secondary roads, 26,591 are local roads, and 4,321 are non-classified roads in Bessarabia.

Until recently there has been no unified system for the upkeep of the roads or for building new main roads. The National-Peasant Government created the autonomous road fund with special resources to secure a national system of public highways which would connect with communication arteries with other countries and withstand the wear and tear of heavy traffic. New roads are to be constructed in Bessarabia.[60] In 1930 the state roads have been controlled by the autonomous state roads board, which is a part of the Ministry of Public Works and Communications. Most of the roads are in bad condition—a circumstance which seriously affects motor traffic, though the development of provincial motor-bus service is very general. In 1930 the number of automobiles, motor-buses, motorcycles, and other kinds of motor vehicles, reached the figure of 41,711, or about 2.45 vehicles per 1,000 inhabitants.

Roumania can boast a very extensive waterways system. The seacoast of the Black Sea, of more than 200 miles, is supplemented by 1,800 miles of river courses navigable for steam craft, which can be doubled by that extent for small boats and rafts. Besides the Danube and the Dniester, the rivers like the Prut, the Siret, the Mureş, the Olt, and the Bistriţa must be considered. What is needed is the increase of transportation facilities for the home distribution of goods and the carrying of products to the seaboard. Roumania's only port on the open sea is Constanţa, which has the largest and best-equipped warehouses and grain elevators in the country. The usefulness of Brăila and Galaţi, the chief Danubian ports, is marred because the ports are ice-blocked for about three months of the year. The most important minor Danubian ports are Reni, Sulina, Chilia Nouă, Giurgiu, and Olteniţa. With the exception of Galaţi, and possibly Brăila, the ports on the Danube lack the machinery and plants necessary for handling grain and goods generally. Several have no railroad connections, and most of them do not even possess proper wharves.

The state gives subventions to the aviation society, formed in 1920, and known as the Compagnie Internationale de Navigation Aérinne, which serves the following lines: Bucharest-Cluj; Bucharest-Iaşi-Chişinău; Bucharest-Constanţa; and Bucharest-Cernăuţi. Connections are established with the routes served by the National Airways Company between Bucharest and Istanbul, and between

[60] On March 7, 1931, the Roumanian Government and the autonomous state highways institution contracted with the Swenska Vägaktiebolaget of Stockholm for resurfacing 750 kilometers of roads, at a total cost of 71,155,840 Swedish crowns, of which 31,181,385.50 crowns are to be paid in cash and 39,974,454.50 crowns in highway bonds. The contract also provides for supplementary work such as gradings, widening of existing roads, construction of sidewalks, small bridges, and drains at a cost of 3,284,750 crowns, to be paid in cash in six yearly instalments. The work is to be completed and paid for within six years.

Bucharest and Paris, through Belgrade, Budapest, Vienna, Prague, Breslau, Nürnberg, and Strassbourg. In June 1931 a new air line was inaugurated between Bucharest and Salonika.

To recapitulate, Roumania is endowed with extensive and varied natural resources and is potentially a country of great economic wealth. While in the past it has been an important supply house of cereals for Europe, there is no doubt that with adequate transportation, greater credit facilities, and additional modernization of the production, a much larger output would be possible. The problem of transportation is pressing. The resulting inability properly to move freight has been serious, and the extent to which foreign and domestic commerce have been hampered has greatly retarded the economic readjustment of the kingdom. Fundamentally, the country's natural resources have as yet been very slightly developed. Roumania is essentially a country of the future, and her resources are awaiting capital to develop them.[61]

---

[61] Professor H. Parker Willis of Columbia University carried out an extensive study of economic and financial conditions of Roumania. Professor F. A. Ogg quotes in *Current History,* March 1931, p. 949, a digest of his report, prepared for the Carnegie Endowment for International Peace. The report was given to the press on January 10, 1931, and its content indicates that while the currency has been stabilized, agrarian reform achieved, and substantial economy effected in the effort to maintain a balanced budget, the country labors under a heavy handicap because of lack of capital. No attempt is being made at present to obtain large sums abroad, but considerable effort is being put forth to interest business men in the development of the country's resources. "The economic opportunities of Roumania," says Dr. Willis, "are vast, and those who have the vision to recognize their possibilities and to aid in realizing them, will reap a large return."

CHAPTER XII

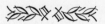

AGRARIAN REFORM

THE story of the agrarian reforms in the territory of Roumania is a long and complicated one. In one sense it shows gradual concessions to the historical processes demanding more democracy for the backbone of the nation—the peasant. Notwithstanding the incorporation of Transylvania and the Banat with their industrial development into the Roumanian state, Roumania is still predominantly agricultural. Agrarian problems naturally assume a vital importance and go straight to the heart of the nation. The great reform of 1917 changed radically the basis of the national life of the country, and Dr. David Mitrany goes so far as to maintain that "among the various social effects of the Great War the downfall of the class of large landowners has been the most outstanding on the Continent. No other effect compares with that either in intensity or extent."[1]

When one studies the problem of the Roumanian farmer, which has been varying under pressures of war and politics, one is amazed at the picture of the great tragedy of social and economic inequality which had pressed down the peasant of Roumania for centuries. Recently we have been given probably the best historical survey of the land and farmers of Roumania by Dr. Mitrany, whose book, here quoted by permission of the Carnegie Endowment for International Peace, its publishers, is eloquently described by Professor J. T. Shotwell as

a large canvas which has here been filled with the figures of those inarticulate masses of men and women to whose fate the historian has been as often indifferent as the politician has been unjust. At last, in this volume the Roumanian peasant speaks for himself to the whole world. And his plea for social, economic, and political justice is, in its very nature, a force which makes for peace.

[1] D. Mitrany, *The Land and the Peasant in Rumania,* p. xxv.

One wonders, however, whether Dr. Mitrany has not dwelt with too great emphasis upon the dark side of the story. The Roumanian peasant of the past centuries had his psychology rooted in long and intimate contact with nature; if the past centuries brought undoubted suffering, they also brought sometimes something of happiness; at any rate the past carried through servitude and oppression the germs also of future liberty.

The most astonishing thing about the history of the wide, complex, and enduring changes in the economic, social, and political transformation of the Roumanian people is the fact that they have still maintained their nationalistic culture, religion, and language. Despite the vicissitudes of history their faith in the land was preserved and even intensified. And today the whole problem of Roumania and every phase of it in its internal and international spheres can be largely explained in terms of the problems of the small peasant and thus also in the terms of agrarian reform. Throughout the evolution of the political régime of Roumania from Turkish suzerainty to 1918, the Roumanian peasants remained in a condition of servitude, practically bound to the landlords. This servitude prevailed generally; only its forms varied.

Dr. Mitrany has distinguished, in broad lines, three main periods in the downward trend of the status of the Roumanian peasantry. During the first period there was but the merest class distinction, based more than anything else on a rudimentary division of functions. But political exigencies coupled with proprietary propulsion gradually changed this. The first Roumanian prince, Mihaiu the Brave, who by uniting under his scepter the three sister countries for a moment realized unconsciously the dream which in later days was greatly cherished by the Roumanians, also must be charged with having further curtailed the peasant yeoman's freedom.

In the second period, the general misery of the peasants was shared by the landlords. The original agrarian system, generally in force under Turkish rule, permitted the peasantry to use such lands as were required to support the families in return for one-tenth of what it produced, which was passed on to the village landlords. Thus formally the peasants were not oppressed, though the peasant informally and practically had to suffer from the abuses of the landlords and had to support the terrible burden of the ever changing princes, the *boiars,* and the Porte. The Ottoman Empire was claiming an ever increasing amount of taxes, and the weight lay heavily on the shoulders of the peasants. Occasionally the peasants tried to escape the excessive taxation by surrendering the ownership of the land to the nearest *boiar* or to a monastery, keeping only the right to use under an obligation to pay the tithe and give days of work. To avoid the personal tax that they still had to pay, the peasants even agreed to give up their individual liberty in favor of the same *boiar* or monastery. At other times, serfdom came about imperceptibly as a result of the administrative and military privileges of the *boiars,* without any formal renunciation on the part of the peasant; in other cases it was violently imposed. With the political decadence of the principalities and in proportion as the produce of the country was more and more sought after by the Ottoman Empire, the position of the serfs became worse and worse.

When the provinces escaped from Turkish rule, strangely enough, the situation of the peasant was not improved. The return of the native princes[2] was followed by the imposition of larger labor dues and by the restrictions of the right of the peasant to his land.[3] Foreign affairs of Europe produced the Adrianople treaty of 1829, which opened to the Moldavian and Wallachian wheat producers the rich grain-markets of Western Europe. Agriculture became very profitable and the landlords began encroaching systematically upon peasant holdings. The situation was no better in Wallachia, and in Moldavia even the number of cattle that the peasant might possess was limited. The revolt of 1821, the Greek Hetaria movement, was really directed against social and economic exploitation by the upper classes.

The occupation of the principalities by the Russian troops made possible the legal regulation of feudal restrictions. In 1831 General Kisseleff, military governor of the principalities, promulgated the "Règlement Organique," which codified the legal position of the serfs and their obligation to the lords. The statutes also levied a tax on farm labor and diverted a great part of that labor to the landlord. For the first time the landlord became lord of the land with the title

[2] The transition from the end of the Turkish rule to its replacement by a Russian protectorate was marked by the treaties of Kutshuk Kainardji of 1772 and of Iași of 1792. The return of native princes materialized in the Convention of 1821.

[3] In 1805 the landlords secured the right to one-fourth of the meadow land. In 1828 to this was added one-third of the cultivable land. For the subsequent period see G. J. Sisesti, "Share Tenancy in Rumania," in the *International Review of Economics* (New Series), 1923, I, 210–26.

of "proprietor." The peasant was confirmed in his right to the land, but the landlord could reserve for himself one-third of the "narrow-estates," where there was not enough ground to satisfy all the inhabitants. The holdings were reduced by more than half.[4] Serfdom was formally abolished, but in fact it was reproduced in another form: the peasant could not move from one village to another, and the landlords acquired the right to conscription of "voluntary servants."[5]

On the eve of national independence the peasant population suffered under the climax of feudal oppression in the provinces. When the second period finished with the formal emancipation of the serfs, in 1864, a large number of the farmers migrated. The discontent was evident in the revolutionary movement in 1848. A provisional government of that year proclaimed the peasant free from labor dues and master of the land he occupied, but the whole question was forgotten in the Russo-Turkish intervention.

During the period of transition, Prince Alexandru Cuza, remembering the peasant rising of 1862, included in his program of reform the abolition of serfdom as one of his fundamental objects. Mihail Kogălniceanu became Prime Minister in 1863 and secularized the lands of the Greek monasteries, which formed about one-fifth of the whole territory. In compliance with the injunction of the Great Powers the peasants were emancipated a year later by an agrarian law of August 24, 1864, a hastily conceived and defective measure. It abolished the provisions of the "Règlement Organique," along with the feudal dues, and gave each cultivator the land he held. In the allotment of land the live stock possessed by the peasant was taken into account and only the heads of families were considered. The right of the peasants to pasture on forest land, and to apply for and to obtain usufruct land on the estates of the *boiars* was sacrificed to the future, while the landowners acquired the right of absolute ownership of the two-thirds remaining and of woodlands and pasturages. All together over 460,000 peasant families were emancipated and became owners of their lands.

The greatest defect of the measure, however, was its unfair application and its failure to provide means for the execution of its provisions. The land parcelled out proved to be inadequate and

---

[4] D. Mitrany, *The Land and the Peasant in Rumania,* p. 28.

[5] There was some difference in the Muntenian statute, which especially curtailed the peasant's right to land.

peasants were compelled to rent additional land from the landowners, not on the basis of rent paid in money, but in contracts for labor. Bad harvests, shortage of grazing land, and lack of money forced the small farmer to sell his labor and to fall more and more into debt. While the small proprietor was free as a citizen, he was not free as a laborer, and he was forced into servitude once more by the landlords. He had to pay the indemnity to the state and the system of labor dues continued as an economic practice. One of the results of 1864 was the rise of a new class of middlemen—generally Jewish —who rented the *boiar* land and lent money to the peasants on very hard terms. The peasants were continually forced by necessity to share tenancy on the lands of the owners of large estates as before and the farm agreement law of 1866 was really the re-establishment of serfdom in a weakened form. The peasants once again were placed at the disposal of the landlords under penal punishment clauses. If the peasant failed to come to work, the law provided that he might be forced to do so by *manu military,* after the mayor's judgment. The peasant again fell into total dependence. To borrow from Dr. Mitrany the epigram of Dobrogeanu-Gherea: "The reform of 1864 carried in its womb the terrible year of 1907."

The third period began with the declaration of constitutional liberties. The new ruling class of Roumania controlled the administrative machinery of the state. The growing corn trade made the landowners ask for more labor and land, which they secured through administrative measures. In 1872 the government made the peasants liable jointly and severally, and it was only in 1882 that compulsion by military force and the clauses relating to joint liability were suppressed.[6] But, in general, this ingenuous system was continued. Before 1908 another type of it appeared—the tithe per area. The two parties to the agreement divided between them the area to be cultivated. The landlord naturally kept the best land for himself and exacted from the peasant the best possible cultivation at the right time. Meanwhile more and more landlords were abandoning their estates and leaving them to tenants, farming speculators.

In the same period, however, the hunger of the peasant for land

---

[6] We must note that before the reform in 1917 the large estates embraced half the cultivated area of the country, and only one-tenth of the farm equipment. That meant, therefore, that farming of large estates had to be done not only by the labor of the peasants, but also with their farm implements. See D. Mitrany, *op. cit.,* pp. 260 ff.

Ion Mihalache, former Minister of Agriculture (in peasant costume which he always wears), dancing the "hora"

Typical Roumanian Peasant House

was appeased from time to time. In 1889, for example, state domains amounting to nearly one-third of the total area of the country were sold in very small lots.

Thus the policy of the kingdom followed two corollary though paradoxical lines. The peasants were endowed with very small lots of lands, and at the same time they were impressed as to their labor and were tied by contracts to the village in order to supply enough labor to the landlords. "It was the Roumanian peasant's refusal to live without land that caused him to live without freedom." His surpluses were not flowing back into the needs of the agricultural system, but to commercial and industrial undertakings, favored by the ruling class of the country.

The revolt of 1907 alarmed the rulers of the country. Never had the peasants seemed so savage as then, and about 10,000 of them had to be killed before they would consent to return to their peaceful work.[7] Hastily new laws were passed. Agricultural contracts were from now on to protect also the peasants. The agreements became public contracts, which had to be approved by communal authorities. The formation of common grazing grounds was provided for. Besides other provisions, favorable now to the small farmers, the rates were fixed district by district and the tithe per area agreements were abolished. After 1908 the only form of share tenancy maintained in Roumania was that of cultivation on the basis of sharing the produce of the joint undertaking. But even then means were found of evading the law, though the creation of the "casa rurală" (rural office) was accepted with hopes. Its main task was to facilitate the passing of various lands into the proprietorship of peasants.

But all these remedies seemed to be insufficient to the farmer, whose one desperate aspiration has been—more land. Industrial products were pushing the domestic agricultural industries out of existence. The growth of the peasant population increased the subdivision of the holdings. The price of land was rising and the prices of the products correspondingly falling. Evidently the whole situation needed a new solution based on a new policy.

Between 1907 and the World War, agitation for reform gathered strength. The campaign of the Roumanian soldiers in Bulgaria in the Second Balkan War of 1912–13 had its effects on the peasant-soldiers. Ion Brătianu acknowledged the need for land reform in a

---

[7] D. Mitrany (*op. cit.*, p. 86) suggests that the real number will never be known, as the official dossiers have disappeared.

letter published in *L'Indépendance Roumaine* (periodical) and the leader of his Liberal Party, disappointed in the poor response of the landlords to the demand for land for village commons, declared that their attitude "justified the application of the expropriation principle."[8] When Roumania joined in the World War, the King promised the soldiers that they would be recompensed for their loyalty in the face of almost overwhelming adversity and declared that at the conclusion of the hostilities they would come into possession of most of the farm land of the country then included in the landed estates. By way of binding this agreement he announced that the royal estates were on that day turned over to the peasants of Roumania. The parliament, which sat at Iaşi during the German occupation of Bucharest, convoked a constituent assembly and this body in June 1917 amended Article 19 of the Constitution. The right to expropriate for reasons of public utility was extended to expropriation for reasons of national utility. It was decreed that all inalienable lands, all lands belonging to foreigners, absenteeists, corporations and institutions, the Crown, and the "casa rurală" should be completely expropriated. The private owners were to furnish two million hectares (nearly five million acres) of cultivable land. The dispossessed owners were to be compensated for their losses.

The main principles of the reform were a bargain between the Liberals and the Conservatives, decided upon in private by Ion Brătianu and Take Ionescu. The Conservatives forced the government to abandon its intention of expropriating the soil, and it is interesting to notice that the constituent assembly had no peasant deputies on its roster of members.

The agricultural development in the provinces naturally was different because of differing political conditions. Transylvania was always a stronghold of the feudal Magyar landlords, even under the Turkish rule between 1526 and 1711. Their serfs were the Roumanian peasants. Only the Saxons had some privileges, and the free peasant of the hills found a market for his products in the Saxon towns. The conditions became worse by 1784. The reforms of Empress Maria Theresa of 1767 and 1769 seem to have been disregarded by the landlords, and even the reforms of Joseph II could

---

[8] Article 19 of the Constitution allowed the expropriation "solely for the requirements of public transport, public health, and the defence of the country." See Mitrany, *The Land and the Peasant in Rumania*, pp. 97 ff.

not stay the desperate, though futile, rising of 1784. The leaders, Horia, Cloşca, and Crişan, were broken on the wheel. As late as 1874 a law was passed regulating the dues of the serfs in kind and labor. The nineteenth century reforms, which followed the abolition of serfdom by the Austrian law of September 7, 1848 (applied to the eastern portion of the monarchy in 1853 and 1854), were applied at the expense of the former serfs. The Roumanian peasant suffered additional disadvantages through national discrimination. The whole state of affairs is admirably summed up by Professor Seton-Watson:

In the case of Transylvania, whatever may be disputed, one thing is indisputable—that the Roumanians have, from the thirteenth to the nineteenth century, occupied the position of mere serfs, and ever since the abolition of feudalism in 1848, the position of political helots.[9]

The condition before 1914 was described by Dr. Oscar Jászi as "the fatal antagonism between the opulent aristocracy and the wretched peasantry." The growing dissatisfaction of the Roumanians, political persecution, and many other abuses provided the atmosphere for the National Assembly of Alba-Iulia, which, on December 1, 1918, declaring the union of Transylvania and the Banat with the Kingdom of Roumania, accepted the principle of expropriation.[10] The quota which could be retained by private estates was limited to a maximum of 300 hectares and depended upon the density of the population and upon the length of the absence of the proprietors from the holdings.

In Bessarabia the distribution of land property dates from the reforms of 1861–66, when the decrees of Alexander II emancipated the peasant and provided him with land in the collective form of the "mir." The land was not made over to the individual peasants, but to local communes, called "mir," whose duty it was to divide it up periodically for cultivation. The ever growing indebtedness of the Russian *boiars* enabled the industrious and enterprising peasantry to purchase property from the large owners, and by the end of the nineteenth century some 800,000 acres had thus passed into peasant

[9] R. W. Seton-Watson, *Roumania and the Great War,* p. 35.

[10] Proclaimed by Decree No. 2911 of 1919, and subsequently amplified by the Law of July, July 30, 1921. All property belonging to institutions, corporations, foreigners, and absentee lords was liable to total expropriation, as well as all private estates leased for farming purposes for more than twelve years between 1900 and 1918.

hands.[11] The so-called Stolypin law of 1906 was intended to further the establishment of individual peasant holdings with the financial help of the Peasant Bank. The law voted by the "Sfatul Țării" on November 27, 1918, accepted the principle of expropriation. On March 4, 1920, the Roumanian parliament passed an agrarian law for Bessarabia. Its provisions were very drastic, and total expropriation of all crown domains, state lands, and holdings of peasants' banks and foreign monasteries was proclaimed.[12]

Bukovina was acquired by Austria at the conclusion of the Russo-Turkish War in 1774. The wretchedness of the peasants convinced the Austrians that a definite legal basis should give the serfs a status corresponding as much as possible to that in force in the territory of the Bohemian crown. The patent of 1782 set a limit to the exactions of the *boiars*. A decree of 1878 attempted to guarantee each individual the land he occupied. But the "community holdings" survived. Meanwhile the territory was losing its Roumanian character. All feudal services were abolished in 1848, but the financial application of the reform was not completed until the early '70's. An Imperial Rescript of 1858 made over to the peasants three-fourths of the area of the province. I. L. Evans has concluded on the basis of his exhaustive study that despite the numerous defects of the Austrian administration the reform "established peasant proprietorship on a much wider scale than was the case in any of the other Provinces of what is now Greater Roumania,"[13] with the sole exception of Dobrogea.

On September 6, 1919, the National Council of Bukovina approved a project for expropriation of land, and on September 23, 1921, an agrarian law for Bukovina was passed by the Roumanian Parliament. The property was expropriated on a sliding scale on lines similar to those adopted in the other Roumanian provinces.

Agrarian reform, as introduced into the Constitution in 1917, was supplemented, strengthened, qualified, and administered under sepa-

[11] I. L. Evans, *The Agrarian Revolution in Roumania,* p. 63.

[12] Holdings of foreigners who had not made a declaration of Roumanian nationality by January 1, 1919, were totally expropriated, as well as holdings of owners who had not farmed their lands at any time between 1905 and 1918 for an uninterrupted period of five years. The act of March 11, 1920, amended the earlier legislation in some respects, and provided that the owners of over 100 hectares could keep 100 hectares (247 acres) of cultivable land, plus vineyards, orchards, and nurseries (see Evans, *op. cit.,* p. 112).

[13] I. L. Evans, *The Agrarian Revolution in Roumania,* p. 57.

rate laws for pre-war Roumania and for each of the provinces incorporated after the war.[14]

To summarize, then, the 1921 law for the Old Kingdom expropriated: (1) All arable land on crown and state domains and in the possession of public institutions; (2) all estates belonging to foreigners; (3) all estates of Roumanian citizens with permanent residence abroad, or who had at no time during the previous ten years farmed their land themselves; and (4) the arable land of private landowners, according to the equipment possessed by them and to the local demand for land, down to the reserved minimum of 100 hectares and up to a maximum of 500 hectares.

The Bessarabian law of 1920 was more drastic, and reduced all estates to a maximum of 100 hectares; furthermore, it included forests, which became the property of the state for the provision of communal woodlands, etc. In Transylvania, the law of 1921 was applied on a similar basis, but the measurements were in jugars. In Bukovina, the law of 1921 was limited in its scope, as peasant property was better represented there; the exempted quota varied from 100 to 250 hectares.

The landlords were compensated in amounts equal to 40 times the rental value of the land in the period 1917–22, and payments were made by the state in bonds bearing 5 per cent interest and redeemable in 40 years. But the depreciation of the leu to about one-fortieth of its value really meant another drastic expropriation. The peasants bear 65 per cent of the compensation, and the remainder is assumed by the state.

The extent of the reform can be made evident by means of statistics. The distribution of arable land before the reform was as follows:[14a]

	Up to 100 hectares	Percentage	Above 100 hectares	Percentage
Old Kingdom	4,593,148	57.5	3,397,851	42.5
Bessarabia	2,337,811	55.9	1,844,539	44.1
Transylvania	4,689,855	63.0	2,751,457	37.0
Bukovina	405,000	78.0	115,000	22.0
Total	12,025,814		8,108,847	

Altogether 6,007,106 hectares have been expropriated, which up

[14] See D. Mitrany, *The Land and the Peasant in Rumania,* p. 122.

[14a] D. Mitrany, "Fresh Start for the Peasants," in *Manchester Guardian,* November 28, 1929, p. 23, also *op. cit.,* pp. 201–25.

to the end of 1927 had been distributed to 1,368,978 peasants as follows:

Division	Hectares
Old Kingdom	2,037,293.04
Transylvania	451,363.96
Bukovina	42,832.25
Bessarabia	1,098,045.50
	3,629,534.75

Not all of the expropriated area has been handed over to individual small holders. A considerable portion of it has been used for communal grazing lands and woodlands, as well as for the creation of a land reserve from which public needs, such as the building of roads, town extensions, model farms, etc., may be satisfied.

The general distribution of arable land shows the following picture:

	Up to 100 hectares	Percentage	Above 100 hectares	Percentage
Old Kingdom ...	7,369,459	92.22	621,450	7.73
Transylvania	3,829,731	91.57	352,619	8.43
Bessarabia	6,353,664	85.38	1,087,648	14.62
Bukovina	480,967	92.49	39,033	7.51
Total	18,033,911		2,100,750	

By 1927 out of the total of 1,979,083 peasants entitled to land 1,368,978 had received a share. The arable area of the whole country was divided as follows:

	Before the Reform		After the Reform	
	Hectares	Percentage	Hectares	Percentage
Small property	12,025,814	59.77	18,033,911	89.56
Large property	8,108,847	40.23	2,100,750	10.44

From these figures we may conclude that the general reform has not been finally achieved. About one-third of the claimants have been left out of the distribution of the expropriated property, and not all of the remaining two-thirds have received what they are to receive. The small property now predominates in the agricultural life of Roumania but in most cases has not reached the necessary economic autonomous level.

The distribution process also came under severe criticism. Not only haste but also inadequate means for the measurement of the land, as well as the complexity of economic criteria of expropriation, aggravated the process. The reform was not without abuses and consequent ill feeling.

The agrarian reform of 1917 was designed primarily to meet political and social exigencies, and not too much attention could be paid to modern economic factors. Notwithstanding this fact, the total agricultural production slumped dangerously, especially in the years following the conclusion of the armistice. Even now the yield per acre is comparatively low.[15] But it must be remembered the decline in production must be considered a result also of the devastation and disorganization by the war and its psychological consequences, as well as of the greater diversification of crops, the perplexities of the actual transferring of the land, and the poverty and low economic standard of the peasants. Last, but not least, the general economic policy of the post-war government, favoring the industrialization of the country and considering the agrarian question solved by the reform, must be taken into consideration.[16]

Several misconceptions regarding the effects of the reform have been effectively disposed of by Dr. Mitrany. The critics of the reform point out that the passage from a large-scale agrarian system to peasant farming will permanently weaken Roumania's economic system. They fail to note the fact that over two-thirds of the arable land belonging to the landlords before the reform was rented by the peasants. Consequently the new system brought about an enormous change in the distribution of property but not a very striking change in the organization of farming. The great landowners, as suggested before, had had to employ the peasants with their implements and teams. Hence the reform could dispose of the landlords as non-essential factors of economic production in Roumania.

Another observable phenomenon is the decline of wheat-growing. The raising of cereal crops is diminishing in average, while artificial grazing and fodder crops are steadily increasing, as they are

---

[15] According to the statistics of the United States Department of Commerce, *Commerce Yearbook 1930,* II, 481, the production of the pre-war and post-war years has been as follows (thousands of units) :

	1909–13*	1923–27	1928	1929
Wheat	158,672	96,979	115,544	101,200
Rye	20,644	8,827	11,483	13,267
Barley	61,677	54,758	69,403	125,873
Oats	59,776	59,065	67,546	93,647
Corn	193,209†	167,921	108,514	251,415

* Four-year average, present boundary.
† Two-year average, present boundary.

[16] The author cannot but refer the reader again to D. Mitrany's *The Land and the Peasant in Rumania,* pp. 281 ff., an excellent analysis of the effects of the reform.

better adapted to a rural economy based largely on the keeping of animals.

Undoubtedly the reform improved the standard of living and raised the level of the most numerous class of Roumania. The growing demand for schools (see Appendix) has shown the growing emancipation of mind, which effects a new political keenness in the peasants.

In conclusion it may be said that whereas the lot of the Roumanian peasant was very hard in past centuries his serfdom was continued and even intensified during the times when the country was nearing political emancipation and consolidation. While the peasant was occasionally granted more land for his use, the amount was never sufficient and the domination of the landlords found expression in an effective way in tying the small farmer to the village and forced labor. Usury and absenteeism were predominant before the war. What is amazing is that the peasant kept his nationalism throughout the centuries of oppression. The World War changed thoroughly the basis of the agrarian system and the agrarian reform in the Old Kingdom and in the new provinces virtually obliterated the landed upper class and substituted for it a class of small landowners, who, however, have not been allowed to benefit from their position, largely because of the economic and social policies of the post-war governments. There was no narrow or selfish economic motive behind the reform, and its beneficial results have practically created a new life and civilization in Roumania. The peasants now have a chance to assert themselves as a strong political class, favoring agrarianism against the mercantilism of their former opponents.

CHAPTER XIII

ECONOMIC POLICY

Agriculture has been for centuries and will in future be the principal occupation of the Roumanian people. Ion Mihalache, Minister of Agriculture in the National-Peasant Government, emphasized the point:

> The form and the organization of the modern State of Rumania and its cultural progress during the last three-quarters of a century has been for the most part due to the part played by agriculture within it. Since Roumania became once again a State until today agriculture has enabled it each year to show a surplus on the balance-sheet of its material wealth, and that surplus has permitted the State to provide Rumania with roads and railways, ports, and administrative and cultural institutions. Equally it has made possible the development of the fundamental conditions of national life, increase of the population, and the consequent increase in the capacity for production on the part of the Rumanian people.[1]

To create a large surplus from agriculture, however, is a slow and occasionally a difficult task, since the variability of returns is a serious question. A slight variation in the rainfall often means a serious loss. Nevertheless, during the thirty years preceding the World War, Roumania succeeded in creating, within her own limitations, several branches of industry connected with agriculture and the natural riches of the soil.[2] The lack of an adequate system of transportation and of economic organization have been serious handicaps, however.

About the '80's of the last century the ruling classes of the kingdom began to entertain the idea of creating a national industry. The general crisis of those days brought about a reduction in exports, and the competition of the overseas countries led to an occasional

---

[1] Ion Mihalache, "Back to the Land," in *Manchester Guardian,* November 28, 1929, p. 39. Quoted by permission.

[2] For an excellent discussion, see L. Pasvolsky, *Economic Nationalism in the Danubian States.*

unfavorable balance of trade. It was believed that decreasing the dependence of Roumania on the outside world would solve the situation, and the remedy suggested to the statesmen of Roumania was the upbuilding of national industries. But there was a considerable lack of the capital needed for fundamental improvements, such as the construction of railways and general economic development. The exports were insufficient to pay for the imports; it was only after the beginning of the present century that exports began to exceed imports. But this surplus had to be used for the payment of interest and amortization, which payments usually exceeded export surpluses.[3] Dr. Pasvolsky estimates that by 1914 the total foreign debt was between 1,500 and 2,000 million lei.[4]

Most of the working capital came from Berlin, Vienna, and Budapest. There have also been investments of French and British capital, but their importance fell behind the German and even the Belgian investments.[5]

On the other hand, there seemed to be several elements in favor of the industrial policy. The influx of foreign capital, the wealth of agricultural products and of the soil, especially in the production of timber and oil, were aided by the advantages of cheap labor and the local markets protected by tariffs, which encouraged national production. An effective system of protection was especially well realized in 1906 and, in general, lower rates were put into effect on raw materials and on machinery necessary for factory installations than on finished products. Dr. Pasvolsky attributes this policy to the spirit of nationalism, "which had wrested political independence from the hands of the Ottoman Empire, and persisted through the three and a half decades of Roumania's pre-war existence as a nation."

In spite of these attempts tending toward the industrialization of the country, Roumania was still, in 1914, a predominantly agricultural state. Dr. Madgearu estimates that at that time about 10 per cent of the working population worked in the industries and that of the estimated national wealth of 21,150 million gold francs only 330 million, or some 1.5 per cent, were invested in industry.[6] The dis-

[3] L. Pasvolsky, *op. cit.,* p. 51.

[4] *Idem.* See references quoted therein and in H. Feis, *Europe the World's Banker, 1870–1914,* pp. 268 ff.

[5] See G. Boncesco, "A Field for American Investments," in *Roumania,* April 1929, pp. 33–38.

[6] M. Virgil Madgearu, "Economic Policy," in *Economic Survey of Roumania* (reprinted from *The Economist,* 1929), p. 8.

proportion was especially evident in the exports. The agricultural products amounted to about 75.7 per cent of the total, while industrial were only 3 per cent.[7]

The economic results of the war fundamentally altered the immediate problems. The administration of the enlarged territory required a new machinery; various currencies needed to be consolidated; and new means of communications needed to be established to correspond to the political system. The economic relations of the new provinces were interrupted and their direction oriented toward their new country. The state was burdened with large foreign and internal debts and other obligations growing out of the far-reaching agrarian reform, which, together with the influence of the war, reduced the general productivity of the farm land. State expenditures outstripped receipts, and there was hardly any liquid capital left in the country. The occupation by the Austro-Hungarian-German armies denuded the country of food and raw materials, and Roumania, one of the great producers of the cereals in the world, had to import cereals to feed its own population.

The strife and final victory necessarily intensified the spirit of nationalism to an extreme degree. The months following the armistice strengthened it. The unsettled domestic conditions and foreign antagonism of Russia and Hungary, as well as the attitude of the Allies at the Peace Conference, convinced Roumanians that the solution of their difficulties depended on their patriotism. In this belief they were supported by the experiences of the war. The impossibility of importing manufactured goods from the Allied countries during the conflict made the leaders of Roumania determined to prevent the recurrence of such a situation if they could do so. In addition, the acquisition of Transylvania and the Banat, more pronouncedly industrial in their character, seemed to be pointing the future road of economic policy which should be followed by the enlarged Roumanian kingdom. To the petroleum industry of the kingdom were added the coal, iron, textile, sugar, chemical, and other industries of the provinces. The Liberal governments decided that it was time to achieve the ideal of national economic self-sufficiency, and thus led Roumania into what Dr. Pasvolsky calls "an uncompromising assertion of economic sovereignty . . . . imbued with a fear of economic colonization."

Dr. Mitrany's excellent study of the agrarian reform in his *The*

[7] *Idem.*

Land and the Peasant in Rumania leaves no room for doubt that the agrarian production of Roumania was disturbed by the reform. But what is more important is that this transition period was hampered by the economic policy of the government. The land was not immediately transferred to the peasants. The damages of the war required capital for the restoration of the agricultural production, which was adjusting only very slowly to the consequences of the reform. But the state was pressing the peasant for the tax money, which was so needed for the upbuilding of their small properties, and was using it as a revenue source. The credit policy removed the possibilities for credits. The large landowners had but little land left for credit and the small farmers, beneficiaries of the reform, were forbidden by law to sell or mortgage their newly acquired land. When some additional working capital could be brought into the country, and the exports of the agricultural produce could be sold for a good price, the government stopped the exports of wheat and of wheat flour, as well as of meat, oats, barley, millet, and caviar. The prices were kept low at home through the maximum prices set by the government, and the wheat growers were unable to recover even their investment from the low official prices. This situation led naturally to passive resistance on the part of the peasants, when the production should really have been increased in order to amend the war ravages. To aggravate the situation, already made harsh by the lack of capital and by the nationalistic policy aiming to restrict the use of foreign capital, the government followed the policy of revalorization of money until the end of 1927. The post-war years in Roumania were thus cursed with a money crisis and high rates of interest, as well as some years of bad harvests, which occasionally forced the government to buy wheat from abroad.[8]

In comparison to the favors granted to industry, agricultural favors came out at the small end of the horn. The credits granted to the latter were insufficient.[9] High import duties on agricultural

---

[8] D. Mitrany, *The Land and the Peasant in Rumania*, p. 302.

[9] Notice the discrepancy of the movement in credit advances, given by *The Near East Year Book, 1927*, p. 297 (in millions of lei):

	1920	1921	1922	1923	1924
Agriculture	879	947	2,021	2,441	2,600
Industry and commerce	864	2,008	6,231	11,680	15,000

Pasvolsky estimates that the transactions of the Society for Industrial Credit reached one milliard lei in 1924, and those of the agricultural lending banks only about 95,000,000 lei.

machines and implements discouraged purchase of these necessities. While the other classes paid taxes on their net income, the farmers had to pay nearly half the value of their gross income. At the same time the farmer had to buy at high prices the products of the domestic industry protected heavily by high tariffs.

We may safely affirm that with the exception of the mining and rural industries the industries of Roumania are not important to the national economy. And yet all ten post-war years seem to have been devoted by the Liberal governments to advancing their interests. To this end the support of all manner of industries by the official policy—many of them, in the opinion of the political opponents of the Liberals, lacking a natural basis for development within the country—was bolstered up by tariffs, modified six times and each time increasing import duties on industrial products, which immediately had the effect of increasing the cost of living. Having set their face against foreign capital, the Liberals encouraged the multiplication of banks largely dependent on the funds of the National Bank and in turn supporting the newly formed industries. "A Law for the Encouragement of the National Industry," originally enacted in 1912, but modified in 1920, provided for certain privileges and exemptions for a period of thirty years to those industries derived from agriculture, or from the soil or subsoil. Native enterprises could purchase factory sites at a low price fixed by the Ministry of Industry and Commerce, while foreigners could rent such sites for a period of ninety-nine years only. The industrial companies were enjoying reductions on railroad rates and some exemption from taxes; machinery, parts, and accessories were exempted from custom duties. Other favors were added later: export of raw materials was prohibited, maximum prices for fuel were fixed, and credit privileges were granted. The surplus for these favors had to come from agriculture, and Dr. Mitrany summarized it well when he said: "Agriculture was mere spectator but had to pay the bill."

In 1923 the government organized the "Societatea Naţională de Credit Industrial" (National Society of Industrial Credit) with a capital of 500 million lei. It was largely backed by the National Bank. The rates were fixed at the maximum of 12 per cent, and compared very favorably with the high rates charged by commercial banks.

The trend of the nationalistic policy became most evident with the passing of the Roumanian Constitution of 1923, which introduced the principle of nationalization of the subsoil. This constitutional provision was immediately followed by the mining law of 1924, which laid down the principle that the exploitation of oilfields would in future be carried out only by "nationalized" companies. The rights of existing companies were safeguarded up to a point, in respect of concessions already granted, but as a mining property is a wasting asset and a company must depend on further extensions to prolong its life, the effect of the provisions restricting further exploitation to companies with 60 per cent of their capital in Roumanian hands, with a Roumanian chairman and a majority of the board Roumanian citizens, was to prevent the future domination of the economic life by foreign enterprises and safeguard national interests.[10]

However, the results have been quite contrary to those expected by the originators of the law. The hope of creating a national petroleum trust which would meet the international trusts in the world's markets and assure an outlet for the native oil industry failed to materialize, mainly because of the resulting curtailment of foreign capital investments in Roumania. Many corporations camouflaged the nationality of their capital structures. Despite the nationalistic character of the law, the production of companies with foreign and mixed capital increased while that of companies with Roumanian capital decreased.

Thus the mining law of 1924, besides causing unnecessary friction between Roumania and foreign capital, worked to the detriment not only of foreign interests but of the interests of the Roumanian people as well.[11]

The coming into power of the National-Peasant Government in 1928 resulted in a thorough reorganization of the economic order of Roumania by legislative reforms and administrative measures; the policy favoring agrarianism supplanted that of industrialism; "the principle of economic interdependence" was substituted for "the illusion of economic self-sufficiency"; and the public undertakings dependent upon departmental bureaucracy and the formalism of the

[10] The United States Department of State repeatedly protested against the provisions of the law and argued that these provisions in effect confiscated rights and investments of the New Jersey Standard Oil Company.

[11] Dr. Virgil Madgearu, *Rumania's New Economic Policy*, pp. 18 ff. This little volume forms the basis of our discussion concerning the economic reforms of the National-Peasant Government.

law of public accountancy were transformed into autonomous public commercial administrations. The central idea of the program was the recognition of the fact that Roumania is primarily an agricultural country, and that agriculture must take precedence in the economic policy of the government.

The application of this policy began with the reorganization of the important properties owned by the state. The Roumanian state owns, besides mineral resources (the entire subsoil wealth, oil, natural gas, coal, salt, etc.), the following enterprises:[12]

	In Gold Lei	In Dollars
Railroads	2,139,500,000	427,900,000
Post, telegraphs, telephones	110,000,000	22,000,000
Seaports	77,400,000	15,480,000
Danube ports	56,000,000	11,200,000
Docks at Galaţi and Brăila	17,000,000	3,400,000
Danube navigation steamship lines...	12,200,000	2,440,000
Maritime steamship lines	5,370,000	1,074,000
Climatic and health resorts	23,500,000	4,700,000
State monopolies	66,900,000	13,380,000
Forests	1,375,000,000	263,000,000
Fisheries	176,500,000	35,300,000
Mines and industrial enterprises	40,000,000	8,000,000
Land and farms	500,000,000	100,000,000
Total	4,599,370,000	907,874,000

Details regarding the annual return on the various properties are presented in the following table (exclusive of the rights on the subsoil in the case of mining and industrial enterprises):

	Value (1927) in Dollars	Percentage Annual Return
Railroads	427,900,000	Deficit
Maritime steamship lines	1,074,000	Deficit
Mining and industrial enterprises	8,000,000	Deficit
Forests	263,000,000	0.06
Fisheries	35,300,000	3.05
Seaports	15,480,000	3.20
Danube ports	11,200,000	0.73
Danube navigation steamship lines	2,440,000	2.20
Climatic and health resorts	4,700,000	0.08
Docks in Galaţi and Brăila	3,400,000	0.08
Post, telegraph, telephone	22,000,000	9.80

[12] *Roumania*, April 1929, p. 93. The wealth of the state before the war was estimated by N. Xenopol at 2,320 million gold lei, equivalent to $464,000,000; the present wealth of the Roumanian state, according to Dr. I. N. Angelescu, reaches the figure of 6,200 million gold lei, or about $1,240,000,000, inclusive of the mining wealth and the state's sovereign rights.

The adverse results of the state's commercial activities after the war induced the government to consider the idea of commercializing all state enterprises. The law of 1924 for the commercialization of state undertakings divided all enterprises belonging to the state into two groups: On the one hand, economic enterprises of general interest, performing public services, concerned with national safety and defense, or being monopolies (tobacco, matches, cigarette paper, playing cards, explosives, salt, and alcohol); these enterprises included railroads, posts, telegraphs, telephones, and, in part at least, the state monopolies department. On the other hand, enterprises of a purely commercial and industrial character which were state-owned but were not monopolies (mines, forests, fisheries, metallurgical works, various industries, river and maritime steamship companies, owned by the state).[13] Special legislation gave the enterprises of the first group autonomy, an independent budget, power to contract loans for equipment, management of commercial lines, etc. They were to be regulated by limited companies, formed by the state and by private individuals. Roumanian capital was to have a majority[14] and the shares were to be inscribed and disposed of by public subscription.

However, the mixed management proved to be no impulse toward the development of the state's properties. Not only prior to the war, but during the years following it as well, the returns have been rather insignificant. In fact the pre-war annual return decreased from 5.4 per cent to 1.5 per cent in 1927, not considering the failure to provide for depreciation or amortization.

The National-Peasant Government passed in 1929 a new commercialization law. Private capital—both domestic and foreign—was enabled to go into partnership with the state in the management and exploitation of the state's wealth on equitable terms. A condition was made that private investors were to participate to the

[13] The state domain comprises: (1) forests, 20 per cent of the wooded surface of the country; (2) fisheries, in the Delta, in the Danubian marshes and in South Bessarabia; (3) mines, coal at Lonea-Petroşani, pyrites at Zlatna, gold and silver at Abrud and Haramb and Luncouil, copper at Altân-Tepe (Dobrogea), methane gas at Cluj, etc.; (4) metallurgical works at Hunedoara, Cujir, Baia-Mare, etc.; (5) river and maritime navigation companies, "Navigaţiunea Fluvială Română" (known as "N.F.R.") and "Serviciul Maritim Român (S.M.R.)"; (6) docks at Brăila, Galaţi, Constanţa; watering places (Mehadia, Sibiu, etc.).

[14] The participation of foreign capital could not exceed 40 per cent of the share capital, and at least two-thirds of the boards had to be Roumanian citizens.

extent of 50 per cent in the company which may be charged with the exploitation of any of the state's property, with the right to elect two-thirds of the board of directors. All existing forms of enterprises were made possible—leases, concessions, public commercial administration, mixed administration, and co-operative enterprises. All the restrictions formerly imposed on foreign capital were completely abolished. To co-ordinate the whole system a superior council for the administration of public properties and enterprises was set up.

On February 7, 1929, the autonomous institute of monopolies was created and the whole system was reorganized on commercial lines. The state transmitted to the institute the exclusive, irrevocable, and non-transferable right of controlling all the monopolies (tobacco, salt, explosives, playing cards, and matches, the match monopoly being operated by the Swedish trust). The bonds of the institute were guaranteed unconditionally by the Roumanian Government; the price of the monopoly concessions was fixed at $300,000,000. The operations of the institute being of a commercial nature, it enjoys all the rights and powers of commercial companies. The institute will liquidate after thirty years and its assets and monopolies will be returned to the state.

The attempt to put the exploitation of state properties on an economic basis began with a radical reform of the mining policy. The new mining law of March 28, 1929, proposed to reorganize the whole mining régime so as to meet the needs of the country and at the same time encourage investments of foreign capital, without encroaching upon the sovereign rights of the state. Foreign capital enjoys full freedom of investment, and the presence of foreign experts among the operating personnel is allowed. Foreign companies are granted the right to use their discretion in the appointment of executives. The director general, the technical director, the general manager, and the members of the board of directors need no longer be of Roumanian nationality, and 25 per cent of the technical, business, and administrative staff can be composed of foreign citizens. A comprehensive cadastral survey of the oil regions is being carried out with the aid of air photography to promote the speedy definition of acquired rights of private owners and of the state. Facilities are granted to prospectors to stimulate the work of exploration on the state's mining domains, and concessions may be obtained by any kind of enterprise constituted by any method and with capital of any nationality. State reserves are being auctioned off in a manner to promote prospecting in localities at a distance from established oil fields.

The inadequacy of the transport system has been one of the principal reasons for the tardy pace of economic reconstruction of Roumania. For years efforts were made periodically to raise a loan with a view to undertaking the repairs and additions necessary to bring it up to the standard required by the growing trade and industry. Traffic has increased since the war and the facilities are being subjected daily to an abnormal strain. The conversion of many of the single lines to double track, especially on international routes, was a necessity. Moreover, because of the new trade currents created by the union of the provinces, several small lines were required to link up the systems in the new provinces with each other and with the Old Kingdom. The present railway system of 6,915 miles does not meet the needs of Greater Roumania.[15] Among the connecting arteries, the Bumbeşti-Livezeni, Buzău-Nehoiaşi, and Dorna Vatra–Iva Mare lines are being constructed and need special funds. Lines with great stations like those at Ploeşti-Braşov and Madefălău–Târgu Ocna must be electrified in view of the increase in traffic. An essential part of the reconstruction program and normal development of the Roumanian railways is the renewal of old rails and the changing of the present type of old rails on many lines, replacing them with a heavier type. There is also need to modify the stations, which do not have sufficient sidings or have too short ones, and to introduce in others modern installations for signaling and for switch centralization.

A large part of the proceeds of the stabilization loan of 1929 was allocated to a general reconstruction of railways: 35 million dollars for capital expenditure and 9 million dollars for paying off overdue debts. The program included relaying some 870 miles of track, double-tracking 214 miles, and improving or adding to bridges, telephone and telegraph systems, rolling stock, and safety devices.[16] A public body, known as the Autonomous Roumanian

[15] The management of the Roumanian State Railways estimates that a normal functioning of the actual system would require 2,800 locomotives and 78,000 cars as compared with the 2,179 locomotives and 58,683 cars circulating in 1929. New rolling stock is bought at present and old locomotives and cars are repaired. However, not all the old cars and locomotives can be repaired, owing to the fact that many of them are obsolete.

[16] See *Roumania,* April 1929, p. 92; and N. Codreanu, "Railways' Diamond Jubilee," in *Manchester Guardian,* November 28, 1929, pp. 43–45, for the details of the program for the construction of new railway lines.

Railways Corporation ("C.F.R."), administered on commercial principles, now manages the state railways. A more efficient accounting system was introduced, as well as monthly publication of receipts and expenditures. Gratuities and reduced tariffs have been abolished. The state pays now for public services. The Minister of Communications has no longer any authority in matters of railroad administration, though the state retains complete control over the program of construction of lines, and over the convention policies of the railroads, either international conventions or conventions between railroads and water-way enterprises.

Until recently there has been no unified organization in charge of the upkeep of the road system or the building of new main roads. Maniu's Government created an autonomous administrative organ, the autonomous road fund, with special resources at its disposal and an independent budget, which is to build in Roumania a national system of public highways, connecting the country with foreign countries, and to modernize the state road system. Mention should be made also of the act dealing with the public commercial administration of state pipe lines, freed from the authority of the railways and also given autonomy.

An important state property is the inundated riverside regions, which require improvement both for agricultural purposes and for fisheries. The act of July 1929 was planned to put a stop to the previous wasteful policy, and created a unified administration under completely autonomous economic and technical direction, a public commercial organization for the exploitation of fisheries and of the inundated regions of the state.

While it has been possible for the railways to carry reasonably well the imports from Western Europe, the situation is different with exports, for they are bulky and heavy and the system cannot very well meet the demands they impose. Hence the encouragement of river and maritime navigation became a part of the program of the National-Peasant Government, which also aimed to make Roumania a transit nation of Europe, owing to the fact that it controls the mouth of the Danube and thus connects the West and East through the tributaries of the Danube and the connecting canals, on the one hand, and the Black Sea, on the other. With the same fundamental lines of policy, the government turned the old general office of ports and waterways, created in 1908, into an autonomous administration, which was to organize exploitation on a commercial basis. Navigation on the Danube has been for some years passing through a severe crisis. To ameliorate the situation the government proceeded to create free zones in the ports of Brăila, Galaţi, Giurgiu, and Constanţa, and large sums have been expended on the construction of the ports. The construction of a canal from Bucharest to the Danube is under way.

In addition, the general direction of the postal, telegraph, and telephone service was also turned into an autonomous organization. The law promulgated on July 3, 1930, authorized the autonomous postal, telegraph, and telephone service to conclude a contract with the International Telephone and Telegraph Corporation of New York City for the development and improvement of the system.[17] This American company was empowered to incorporate a Roumanian subsidiary, with headquarters at Bucharest, which is to develop a system of urban, interurban, rural, and international telephones, as well as a service by wire, cable, and wireless. The new company was granted the exclusive right to exploit telephones, and took over, with the exception of the railway and state military telephones, the existing public telephone facilities upon payment to the state of the total value of outstanding investments.[18]

Another consequence of the new economic policy of the National-Peasant Government was the passing of the power law in 1930. It purports to regulate the generation, transmission, and distribution of electrical energy by means of concessions which are to be granted either by the state or by its administrative subdivisions under the advice of the national power board. The law was obviously intended to foster the development of the country's water power and to favor the installation of steam-generating stations burning cheap or run-of-mine coal at the mines. The construction and exploitation of hydroelectric or thermal generating stations are exclusive rights of the state, and may be transferred through concessions. The law

[17] See a pamphlet published by the information department of the International Telephone and Telegraph Corporation, 67 Broad Street, New York City, entitled "Rumania," p. 31. Additional information and details can be found in *Roumania,* 1930, VI, 82–83.

[18] The state is to receive 10 per cent of the net annual profits, provided this sum equals or exceeds 4 per cent of the gross after deduction of dividends and interests. Provision is made that after twenty years, at the government's option and upon reimbursement of the existing investments, calculated in gold lei, and upon payment of a premium of 15 per cent thereof, the service may revert to the state. In emergencies affecting the safety of the government the state may temporarily operate all telephone service.

requires, however, that even the building of individual plants should be authorized by the state. Thermic generating stations may also be ceded for not more than 60 years, and, as in the case of hydroelectric stations, at the expiration of the concession, lands, buildings, and equipment are to revert to the state without indemnity except for investments made during the last ten years. The transmission of energy constitutes also an exclusive state right, transferable by concession to private enterprises, the maximum term of such a concession being 50 years. Exclusive concessions may be granted to individuals or companies in a position to offer certain financial guaranties and to assume the obligation to build on the same stream or river hydroelectric generating stations of at least 10,000 horsepower capacity.[19]

Another corollary of the new orientation was the reduction of the general level of Roumanian tariffs. In fact, Roumania was the first country to reduce her tariffs in accordance with the resolutions passed in 1927 at the economic conference convened by the League of Nations.

Enough has probably been said of the reform of the National-Peasant Government to intimate the radical departure from the

[19] See S. T. Drutzu, "Developing Roumania's Power Resources," in *Roumania*, 1930, VI, 20–29. According to Engineer Drutzu, Roumania's power supply on December 31, 1929, was 1,167,300 installed horsepower, or 46.85 horsepower per thousand population. We must notice that in the United States this ratio in 1929 was 547 horsepower.

This total Roumanian capacity as stated by this author comprised:

	Horsepower	Percentage
Steam engines and turbines	632,200	55.1
Gas engines	40,400	3.5
Oil engines	406,000	34.8
Water turbines	88,700	7.6
Total	1,167,300	100.0

In 1928 the distribution of prime movers among the chief Roumanian industries was:

Industry	Steam	Gas	Oil	Hydro	Total	Percentage
Foodstuffs	87,000	7,480	168,000	16,330	278,810	23.9
Light and power	149,600	1,380	71,500	38,950	261,430	22.4
Agriculture	75,600	327	48,400	.....	124,330	10.7
Lumber	80,300	345	5,670	4,800	91,120	7.8
Manufactures and mechanical shops	36,000	10,500	28,600	13,400	88,500	7.6
Oil and refining	33,800	14,800	27,500	.....	76,100	6.5
Total	462,300	34,832	349,670	73,480	920,290	78.9
All others	169,900	5,570	56,330	15,220	247,010	21.1
Grand total	632,200	40,402	406,000	88,700	167,300	100.0

methods used by previous governments. As a matter of fact, however, the hopes of the new government did not materially differ from what the Brătianus, supported by the Liberal Party, had been striving to bring about. Only their methods and their outlook on the problem of economics were different. To pass judgment on the new experiments would be very difficult. The time has been too short for full realization of many plans, and the good will of the National-Peasant Government could not dispose of the results of the policy of the past. Furthermore the spell of economic depression of the world has spread like an epidemic to Roumania, which could not expect to be immune, and experiments of any kind cannot be expected to work out favorably in a short time under such conditions.

Fundamentally, the National-Peasant Government tended to transform public undertakings dependent upon departmental bureaucracy into autonomous administrations conducted according to commercial principles. Secondly, the new policy endeavored to strike a reasonable balance between a proper conservation of Roumanian interests and friendly co-operation with foreign capital. The conclusion of a foreign loan in February 1929 with an international banking group headed by the Bank of France for a par value of $72,500,000 and with the Swedish Match Company for $30,000,000, enabled the government to give up entirely the revalorization policy of the former government in favor of the stabilization of the currency. The rest of the proceeds of the loan were used mostly for the stabilization of the railroads and for other public reconstruction works. Thus the nationalistic economic policy was supplanted by the ideal of international economic co-operation.

The third principle and the central idea of the National-Peasant Party was the belief that Roumania, being an agricultural country, must give precedence to agriculture in the economic policy of her government. Thus the government passed the law concerning primary agricultural education and popular instruction in the technique of farming, the law as to higher agricultural education intended to form leaders fully competent to deal with all agricultural problems and to educate workers in scientific research, and the law abolishing the restrictions placed on the transfer of peasant property. Great efforts were made to reorganize agricultural co-operation. A central co-operative office for imports and exports was set up with financial aid from the Central Co-operative Bank in order to facilitate the sale of harvests and the supply of tools, machinery, and seeds to farmers. The state and the federation of co-operatives participated in the creation of this Central Co-operative Bank. An act for the regulation of land transfer was passed in order to keep the land in the hands of the actual cultivators and to avoid land cornering and speculation.

Dr. Virgil Madgearu attributes, as does Dr. Mitrany, the qualitative and quantitative deterioration of post-war agricultural production of Roumania not entirely to the easy and hasty formula that the agrarian reform, by dividing up the land among peasants, had disorganized production. To him

the real cause lay in the inadequacy of the country's agrarian policy, which consisted only in giving land to the peasants without simultaneously organizing agricultural production, making provision for agricultural credits, and directing the disposal of agricultural produce.[20]

The effects of the usurious interest and the impossibility of disposing of his produce, owing to such causes as difficulties of transportation and the export taxes, combined with bad harvests, brought the Roumanian farmer to a condition of poverty such as in 1928 caused the farmers of twenty-eight countries to appeal to the state for aid.[21] Notwithstanding the important part played by agriculture in Roumania, the country is still seriously handicapped by inadequate provision of agricultural credit.

The first attempt to deal with the need was made before the war. In 1873 the "Crédit Foncier Rural" (Rural Land Credit Bank), which still exists, was established, with the purpose of aiding the owners of large properties.[22] In 1923 this institution was changed to "The Private Rural Land Credit Institute," and its functions were extended to a considerable degree. But owing to the serious insufficiency of capital, the agriculturist is still left at the mercy of usurious interests.

In 1883 the so-called popular banks came into existence. In 1881 the agricultural credit banks were founded, and were replaced in 1892 by the "Crédit Agricole," which also was not a success, being too stiffly bound by tradition and the old banking laws; it was absorbed in 1903 by the central organization of the popular banks, and

[20] Dr. Virgil Madgearu, *Rumania's New Economic Policy,* p. 1.

[21] *Idem.*

[22] Based on Banque Marmorosch, Blank & Cie, *Les Forces économiques de la Roumanie en 1929,* "Le Crédit agricole en Roumanie," pp. 123–28.

went into liquidation in 1912. The Agricultural Bank, established by a law of 1894, modified in 1906, 1912, and 1913, was to open its credits both for large landowners and for small farmers who had been excluded from the operations of the Crédit Foncier Rural; but after 1913 its operations were restricted to purely banking business. In 1905 the "county banks for loans on pledge" were founded to grant short-term credits; their borrowings are almost exclusively confined to the National Bank. After the revolution of 1907 the "Casa Rurală" was created by a law (1908, subsequently modified in 1910 and 1914); it had as its main object the purchase of large properties and their sale in small lots to peasants. In 1915 the state founded a state institution, known as the "loan against security bank for agriculture and industry," with branches in different districts; it granted fixed-term loans secured on agricultural products. A rural credit act of 1923 provided a large framework for agricultural credits, but it limited itself to the Old Kingdom and was handicapped by the general shortage of capital. In 1924 the state authorized the creation of the agricultural credit banks; they secure their borrowings from the Crédit Foncier Rural and grant short-term loans.

In July 1929 the National-Peasant Government passed a comprehensive act concerning the organization of rural mortgages and agricultural credits. A Central Co-operative Bank was founded, replacing the "Casa Centrală a Băncilor Populare," with a capital of 1,000,000,000 lei, half subscribed by the state and half by the National Bank and co-operative societies.[23] The bank was to organize short-term credits through the people's banks and mutual rural mortgage credit societies. Two types of agricultural credit institutions were set up: (1) mutual rural mortgage credit companies with a minimum capital of 555,000,000 lei; (2) agricultural credit companies with a minimum capital of 500,000,000 lei. The operations of both credit companies are limited to credit transactions. Short-term credits up to a maximum of a year and up to the maximum of double the share capital of the borrowing banks are granted to the popular banks only through the intermediary of the Central Co-operative Bank. The authorization of the issue of debentures as a means of procuring capital is designed to meet the necessity of mobilizing this capital, especially on foreign markets. The mortgage bonds are guaranteed and enjoy exemption from taxation. Other

[23] See Madgearu, *Rumania's New Economic Policy,* pp. 6–10.

advantages, especially in the formalities of organization and operation, were granted with a view to attracting foreign capital. The act
also modified the provisions of the law for agrarian reform by
permitting the alienation of plots acquired by new owners to Roumanian cultivators, subject to the condition that the buyer should not
possess more than 25 hectares.

In June 1930 a special law formed the "Temporary Mortgage
Loan Institute," with a capital of 100,000,000 lei, for the purpose
of converting mortgages into five-year loans at 12 per cent interest.
The institute may issue debentures up to 500,000,000 lei, bearing
interest at not more than 9 per cent, tax free, under a state guaranty.

In March 1931 a law authorized the formation of the "Crédit
Agricole Hypothécaire," with a total capital of 330 million lei, 170
million of which was subscribed by the Roumanian state, 24 million
by the International Telephone and Telegraph Corporation, and the
rest by foreign capital. The object of this bank is to issue redeemable
loans against mortgages of agriculture, buildings, etc., on long or
short terms. This "Crédit" is authorized to issue bonds up to ten
times the value of the nominal subscribed capital. The Roumanian
state guarantees a 7 per cent annual interest on the preferred shares,
free of all Roumanian taxes, and also guarantees the service, both
interest and amortization, of any future bonds. This institution and
the "Banque d'Agriculture," founded in 1931, also under the auspices of the state, are the only source of cheap and extended credit
for the Roumanian peasant.

The solution of the question of agrarian credits in Roumania is
retarded by the absence of reliable statistical data concerning the
debts burdening the Roumanian agriculture. The total of agricultural credits afforded by the state-controlled financial institutions
before July 1931 was estimated at about 7,830,000,000 lei. To this
amount must be added the 20 milliards loaned by private banks in
the form of hypothecary credit, and 8 to 10 milliard lei of loans contracted by the agriculturist from other sources. Thus the total figure
of agricultural indebtedness reaches from 36 to 38 milliard lei, and
there being more than 12 million hectares of cultivated land in Roumania this amount represents a debt of 3,000–3,200 lei on the average upon each hectare of cultivated land.[24]

[24] *Central European Observer,* 1931, IX, 559. Another authority estimates that
the average per hectare indebtedness of farm holders in Roumania is $24.40, as
compared with $33.74 in Hungary, $59.00 in Yugoslavia, $10.97 in Bulgaria, and

The co-operative system of Roumania was thoroughly reorganized in 1929. The movement dates back to the nineteenth century when a number of credit co-operative societies, known as the people's banks, were founded. About 1890 village priests and teachers became interested in the peasant-credit problem, and the first "popular bank" was formed in 1891. In 1892 there were two of these banks. Then the idea spread very quickly; in 1904 there were 1,625 popular banks in Roumania, with a membership of 121,786 and a paid-up capital of 6,850,976 lei. In 1903 a very important step was taken —the organization of a central office and clearing-house, called "Casa Centrală a Băncilor Populare şi Cooperativelor Sătești" (The Central Office of the Popular Banks and Village Co-operatives), in order to co-ordinate the movement and link up the banks among themselves. But the funds at the disposal of the co-operatives were insufficient and the peasant had recourse to usurers. Between the central office and the local village banks were district or regional banks ("federale"), acting as clearing-houses; they reported to the popular banks' commission at Bucharest. This law of 1903 was applied in 1905 to all rural co-operatives for production and consumption, and in 1909 to urban co-operatives of artisans and laborers. In 1912 the Central Institute of Trades, Credit, and Workmen's Insurance was formed.

The decree-law of January 3, 1919, transformed the central office into "The Central Office of Peasant Co-operation and Resettlement,"[25] three of its sections to control and guide the co-operative movement and the other two sections to supervise the execution of the agrarian reform. Each of the first three sections was autonomous, with its own capital and an administrative council. A general council co-ordinated the work of the whole central office. In 1928

$10.24 in Poland. According to Dr. N. Cornățeanu of the Bucharest Agronomical Institute, of 7,767 farms in sixty departments, only 11.86 per cent were free of debt in 1930. The remainder showed indebtedness ranging from 1,000 to 20,000 lei and more per hectare. The Government of Iorga is attempting to facilitate short-term mortgage loans to farmers and proposes to convert all farm debts by voluntary agreements. A new Roumanian Bank of Agriculture was incorporated under state auspices on May 18, 1931, with a capital of 690 million lei, which may be increased to two billion lei before the end of 1931. The bank is to take over the farmers' obligations to commercial banks and extend to them, in proportion to their holdings, new credits on more favorable terms. The state guarantees a dividend of 7 per cent for a period of thirty-three years.

[25] For a detailed discussion see D. Mitrany, *The Land and the Peasant in Rumania*, pp. 373 ff.

only the central of the popular banks and the central of the co-operatives were left in existence.

The development of the popular banks since the enactment of the law of 1903 is shown in the following table:[26]

Year	Number of Banks	Membership	Paid-up Capital, Lei	Balance-Sheet Total, Lei
1904	1,625	121,786	6,850,976	10,168,811
1905	1,849	198,411	13,665,824	16,703,135
1906	2,021	240,253	18,509,519	27,275,474
1907	2,223	295,325	27,746,241	41,153,303
1908	2,410	346,707	37,851,898	58,670,708
1910	2,656	454,187	61,016,395	93,567,883
1913	2,901	583,632	107,142,203	170,790,003
1918	2,965	641,359	186,438,528	325,265,138
1919	3,114	678,061	243,863,256	482,217,716
1920	3,194	752,846	301,850,404	646,304,101
1921	3,211	705,150	348,062,894	813,459,882
1922	3,213	717,507	398,974,921	1,064,029,394
1923	3,747	825,879	478,915,265	1,507,952,912
1924	3,956	847,217	584,034,834	1,894,469,322
1925	4,207	886,844	745,356,714	2,709,844,978
1926	4,413	915,388	971,746,812	3,608,670,423
1927	4,766	962,515	1,265,465,317	4,414,494,398
1928	4,743	1,013,970	1,563,348,748	5,313,797,056
1929	4,757	1,003,082	1,801,800,000	....

While the movement would seem to have increased since the war, financially it is much weaker, especially in view of the fact that the figures relating to capital must be considered in relation to the depreciation of the currency, and that the co-operatives are confronted with greater tasks since the last land reform.

The dissatisfaction of the National-Peasant Government was evident from the law of March 1929, dealing with the formation, activities, and administration of co-operative societies. All co-operatives must group themselves into unions, or federations. These unions are completely autonomous institutions, charged not only with general control but with the organization of co-operative cultural activities, with directing the activities of the affiliated associations in every respect, and with organizing legal and technical assistance for them.[27] The unions may be organized regionally or by categories, and they are controlled by the National Office of Rou-

[26] *Annuaire statistique de la Roumanie 1929*, p. 122.

[27] See D. Mitrany, *op. cit.*, pp. 409–11, note 3; V. Madgearu, *op. cit.*, pp. 7–14; G. Mladenaz, "Rationalising the Co-operative Organisations," in *Manchester Guardian*, November 28, 1929, p. 41.

manian Co-operation, an autonomous institution under the Ministry of Labor, Health, and Social Welfare. Alongside the unions and the national office the co-operatives are grouped in regional credit federations financed by the Central Co-operative Bank, an institution created by the new law. The bank, an autonomous institution and a purely banking organization, with a capital of 500,000,000 lei, with subscriptions also of co-operative societies and their unions, may perform all sorts of banking transactions for the benefit of the affiliated co-operatives. The bank is managed by four delegates of the Ministries of Finance, Agriculture, and Labor and the National Bank, and by five delegates elected by the co-operative societies and unions.

By a law of August 1929 a new financial organization, the Land and Agricultural Mortgage Bank, was established. The law provides for the formation of rural land credit institutes which may be created of groups not less than 100 rural landowners, whose properties shall together be of not less value than 50 millions of lei; their operations are restricted to the granting of mortgage and security loans and to general banking business on behalf of members. The law, furthermore, creates an agricultural credit institute, with a capital of 500 million lei, authorized to grant long-term loans, short-term credits secured on crops or agricultural machinery, and personal loans granted through the popular banks. The capital is derived from share subscriptions and the issue of land bonds.[28]

Alongside the co-operative credit societies there have developed rural consumers' and producers' co-operatives. At the end of 1928 there were 169 bee-keeping, vineyard, mineral water, dairying, and other co-operatives in Roumania with 18,665 members;[29] and 2,155 consumers' co-operatives, with 239,900 members. There has been a marked development as regards the forestry co-operatives, which numbered 492 in that year, with 62,401 members. There were 351 land purchase co-operatives with 30,732 members. In Transylvania there are 446 consumers' co-operatives with 102,500 members, affiliated to the "Hangya" central body, in addition to 289 Hungarian credit co-operatives affiliated to the alliance of savings and credit

[28] The intention of the law is to attract foreign capital. The loan of 200 million French francs was subsequently granted by the Banque d'Acceptations de Paris.

[29] *Annuaire statistique de la Roumanie 1929*, pp. 127 ff. See G. Mladenaz, *op. cit.*

co-operatives (Cluj), together with a producers' co-operative affiliated to this alliance. These co-operatives boast a total membership of 86,000 and accumulated funds of 26,000,000 lei, with deposits at interest amounting to 144,000,000 lei.[30] The Saxon co-operatives of Transylvania number 185 credit co-operatives, 81 consumers' co-operatives, four co-operative wine vaults, and a co-operative mill, with a total membership of 30,000. Their funds amount to 6,000,000 lei and their deposits to 150,000,000 lei. In Bessarabia a union of Jewish co-operatives exists with about 30,000 members and 40 credit co-operatives. Urban co-operation is very little developed. The Souabian co-operatives of the Banat, and the German, Polish, and Ruthenian co-operatives of Bukovina are of lesser importance.[31]

To sum up, it may be said that before the war Roumania was primarily an agricultural country but several branches of industry connected with agriculture and the natural riches of the soil were in existence. The nationalist economic tendencies of the ruling classes, intensified by the war, and the addition of Transylvanian and Banat industries, gave a chance to the post-war Liberal governments to foster systematically the industrialization of the country. Despite the fact that the nation's capital was hardly sufficient to finance the economic system of the country, exhausted by war, the policy of revalorization was pursued, and the diminished resources of the state were pressed into the service of the new industries and the nationalization of the existing industrial undertakings.

The conception of the National-Liberal Party of the state as an instrument of domination was opposed by the National-Peasant Party, which looks upon the state as a regulator of the nation's labors. The economic policy of the National-Peasant group is in general oriented in favor of agriculture instead of industrialism; they considered that sacrifices should be made only for the industries which use as material agricultural produce and which concern national defense, that the deception of economic self-sufficiency should be supplanted by the principle of economic reciprocity and interrelation. In short, the policy of the National-Peasant Government was a program favoring agricultural organization, agricultural edu-

[30] G. Mladenaz, op. cit.

[31] Co-operation is today a prescribed course in the Roumanian commercial high school, and there is an academy of co-operation in Bucharest with about 100 students.

cation, credit facilities, all kinds of co-operatives, the co-operation of science in the rationalization of agricultural work and in the industrialization of agricultural produce, and equal treatment of foreign and domestic capital.[32]

[32] Some authorities are convinced that Roumania will eventually have to follow the policy of industrialization. L. Pasvolsky (*op. cit.*, p. 439) came to the conclusion that "the population problem coupled with the existence of natural resources, indicates for Roumania a policy of industrialization. The fact that over one-half of the peasants have no land is a factor of cardinal importance in the economic situation. Nothing but industrial development can provide them with a means of livelihood, and it is toward industrial development that the country has been tending more and more." Quoted by permission of the Macmillan Company, publishers.

CHAPTER XIV

COMMERCIAL POLICY

ROUMANIA did not begin her independent commercial policy until 1875, when a treaty of commerce was signed with Austria-Hungary based on the most-favored-nation principle. The empire was granted various advantages,[1] but allowed to Roumania only the importation of cereals. The convention was indeed very advantageous to the Habsburg Monarchy, though not exactly so to Roumania. It was bitterly opposed by the Liberals on the ground that the arrangements would destroy domestic industry. Under the fire of the opposition the Conservative Government had to resign and the new Liberal Cabinet prepared a new tariff which raised the rates by about fifteen per cent.

Because of political considerations Russia was granted the same favors as Vienna in a treaty which lasted from 1876 to 1886. As Bucharest also needed German support, a very disadvantageous treaty was signed in 1877, which came into force in 1881 and lasted until 1891. Then followed treaties with Switzerland, Greece, Italy, England, Belgium, and Holland. Roumania increased the volume of her exports, but her home industry suffered. Furthermore, since imports exceeded exports, the balance of trade was adverse.

The trend of the commercial policy of Roumania began to change with the German restrictions on the importation of Roumanian cattle in 1879 and with the similar policy followed by Austria-Hungary in 1882. The Roumanian Government had to denounce the Austro-Hungarian convention under the pressure of agricultural interests, industrialists, and protectionists. The general tariff of 1886 did not concern the countries with which Roumania still had unexpired

[1] See Dr. Cornélius G. Antonescu, *Die Rumänische Handelspolitik von 1875– 1915;* C. G. Rommenhoeller, *La Grande-Roumanie,* chapter xvi, "La Politique commerciale de la Roumanie de 1875 à 1925."

treaties, but the policy of "free-exchange" was given up and the new rates marked the beginning of the Roumanian protectionist policy. Up to 1891 Vienna, under the influence exerted by the Hungarian landowners, fought a customs war with Bucharest which did considerable damage to the Roumanian cattle industry. Up to that time Austria-Hungary had imported more than 70 per cent of the Roumanian cattle exports. Though subsequently the exports from Roumania to Turkey and Italy increased, the former export figures could not be reached.

However, beneficial results of the Austro-Hungarian-Roumanian difficulties were felt by home industry, which was no longer hampered by foreign competition. The German Empire as well as England, which supplied the country with textiles, benefited from the situation. During 1886–87, Roumania concluded new commercial treaties with Switzerland, Russia, England, France, Germany, and Turkey, and one in 1893 with Austria-Hungary. Of the greatest importance was the German treaty of 1892, renewed in 1893, 1901, and 1904, which opened the Reich to Roumanian wheat. Roumania, on the other hand, gave up her tariff rates on industrial products in 1891, and gradually came under the growing influence of German capital and cultural relations. Professor H. Feis estimates in his *Europe: the World's Banker 1870–1914* that "of the investments in the Balkan states, almost half of the total was in Roumania."[2]

Subsequently treaties with the most-favored-nation clause were signed with Austria-Hungary (1893), Turkey (1901), Italy (1892), England (1892), France (1893), Switzerland (1893), Belgium (1894), Bulgaria (the only provisional treaty, 1895), Holland (1899), and Greece (1901). New ones were signed after 1900, most of them containing the most-favored-nation clause. Up to the World War the commercial policy of Roumania was based on the tariff of 1906 and the treaties of commerce in which the German and Austro-Hungarian governments seem to have received greatest concessions. On the whole, the pre-war commercial policy was neither protectionist nor free; Roumania simply followed the policy dictated by the exigencies of the times. Generally, duties on machinery necessary for factory installation and on raw material were lowered rather than those on finished products.

When Roumania decided to participate in the World War, the

[2] P. 75.

conventions with the Central Powers were cancelled, while those with the Allied Powers could not be put into effect, despite the fact that another agreement was signed with England.

The war caused enormous destruction. The effects of the agrarian reform created a new situation, and the acquisition of the new provinces profoundly modified the structure of the national economy. The trend of commercial policy was reflecting the situation.

At the beginning of 1919 a royal decree inaugurated a system of restrictions on foreign imports. In April 1920 the tariff was modified in order to correspond to the depreciated currency. The system of licensing was inaugurated for both exports and imports, which culminated in export taxes. They were almost completely given up by 1923. In 1924 the rates were multiplied by 30 and made payable in gold. A minimum tariff rate was conceded to the countries granting the same privilege to Roumania. But only two treaties were concluded up to 1928, those with Poland and Czechoslovakia, and sixteen provisional agreements with France, Italy, Switzerland, Austria, Greece, Spain, the United States, and others.

The Liberal Government evidently tried to protect the domestic industry and to prevent the adverse balance of trade. While the country had only two years of unfavorable balance of trade from 1900 to 1913,[3] its post-war trade balances showed imports far in excess of its exports.

The value of the leu decreased by 1926 to about one forty-fifth of its original value. By the decree of March 26, 1926, put in force as of April 1, 1926, the tariff rates were raised again from 50 to 100 per cent. On April 10, 1927, a new tariff was promulgated which contained maximum and minimum rates. The general rates, increased by 50 per cent, were in operation against the states failing to apply their minimum rates to Roumanian goods. The minimum rates could be raised again at any time by the Roumanian authorities. An exaggerated protection was granted to national industries. As the minimum duties could not be modified through commercial conventions, the tariff was altogether unsatisfactory as an instrument of negotiations for securing markets for Roumanian exports.

The Government of Maniu made substantial modifications in the tariff. The tariff law became effective on August 1, 1929. It differs fundamentally from its predecessors in that whereas the past

---

[3] L. Pasvolsky, *Economic Nationalism of the Danubian States,* pp. 451–52.

measures were based on the conviction that the interests of the Roumanian industrial production should be defended against foreign capital the present measure grants priority to agriculture.[4] A certain elasticity was given to its application. The government announced in February 1930 that the minimum rates would remain in effect for all countries until May 1. After that date these, or even more advantageous rates, were to apply to countries which had entered into trade agreements with Roumania by that time. Minimum rates were designed to give reasonable protection to national production, industrial and agricultural, and, on the other hand, general rates, more or less flexible, and as such useful in future negotiations were established. The government made it plain that it could not agree unconditionally to the free entry of foreign manufactures, as but few of the domestic industries could survive unrestricted competition. The guaranty that Roumanian grain, lumber, and petroleum and other underground riches would find a foreign market imposed itself, therefore, as a prerequisite to any concessions to be granted to foreign manufactures.

As a preliminary to international trade agreements, Roumanian export duties and prohibitions were abolished or reduced; moreover, the new tariff brought about a reduction of import duties on many articles and a stable customs régime.

Immediately after the tariff was voted, the Roumanian Government made arrangements with the Polish Government for the transit of the products of Roumania through Poland toward Austria, Czechoslovakia, and Germany as well as through the northern countries by way of the Polish port, Gdynia. Through the free zones act, commercial interests abroad were to be attracted to the Roumanian Danubian and Black Sea ports.

Meanwhile, during the first months of 1930, a new situation developed in Europe. Some of the best customers for Roumanian cereals created serious obstacles to the development of Roumania's export trade by inaugurating a system of agricultural protection. Among these were Germany, Czechoslovakia, and Austria, in addition to France, Poland, and Italy. The world-wide agricultural crisis had been felt in Roumania for some time and the new tariffs were especially harmful now, for cereal overproduction had become apparent.

[4] See Dr. Virgil Madgearu, *Rumania's New Economic Policy*, chapter iii, "The New Customs Tariff," pp. 38–46.

The Roumanian Government was disappointed. It had embodied
the conclusions of the Geneva economic conference of 1927 in the
new tariff, and the promised new trade facilities were not forthcoming. Dr. Madgearu, therefore, had the parliament pass a law au-
thorizing the government to levy double the taxes specified in the
1929 tariff and to resort to retaliatory measures of prohibition or
restriction. It was under these inauspicious circumstances that a
number of trade negotiations were pursued.[5] Conventions were
signed with Turkey, Italy, Norway, Sweden, Czechoslovakia, England, Hungary (to become effective after settlement of minor points
in dispute), and France. By the end of 1930 sixteen short-term
agreements were concluded, including one with the United States.
It seems, however, that the agricultural crisis has continued with
unabated force, and the agricultural states are again (1931) considering new measures for abating the crisis. On June 22, 1931,
Roumania and Germany signed an agreement based on preferential
tariff rates—a policy favored by the Government of Roumania since
1930.

Before the World War, foreign trade of Roumania showed a
favorable balance of trade from 1900 to 1913 with the exception of
but two years, 1904 and 1908.[6] Up to 1914 the average excess of
exports over imports was nearly $15,000,000 a year (74,000,000
lei). On the basis of their exports to Roumania in 1910–14, the
first five countries were Germany, Austria-Hungary, England,
France, and Italy. The United States had sixth place in this order
in 1914. In the same period the best customers of Roumania were:
Belgium, the Netherlands, Austria-Hungary, Italy, and Germany;
exports to the United States were negligible. In value, the chief
articles of Roumanian imports were metal and manufactures of
metal, vegetable textiles and their manufactures, machines, and wool
and hair and manufactures of hair. The exports consisted largely
of cereals but also included petroleum, bitumens, vegetables, flower
seeds and plants, timber, and wood and manufactures of wood.

The destruction of the war, the results of the agrarian reform
and the modification of the national economic structure by the acquisition of the provinces, had a marked influence on the trade, which

[5] See André Tibal, "Roumania's Trade Conventions," in *Roumania,* 1930, VI,
37–41, and a list of the trade conventions and agreements on p. 80.

[6] See U.S. Department of Commerce, *Rumania: An Economic Handbook,*
p. 138.

Galați Harbor and Docks

Port of Constanța

even today compares unfavorably with that of the Old Kingdom if we consider the increases of territory and population.

The evolution of the foreign trade is given below (in millions of lei):

Year	Imports	Exports	Balance
1919	3,762,300	104,385	−3,657,915
1920	6,980,290	3,447,848	−3,532,442
1921	12,145,404	8,263,009	−3,882,395
1922	12,325,366	14,039,296	+1,713,930
1923	19,515,026	24,594,129	+5,079,103
1924	26,264,682	28,361,044	+2,096,362
1925	29,912,645	29,126,824	− 785,821
1926	37,135,032	38,223,520	+1,088,488
1927	33,841,804	38,110,810	+4,269,006
1928	32,145,101	26,919,256	−5,225,845
1929	29,896,504	28,914,934	− 981,570
1930	22,468,000	28,495,000	+6,027,000

Dr. Colescu attempted the difficult task of computing the value of the exports and imports in terms of the dollar under a very unstable rate of exchange of the leu with these results[7] (value in dollars):[8]

	Imports	Exports	Balance
1919	209,020,000	5,800,000	−203,220,000
1920	126,914,372	62,687,413	− 64,226,959
1921	141,225,634	96,000,000	− 45,225,634
1922	82,170,000	93,600,000	+ 11,430,000
1923	95,837,650	121,233,837	+ 25,396,187
Media	131,033,531	75,864,250	− 55,169,281

---

[7] Dr. L. Colescu, "The Balance of Trade," in *Manchester Guardian,* November 28, 1929, p. 46. The reader should consult Colescu's excellent analytical article. The 1929 figures are taken from *Commerce Yearbook 1930,* II, 485, which provides us with the following table (we must notice, however, that these figures differ slightly from those supplied by Dr. Colescu):

	Thousands of Lei		Thousands of Dollars	
Year	Imports	Exports	Imports	Exports
1921	12,145,405	8,263,009	152,060	103,453
1922	12,325,366	14,039,296	85,895	97,840
1923	19,516,026	24,594,129	96,351	121,421
1924	26,260,584	28,361,044	130,830	141,295
1925	29,912,645	29,126,824	144,538	140,741
1926	37,135,032	38,223,521	171,564	176,593
1927	33,428,547	37,703,178	201,908	227,727
1928	32,145,101	26,919,257	197,049	165,015
1929	29,896,504	28,914,933	178,183	172,333

[8] The rate of exchange (lei to the dollar) used by Dr. Colescu was as follows:

Pre-war	5	1922	150	1926	220
1919	18	1923	203	1927	167
1920	55	1924	202	1928	163.70
1921	86	1925	208		

	Imports	Exports	Balance
1924	129,665,590	137,790,000	+ 8,124,410
1925	144,701,000	139,543,000	− 5,158,000
1926	168,800,000	173,750,000	+ 4,950,000
1927	202,640,000	225,700,000	+ 23,060,000
1928	196,300,000	164,400,000	− 31,900,000
1929	178,183,000	172,333,000	− 5,850,000

The high imports in the years immediately after the war are partly justified by the exhaustion of the war-torn country and the shortage of foods and other necessities. On the whole, the exports have been rising irregularly, and in 1922 a favorable balance was reached which lasted until 1927 with the exception of the year 1925. The unfavorable balance of 1928, which was due to the failure of the maize crop and a weak harvest of the previous year, in addition to the rising value of the leu and the low world prices of cereals and oil, was radically reduced in 1929.

Roumania's main export is still the cereals, followed, considering the value of exports, by petroleum products, timber, cattle, and meat.[9]

On the whole, the direction of Roumanian exports into Central Europe has remained the same as before the war. It is evident from the following table[10] that Germany, Austria, Hungary, Poland, and Czechoslovakia absorbed a little over 50 per cent of the value of the Roumanian export trade:

Destination	Percentage of Total			
	1913	1923	1925	1927
Belgium	27.0	15.6	2.54	2.34
Austro-Hungarian Monarchy.	14.3	....	....	....
Austria	....	10.4	14.92	7.34
Poland	....	2.4	3.49	8.20
Czechoslovakia	....	4.4	9.41	2.85
Hungary	....	12.5	11.84	17.80
Italy	10.6	4.3	4.14	8.67
France	9.5	10.6	5.72	3.55
Germany	7.8	7.3	8.45	14.67
Great Britain	6.7	4.8	8.13	5.68
Turkey	5.5	2.2	1.81	1.43
Egypt	3.5	3.0	4.77	5.95

---

[9] According to *Roumania,* 1931, VII, 64–65, principal products exported during 1930 were as follows:

	Tons		Tons		Head
Grains		Lumber		Livestock	
Wheat	336,183	Firewood	673,722	Cattle	125,159
Rye	29,114	Timber	94,516	Hogs	97,694
Barley	1,442,911	Planks	749,676		
Oats	94,051	Petroleum and			
Maize	1,180,797	by-products	3,855,521		

[10] *Les Forces économiques de la Roumanie en 1929,* p. 87.

It should be noticed that the members of the Little Entente have comparatively little trade with Roumania.

The value of imports showed a steady irregular decrease after 1919 up to 1923, then began to rise again, and reached the highest mark in 1927. They consist mainly of textiles, metals and mining products, machinery and woollen goods. Germany is evidently making every effort to regain her influence in the Roumanian markets, with her exports mainly of metal goods and coal, together with machinery. A comparison with the pre-war imports gives every indication that the importation of metal goods will be supplanted by the products of the Banat and Transylvania, and the first place on the import list will be taken by the textiles.

The distribution of the value of the imports among the several countries is as follows:[11]

Destination	Percentage of Total			
	1912	1923	1925	1927
Germany	40.3	22.7	16.70	22.29
Austro-Hungarian Monarchy	23.4	....	.....	.....
Austria	....	15.6	16.54	13.30
Poland	....	13.8	5.58	7.45
Czechoslovakia	....	8.3	14.28	14.24
Hungary	....	5.0	3.96	3.73
Great Britain	9.4	9.2	10.54	8.40
France	5.8	6.6	7.80	7.73
United States	5.4	1.6	1.88	2.91
Italy	3.7	7.5	10.98	8.73
Belgium	2.8	1.8	2.26	2.58

In comparison with the pre-war foreign trade, the post-war trade of Roumania has decreased in extent. Dr. Colescu estimates that the annual pre-war importation amounted in value to $15 per member of the population, while today it is only $10. On the export side the figure before the war amounted to $16.10 per person, and today is only $9.50.

Though the adverse balance of trade was reduced in 1929 by 82 per cent from that of 1928, the economic situation became even more difficult after that period, owing to the inordinately low market prices for cereals, which handicapped exports, and to the heavy indebtedness among the farmers resulting from the subnormal crop of 1927 and the serious crop failure of 1928. In 1930 Roumania's foreign trade closed with a favorable balance of 6,027 million lei,

[11] *Idem.*

as compared with an adverse balance of 981 millions in the preceding year.[12] The exports were largely in excess of the preceding year as far as quantity is concerned, owing to the big drop in the prices of agricultural products and timber. On the other hand, the imports declined in a noticeable way. While the exports increased in bulk by some 30 per cent, the imports declined to approximately the same extent.

It is a matter of interest to notice that Roumanian trade with the United States is expanding.[13] American exports to Roumania increased in 1929 by 4 per cent in contrast to the 7 per cent decline in Roumania's total imports that year. The exports of American industrial machinery more than doubled between 1927 and 1929. The principal Roumanian exports to the United States, consisting of

[12] *Central European Observer,* 1931, IX, 252. The main categories of the exports were as follows:

Live stock	1,701,000,000 lei	6 % of total
Timber	2,846,000,000 lei	10 % of total
Oil and derivatives...........	10,385,000,000 lei	36.4% of total
Cereals	9,889,000,000 lei	24.6% of total
Other agricultural products....	3,674,000,000 lei	13 % of total
Total	28,495,000,000 lei	

[13] U.S. Department of Commerce, *Commerce Reports,* 1930, September 15, No. 37, p. 639. The evolution of the trade with the United States is evident from the following table (in dollars) covering imports into Roumania by categories, also total imports and total exports to the United States:

Imports	1922	1923	1924	1925
Animals and products..........$	9,735	$ 6,403	$ 80,371	$ 69,081
Vegetable products	529,852	80,127	69,444	181,677
Textiles	767,519	172,112	71,399	78,391
Wood and paper...............	......	......	11,119	26,088
Non-metallic minerals	81,981	38,328	82,482	86,328
Metals and manufactures.......	436,914	224,070	194,903	382,278
Machinery and vehicles........	505,152	612,919	632,834	1,318,512
Chemicals and by-products......	......	......	14,422	19,902
Miscellaneous	73,816	43,371	31,737	36,807
Total imports	$2,404,969	$1,177,330	$1,188,711	$2,199,064
Total exports	$ 499,941	$ 336,440	$ 99,427	$ 302,259

Imports	1926	1927	1928	1929
Animals and products..........$	44,218	$ 12,035	$ 25,970	$ 50,914
Vegetable products	103,287	366,672	679,577	786,407
Textiles	58,283	33,185	62,480	55,491
Wood and paper..............	6,628	24,321	9,820	22,837
Non-metallic minerals	119,280	227,254	262,745	312,958
Metals and manufactures.......	499,749	434,050	994,092	982,559
Machinery and vehicles........	2,205,037	3,717,409	7,165,597	7,250,277
Chemicals and by-products......	20,572	23,886	105,719	183,310
Miscellaneous	53,205	84,261	121,320	145,000
Total imports	$3,110,259	$4,923,073	$9,427,320	$9,789,753
Total exports	$1,097,933	$ 649,412	$ 677,174	$ 558,826

walnuts, fur skins, beet pulp, glue, and beans, have for some years maintained the same level.[14]

In April 1931 a National Export Institute under the Ministry of Industry and Commerce was established. Its main purpose is to seek all possible means of increasing the exports, to assist in bringing about the standardization of Roumanian products for export, and to study foreign markets and foreign methods of competition.

To sum up, it may be said that on the whole the pre-war commercial policy of Roumania was neither protectionist nor free. Roumania simply followed the policy dictated by the exigencies of the times. The post-war trade balances showed, in general, imports far in excess of exports. The high tariff rates were modified by the Government of Maniu and new commercial agreements have been concluded. The unfavorable balance of trade in 1928 and 1929 presents a problem which must be examined as an element in a larger situation. The world-wide depression determines the situation of today. There is no doubt that the recovery of the buying power of Europe will increase the utility of Roumania's considerable natural resources. Large investments of foreign capital, coupled with favorable commercial treaties, are bound to bring about domestic prosperity, based on a favorable balance of trade, while the country is groping to find means by which to dispose of her surplus wheat. It is an unalterable fact that the Roumanian trade problem, which is for the most part due to the lack of world markets for grain, is linked with the larger world economic problem today engaging the most serious attention not only of governments but also of bankers throughout Europe and the world.

[14] On August 20, 1930, a commercial treaty with the United States was signed at Bucharest providing for most-favored-nation treatment in trade between the two countries.

CHAPTER XV

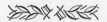

FINANCIAL SYSTEM

CURRENCY

THE fundamental factor in Roumanian foreign exchange is the grain harvest and the facilities for moving it at home and abroad. The amounts received ordinarily pay for the imports and leave considerable surplus. Up to the World War the transportation system of the Old Kingdom and its cereal production were good enough to stabilize the leu, the Roumanian monetary unit.

Before the war the leu was equal in value to French, Belgian, and Swiss francs and to the Italian lira, or to 19.3 cents United States currency. Though not a member of the Latin Monetary Union, Old Roumania adopted practically all its regulations. The gold standard was legalized. The National Bank issued banknotes in the values of 20, 100, and 1,000 lei. The issue had to be covered by 33 per cent gold; in the normal years 1908–13 the gold reserve ran as high as 47 to 50 per cent.

With the exception of two years the country had from 1900 to 1913 a favorable balance of trade. However, the war forced large purchases abroad, which continued steadily to depress the value of the leu. In addition, currency inflation to meet the war expenses of the government and the dumping of foreign goods after the armistice were important factors. During the occupation the Germans issued some 2,500,000,000 lei; they also secured large sums of Roumanian gold by the sale to the peasants of goods, especially sugar, of which there was a scarcity. Furthermore, on taking over the new territories, the Roumanian Government had to deal with about 8,500,000,000 Austrian kronen (exchanged by the government at about 4,250,000,000 lei) and an estimated total of nearly 2 billion Russian rubles (worth about 1,250,000,000 lei). Besides, the bullion of the National Bank, with much property in jewels, treasure, and objects of art, was sent to Moscow for safety and has been considered irrevocably lost since the accession of the Soviet Government. Its value has been estimated at 315,000,000 gold lei.

The unification of the country made it necessary to issue new bills, a process begun before the end of 1918 by the National Bank and which provided also for the absorption of other currencies. But the decline of the leu was rapid. While in 1914 the circulation amounted to 578,244,000 lei, it increased in 1918 to 2,489,145,000 and in 1922 to 15,170,000,000.[1] By March 1919, the value of the leu was still officially nine to the United States dollar. The average for 1920 was 58.50 to the dollar, and on January 1, 1921, lei were selling at 70 to the dollar.[2] From 1923 to 1928 the leu varied between two distant limits—184 to 235 to the dollar. The circulation increased in that time over 21 milliards.

A policy of expediency seems to have been the major cause of the depreciation. The figures of expenditures were artificially reduced by the postponement of arrangements in respect to the foreign debt. And while the country needed the greatest financial expansion after the war ravages, the policy of revalorization reduced the volume of circulation in the country. At the same time an attempt was made to prevent prices at home from rising to the world level.

The financial and commercial crisis of 1927 and 1928 brought a change in monetary policy and a foreign loan was admitted to be indispensable for stabilization. The National-Peasant Government succeeded in officially stabilizing the leu on February 7, 1929, at $0.00598 United States currency. The National Bank is under legal obligation to redeem its notes in gold or gold exchange in minimum amounts of 100,000 lei, and it must maintain against its notes and other demand liabilities a reserve of 35 per cent in gold or gold exchange, five-sevenths of which must be gold.[3]

[1] U.S. Department of Commerce, *Rumania: An Economic Handbook,* p. 42.
[2] *Idem.*
[3] *Commerce Yearbook 1930,* II, 488. Note circulation and reserves as given in the table following are in terms of the new currency (millions of lei):

	Notes	Gold Reserves at Home	Gold Reserves Abroad
1913	437	4,887	....
1922	15,162	1,268	5,760
1923	17,917	4,105	3,644
1924	19,397	4,349	3,644
1926	20,951	4,644	3,644
1927	21,025	4,848	3,644
1928	21,321	5,064	3,654
1929	21,150	5,266	3,919

The stabilization of the Roumanian exchange so far has continued with exactness, and continued stability is assured.[4] But a general shortage of money and credit continues. Though the official discount rate is 9 per cent, the agriculturists, for example, cannot borrow money unless they pay from 18 to 50 per cent. On the whole, the loan of 1929 failed to restore the economic situation, owing to the subsequent outflow of foreign exchange and to the very low prices obtainable for Roumania's principal products. Roumania's national capital is small and overburdened with debts, and her liquid cash is insignificant. The country needs foreign loans.

BUDGET

Following the serious crisis of 1899, the state effected a number of economies in its budget and from 1901 to the World War Roumania's budget of ordinary expenditures was more than balanced by receipts. Such loans as were incurred were designed mainly for extraordinary expenditures or for refunding.

The World War seriously disorganized the state finances of Roumania, and the incorporation of the new provinces and the depreciation of the currency added fresh complications. The inevitable result was a large excess of expenditures over revenues. Up to 1920 no government reported any budget to the parliament. The first budget without a deficit was introduced by Titulescu in 1921–22, but the year finished again with a large deficit. New taxes were imposed, the taxation system of the country was unified, and certain state enterprises which had formerly been included in the budget were reorganized and dissociated from the state budget in 1926, when it was decided to adopt separate budgets for the autonomous departments. It seems, however, that the budget figures were balanced on paper only, and a large number of claims against the state were left in abeyance. All this was due to the fall of the leu, decreased production, and the deficiencies of the fiscal system. Another step forward was taken in 1923 when the budgetary year was made to correspond with the calendar year.

---

[4] After many weeks of negotiations, arrangements were completed in Paris on March 10, 1931, for a French loan to the Roumanian Government. According to *New York Times,* March 11, 1931, various liquidation operations in connection with the loan of $50,000,000 will reduce the amount which the Roumanian Government will actually receive to a sum not in excess of $26,000,000. This loan is the second part of the previous stabilization loan of 1929.

In 1928 the actual budget deficit figure stood at 4,000,000,000 lei. In 1929 the state budget was slightly reduced, to 37,700 millions of lei (an equivalent of $224,700,000). In compliance with the terms of the stabilization loan of 1929 the taxes were increased, but the insufficiency of the measure led to the passing of a law late in the year reducing budget expenditures. The actual deficit was reduced to about 1,000,000,000 lei. All state enterprises have been placed under their own budgets since March 1929. The 1930 figures were again reduced, this time to 37,450 million lei.[5]

For the first time since the war it was then possible to base the budget on scientific estimates as a result of a stabilized currency; in addition, provisions were made for the payment of all debts and liabilities remaining over from previous financial years. The stabilization loan provided 3,908,611,034 lei to meet various debts of the state; but an additional 2,033,367,476 lei were required to meet all liabilities together with 250,000,000 lei needed at the end of 1928 to meet the needs of impoverished districts. These sums added to the difficulty of creating budgetary equilibrium in that year. The excess of receipts over disbursements registered during the first six months of 1930 was not maintained during the second half, owing to economic depression and the decreased prices of cereals; nevertheless, important reductions in expenditures were made and supplementary revenues were created so as to cover the deficit of about 3,000 million lei.

The 1931 budget aggregates 31,800 million lei, corresponding

---

[5] *Commerce Yearbook 1930* (II, 487) gives the following figures of receipts and expenditures (millions of lei):

	1928 Budget	1929 Budget	1930 Budget
Receipts	38,350	37,700	37,450
Direct taxes	7,282	7,502	8,897
Indirect taxes	15,297	11,992	13,606
Stamp and registration	3,600	4,500	4,500
Monopolies (gross)	7,462	7,980	4,380 (net)
All other	4,709	5,726	6,067
Equivalent receipts	($235,000,000)	($225,000,000)	($224,000,000)
Expenditures	38,350	37,700	37,450
Debt service	5,816	6,403	6,251
National defense	7,830	7,994	9,093
Public instruction	6,028	6,153	6,846
Ministry of finance	8,920	11,984	13,379
All other	9,756	5,166	1,881
Equivalent expenditures	($235,000,000)	($225,000,000)	($224,000,000)

approximately to the actual receipts of 1930.[6] It was divided into two parts: the ordinary budget, restricted to current expenses of the state; and the extraordinary budget, which will account not only for the extraordinary and non-recurring expenditure but also for the liquidation of the state's internal indebtedness.[7] Extraordinary ex-

[6] Details of the 1930 budget were as follows (*Roumania*, 1931, VII, 55):

	Receipt Estimates	Actual Receipts January–June	July–December	Total Receipts 1930
Direct taxes	9,487,000,000	3,653,966,151	5,424,329,200	9,078,295,351
Indirect taxes				
Customs	7,360,000,000	2,145,010,721	2,160,689,583	4,305,700,304
Beverages	1,330,000,000	309,252,377	368,591,501	677,843,878
Turnover tax	2,200,000,000	951,838,053	1,018,550,580	1,970,388,633
Amusements	150,000,000	50,600,979	44,722,493	95,323,472
Excise	2,566,000,000	868,444,701	1,481,763,470	2,350,208,171
Stamp tax	4,500,000,000	2,030,163,890	1,909,535,727	3,939,699,617
State monopolies	4,380,000,000	2,052,867,432	2,369,516,878	4,422,384,310
State properties	2,602,000,000	485,200,932	1,047,206,610	1,532,407,542
Miscellaneous	2,875,000,000	735,200,488	1,948,405,002	2,683,605,490
Exceptional	....	436,025,071	361,984,894	798,009,965
Total lei	37,450,000,000	13,718,570,795	18,135,295,938	31,853,866,733

		Disbursements		
Ministries of:	Estimates	Authorized	Effected
Army	9,092,700,000	7,968,588,208	7,484,589,634
Finance	12,104,875,926	11,742,381,482	11,208,099,541
Education	6,856,270,453	6,583,402,012	6,543,921,809
Interior	2,004,100,257	1,933,573,529	1,803,516,398
Public Works	150,954,402	113,633,119	107,385,754
Justice	1,403,697,843	1,334,516,628	1,282,948,164
Agriculture	1,167,773,000	1,021,368,224	997,885,408
Foreign Affairs	345,465,000	365,053,196	361,642,129
Labor and Health	1,570,188,826	1,433,871,019	1,387,290,414
Industry	571,199,371	513,130,050	512,428,490
Council of Ministers	114,256,336	112,356,747	112,356,747
Contingency fund	300,000,000	100,000,000	....
Overdue accounts	1,768,519,586	....	....
Total lei	37,450,000,000	33,221,874,214	31,802,064,488

[7] *Ibid.*, pp. 55–56. The treasury announced that hereafter revenue estimates are to be based on the average actual receipts of the preceding three years. The 1931 budget is as follows:

Receipts		Disbursements	
		Ministries of:	
Direct taxes	9,310,000,000	Army	10,204,029,661
Indirect taxes		Finance	12,289,590,039
Customs	4,575,000,000	Education	6,419,666,327
Beverages	1,250,000,000	Interior	1,716,234,526
Turnover	2,000,000,000	Public Works	131,857,420
Amusements	100,000,000	Justice	1,314,876,270
Excise	2,589,960,546	Agriculture	919,680,116
Stamp tax	4,150,000,000	Foreign Affairs	262,140,000
State monopolies	4,452,000,000	Labor and Health	1,267,659,541
State properties	1,793,418,269	Industry	405,028,771
Miscellaneous	1,659,574,856	Council of Ministers	75,191,000
Exceptional	3,426,000,000	Contingency fund	300,000,000
Total lei	36,305,953,671	Total lei	35,305,953,671

penditure will be incurred only to the extent that revenue from extraordinary sources is available. The source of all foreign debts and consolidated loans is to be incorporated in the ordinary budget.

The present high rates of taxation are said to be having disastrous effects; the prices of Roumania's products have considerably diminished, but taxation, in general, is increasing. Balanced budgets, however, are necessary for the stabilization of economic conditions of Roumania, which at the present time will be achieved only through heavy sacrifices, owing to the heritage of the post-war years and the world-wide depression of today.

Public Debt

The burden of national debt in Roumania is not so serious as is sometimes supposed. The total of both internal and external indebtedness up to 1930 was the equivalent of 4,614 million gold francs, which represents a burden of 256 gold francs per head of population, a more favorable state of affairs than exists in the neighboring countries. On January 1, 1930, the total debt was:[8]

In foreign currency:	Lei
Pre-war debt	19,310,984,827
War and post-war debts	116,655,790,233
Payable in lei:	
Pre-war debt	885,529,007
Post-war debt	11,979,882,295
Total	148,832,186,372

The total was equivalent to 4,613,797,778 gold francs, distributed over a population of about 18,176,000. On January 1, 1931, the public debt amounted to 185,526,481,269 lei.

Banking

The post-war situation of commercial banking in Roumania is different in great degree from that of the pre-war period. From this point of view we can divide the history of banking into two periods—one up to 1918 and the other from 1918 to the present time.

[8] *Central European Observer,* 1931, IX, 238; *Annuaire statistique de la Roumanie 1929,* p. 417. According to *Commerce Yearbook 1930* (II, 487), the total debt, January 1, 1930, amounted to $1,021,690,000; the external debt stood at $917,176,000. The debt due to the United States Government was $65,120,000.

Up to the beginning of the nineteenth century there had been no banks or banking institutions in the Old Kingdom in the ordinary sense of the phrase.[9] Toward the middle of that century bankers, operating with their own capital only, owing to the scarcity of deposits, began to operate in exchange transactions, as there was a great variety of currencies. One of the first bankers was I. Marmorosch at Bucharest, whose enterprise became one of the principal Roumanian banking establishments, the Bank of Marmorosch, Blank & Company. The economic advance of the period and the political consolidation of the country created the need of an issue and discount bank. In 1857 the "Banca Moldova" was founded at Iași by a German, but it went bankrupt in three years. In the next ten years all sorts of proposals were made to create a bank of issue and discount. Finally, in 1867 a national currency system was adopted, and in 1880 the "Banca Națională" (National Bank of Roumania), was founded by private capitalists with a capitalization of 1,200,000 lei, which was subsequently increased to 12,000,000 lei. After that the growth of other commercial banks was phenomenal, and in 1913 the Old Kingdom had 197 commercial banks, with a total paid-up capital of 215,803,000 lei (approximately $41,650,000),[10] of which more than 105 millions of capital and reserves were foreign.[11] Of this number 39 were located at Bucharest, 158 were corporations, and 39 were organized on a mutual or co-operative basis.

Approximately 300 million gold francs were borrowed from Berlin, Belgium, Austria-Hungary, and elsewhere.[12] The main policies of that period were to foster the development of the country, including agricultural credits, and to aid indigenous industries.

Transylvania, at the moment of reunion with her mother country, had an important banking organization, scattered throughout the territory according to the varied ethnic groups in the province. The Roumanian population, though forming the great majority, had no important financial organization of its own because of the objections

[9] See "Rumania's 'Big Six,'" in *Manchester Guardian,* November 28, 1929, p. 36.

[10] U.S. Department of Commerce, *Rumania: An Economic Handbook,* p. 30; *Manchester Guardian,* November 28, 1929, p. 36; and see C. G. Rommenhoeller, *La Grande Roumanie,* pp. 606–16.

[11] Rommenhoeller, *op. cit.,* p. 614; see D. Kastris, *Les Capitaux étrangers dans la finance Roumaine.*

[12] See H. Feis, *Europe: The World's Banker 1870–1914,* pp. 268–72.

of the Hungarian Government, which feared that serious political consequences would follow in the wake of financial emancipation. The Roumanian credit unions, modelled upon the Schultze-Delitzsch co-operatives, disappeared completely under political pressure. In their place, the "Banca Albina," the first Roumanian institution, was organized in 1872, and succeeded in establishing credit institutions over the territory. Bukovina was limited to banks of a purely local character, in which the Roumanian element was not represented, and all the needs of the territory were served by the branches of the principal Viennese banks. In Bessarabia could be found branches of St. Petersburg and Odessa banks and small local banks, in addition to some co-operative organizations.

The unification of the country completely changed the whole situation. The entire system had to adjust itself to the new political, economic, and financial situation of Greater Roumania. The war interrupted foreign credits of Berlin, Vienna, Budapest, Odessa, and St. Petersburg. The devastation of war almost completely destroyed the liquid capital resources. Currency was disorganized. The results of the agrarian reform and the loss of the gold reserve made themselves felt. Financial relations with England and France were not opened immediately. The currency inflation was accompanied by a corresponding fall in securities. From the second half of 1918 the banks had to adapt themselves to the increased financial demands and new needs of the national economy.

As early as June 1920 the banking situation of the Old Kingdom had changed through the addition of 62 banking corporations and 18 mutual (co-operative) banks, and through increases in capitalization by many of the older institutions, the multiplication being largely the result of the depreciating currency. Altogether there were some 972 banks in the whole country at that time with paid-up capital of 1,398,700,000 lei.[13] At the end of 1928 there were 1,112 banking corporations with a capital of 10,000 million lei and 2,569 millions of lei of reserve funds.[14]

On the whole, the banking resources have shown a considerable capacity for expansion, but the operating capital resources have remained very meager.[15] The increase of territory and the economic

---

[13] U.S. Department of Commerce, *op. cit.,* p. 30.

[14] Banque Marmorosch, Blank & Cie., *Les Forces économiques de la Roumanie en 1930,* p. 132.

[15] L. Pasvolsky, *Economic Nationalism of the Danubian States,* p. 435.

policy of the government increased the requirements for operating capital, but the accumulation of capital was, on the other hand, small. The result has been a high credit rate, and the problem which has confronted the country has been whether Roumania should develop slowly by her own means or advance more rapidly with the aid of foreign capital. The first policy was adopted by the governments after the war.

We shall now consider briefly the principal institutions of the country.[16]

There are in the provinces credit institutions, the ethnical character of which corresponds to the ethnical nature of certain districts. The most powerful banks of Transylvania belong to the Saxons: the "Bodenkreditanstalt" of Sibiu; the "Kronstädter Allgemeine Sparkasse" of Braşov; and the "Hermannstädter Allgemeine Sparkasse" of Sibiu. The principal Souabian credit organizations of the same province are the "Schwäbische Zentral Bank" and the "Erste Temesvarer Sparkassa" of Timişoara. The chief Hungarian bank is the "Aradi Polgári Takarékpénztár" of Arad. In the Bukovina there are no minority banks. The more important banks were mostly operated from Vienna. The "Bürgerliche Bank" and the "Bukowiner Landwirtschafts Bank" of Cernăuţi deserve mention. In Bessarabia banking, prior to the union with Roumania, was of an elementary nature. Most of these institutions of the provinces were dependent on the financial institutions of Austria-Hungary and Russia. Today the provinces still have a number of Russian, Austrian, and Hungarian banks, some of which are adapting themselves to the new conditions. The principal institutions are the "Wiener Bank Verein" of Cernăuţi, the "Banque Générale de Crédit Hongroise" of Braşov, and the "Banque Commerciale Hongroise de Pest." The following principal provincial banks have been able to reestablish their position: the "Banca Agrară" of Cluj; the "Banca de Est" of Cernăuţi; the "Banca Creditul Besarabean" of Chişinău; and the "Banca Iaşilor" of Iaşi. In addition, there are four leading provincial banks, which surpass in importance many of the financial institutions of Bucharest: the "Banca Albina" of Sibiu; the "Banca

---

[16] Based on G. Leonhardt (ed.), *Compass Finanzielles Jahrbuch 1930*, "Rumänien" (Compassverlag, Wien, 1930). See also Aristide Blank, "Banking," in "Economic Survey of Roumania," reprinted from *The Economist*, 1929, pp. 20–24; and C. G. Rommenhoeller, *op. cit.*, pp. 606 ff.

Comerțului" of Craiova; the "Banca Moldova" of Iași; and the "Banca Timişoarei" of Timişoara.

Mr. Blank divides the Bucharest principal banks into two categories: those which limit their sphere to banking activities alone, and the other six banks, which are intimately connected with the industrial and commercial undertakings of Roumania. These latter six leading banks deserve our attention.

The "Banca Marmorosch, Blank & Cie." was founded in 1848 by Jacob Marmorosch with the aid of foreign capital. Although from October 1931 to March 1932 its doors were closed as a result of the failure of the Austrian Creditanstalt, it is one of the largest commercial banks of Roumania and has steadily been increasing the number of its operations in the fields of industry, commerce, and rail and air transportation. About 78 per cent of the capital is owned by Roumanians, the remainder being almost exclusively in French hands. It has branches and agencies in numerous foreign cities, including New York. The bank promotes metallurgical factories, beet-sugar refineries, breweries, forest undertakings, sea-transport companies, petroleum enterprises, etc.

The "Banca Românească," organized in 1911, has close relations with the financiers of the Liberal Party. It plays a leading part in the coal and metallurgical industries and has several subsidiary institutions with holdings in petroleum, lumber, and coal concerns.

The "Banca Comercială Română" co-operates closely with French capital and specializes in the granting of commercial credits. Unlike the other banks, it has kept aloof from direct participation in industrial establishments.

The "Banca Chrissoveloni" is supported by the Nieder-Oester-reichische Eskompto Gesellschaft of Vienna, the Banque de Bruxelles, Hambros Bank of London, and Harriman of New York. It is particularly interested in electrification through the utilization of the country's water resources.

The "Banca de Credit Român" was originally financed by Austrian capital and sequestrated during the war. In association with the Credit Anstalt of Vienna and Mendelssohn of Berlin it enjoyed a rapid development after the war and has interests in the textile and metallurgical industries.

The "Banca Comercială Italiană și Română" is really a branch of the powerful Banca Commerciale Italiana of Milan and is actively interested in Roumanian business and occasionally advances money to the Roumanian treasury.

The balance sheet of ten great Roumanian banks at the end of 1929 was as follows (in millions of lei) :

Bank	1920	1929	Percentage Dividends 1920	Percentage Dividends 1929
Marmorosch, Blank & Cie............	1,786	4,038	20	25.3
Românească	1,101	3,554	14	21
Chrissoveloni	220	2,720	12	5
Comercială Romàna	420	3,111	10	17
de Credit Român...................	490	3,462	12	18
Generală a Țarii Românești.........	534	1,397	16	14
Agricola	414	496	15	..
de Scont a României...............	270	887	15	9
Comerțului, Craiova...............	199	838	14	20
Timișoarei, Timișoara.............	118	836	12	28
Total	5,552	21,439		

The "Banca Națională" was founded by a law of April 17, 1880, as a discount and currency bank, with the exclusive right of issuing notes, and is now the principal fiscal agent of the nation. During the war the National Bank provided the government repeatedly with loans, the funds for which were obtained by the issue of paper currency. This means of obtaining capital caused the inflation of the currency, which at one time fell as low as 224 lei to the dollar as compared to the pre-war parity of about 5 lei to the dollar. On May 2, 1925, an agreement was reached between the Roumanian Government and the National Bank to create a liquidation fund for the purpose of gradually redeeming the notes in circulation issued on the account of the state. As a result of this agreement, the Roumanian leu regained some of its former value. The notes were to be withdrawn during a period of from 15 to 20 years. The capital of the bank was increased to 100,000,000 lei and the government, as before, retained a one-third interest.[17] However, the financial situation became worse in 1928 and the deficits naturally increased the floating debt and indebtedness of the state to the National Bank.

By the terms of the loan concluded on February 7, 1929, $25,000,000 was assigned for the stabilization of the currency through the National Bank of Roumania, the leu was stabilized at a

---

[17] The bank is operated as a corporation, with the government holding one-third of the stock and enjoying appointive power so far as the Governor of the bank apart from its Board of Directors is concerned.

value of $0.006, the note-issue privilege of the bank was reaffirmed, and the gold reserve was fixed at not less than 35 per cent of all outstanding demand obligations of the bank. The capital was increased to 600,000,000 lei ($3,600,000) from 100,000,000 lei; the debts of the state for treasury notes in circulation and the bank's advances to semi-official credit institutions were paid off.[18] The operations of the bank were placed under the supervision of Messrs. Charles Rist and Roger Auboin. The balance sheet was adjusted and the item of the gold reserves held in Russia was eliminated. The whole reorganization was based on the model of the statutes of the National Bank of Belgium. The bank is no longer permitted to make advances to the government, with the exception of an annual advance to the treasury of two milliards of lei repayable in the second half of each year. Only short-term discount operations are allowed, which affects favorably its control over the note circulation.[19]

Note circulation and reserves, as given in the following table, are in terms of the new currency (millions of lei) :[20]

Year	Notes	Gold Reserve at Home	Gold Reserve Abroad
1913	437	4,887	....
1922	15,162	1,268	5,760
1923	17,917	4,105	3,644
1924	19,397	4,349	3,644
1926	20,951	4,644	3,644
1927	21,025	4,848	3,644
1928	21,321	5,064	3,654
1929	21,150	5,266	3,919

[18] U.S. Department of Commerce, *Commerce Yearbook 1930,* II, 486–87.

[19] See Professor C. Rist and Roger Auboin, "Six Months after Stabilization," in *Manchester Guardian,* November 28, 1929, p. 33, and Costin Stoicescu, "Leu Weathers the Crisis," *ibid.,* p. 32. The National Bank is required to redeem its notes at its head office on demand at its option in legal tender, gold coin, gold bullion, or foreign exchange convertible into gold, without limitation as to quantity, provided redemption for no amount less than 100,000 lei be demanded at a time; it must hold a reserve in gold or in foreign exchange which is by law and in practice convertible into exportable gold to at least 35 per cent of its sight liabilities. At least 25 per cent of the sight liabilities must be covered by gold in its own vaults or on immediately callable deposit in foreign countries. The sight liabilities in excess of that portion covered as above, with the state debt to the bank and the short-term advances to the Treasury subtracted, must be covered to their full value by the bank's other immediately realizable assets. The bank is not required to purchase either gold or foreign exchange on demand at a fixed price. The monetary law of February 7, 1929, does not provide for gold coin. There is, moreover, no mint in Roumania, subsidiary coin being minted abroad. The export of gold is prohibited.

[20] *Commerce Yearbook 1930,* II, 488.

In general, the development of post-war banking of Roumania has been rather unsound. Professor H. Parker Willis of Columbia University states that

the points at which the present organization of Roumania is most defective are capital equipment and banking credit. Her supply of capital is severely restricted, and her equipment in most cases antiquated. Her banking system is obsolete, inadequate and badly managed. It is a condition that calls for an immediate and extensive supply of capital from outside; it also calls for the modernization of the banking system within Roumania herself. These measures will have to be effected before she really becomes able to supply the European world with the materials of which that world stands in such great need.[21]

In 1930 and in 1931 Roumania suffered a stringent banking crisis, owing to the too close association between banks and industrial undertakings. The run of depositors found the banks unprepared. A number of provincial banks failed. The situation was affected to a particularly great extent by Soviet dumping of grain, timber, and oil in world markets.

INDUSTRIAL CREDIT

In order to facilitate the development of industries and to provide credit facilities for existing establishments, the "Societatea Naţională de Credit Industrial" (National Society for Industrial Credit), was created by a special act of government in 1923 with a capital of 500 million lei. Twenty per cent was subscribed by the government, thirty per cent by the National Bank, and the rest by banking institutions and private individuals. The state guaranteed the bonds as well as their interests. The society was to pay for 30 years only one-half of the ordinary dues, stamp duties, and registration fees. It has a prior claim in regard to the property of debtors for the recovery of money due to it over all other creditors, the state alone excepted.

The purpose of the society is to grant mortgage loans to industrial establishments and to assist in the establishment of the new Roumanian industrial enterprises. The society also has the right to receive time deposits and the privilege of rediscount with the Central Bank, and is allowed to issue its bonds bearing interest at a rate not greater than twelve per cent. With the accession of the National-Peasant Government the stabilization plan left as its sole resource a credit

---

[21] "Roumania and American Capital," in *Roumania,* 1931, VII, 26–31.

opened at the National Bank and carried over to a special state account when the stabilization plan came into force. It seems that an assistance of long-term credits to industry is needed which the society cannot supply without a loan from some foreign consortium.

During 1928 the society loaned 3,181,000,000 lei. From 1924 to 1929 a total of 10,171 million of credit was applied for, one of 4,587 million was authorized, and one of 2,513 million granted. In 1930 the society made a net profit of 60,000,000 lei and paid a dividend of eight per cent. Its balance sheet stood at the end of 1929 as follows (in millions of lei) :

Capital	500
Reserves	134
Deposits	60
Bonds	250
Rediscounts	1,006
Liabilities to the state according to the stabilization plan	628
Total	2,578

To sum up, it may be said that the disorganization of the economic life of the enlarged kingdom of Roumania was the chief cause of the financial distress of the country. The policy of expediency and rapid industrialization, together with the deflation of the leu, has been succeeded in the last two years by stabilization, which has enabled the government to prepare a definite budget according to a fixed standard and has placed it in a position, for the first time since the war, to calculate with a comparative degree of accuracy its receipts and expenditures. However, the budgetary deficits are still large.

Currency inflation and rising prices induced an unhealthy stimulation in industrial investments. The present task of the banks is to reduce the frozen investments in various holdings and subsidiaries. Increased attention is being paid to the agricultural credits. With the stabilization of the currency and the finances placed on a sound basis, a surer foundation is provided for the future. But lack of capital is a dead weight on the whole economic system of Roumania.

PART V

CONCLUSION

CHAPTER XVI

CONCLUDING OBSERVATIONS

THE story of the rise of Roumania to the status of independence and ultimately to the fulfillment of her nationalistic ideal—the formation of Greater Roumania—is intensely dramatic, with elements of both tragedy and glory. The principles of nationalism and democracy which have been shaping the development of Europe since the fifteenth century, with the philosophical tendencies of humanism, resulting in the creation of modern constitutionalism, were slow to reach the part of Europe in which Roumania is located.[1] The political experiment of the kingdom was handicapped from the beginning by the inexperience of its people and by the heritage left by the oppression from without and from within. In fact, the ideals of political democracy could not be realized without social democracy, and that was impossible until after the great agrarian reform of 1917. Political life was naturally undeveloped and the economic development absorbed all the energies of the leading classes, who, in their semi-feudal world, had to work out the progress of the nation without the aid of a politically-minded middle class.

The spiritual revolution of the Roumanian people, as we have tried to show in the preceding pages, put Roumania in the camp of Western Powers. While much has been left from the previous Eastern influences, on the whole the nationalistic rebirth went through the same political and social revolution that Western Europe had already experienced. Because of the delay, Roumania has paid and is still paying a great price. On the eve of the World War Roumania stood culturally and politically in the Western camp but economically more or less under the domination of the Central Powers. When the World War broke out, Roumania had to make

[1] See a fine discussion of *The Problem of the Small Nations after the World War,* a lecture delivered by Dr. Edward Beneš, Czechoslovak Foreign Minister, on December 2, 1925, at King's College (published by the School of Slavonic Studies in the University of London, King's College, 1925).

a decision which was to have most fateful consequences. But the answer in favor of the Allies was to be expected. For despite the fact that Berlin and Vienna had spread their influences to the Court of Bucharest and had large followings in the leading classes of the Roumanian citizens, there was nevertheless remaining one great and consuming passion in the mind of the Roumanian—the desire to include within "România Mare" all the Roumanians then subject to Austria-Hungary, to realize a national unity denied them by the heavy hand of the Habsburgs.

But political principles were not the only ones involved in the struggle. Democracy and social ideals made their demands under the influence of the conditions of the war and the Russian upheaval.

When the war was over, Roumania was panting for breath from sheer exhaustion of her resources. But politically she had gambled with the right side and her boundaries included everything that the most ardent nationalist could desire. Socially, the agrarian reform became a part of the fundamental law of the land and there was no question but that it meant the death-knell for the landlords, together with the semi-feudal practices accompanying the pre-war conditions. Roumania stood with both feet on the principles of democracy and was willing to acknowledge them in practice. But she soon found that their practical application was not easy and it took another ten years for most of the democratic principles, embodied in the new constitution, to be partly applied in practice.

Concurrently, the enthusiasm of the armistice could not offset the damages of the past years and could not dispose of the numerous other problems pressing for solution the moment they became a part of the new system, the new structure of Greater Roumania. Post-war psychology, neighbors who were openly hostile, the lack of political experience of the masses, an unstable currency, economic chaos, irredentism of some of the new alien minorities, limited financial resources, inadequate education on the part of the lower classes, and the headache of the whole world, the effects of which are still felt by every country of the world—all these have placed a heavy demand upon the Roumanian people in their attempt to acquit themselves with honor. Yet it is a matter of record that the Roumanian state has done more than survive; it has established itself securely in the confidence of its own people and in the confidence of the world. The faith and hope which the Roumanians themselves repose in the future of their country is amazing; one might almost characterize it as an act of faith, born of the long-cherished nationalism which now seems so real after centuries of oppression.

Roumania recognizes that to continue on this road of national greatness requires the mutual efforts of all Roumanian citizens and the good will of Roumania's neighbors. Every Roumanian must continue his efforts to orient himself in the problems of democracy, rejecting the impositions of the past. To be imbued with democracy Roumania must emphasize civic education. The absorption of the intelligentsia in the services of the state and in politics must be correlated with a redirection of the new classes into the economic life of the nation. Thus not only would many economic and political problems be solved, but a new and larger political middle class would be created which would become a regulator of sufficient strength to keep class opposition within safe limits. If society is divided into two political and economic classes only, differences of opinion on all subjects are likely to follow a horizontal line of cleavage. If there are more classes, vertical divisions are more common and society will divide on different questions, thus relieving the intensity of the antagonism between political and economic classes.

Then there is the ever troublesome problem of minorities. If self-training and self-education of the masses of the Roumanian nation is necessary for civic advancement and political and economic growth, the same applies to the problem of minorities. If the laws of Roumania are made for all Roumania, then there is the necessity that the laws be obeyed by the minorities, some of whom do not sympathize with the new political system of which they are a part. The minorities groups cannot demand that special privileges be given them and even the greatest republic of the world, the United States of America, does not give them. The minorities must identify themselves with the new system, they must understand the problems and interests of their new country, and must feel that the new day is also their own new opportunity. Otherwise constant irritation will arise, and irritated minds are not apt to be impartial and are quite apt to exaggerate their own point of view. This is acknowledged even by the bitterest critics of Roumania, the Jews. The official representatives of this group, which takes upon itself the protection of the interests of Roumanian Jews from abroad, wrote recently:[2]

[2] M. D. Waldman, "Report of the Secretary on European Conditions to the Members of the American Jewish Committee," reprinted in the American Jewish Committee, *Twenty-Fourth Annual Report* (New York, 1931), p. 107.

Brăila Docks on the Danube

Brașov Airplane Factory

I desire to point out that publicity though sometimes a powerful instrument is a double edged sword and when indulged in to excess is likely to work great injury. I cannot escape the conviction that publicity, especially in relation to the troubles of the Jews of Eastern Europe, has frequently been thoughtlessly resorted to and, may I say brutally, that it sometimes appears as if it has been exploited for personal ambitions, or for the prestige of certain organizations.

It is of course true that if there are certain obligations of moderation on the minorities, there are also the obligations of the majority. The Roumanian Government is undoubtedly attempting to follow principles of justice and wisdom. But, of course, the minorities and the majorities will always have their differences on the definition of what is "justice and wisdom." The fundamental need is moderation and sensible views on both sides; if these are exercised, the international problem of minorities will advance far toward its own solution.

And then there is the third precept which will help to solve the problem of minorities—one which is seldom thought of. No Roumanian objects to any criticism of acts thought contrary to the trends of modern civilization. But such criticism should be tolerant and aware of the facts in the situation and not based on sensational reports from unwarranted and irresponsible sources. If an excess occurs—and is there a country where we do not hear about excesses? —foreign critics must not indict the whole country for the single occurrence. There exists in Roumania, as there exists everywhere in the civilized world, a powerful body of liberal opinion which strongly condemns such excesses. A Roumanian student, trained in this country, and now one of the leading members of the administrative system of Roumania, makes this point very clear. He says:

The headlines of newspapers are sometimes so worded as to give the false impression of associating persecution and the rest with the whole country, to which I object in the same way that you, as an internationally minded person, would object when lynching would be laid at the door of the whole of the United States and the whole country blamed for it when it is quite clear to anyone that the name of the United States could not possibly be associated with the Ku Klux Klan any more than the name of Roumania with the Anti-Semitic League.

In foreign policy Roumania is in a difficult situation. Her political and economic consolidation has been delayed by the sense of insecurity from two sides. But she has followed fundamental principles of international relations, based primarily on the security of the state and on the principles of international co-operation expressed in the Covenant of the League of Nations. But economically the official policy of the country has not until recently tried to fit world economic and financial conditions.

It is undoubtedly true that the ruling classes of Roumania and the bureaucracy have been governed by patriotic rather than selfish reasons. But their idealism unfortunately has not always produced the desired results. Instead it has seemed to lead most markedly to an increase in the administrative functions of the state. In view of the conditions of the state the system no doubt seemed necessary to them, and it must be said that the steady inclusion of younger elements has had beneficial influence on the administrative *esprit de corps*. But it has also created the problem of a spirit of caste, accompanied by over-emphasis on administrative routines, which will have to be solved in the future by the reduction of the numbers in public service and by an increase in the spirit of political and economic initiative on the part of the citizenry at large. But, on the other hand, the Roumanian bureaucracy must be credited with great skill and capacity, a capacity which is hampered by the low salaries of the officials, with consequent demoralizing effects, and by frequent turnovers coming on the heels of political changes in the cabinets.

The greatest of all Roumanian problems is the necessity compelling every person in Roumania to raise the economic level of the country. The rich resources need a systematic and steady exploitation, which cannot materialize without foreign help and capital. The surpluses of the agricultural classes, which are the backbone of the kingdom, have hitherto been diverted to the industrialization policy of the country. But a considerable failure of this policy seems to prove that the policy of the National-Peasant Government, favoring foreign help, will have to be followed in the future. That does not, of course, imply that the vast natural resources of Roumania are to be alienated for a few temporary advantages. A turn for the better in agricultural conditions, however, depends largely on an improvement in the international situation.

But, ultimately, Roumania must depend upon herself and upon her internal strength. The minorities problem, the world-wide depression with its effects on Roumania, the evil influences of the war, the political and social differences, and other numerous difficulties, will in the end be solved by careful, detailed, and daily work on the part of each Roumanian citizen. The awareness of duties will eventually overcome the difficulties. Probably too much is expected of the state in our modern world, and Roumania is no exception. The formal statement of democratic principles in constitutional documents does not solve actualities. The essence lies, in the final analysis, as President Masaryk of Czechoslovakia once said, in "the concord of people, their peaceful association, love, and humanity." The Roumanian nation is united in the belief of her people in the mission of their state. The Roumanian citizens are very earnest in trying to set their house in order. The prospect is one of prosperity and the enjoyment of the things that make life worth while.

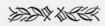

APPENDIX
BIBLIOGRAPHY
INDEX

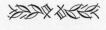

APPENDIX

A. The Roumanian Press

THE first Roumanian newspapers began to appear irregularly at the end of the eighteenth century and during the occupations of the principalities by Russia from 1828 to 1832. It was not, however, until 1877 that a serious attempt was made to raise the standard of journalism of Bucharest, which so far had followed the easy process of translating news from foreign periodicals and depending on the news coming from Vienna and Budapest.

A new chapter in the history of Roumanian journalism started with the publication of *România Liberă* (Independent Roumania) on May 15, 1877, by D. A. Laurian and Professor Şt. Mihăilescu. Here important writers like Barbu Delavrancea, Al. Vlăhuţă, Duiliu Zamfirescu, and others, began to publish their articles. Another step in the improvement of the journalistic profession was taken by a Frenchman, E. Galli, on June 2, 1877, when his periodical *L'Orient,* continued today in *L'Indépendance Roumaine,* introduced a section of journalistic information and reports. Above the general mediocrity of the press *Basarabia,* published bi-weekly in Iaşi after 1879, stood out. It was the first Socialist periodical, but, as its title indicates, it also had nationalistic tendencies which were reflected in protests against the retention of Bessarabia by Russia.

Under the leadership of Constantin A. Rosetti a wing of the Liberal Party edited *Românul,* agitating for the revision of the constitution during 1883–84, and favoring the extension of universal suffrage. A year later a young Socialist, Ion Nădejde, started a Socialist agitation with his *Contemporanul* at Iaşi.

A real change in the situation began with the publication of *Epoca* and *Lupta* (Fight), both elevating the cultural level of the press of Roumania. *Epoca* first appeared on the streets of Bucharest on November 16, 1885, as an organ of the Conservative Party and as such against the Liberal Government. The same policy was followed by the radical and anti-dynastic *Lupta* of Gheorghe Panu, in Iaşi. It soon became popular in Bucharest and together with the *Epoca* it led popular attacks against the Liberal Government, which resigned in 1888. But both newspapers retained their aggressiveness and stayed in the same political camp, *Epoca* standing on the right and *Lupta* on the left of the new Conservative Government.

As the public was becoming accustomed to the general tone of both periodicals, a new newspaper, *Adevĕrul,* following the aggressive tendencies of *Lupta* and *Epoca,* came out on August 15, 1888. It appeared to be very strongly republican, and despite the fact that there was no republican orientation in Roumania, became very popular, thanks to its entertaining and bold policy.

In the pre-war years, the Roumanian press, with very few exceptions, was in the hands of the political organizations. The chief organs of the Liberal Party were *L'Indépendance Roumaine* and *Viitorul* (Future). The Old Conservatives controlled *La Politique* and *Epoca.* Take Ionescu was propounding his program in *La Roumanie* and *Acţiunea.* He was supported by *Adevĕrul* and *Dimineaţa.* The largest circulation was achieved by *Universul,* an independent daily. Much interesting matter was found in the weekly, *Noua Revistă Română,* started by University Professor Rădulescu-Motru. The German community read two dailies, *Bukarester Tageblatt* and *Rumänischer Lloyd.* Professor Iorga's nationalistic policy found its expression in *Neamul Românesc.* During the war, the Germanophile tendencies were represented by *Gazeta Bucureştilor* and *Lumina.*

During the post-war economic and financial crisis a number of periodicals disappeared after a brief span of existence. According to the latest statistics Roumania has 709 newspapers and 554 periodicals; of the newspapers 505 are in the Roumanian language, 7 in French, 112 in Hungarian, 72 in German, 5 in Russian, 2 in Bulgarian, and 8 in Yiddish. Of the total number, 160 are political and general newspapers. The most important periodicals appear in Bucharest, viz., 91 newspapers in Roumanian, in addition to 5 other newspapers, and 227 periodicals, 215 of which are printed in Roumanian, 2 in Hungarian, 7 in French, and 3 in German.[1]

The most important Roumanian newspapers today are as follows: *Universul,* founded in 1882 by an Italian, L. Cazzavillan, as an organ of publicity, rapidly gained general popularity under the able journalist Steinberg. Its columns are devoted more or less to pure

---

[1] See *The Near East Year Book, 1927,* pp. 267–71.

information, and as an independent daily it has had very little influence on politics. Former Minister Stelian Popescu is its editor and proprietor. The morning edition has more than 100,000 circulation. The main political contributors are Romulus Seișanu, Mihail Mora, Cecropide, V. Ionescu-Vion, and Constantin Bacalbașa, who was for many years in charge of *Patriotul* and is the author of several plays as well as of a volume, *Bucharest of Yesterday and Today.* *Universul* is probably the most informative general newspaper of Roumania, with conservative nationalist leanings.

An encyclopedic journal, *Dimineața* (Morning), was founded in 1904 by Constantin Mille. Its morning circulation exceeds that of *Universul.* The Adevěrul Company, which owns it, publishes various literary and cultural periodicals,[2] as well as a very popular political and democratic evening journal, *Adevěrul* (Truth), since 1888. The direction of the two dailies passed in 1922 from Const. Mille to I. Rosenthal, and after 1924 to C. Graur and B. Brănișteanu, who have been supporting the democratic parties against the Liberals.

Cuvântul (Word) was founded in 1924 by a rich engineer and deputy, the late Titus Enacovici. Its independent and critical attitude attracted to it a number of well-known writers and newspapermen of the younger Roumanian nationalist generation. The actual editor, Nae Ionescu, supported Prince Carol, and is well informed concerning the political undercurrents.

Argus, a daily of commerce and industry, serves the interests of business and finance. The editor, Grigore Gafencu, tries to steer away from political controversies. Among his distinguished collaborators should be mentioned a vigorous journalist, T. Pizani, former editor of *Epoca,* two former cabinet members, Manoilescu and Garoflid, A. Corteanu, and Viator.

Epoca is a personal organ of Grigore Filipescu who favors dictatorship. *Miscarea* (Movement) serves as the official organ of Gheorghe Brătianu. Another dissident faction of the Liberal Party is supported by *Omul Liber* (Free Man), a private organ of Jean Th. Florescu.

The former official organ of the Peasant Party of Roumania, *Aurora* (Dawn), is sustaining the vacillating policy of Dr. N. Lupu, who resigned from the National-Peasant Party after the Peasant

---

[2] The *Biblioteca Dimineței* (Morning Library); the *Pandectete Săptămânale* (Weekly Pandects); the *Dimineața Copiilor* (Morning of Children).

Party was fused with the Nationalists. His collaborators were Constantin Sharf, an ironic analyst, Adolphe Clarnet, interested in foreign policy, and Tudor Teodorescu-Branişte, an able polemical writer.

The Bucharest organ of the National-Peasant Party is *Dreptatea* (Justice), edited by G. Ştefanescu. Another official organ of the party is the daily *Patria* of Cluj, a leading provincial journal since 1919, the director of which was a Transylvanian writer Ion Agârbiceanu. The oldest Roumanian newspaper of Transylvania and the organ of the National Party is *Gazeta Transilvaniei,* founded in 1838, which, however, for financial reasons, appears only three times a week.

Lupta (Struggle) is one of the creations of Const. Mille, former director of *Dimineaţa* and *Adevěrul.* It has democratic leanings.

The National-Liberal Party publishes *Viitorul* (Future), the Roumanian counterpart of *L'Indépendance Roumaine.* The editor, Alex. Mavrodi, is aided by Gr. Ţauseanu, Ion Foti, and Aureal Marcu. The second paper is one of the oldest Roumanian newspapers, dating from 1877; it is edited, primarily for foreign readers, by Dr. R. Berkovitz. In Transylvania the Liberal Party is supported by *Gazeta Transilvaniei,* printed at Braşov. The Liberal Party issues also the following publications in the provinces: *Mişcarea* in Iaşi, *Dunărea de Jos* in Brăila, *Glasul Bucovinei* in Cernăuţi, and *Dreptatea* in Chişinău.

The People's Party expresses its views through the medium of *Îndreptarea* (Guidance), which has been appearing since 1919 in afternoon editions of about 15,000, under the directorship of Dr. Anton Bărdescu.

A frank discussion of political points of view has been started in a new daily, *Curentul.* Pamfil Şeicaru, its editor, discusses freely all Roumanian political personalities, and his independent attitude provides a counterbalance to the other partisan periodicals.

Neamul Românesc (The Roumanian Nation) was founded by Professor Nicolae Iorga, whose idealism and nationalism it expresses. It is directed by N. Georgescu. Former Minister Jean Th. Florescu created *La Roumanie Nouvelle,* a review interested in political and economic interpretations.

The Roumanian Socialists have no dailies and limit themselves to weeklies, *Socialismul* in Bucharest and *Tribuna Socialistă* in Cluj. However, the organ of the Social-Democratic camp of Bukovina, *Vorwärts,* appears daily in Cernăuţi, and *Arbeiter Zeitung* in

Timişoara is the daily organ of the Social-Democratic Party of the Banat.

The press of the minorities of Roumania is located especially among the Magyar and German populations of Transylvania. The leading journal of the Hungarian irredentist movement and the central organ of the conservative group of the Magyar Party is *Ellenzék,* published for nearly fifty years in Cluj. The most extreme chauvinistic views are propounded by *Brassói Lapok* in Braşov. *Keleti Ujság* (Morning News), also of Cluj, is the organ of the industrialists. Numerous Magyar periodicals also appear in Arad, Satu-Mare, and Timişoara.

Among the German periodical publications *Deutsche Tagepost* of Sibiu (Hermannstadt), founded in 1874, stands out. It has aimed to represent the democratic section of the Saxons. *Siebenbürgish Deutsches Tageblatt* of the same city is the official organ of the German Party with conservative leanings, as represented by the leaders of the group, Dr. Hans Otto Roth and Heinrich Plattner. The oldest organ of the German-Saxon Party of Transylvania is, however, *Kronstädter Zeitung,* published for over ninety years in Braşov. The central organ of the Germans of the German-Souabian Party of the Banat is *Banater Deutsche Zeitung* (formerly *Schwabische Volkpresse*) of Timişoara, existing from 1919, whose director is Senator Karl von Möller. *Temesvárer Zeitung* also has had a long existence and provides local information for the Germans of the Banat. Other German papers, especially in Cernăuţi, as well as the Russian dailies of Chişinău, have only local importance. *Bukarester Tageblatt* is the only Bucharest newspaper published in German.

Curierul Izraelit serves the Jewish communities in the Old Kingdom. The Cluj *Uj Kelet* (Morning) is the official Zionist organ.

Some leading political reviews may be mentioned. Ion Mihalache, former Minister of Agriculture, leads *Ţărănismul.* Mihalache, who made the peasant costume a familiar sight in the Council of State, appeals to the farmers by his simple, often humorous, always sincere articles. The Liberals support the publication of the monthlies, *Democraţia* and *La Roumanie Nouvelle.* A famous Roumanian poet, Octavian Goga, is the founder of *Ţara Noastră* (Our Mother Country), a weekly review of Cluj. *Societatea de Mâine* (Society of Tomorrow), an independent and able political review, appears in the same city.

On the whole, the tendencies, the character, and the influence of the Roumanian press are such as not to indulge unduly in retrospection and avoid deep analysis. Each newspaper usually carries one or more editorials on current politics and numerous comments on sensational political gossip. Occasionally personal abuse runs to a higher pitch and the tone of reckless and sweeping statement is generally sharp and extravagant.[3] Slanderous reports about men in public life are freely printed. But in comparison with the press of other Southeastern European countries, Roumanian journalism has gained for itself an honorable place. Its influence at home is important and the newspapers are read with interest even by the lowest classes of the nation. Hence political education of the Roumanian people will be largely determined in the future by the high standards of Roumanian journalists and political writers.

In order to collect and distribute accurate information pertaining to all fields of Roumanian activity for the use of Americans interested in Roumania, the Society of Friends of Roumania was incorporated on September 13, 1920, under the laws of the State of New York by a group of prominent Americans and Roumanians, including William Nelson Cromwell, T. Tileston Wells, John W. Riddle, Nicholas Lahovary, John Foster Dulles, Clarence Mackay, James Gerard, Henry Clews, Percival Farquhar, and Edward P. Mellon. Beginning with 1925 the society has published a quarterly bulletin containing information of interest and value to bankers, traders, and manufacturers who contemplate doing business in Roumania and also to tourists who were preparing to visit this kingdom. A similar society with reciprocal aims was inaugurated in Bucharest.

During Queen Marie's visit to the United States in October 1926 a publication in folio form, illustrated with portraits and scenes, took the place of the usual quarterly bulletin of the society and presented, aside from economic and financial information, a number of articles of particular and general interest by well-known writers more in keeping with the established conception of a review and magazine. Subsequent issues of the bulletins of the Society of Friends of Roumania have retained to a certain extent the character of the bulletin dedicated to Queen Marie, including more and more reading matter of popular interest with illustrations of the same character. The reproduced typewritten page gave place to a printed

[3] In 1930 a law was passed to check the circulation and printing of news of an alarmist tendency, especially regarding false financial and economic information.

format, and the name *Roumania* was substituted for *Bulletin*. With the January-February-March 1929 number of *Roumania,* the quarterly formally entered the field of magazine publication and was placed on sale where publications of an international character are usually offered.

For an account of Roumanian literature the reader is referred to C. U. Clark, *Greater Roumania,* chapter xv, "Roumanian Literature"; L. Feraru, *The Development of Roumanian Poetry,* The Institute of Rumanian Culture, Columbia University, 1929; J. S. Rouček, "Post-War Roumanian Literature," in *Books Abroad,* 1932, VI, 11–13.

B. The Educational System of Roumania

The school is one of Roumania's major social institutions. Universal education is a necessity in a country attempting to apply the principles of democracy. Consequently a political democracy cannot flourish unless political and social intelligence is developed in the electorate. The school must educate for citizenship as well as for the occupations and professions.

The Roumanian educational system bears the influences of culture of twenty-five centuries, in addition to the influence of Latin culture, the impress of which was somewhat abrogated under the Slavonic influence of the church during the Middle Ages and the subsequent Greek religious predominance but is again strongly noticeable after the vogue of the neo-Hellenic literature at the end of the eighteenth century. Professor Iorga has characterized the present system by saying:

In our school has reigned until now the spirit of domination. First of all the system of French barracks from the times of the second Empire has dominated, on which was superimposed the German pedagogical regulation. These two systems should now be abandoned.

The origin of the grammar school system in the Old Kingdom dates back to the first half of the nineteenth century. In 1838 the first Wallachian official decrees were promulgated, giving directions for the organization and the upbuilding of schools attended not for the whole year but only during the winter season. The first schools were to be set up by the *boiars*. The result was 29 grammar schools, and between 1838 and 1864, 259 additional schools came into being. The creation of schools in Moldavia was imposed by the state as early as 1832, but up to 1859 only 25 grammar schools had been established in villages and 30 in the cities.

. The educational acts of 1864 created the principle of free and compulsory education "where schools were available" under state supervision. These principles were included in the constitution of 1866. But because of financial and organization deficiencies the law could not be applied very effectively. The foundations of the present Roumanian system were laid by the decrees of 1896, supplemented in 1901, 1903, and 1908. The requirement of four years' attendance was introduced and the state imposed on itself the obligation to support and extend education and to provide for the training of teachers.

In Transylvania each commune having more than thirty children had to establish and support a school. The Magyar government granted the schools, which were not directly supported by it, certain aids if the Magyar language and nationalistic spirit were taught. The Roumanian schools were mostly the products of the church and controlled by it. In 1918 there were in Transylvania, according to Professor Sylvius Dragomir, 2,392 Roumanian primary schools for 2,930,120 Roumanians. Not a single one was supported by the Hungarian state. According to the same authority there was one primary school for each 1,229 Roumanians, in contrast to one primary school for each 504 Hungarians, 890 Saxons, and 10,847 Souabians. In Bukovina the policy of the government was that of steadily reducing the employment of the Roumanian language. In 1914, 179 Roumanian schools with 35,131 pupils belonged to the Bukovinian school system, which had a total of 541 schools. In Bessarabia the conditions were much worse when the province joined Roumania in 1917. Only private Roumanian schools were allowed and the teaching in this language was limited to the first two years of such schools.

Though the development of education in Roumania was rapid after 1896, the number of illiterates remained rather large. Their number, for example, in pre-war Roumania was 43 per cent, in Transylvania 40 per cent, in the Bukovina 60 per cent, and in Bessarabia 40 per cent of the entire population.

The conditions of the educational structure changed fundamentally after the war; the increase in the number of schools and pupils and of teachers is remarkable. Statistics of 1921 show that in that year out of some 2,500,000 children of school age (7 to 12 inclusive) over one million did not attend school. The estimated number of primary schools was 13,398, of teachers 25,745, and of pupils 1,516,198.[1] In 1928, these figures had increased to a remarkable extent. There were then 16,824 schools, 52,995 teachers, and 2,216,206 pupils.[2]

As compared with the old régime, the number of the minorities schools supported by the Roumanian Government has increased. While the Magyar government did not support one school teaching the Roumanian language, the Roumanian Government spends, in addition to extraordinary appropriations, 130 million lei annually for Hungarian and German primary state schools. In 1929, the National-Peasant Government granted 25 million lei to the minority and confessional schools and five million lei to German schools.

The educational policy of the Roumanian Government has been based on the desire to make up for the lost time of the past and to retain Roumanian control of every school. All teachers now have to pass an examination in the Roumanian language. The greatest deficiency of the system has been its disunity. The Liberal Government undertook during its régime (1922–26) to unify the entire school system. New schools were founded. Dr. C. Angelescu reorganized the system by an official decree of July 24, 1924. The four-year term of the primary school was lengthened by three years for additional education in civic and practical subjects. However, pupils desiring to attend the higher schools need spend only four years in the primary school. For children of from five to seven years of age kindergartens were introduced. Adult courses were organized, and the training period of teachers in normal schools was lengthened.

The educational system of Roumania is divided into four categories: elementary, secondary, graduate, and superior. Compulsory education is applied only to the elementary schools.[3]

[1] *The Near East Year Book, 1927,* p. 402.

[2] *Roumania,* 1930, VI, 59. See also *School and Society,* 1928, 474–75; and *Central European Observer,* 1931, IX, 473.

[3] See J. S. Rouček, "Recent Tendencies of the Roumanian Educational System," in *School and Society,* 1931, XXXIV, 373–75. The table below, based on *Annuaire Statistique de la Roumanie 1929,* pp. 435–54, shows the number of schools and matriculated pupils as well as the total number of teachers for the school year ending June 30, 1928:

	Old Kingdom		Transylvania		Bessarabia		Bukovina		Total
	Schools	Pupils	Schools	Pupils	Schools	Pupils	Schools	Pupils	Teachers
Kindergarten	611	36,926	487	36,565	422	24,047	56	5,134	1,855
Primary, rural.....	7,058	789,025	3,826	347,821	1,919	259,411	477	78,451	31,929
Primary, urban....	625	112,248	160	36,977	188	33,733	65	16,216	5,409

Primary schools are attended by children of from five to twelve years of age, their first two years being spent in a kindergarten. The curriculum is uniform throughout the country and comprises the teaching of reading and writing, history and geography of Roumania, arithmetic, grammar, and an art or craft as chosen. The parents supply their offspring with school books and other things necessary for the children's training.

Secondary schools comprise normal schools, high schools, seminaries, trade schools, high schools for arts and crafts, elementary agriculture, viticulture, arts, professional and domestic science, and private schools.

Normal schools in 1928 numbered 60 for boys and 36 for girls training rural teachers. Graduates of primary schools are granted admission by certificate. Since 1924 the training covers seven years. Pedagogical methods are especially emphasized, in addition to the history and geography of the country, literary knowledge of the language, physics, chemistry, natural sciences, child psychology, singing, physical education, folk-lore and folk dances, and appreciation of art, including Roumanian peasant art. After their graduation, the new teachers are appointed by the Ministry of Education to rural schools, and must pass an examination after three years and prior to permanent appointment. But the lack of a sufficient number of teachers is still evident. Supplementary summer vacation courses,

	Old Kingdom		Transylvania		Bessarabia		Bukovina		Total
	Schools	Pupils	Schools	Pupils	Schools	Pupils	Schools	Pupils	Teachers
Secondary*	483	117,235	112	230,086	38	42,391	245	9,364	11,615
Seminaries	14	3,982	...	...	3	802	...	...	344
Faculties of:									
Law	2	9,453	1	1,147	...	...	1	564	98
Philosophy	2	6,999	1	580	...	...	1	372	169
Sciences	2	3,517	1	339	...	...	1	218	396
Medicine	2	2,189	1	137	...	...	...	...	704†
Pharmacy	2	1,101	1	137	...	...	...	...	...
Theology	1	1,214	...	...	1	551	...	...	28
Academies of:									
Agriculture	...	...	1	77	...	...	...	...	21
Law	...	...	1	274	...	...	...	...	12
Commerce	1	1,794	...	...	...	...	...	...	24‡
Schools of:									
Engineering ...	1	857	1	263	...	...	...	...	165
Veterinary, Med.	1	300	...	...	...	...	...	...	53
Architecture ...	1	49	1	251	...	...	...	...	19
Music and drama	2	1,777	1	91	...	...	1	313	116
Beaux-Arts ...	2	359	...	...	...	...	...	...	38
Total	8,810	1,089,025	4,596	655,614	2,571	360,935	847	110,632	52,995

* School year 1926–27.
† Medicine and Pharmacy combined.
‡ For Transylvania only.

cultural circles, and regular conferences have been organized since 1924, in addition to a special pedagogical faculty at Bucharest University.

Since 1924 secondary education has been uniform. The courses give general knowledge rather than specialized instruction. The graduation diploma from a primary school and the passing of an oral and written examination is required for entrance into the high school. At the end of the seventh year the students successfully examined receive a "high-school studies certificate." In order to be able to enter a university or other higher educational institution, the passing of the dreaded "baccalaureate" examination is necessary. In 1928 and 1929 secondary education was divided into the gymnasium or lower grades, with three years of study, and the higher grades, covering four years.

In 1928 there were 495 commercial schools, 1,396 trade schools, and 872 professional schools for girls. Trade schools were especially favored by the National-Peasant Government, as it felt that there were too many graduates of the high schools and not enough graduates in practical subjects. Those who are interested in manual work, home life, or out-of-door occupations, have access to the high schools for arts and crafts, elementary agriculture, viticulture, arts, and professional and domestic science.

Private education plays a very important part in Roumania, and has been the pioneer along lines of cultural progress in Roumania. In 1924 a bill was approved for the recognition of the minorities' rights to their own churches and schools, subject to having their programs approved by the Ministry of Education, a topic mentioned in our chapter concerning minorities. Then there are 16 theological seminaries giving from six to eight years of training.

Graduate and post-graduate education was reorganized after the war on the French model and at the present time the government is considering another reorganization concerning years of study, subjects, and the granting of diplomas and degrees.

Today Roumania has four universities in the cities of Bucharest (founded in 1863), Iaşi, Cluj, and Cernăuţi, in addition to the law academy at Oradea Mare and the polytechnic institutes at Bucharest and Timişoara. Bucharest University includes six faculties, viz., those of laws, philosophy and literature, theology, science, medicine and pharmacy, and veterinary medicine. The University of Iaşi has no faculty of veterinary medicine and its theological faculty is located at Chişinău; the University of Cluj comprises faculties of philosophy, law, medicine and pharmacy, and science; and the University of Cernăuţi those of philosophy and literature, theology, law, and science. The medical faculty of Bucharest is one of the best institutions of its kind in the Balkans.

The graduates from these universities must include in their studies special pedagogical courses and must pass a special examination in their chosen field in order to receive appointments in secondary schools. Permanent appointments are granted after a three years' probationary period. There are no residence requirements for a doctorate. A successful defense of the original thesis before the university council is essential, and it is expected that every student shall be familiar with the scientific approach to his problem.

The Roumanian student bodies of the universities play a very important part in Roumanian political and social life. Recently groups of students have formed special circles for the purpose of giving practical as well as cultural instruction to the peasants. Otherwise there is an absence of social activities, physical education, and sports. In contrast to American student life, there are no opportunities for developing friendly relations between the students and the professors.

In 1924 the French Government instituted "L'Institut Français des Hautes Études en Roumanie," whose lecturers change every year. It has no specified program.

In addition there are three conservatories of music, at Bucharest, Chişinău, and Iaşi; two schools of plastic art and two dramatic schools, at Bucharest and Iaşi; an agricultural and a commercial academy at Bucharest; and a Mohammedan seminary.

Roumanian scientific life is centered in the Academia Română (Roumanian Academy) at Bucharest. It was founded with state help in 1866, and the government nominated its first members from all Roumanians, including those living outside the kingdom's borders, aiming thus to show the unity of the nation. The later members have been appointed by the academy itself, which is an entirely autonomous body subsidized by the state. It is organized on the model of the Institut de France.

The first aim of the academy was to unify the literary language of all Roumanian provinces and to introduce a uniform orthography. In addition, the academy publishes various periodicals, annual reports, and annals of its various sections. The historical section edits the sources of Roumanian history, naming its publications after the founder of this series, E. Hurmuzachi. The literary section publishes ethnographic works, *Din Viaţa Poporului Român*. The academy has its own library of more than 200,000 volumes and 8,000 manuscripts.

A fine type of academic work is produced by the Institutul Social Român (Roumanian Social Institute), founded in 1921 for research work in the social sciences in Roumania and to make the results of its efforts known in order to further social reforms. Dr. D. Gusti, Professor of Sociology in the University of Bucharest, is its president and edits *Arhiva* (The Archives).[4]

Much attention is paid in Roumania to the education of the masses.[5] Private organizations, as well as the Ministries of Education, of Agriculture, of War, and of Labor all have systematic programs for adult education. Thus the Ministry of Agriculture offers courses in agricultural subjects, and the law of 1924 also provided for the creation of schools and courses for adults with compulsory attendance for from four to six months yearly in certain circumstances and in the case of the illiterate for three full years.

The Ministry of Education supports a special institution, "Casa Şcoalelor şi Culturei Poporului" (The House of Schools and Popular Culture), which organizes popular lectures, celebrations, libraries, and agricultural instructions. It has founded about 15,000 libraries and supports over 500 cultural societies. It prints popular books for distribution at a low price, and buys other books with its own means and distributes them among the libraries.

Great strides in popular education have been due to private initiative. Teachers, priests, students, and others have founded numerous societies, libraries, music organizations, and printing offices, spreading popular literature among the people on the basis of the recommendations of the cultural institutions of Bucharest.

Among the oldest and the most important cultural associations is the Transylvanian "Asociaţia Pentru Literatura Românească şi Cultura Poporului Român" (Society for Roumanian Literature and Roumanian Culture), known briefly as "Astra," founded in 1861, which tried to uplift the national sentiment of the Roumanians in

---

[4] For further information on the subject, see a fine summary in R. J. Kerner, *Social Sciences in the Balkans and Turkey.*

[5] See *The Near East Year Book, 1927,* pp. 404, 420–23; D. Mitrany, *The Land and the Peasant in Rumania,* pp. 509–25.

Transylvania during the Magyar oppression. It published a periodical, *Transilvania,* and a collection of popular books (*Biblioteca Populară*). It has today about 110 branches throughout Transylvania and continues its splendid work in the other provinces of Roumania by offering special courses for illiterates, forming study groups and organizing lectures.

A similar institution is the "Liga Culturală" (Cultural League for the Cultural Unity of All Roumanians), founded in 1894 during the severest persecution of the Transylvanian Roumanians. Professor Nicolae Iorga is its president now. Before the war this league took care of the refugee Roumanians suffering under foreign domination, granted material help, sent books to Transylvania, organized lectures, exhibitions, and national celebrations, and founded libraries. Today it has about 66 branches throughout Roumania and its aim is to widen the cultural standard of all Roumanians and to support the nationalistic conscience. Dr. Iorga organizes summer courses every year at Vălenii-de-Munte, which even before the war was the meeting place of the young knowledge-hungry Roumanians from all parts of the country.[6] The lectures are given without official credit, and poor students are supported by contributions which Iorga raises from state grants and otherwise. For the purpose of making worthwhile material available to the masses, a printing office "Datina Românească," is maintained at the same place.

Other institutions interested in popular education are the so-called "Casele Naționale" (National Houses), originating in 1920 under the leadership of General Manoilescu. Their center is Bucharest. Every branch has a library, a recreation hall, a theater, and workshops for peasant art. The casele arranges celebrations, lectures, exhibitions, and grants prizes. Besides publishing educational books, the organization edits its own periodical.

A similar type of endeavor is followed by the "King Carol Cultural Endowment." So far it has established about 600 "cultural houses" throughout the country and has published three periodicals: *Albina* (The Bee) for the general masses; *Ramura* (The Branch) for teachers and priests; and *Gândirea* (Thinking), a literary review.

Finally, the law provides that every village teacher must arrange a number of lectures, theatrical performances, etc., each year.

---

[6] See J. S. Rouček, "The People's University—Professor Iorga's Experiment at Vălenii-de-Munte, Roumania," in *School and Society,* 1931, XXXIV, 199–200.

Furthermore, village priests must assemble every three weeks and hold a joint service.

The organization of radio broadcasting in Roumania dates back to 1925. The National-Peasant Government provided an annual subsidy for the Broadcasting Corporation, formed in 1926. The Ministry of Public Instruction introduced a course in radio broadcasting in the secondary schools, and decided to provide receiving sets for the schools and to arrange with the company for the broadcasting of special school programs. The Roumanian monopolies institute took steps to provide village libraries with receiving equipment, while the Ministry of Interior recommended to district prefects the acquisition and installation of receiving sets in the principal towns and villages. Finally, for the benefit of the industrial working classes, the Ministry of Labor is studying, through the newly created division of people's education, the arrangement of special programs and the installation of receiving apparatus in working communities. The creation of a "Radiophonic Little Entente" enables the co-ordination of the radio programs of Yugoslavia, Czechoslovakia, Poland, and Roumania.

BIBLIOGRAPHY

THIS bibliography is by no means exhaustive. A comprehensive list of references to the material covering so broad a field would itself assume the proportions of a book. The selection here furnished will acquaint the general reader with general and specific information on Roumania, and will help those seeking further information on individual topics to find ready references and others to follow up more detailed lines of inquiry. Other bibliographies, limited to special fields, can also be found in the following publications: Oscar Jászi, *The Dissolution of the Habsburg Monarchy* (Chicago, 1929), pp. 461–80; nearly all of R. W. Seton-Watson's works mentioned below; N. Iorga, *A History of Roumania* (London, 1925), pp. 274–77; C. U. Clark, *Greater Roumania* (New York, 1922), pp. 455–59; *Bessarabia* (New York, 1927), pp. 299–316; A. Popovici, *The Political Status of Bessarabia* (Washington, D.C., 1931), pp. 266–75; D. Mitrany, *The Land and the Peasant in Rumania* (London and New Haven, 1930), pp. 594–611; A. Rally et G. H. Rally, *Bibliographie Franco-Roumaine* (Paris, 1930), 2 volumes. Also Léon Savadjian, editor, *Bibliographie Balkanique 1920–1930* (*Revue des Balkans,* 71 Rue de Rennes, Paris, 1931) contains a classified bibliography; and *A Guide to Historical Literature* (New York, 1931), pp. 829–33, is a work valuable not only for its bibliography but as an analytical guide to the study of Roumania.

A. General Works

Ancel, J., *Peuples et Nations des Balkans,* Paris, 1926

Arion, C., *La Situation économique et sociale des paysans en Roumanie,* Paris, 1861, 1895

Bailey, W. F., and Bates, J. V., "Places and Peoples on the Roumanian Danube," *Fortnightly Review,* 1916, CVI, 795–807

"The Roumanian Danube from Widdin to the Black Sea," *ibid.,* pp. 960–73

Bellessort, A., *La Roumanie contemporaine,* Paris, 1905

Benger, G., *Roumänien, am Land der Zukumft,* Stuttgart, 1896

Roumania in 1900, London, 1900

Beza, M., *Papers on Roumanian People and Literature,* London, 1920

Bowman, I., *The New World,* Yonkers-on-Hudson, 1921, 1924, 1928

Brilliant, O., *Roumania,* New York, 1915

Chamberlain, J. P., *The Danube,* Washington, D.C., 1918

Chater, M., "The Danube, Highway of Races," *National Geographic Magazine,* 1929, LVI, 643–98

Chopin, J., *De l'Elbe aux Balkans,* Paris, 1929
Ciobanu, S., *La Continuité Roumaine dans la Bessarabie,* Bucarest, 1920
Cioriceanu, G. D., *L'Évolution du peuplement dans les terres Roumaines,* Paris, 1928
Clark, C. U., *Bessarabia,* New York, 1927
　　Greater Roumania, New York, 1922
Commene, N. P., *La Dobrogea,* Paris, 1918
　　La Roumanie à travers les ages, Paris, 1919
Dawson, T., *The New Roumania,* London, 1928
D'Ormesson, *Nos Illusions sur l'Europe Centrale,* Paris, 1923
Dungern, O. V., *Rumänien,* Gotha, 1916
Evelpidi, C., *Les États Balkaniques,* Paris, 1930
Gayda, V., *Modern Austria, Her Racial and Social Problems,* London, 1915
Gerando, A. de, *La Transylvanie et ses habitants,* Paris, 1845
Gerard, E., "Transylvanian People," *Contemporary Review,* 1887, LI, 327–46
Gheyn, A. von, *Les Populations Danubiennes,* Gand, 1886
Gillard, M., *La Roumanie Nouvelle,* Paris, 1922
Gordon, W., *Roumania Yesterday and Today,* London, 1918
Great Britain, Admiralty, *A Handbook of Roumania,* London, 1920
Great Britain, Foreign Office, *Peace Handbooks:* No. 5, "Bukovina"; No. 6, "Transylvania and the Banat"; No. 15, "The Eastern Question"; No. 16, "Turkey in Europe"; No. 23, "Rumania"; No. 51, "Bessarabia"; No. 149, "International Rivers"; No. 151, "International Congresses"; No. 153, "The Congress of Vienna"; No. 154, "The Congress of Berlin." London, 1920
Grothe, H., *Zur Landeskunde von Rumänien,* Halle, 1907
Gubernatis, Conte, A. de, *La Roumanie et les Roumains,* Florence, 1898
Guerin, T., *Caps and Gowns of Europe* (New York, 1929), pp. 191–207
Henke, *Rumänien, Land und Volk,* Leipzig, 1877
Hunfalvy, P., *Die Rumänien und Ihre Ansprüche,* Vienna, 1883
Hurst, A. H., *Roumania and Great Britain,* London, 1916
L'Illustration (special numbers on Roumania), Paris, February 1925, September 1929
International Telephone and Telegraph Corporation, *Rumania,* New York, 1930
Iorga, N., *Cinq Conférences sur le Sud-Est de l'Europe,* Paris, 1924
　　"Rumania's Peasants," *Living Age,* 1922, CCCXIII, 296
Kerner, R. J., *Social Sciences in the Balkans and Turkey,* Berkeley (California), 1930
Kirke, D., *Domestic Life in Roumania,* London, 1916
Laveleye, E., *La Peninsula des Balkans,* 2 vols., Paris, 1886
Leger, L., *La Save, le Danube, et le Balkan,* Paris, 1884
Lockhart, D., *Seeds of War,* London, 1925
Lupu, N., *La Roumanie Nouvelle et ses problèmes vitaux,* Paris, 1919
Lyde, A. W., and Mockler-Ferryman, A. T., *A Military Geography of the Balkan Peninsula,* London, 1905
Macůrek, Dr. Josef, *Rumunsko ve Své Minulosti i Přítomnosti,* Praha (Czechoslovakia), 1930

Maican, J. C., *La Question du Danube,* Paris, 1904

Manchester Guardian, Roumanian Supplement, November 28, 1929

Martineau, P., *Roumania and Her Rulers,* London, 1927

Martonne, E. de, "The Carpathians: Physiographic Features Controlling Human Geography," *Geographic Review,* 1917, III, 417–37

"Essai de Carte Ethnographique des Pays Roumains," *Annales de Géographie,* 1920, XXIX, 81–98

"La Nouvelle Roumanie," *Annales de Géographie,* 1921, XXX, 1–31

La Nouvelle Roumanie dans la Nouvelle Europe, Bucarest, 1922

"La Roumanie et son rôle dans l'Europe Orientale," *La Géographie,* 1914–15, XXX, 241–50

"La Transylvanie," *Bulletin de la Société de Géographie de Lille,* 1922, LXIV, 93–102

La Valachie, Paris, 1902

Miller, W., *The Balkans,* London, 1896

Mousset, A., *L'Europe Balkanique de 1925 à 1928,* Paris, 1928

Muzet, A., *La Roumanie Nouvelle,* Paris, 1920

Nacion, J. J., *La Dobrudja économique et sociale,* Paris, 1886

Neugebauer, I., *Beschreibung der Moldau und der Walachei,* Breslau, 1854

Newbigin, M. I., *Geographical Aspects of Balkan Problems,* New York, 1915

Pantazzi, E. G., *Roumania in Light and Shadow,* London, 1921

Parkinson, M., *Twenty Years in Roumania,* London, 1921

Pernot, M., *Les Balkans nouveaux,* Paris, 1929

Peytavi de Faugères, G., *Roumania Terre Latine,* Paris, 1929

Pittard, E., *Dans la Dobrudja,* Geneva, 1902

Les Peuples des Balkans, Paris, 1916

"Les Peuples de la Peninsula des Balkans," *Revue Générale des Sciences,* 1915, XXVI, 665–75

La Roumanie—Valachie, Moldavie, Dobrudja, Paris, 1917

Pointe, H. Le, *La Roumanie moderne,* Paris, 1910

Prager Presse, December 8, 1923; March 14, 1926; May 5, 1929

Quinet, E., *Les Roumains,* Paris, 1857

Roger, N., *La Nouvelle Roumanie* (reprint from *Revue des Deux Mondes*), Vălenii-de-Munte, 1926

Rommenhoeller, C. G., *La Grande-Roumanie,* La Haye, 1926

Sanders, E. M., "The New Rumanian State," *Geographical Review,* 1923, XIII, 377–97

Schmalz, F., *Grossrumänien, Wirtschaftlich, Politisch und Kulturell,* Gotha, 1921

Schwartz, B., *Aus der Dobrudscha,* Leipzig, 1888

Seraphim, Dr. P. H., *Rumänien,* Breslau, 1927

Seurre, J., *En Roumanie,* Paris, 1928

Society of Friends of Roumania, *Bulletin,* October 18, 1926

Stahel de Capitani, H., *Rumänien,* Zürich, 1925

Stephens, J. S., *Danger Zones of Europe,* London, 1929

Sturdza, A. A. C., *La Roumanie et les Roumains,* Paris, 1910

Le Terre et la race Roumaines depuis leur origines jusqu'à nos jours, Paris, 1904

Tabbe, P., *La Vivante Roumanie,* Paris, 1913

Tibal, A., *La Roumanie,* Paris, 1931

Tribune de Genève, Supplément illustré, "Roumanie," May 8, 1924

U.S. Department of Commerce, Bureau of Foreign and Domestic Commerce, Special Agents Series, No. 222, *Rumania: An Economic Handbook,* Washington, D.C., 1924

Vacaresco, H., "Marriages in Roumania," *Fortnightly Review,* 1916, CV, 360–64

Vaillant, J. A., *La Roumanie, ou l'histoire, langue, littérature, orographie, statistique des peuples de la langue d'or, Ardéliens, Valaques et Moldaves, Résumés sous le nom de Romans,* Paris, 1845

Völkermagazin, May 1929, "Rumänien"

Wace, A. J. B., and Thompson, M., *The Nomads of the Balkans,* London, 1914

Xenopol, A. D., *Les Roumains, l'histoire, l'état materiel et intellectuel,* Paris, 1909

   La Richesse de la Roumanie, Bucarest, 1916

B. History

Amouretti, L., *Les Roumains de Hongrie,* Paris, 1894

D'Arges, J., *Le Procès d'une nation (Les Roumains de Transylvanie),* Paris, 1894

Auerbach, B., *Les Races et les nationalités en Autriche-Hongrie,* Paris, 1898

Aulneau, J., *Histoire de l'Europe Centrale,* Paris, 1926

Bănescu, N., *Historical Survey of the Rumanian People,* Bucharest, 1926

Bergner, R., *Siebenbürgen, Eine Darstellung des Landes und der Leute,* Leipzig, 1884

Berry, J., "Transylvania and Its Relations to Ancient Dacia and Modern Rumania," *Geographical Journal,* 1919, LIII, 129–52

Bertha, A. de, *Magyars et Roumains devant l'histoire,* Paris, 1899

Beza, M., "Roumanian Chroniclers," *Slavonic Review,* 1930, IX, 124–32

Bibesco, G., *Histoire d'une frontière: La Roumanie sur la rive droite du Danube,* Paris, 1883

   Roumanie d'Adrianople à Balta-Liman, 1829–1849, règne de Bibesco, 2 vols., Paris, 1893–1894

Bidermann, *Die Bukovina unter Österreichischer Verwaltung (1775–1875),* Wien, 1875

Bielz, E. A., *Siebenbürgen,* Hermannstadt, 1903

Boehm, L., *Geschichte der Temesvarer Banats,* 2 vols., Leipzig, 1861

Böldényi, M. J., *Le Magyarisme ou la guerre des nationalités en Hongrie,* Paris, 1850

Bowen, F., *Hungary. The Rebellion of the Slavonic, Wallachian and German Hungarians against the Magyars,* Cambridge (Mass.), 1851

Bratianu, I., *L'Autriche dans les Principautés Roumaines,* Paris, 1858

   Mémoire sur l'Empire d'Autriche dans la question d'Orient, Paris, 1855

Brosteanu, P., and Maniu, V., *Zur Geschichtsforschung über die Rumänen,* Reschitza, 1885

Brote, E., *Die Rumänische Frage in Siebenbürgen und Ungarn,* Berlin, 1895

Carra, J. L., *Histoire de la Moldavie et la Valachie, avec une dissertation sur l'état actuel de ces deux provinces,* Jassy, 1777

Cogalniceanu, M., *Histoire de la Dacie, des Valaques Transdanubiens et de la Valachie,* Berlin, 1854

Colson, F., *Nationalité et régénération des paysans Moldovalaques,* Paris, 1862

Corwan, N., "Deux Documents sur le choix d'un Prince Etranger en 1856," *Revue Historique du Sud-Est Européen,* 1930, VII, 78–85

Creanga, G. C., *Grundbesitzverteilung und Bauernfrage in Rumänien,* Leipzig, 1907

Damé, F., *Histoire de la Roumanie contemporaine depuis l'avènement des princes indigènes jusqu'à nos jours, 1882–1900,* Paris, 1900

Djuvara, T. G. (editor), *Traités, conventions, et arrangements internationaux de la Roumanie actuellement en vigueur,* Paris, 1888

Duggan, S. P. H., *The Eastern Question: A Study in Diplomacy,* New York, 1902

East, W. G., *The Union of Moldavia and Wallachia, 1859,* Cambridge, 1929

Filitti, J. G., *Les Principautés Roumaines sous l'occupation Russe,* Bucarest, 1904

Fotino, Dr. Georges, *Contribution à l'étude des origines de l'ancient droit contumier Roumain. Un chapitre de l'histoire de la propriété au Moyen Age,* Paris, 1925

Gherghel, I., *Zur Geschichte Siebenbürgens,* Wien, 1891

Ghica, J. T., *Les Roumains de Transylvanie et de Hongrie,* Paris, 1896

Golesco, A. G., *De l'Abolition du servage dans les Principautés Danubiennes,* Paris, 1856

Hajdeu, B. P., *Histoire critique des Roumains,* Paris, 1873

Hajnal, Dr. H., *The Danube: Its Historical, Political and Economic Importance,* The Hague, 1920

Henry, P., *L'Abdication du Prince Cuza et l'avènement de la dynastie de Hohenzollern au trône de Roumanie,* Paris, 1931

Holland, I. E., *The European Concert in the Eastern Question,* Oxford, 1885

Hunfalvy, *Die Rumänen und Ihre Anspruche,* Vienna, 1883

Hurmuzachi, Baron E., *Fragmente zur Geschichte der Rumänen* (translation by A. D. Sturdza), 5 vols., Buckarest, 1878–1887

Iorga, N., *Geschichte des Rumänischen Volkes in Rahmen seiner Staatsbildungen,* 2 vols., Gotha, 1905

Geschichte des Osmanischen Reiches, 5 vols., Gotha, 1908–1913

Les Roumains et le nouvel état des choses en Orient, Vălenii-de-Munte, 1912

Histoire des Roumains de Transylvanie et de Hongrie, 2 vols., Bucarest, 1915–1916

Histoire des relations Russo-Roumaines, Jassy, 1917

Pages Roumaines, Paris, 1918

Histoire des relations entre la France et les Roumains, Paris, 1918

Iorga, N., *Relations entre les Grecs et les Roumains*, Bucarest, 1922
   Relations entre les Serbes et les Roumains, Bucarest, 1922
   Études Roumaines, 2 vols., Paris, 1923–24
   Histoire des états Balkaniques jusqu'à 1924, Paris, 1925
   *Les Ecrivains réalistes en Roumanie comme témoins du changement de
      milieu au XIXe siècle*, Paris, 1925
   A History of Roumania (translation by J. McCabe), London, 1925
   Geschichte der Rumänen und Ihrer Kultur, Hermannstadt, 1929
   Polonais et Roumains: Relations politiques, économiques et culturales,
      Bucharest, 1921
   Les Eléments originaux de l'ancienne civilisation Roumaine, Iassy,
      1911
   *Histoire des Roumains de Bukovine, à partir de l'annexion Austrichienne
      (1775–1914)*, Iassy, 1917
   La Politique de Michel-le-Brave, ses origines et son importance actuelle,
      Iassy, 1918
   *Correspondance diplomatique Roumaine sous le Roi Charles Ier (1886–
      1890)*, Paris, 1923
Jászi, O., *The Dissolution of the Habsburg Monarchy*, Chicago, 1929
Kaindl, R. F., *Geschichte der Deutschen in den Karpathenländern*, 2 vols.,
      Gotha, 1907
   Geschichte der Bukowina, Czernovitz, 1904
Klapka, G., *Der Nationalkrieg in Ungarn und Siebenbürgen in den Jahren
      1848 bis 49*, Leipzig, 1851
Lindenberg, P., *König Karl von Rumänien: ein Liebensbild dargestellt unter
      Mittarbeit des Königs*, Berlin, 1923
Miller, W., *The Balkans*, New York, 1896
Minchin, J. G. G., *The Growth of Freedom in the Balkan Peninsula*, London,
      1886
Mitrany, D., "Rumania: Her History and Politics." N. Forbes and Others,
      *The Balkans: A History of Bulgaria, Serbia, Greece, Roumania,
      Turkey*, Oxford, 1915, pp. 251–318
Murray, W. S., *The Making of the Balkan States*, New York (Columbia
      University, Vol. 39, No. 102, *Studies in History, Economics, and
      Public Law*), 1910–1911
Noyes, J. O., *Roumania: The Border Land of the Christian and the Turk*,
      New York, 1858
Pârvan, V., *Dacia*, Cambridge, 1928
Petrescu, G., Sturdza, D. A., Sturdza, D. C., Colescu-Vartic, G. (editors),
      *Actes et documents relatifs à l'histoire de la régénération de la Rou-
      manie*, 10 vols. in 12 parts, Bucureşti, 1888–1909
Pic, J. L., *Über die Abstammung der Rumänien*, Leipzig, 1880
Picot, E. (editor), *Chronique de Moldavie depuis le milieu du XIVe siècle
      jusqu'à l'an 1594*, Paris, 1878
   Les Roumains de la Macédoine, Paris, 1875
Regnault, E., *Histoire politique et sociale des Principautés Danubiennes*,
      Paris, 1855
René, G., *Question d'Autriche, Hongrie et question d'Orient*, Paris, 1904

Riker, T. W., "The Concert of Europe and Moldavia in 1857," *English Historical Review,* 1927, XLII, 227–44
"The Pact of Osborne," *American Historical Review,* 1929, XXXIV, 237–49
Rosetti, R., "Rumania's Share in the War of 1877," *Slavonic Review,* 1930, VIII, 548–77
Russian Politics at Work in the Rumanian Countries, Bucharest, 1914
Salaberry, Comte de, *Essai sur la Valachie et la Moldavie,* Paris, 1821
Schevill, F., *The History of the Balkan Peninsula,* New York, 1922
Schüler, F. von, *Siebenbürgische Rechtsgeschichte,* 3 vols., Hermannstadt, 1867–1868
Schwicker, J. H., *Die Nationalpolitischen Anspruche der Rumänen in Ungarn,* Leipzig, 1894
Seton-Watson, R. W., *Europe in the Melting Pot,* London, 1919
Corruption and Reform in Hungary, London, 1911
German, Slav and Magyar, London, 1916
The Historian as a Political Force in Central Europe, London, 1922
Racial Problems in Hungary, London, 1908
Roumania and the Great War, London, 1915
"Roumanian Origins," *History,* 1923, VII–VIII, 241–55
Slavici, J., *Die Rumänen in Ungarn, Siebenbürgen und der Bukowina,* Wien, 1881
Sosnovsky, T. von, *Die Balkanpolitik Oesterreich-Ungarns seit 1866,* Stuttgart, 1913–1914
Stephens, H. M., "Modern Historians and Small Nationalities," *Contemporary Review,* 1887, LII, 107–21
Sturdza, A. A. C., *La Terre et la race Roumaines depuis leur origines jusqu'à nos jours,* Paris, 1904
La Roumanie moderne comme facteur de la civilisation en Orient, Paris, 1902
De l'histoire diplomatique des Roumains, 1821–1858: Règne de Michel Sturdza, Prince Régnant de Moldavie, 1834–1849, Paris, 1907
Sulzer, F. J., *Geschichte des Transalpinischen Daciens,* 3 vols., Vienna, 1781–82
Teutsch, G. D., *Geschichte der Siebenbürgen Sachsen,* Kronstadt, 1899
Vacaresco, H., "La Mystique nationale Roumaine aux environs de 1848," *Revue d'histoire diplomatique,* 1919, XLIII, 8–19
Wagner, P. V., *Das Banat in Spiegel der Geschichte,* Novisad, 1930
Weiss, J., *Die Dobrudscha in Altertum: Historiche Landschaftskunde,* Sarajevo, 1911
Wilkinson, W., *An Account of Wallachia and Moldavia,* London, 1820
Witte, Baron J. de, *Quinze Ans d'histoire (1866–1881): d'Après les Memoires du Roie de Roumanie,* Paris, 1905
Xénopol, A. D., *Histoire des Roumains,* 2 vols., Paris, 1896
Les Roumains, Paris, 1909
Une Énigme historique. Les Roumains au Moyen-Age, Paris, 1885
Ypsilanti, N., *Mémoires* (edited by D. G. Kambouroglous), Athènes and Paris, 1901

C. Independent Roumania up to the World War

D'Arges, J., *Le Procès d'une nation. Les Roumains de Transylvanie*, Paris, 1894
Barber, J. E., "Roumanian Policy and the Peace of Europe," *Nineteenth Century and After*, 1913, LXXIII, 548–63
Barbulescu, I., *Relations des Roumains avec les Serbes, les Bulgares, les Grecs et la Croatie*, Jassy, 1912
Beksics, G., *La Question Roumaine et le lutte des races en Orient*, Paris, 1895
Bibesco, Princess M., "The Vocation of a King," *Saturday Evening Post*, October 10, 1931, CCIV, 42 ff.
Blech, E. C., "The Balkan Lands," *Cambridge Modern History*, II, 643–47
Brote, E., *Die Rumänische Frage in Siebenbürgen und Ungarn*, Berlin, 1895
Ciobanu, St., *La Continuité Roumaine dans la Bessarabie, annexé en 1812 par la Russie*, Bucarest, 1920
Damé, F., *Histoire de la Roumanie contemporaine depuis l'avènement des princes indigenes jusqu'à nos jours (1822–1900)*, Paris, 1900
Delavrancea, B., *La Question nationale, le rôle et les droits des Roumains d'au-delà des Carpathes*, Bucarest, 1894
Drossos, D. J., *La Fondation de l'Alliance Balkanique*, Athens, 1929
Eliade, O., *De l'Influence Française sur l'esprit public en Roumanie*, Paris, 1898
International Inquiry Commission, *Causes and Conduct of the Balkan Wars* (Bulletin No. 4 of the Carnegie Endowment for International Peace, Division of Intercourse and Education), Washington, D.C., 1914
Hevesy, A. de, *L'Agonie d'un Empire: L'Autriche-Hongrie*, Paris, 1923
Ionescu, T., *La Politique etrangère de la Roumanie*, Bucarest, 1891
Iorga, N., *Le Hongrois et la nationalité Roumaine en 1909. Les dernières elections en Hongrie et les Roumains*, Vălenii-de-Munte, 1909–1910
Joerg, W. L. G., "The New Boundaries of the Balkan States and Their Significance," *Bulletin of American Geographical Society*, 1913, XLV, 819–30
Marriot, J. A. R., *The Eastern Question: A Study in Diplomacy*, Oxford, 1918
Medlicott, W. N., "Diplomatic Relations after the Congress of Berlin," *Slavonic Review*, 1929–30, VIII, 66–79
Nistor, I., *Der Nationale Kampf in der Bukovina mit besonderer Berücksichtigung der Rumänen und Ruthenen historisch Dargestellt*, Bukarest, 1918
Popovici, A. C., *La Question Roumaine en Transylvanie et en Hongrie*, Paris, 1918
Pribram, A. F., *Austrian Foreign Policy, 1908–1918*, London, 1923
    The Secret Treaties of Austria-Hungary (edited by A. C. Coolidge), 2 vols., Cambridge, 1920–21
Programmes politiques des Roumains de la Transylvanie, Bucharest, 1894
Redlich, J., "Hapsburg Policy in the Balkans before the War," *Foreign Affairs*, 1928, VI, 645–57
Rosetti, R., "Roumania's Share in the War of 1877," *Slavonic Review*, 1929–30, VIII, 546–77

Die Rumänische Frage in Siebenbürgen und Ungarn (Replic der Rumänischen Academischen Jugend Siebenbürgens u. Ungarns zu der von der Magyarischen Academischen Jugend veröffentlichten "Antwort" auf die "Denkschrift" der Studierenden der Universitäten Rumäniens), Wien, Budapest, Graz, Klausenburg, 1892

Schurman, J. G., *The Balkan Wars 1912–1913,* Princeton, 1914

Seton-Watson, R. W., "Transylvania in the Nineteenth Century," *Slavonic Review,* 1924–25, III, 304–19

"Transylvania since 1867," *ibid.,* IV, 101–23

Siebert, D. de, and Schreiner, G., *Entente Diplomacy and the World, 1909–1914,* New York, 1922

Singleton, E., *Turkey and the Balkan States,* New York, 1908

Steed, H. W., *The Habsburg Monarchy,* London, 1919

Street, C. J. C., *Hungary and Democracy,* London, 1923

Sturdza, D. A., *Europa, Russland und Rumänien,* Berlin, 1915

Whitman, S. (editor), *Reminiscences of the King of Roumania,* London, 1899

D. WORLD WAR AND NATIONAL UNIFICATION

American Jewish Congress, *Memorials Submitted to President Wilson Concerning the Status of the Jews in Eastern Europe and in Palestine on March 2, 1919,* New York

Antipa, G., *L'Occupation enemie de la Roumanie et ses consequences économiques et sociales,* New Haven, 1930

Auerbach, B., *L'Autriche et la Hongrie pendant la guerre,* Paris, 1925

Babel, A., *La Bessarabie,* Paris, 1926

Baernreither, J. M., *Fragments of a Political Diary,* New York, 1930

Baker, R. S., *Woodrow Wilson and the World Settlement,* 3 vols., New York, 1922

Barnes, H. E., "The Problem of the New Small National States in Central and Southern Europe: A Summary Survey," *Journal of International Relations,* 1919, X, 99–137

Basilescu, N., *La Roumanie dans la guerre et la paix,* 2 vols., Paris, 1919

Beneš, Dr. E., *My War Memoirs,* Boston and New York, 1928

Berindey, A., *La Situation économique et financière de la Roumanie sous l'occupation Allemande,* Paris, 1921

Bertrand, P., *L'Autriche-Hongrie contre ses sujets,* Paris, 1917

Bibesco, Princess M., *Une Victime royale: Ferdinand de Roumanie,* Paris, 1927

Buchan, J. (editor), *Bulgaria and Roumania,* London, 1924

Buchan, J., in *Nelson's History of the War:* Vol. XV, "Brusilov's Offensive and the Intervention of Rumania"; Vol. XVII, "From the Opening of the Rumanian Campaign to the Change of Governments in Britain"; Vol. XVIII, "The End of the Rumanian Retreat," and "The Clearing of Sinaia and the Fall of Bagdad," London, 1914–1919

History of the Great War, 4 vols., New York, 1922

Buday, L., *The Economic Unity of Hungary,* Budapest, 1919

Dismembered Hungary, London, 1922

Burian, Graf S., *Austria in Dissolution,* New York, 1925
Buxton, N., and Lesse, C. L., *Balkan Problems and European Peace,* London, 1919
Carossa, H., *A Roumanian Diary,* New York, 1930
Carp, P. P., *Auswärtige Politik und Agrarreform,* Bukarest, 1917
Chélard, R., *Responsibilité de la Hongrie dans la guerre mondiale,* Paris, 1930
Casso, L., *La Russie au Danube et l'organisation de la Bessarabie*
Commène, N. S., *Notes sur la Guerre Roumaine (1916–17),* Lausanne, 1917
Creanga, G. D., *Les Finances Roumaines sous le régime de l'occupation de la paix Allemande,* Paris, 1919
Cvijic, J., *La Question du Banat, de la Batchka et la Baranya,* Paris, 1919
Czernin, Count O., *In the World War,* New York, 1919
Danilov, General J., "Les Tentatives de Constitution d'un 'Bloc Balkanique' en 1914–1915," *Le Monde Slave,* May 1928, pp. 202–29; *ibid.,* June 1928, pp. 352–78
Diamandy, C. J., "La Grande Guerre vue de versant Oriental: l'entrevue de Constantza," *Revue des Deux Mondes,* 1928, XLIII, 132–37
Dillon, E. J., *The Inside Story of the Peace Conference,* New York, 1920
Djuvara, M., *La Guerre Roumaine 1916–1918,* Paris, 1919
Dominian, L., *Frontiers of Language and Nationality,* New York, 1917
    The Nationality Map of Europe (World Peace Foundation, I, No. 2), Boston, 1917
Draghicesco, D., and Murgoci, G., *Les Roumains d'Ukraine,* Paris, 1919
Fay, S. B., *The Origins of the World War,* 2 vols., New York, 1928
Feinberg, N., *La Question des minorités à la Conférence de la Paix de 1919–1920 et l'action Juive en faveur de la protection internationale des minorités,* Paris, 1929
Gavanesco, J., *L'Âme Roumaine dans la guerre mondiale,* Paris, 1919
Glaise-Horstenau, Ed. von, *The Collapse of the Austro-Hungarian Empire,* London, 1930
Gooch, G. P., *Recent Revelations of European Diplomacy,* London, 1930
Gratz, Dr. G., and Schüller, R., *The Economic Policy of Austria-Hungary during the War in Its External Relations,* New Haven, 1928
Gueschoff, J. E., *L'Alliance Balkanique,* Paris, 1915
Haskins, C. H., and Lord, R. H., *Some Problems of the Peace Conference,* Cambridge (Mass.), 1920
Hayes, C. J. H., *A Brief History of the Great War,* New York, 1920
Herron, G. D., "The New Roumania," *New Europe,* 1919, XII, 282–84
House, E. M., and Seymour, C. (editors), *What Really Happened at Paris,* New York, 1921
Howard, H. N., *The Partition of Turkey, 1913–1923,* Norman (Okla.), 1931
Hungary, Ministry of Foreign Affairs, *The Hungarian Negotiations,* 3 vols., Budapest, 1921
Iancovici, D., *La Paix de Bucarest,* Paris, 1918
Ionescu, T., *Some Personal Impressions,* London, 1919
    The Policy of National Instinct, London, 1916
Ionesco-Sisesti, G., *L'Agriculture de la Roumanie pendant la guerre,* Paris, 1929

Iorga, N., "The Attitude of Roumania," *Quarterly Review,* 1915, CCXXIII, 439–50

Jászi, O., *Revolution and Counter-Revolution in Hungary,* London, 1924

Johnson, D. W., "The Conquest of Roumania," *Geographical Review,* 1917, III, 438–56

Die Juden im Kriege. Denkschrift des Jüdischen Sozialistischen Arbeiterverbandes Poale Sion an das Internationale Sozialistiche Bureau, Haag, 1915

Kautsky, K., Montgelas, M., and Schüking, W., *Die Deutsche Dokumente zum Kriegsausbruch,* 4 vols., Charlottenburg, 1919

Kerner, R. J., "Austrian Plans for a Balkan Settlement," *New Europe,* 1920, XVI, 280–84

"Austro-Hungarian War Aims in the Winter of 1915–1916 as Revealed by Secret Documents," *Journal of International Relations,* 1920, X, 444–70

Kiritesco, C., *Histoire de la Guerre Roumaine,* 2 vols., Paris, 1925

La Roumanie dans la guerre mondiale (1916–1919), Bucarest, 1927

Kleinwaechter, F., *Der Untergang der Oesterreichisch-Ungarischen Monarchie,* Leipzig, 1920

Knight, M. M., "Conditions within Roumania and Turkey"; "Roumania vs. the Peace Conference"; "Transylvania," *Journal of International Relations,* 1919–1920, X, 13–25, 256–69, 425–43

Kohler, M. J., "Jewish Rights at International Congresses," *American Jewish Historical Society Publications,* No. 26, Philadelphia, 1918, pp. 33–125; *American Jewish Yearbook,* 5678 (1917–18), pp. 106–60

"The Peace Conference and Rights of Minorities," *ibid.,* 5681 (1920–21), pp. 101–30

Kohler, M. J., and Wolf, S., *Jewish Disabilities in the Balkan States,* New York, 1916

La Gorce, J. O., "Roumania and Its Rubicon," *National Geographic Magazine,* 1916, XXX, 185–202

Larcher, M., *La Grande Guerre dans les Balkans,* Paris, 1929

Lederbur, W., *Friedensvertrag mit Rumänien,* Wien, 1918

Luzatti, L., *God in Freedom,* New York, 1930

Mantoux, P., "L'Histoire à la Conférence de la Paix," *L'Esprit international,* 1929, III, 39–50

Martin, L., "Maps Showing Territorial Changes since the World War," *International Conciliation,* May 1924, No. 198

Masaryk, T. G., *The Making of a State,* New York, 1927

Miller, D. H., *The Drafting of the Covenant,* 2 vols., New York, 1928

My Diary at the Conference of Paris, with Documents, 22 vols., New York, 1928

Mirkine-Guetsevitch (editor), "Documents: Entrée en Guerre de la Roumanie," *Le Monde Slave,* September 1928, pp. 423–71; "Documents: La Diplomatie Russe dans les Balkans pendant la Grande Guerre," *ibid.,* March 1928, pp. 433–51

Negulescu, G., *Rumania's Sacrifice: Her Past, Present and Future,* New York, 1918

Nowak, K. F., *The Collapse of Central Europe,* New York, 1924

Pelivan, I. G., *Les Droits des Roumains sur la Bessarabie,* Bucarest, 1919

Petrescu-Commin, N. M., *Notes sur la Guerre Roumaine (1916–1917),* Lausanne, 1917

Russu, M., *Situation juridique des Roumains en Transylvanie,* Paris, 1916

Schmitt, B. E., *The Coming of the War,* 2 vols., New York, 1930

Schüking, W. (editor), *Kommentar zum Friedensverträge,* 5 vols., Berlin, 1920–2

Serbesco, S., *La Roumanie et la guerre,* Paris, 1919

Seton-Watson, R. W., "Wilhelm II's Balkan Policy," *Slavonic Review,* 1928–29, VII, 1–29

Seymour, C., *The Intimate Papers of Colonel House,* Boston and New York, 1928

Sirianu, M. R., *La Question de Transylvanie et l'unité politique de la Roumanie,* Paris, 1916

Sosnovsky, T. von, "The Balkan Policy of the Habsburg Empire," *Contemporary Review,* 1914, CVI, 215–22

Szilassy, Baron J. von, *Der Untergang der Donau Monarchie,* Berlin, 1921

Temperley, H. W. V. (editor), *History of the Peace Conference of Paris,* 6 vols., London, 1920–24

Temperley, H. W. V., "How the Hungarian Frontiers Were Drawn," *Foreign Affairs,* 1928, VI, 432–47

Thomas, A., *La Roumanie et la guerre,* Paris, 1919

Thompson, C. T., *The Peace Conference Day by Day,* New York, 1920

Tisza, Comte E., *Lettres de guerre (1914–1916),* Paris, 1931

Toporul, J., *La Situation de la Bessarabie et de Bukovine comme elle présente au point de vue du droit public et international,* Léopol, 1926

Toynbee, A. J., *Nationality and the War,* London, 1915

Ursu, J., *Pourquoi la Roumanie a fait la guerre,* Paris, 1918

Vilburg, G., *Rumänische Etappe der Weltkrieg Wie Ich Ihn Sah,* Münich, 1930

Vinogradski, A. N., *La Guerre sur le front Oriental,* Paris, 1926

Vopička, C. J., *Secrets of the Balkans,* Chicago, 1921

Wallis, B. C., "The Dismemberment of Hungary," *Geographical Review,* 1921, II, 426–29

Wedel, O. H., "Austro-Hungarian Diplomatic Documents," *Journal of Modern History,* 1931, III, 84–107

Wolf, L., *Notes on the Diplomatic History of the Jewish Question,* London, 1919

Woods, H. C., "The Balkans, Macedonia and the War," *Geographical Review,* 1918, VI, 19–36

Young, G., *Nationalism and War in the Near East,* Oxford, 1915

E. Foreign and Internal Policy of Post-War Roumania

Abedeano, B. C., *Les Relations historiques et politiques des Roumains avec les Serbes, des temps les plus jusqu'à nos jours,* Bucarest, 1930

Adamov, E. A., "Le Problème Bessarabien et les relations Russo-Roumaines," *Le Monde Slave,* 1929, I, 65–106

Alsberg, H. G., "The Roumanian Muddle," *Nation*, 1920, CX, 213–14

Alvarez, A., *Agrarian Reform in Roumania and the Case of the Hungarian Optants in Transylvania before the League of Nations*, Paris, 1927

Ancel, J., *Les Balkans face à l'Italie*, Paris, 1928

Apponyi, A., *Justice for Hungary*, London, 1928

Armstrong, H. F., *The New Balkans*, New York, 1926
Where the East Begins, New York, 1929

Asmead-Bartlett, E., *The Tragedy of Central Europe*, London, 1923

Babel, A., *La Bessarabie*, Paris, 1926

Barolin, C., and Schwechner, K., *Für und Wieder die Donauföderation*, Wien, 1926

Beneš, E., "The Little Entente," *Foreign Affairs*, 1922, I, 66–72
"La Petite Entente," *L'Esprit International*, 1927, I, 300–310
The Diplomatic Struggle for European Security and the Stabilization of Peace, Prague, 1925

Bibesco, Princess Marthe, *Some Royalties and a Prime Minister* (chap. vii, "When Michael of Rumania, Aged Five, Became a King"), New York, 1930

Boldur, A., *La Bessarabie et les relations Russo-Roumaines; la question Bessarabienne et le droit international*, Paris, 1927

Booth, C. D., "The Political Situation in Southeastern Europe," *Journal of the Royal Institute of International Affairs*, 1929, VIII, 318–43, 445–57

Bosiano, C., *La Politique paysanne en Roumanie*, Paris, 1920

Braunias, K., "Die Wahlreformen der Jahre 1925 und 1926," *Zeitschrift für Politik*, 1927, Heft I, 47–63

Brunet, R., "La Réforme agraire et les intérêts privés Hongrois en Transylvanie," *Journal du Droit International*, 1927, pp. 319–45

Buell, R. L., *International Relations*, New York, 1929
Europe: A History of Ten Years, New York, 1928

Bulletin of International News, 1928–29, V, 601–608, "The New Régime in Rumania"

Chamberlain, J. P., *The Danube*, Washington, D.C., 1918
The Régime of the International Rivers: Danube and Rhine, New York, 1923

Codresco, F., *La Petite Entente*, Paris, 1930

Conwell-Evans, T. P., *The League Council in Action*, Oxford, 1929

Crane, J. O., *The Little Entente*, New York, 1930

Csikay, P. de, *L'Europe centrale, économique et sociale*, Paris, 1931

Currey, M., *The Hungaro-Rumanian Dispute*, London, 1929

Czechoslovak White Books: *Documents diplomatiques concernant les tentatives de restauration des Habsbourgs sur le trône de Hongrie*, Prague, 1922; *Documents diplomatiques relatifs aux conventions d'alliance conclues par la République Tchécoslovaque avec le Royaume des Serbes, Croates et Slovènes et le Royaume de Roumanie*, Prague, 1923

Danielopol, G. D., and Others, *La Loi agraire. L'expropriation des sujets étrangères en Roumanie*, Bucarest, 1921

Dascovici, N., *Le Réforme agraire en Roumanie et les optants Hongrois de Transylvanie devant la Société des Nations,* Paris, 1924

Donals, Sir Robert, *The Tragedy of Trianon,* London, 1928

Dugdale, B., *The Hungaro-Roumanian Dispute: the Optants' Case before the League,* London, 1928

Dunlop, R., "Last of the Habsburgs," *Contemporary Review,* 1929, CXXXVI, 47–53

Eisenmann, L., and Others, *Les Problèmes de l'Europe Centrale,* Paris, 1923

Fischer, L., *The Soviets in World Affairs,* London, 1930

Floresco, S., *L'Affaire Carol,* Paris, 1928

Foreign Policy Association, *Information Service,* Vol. 3, No. 24, February 3, 1928, "Post-War Rumania"; *ibid.,* Vol. 4, No. 12, August 17, 1928, "Obstacles to Balkan Co-operation"; *ibid.,* Vol. 4, No. 14, September 14, 1928, "The Little Entente"; *ibid.,* Vol. 6, No. 5, May 14, 1930, "The Reparation Settlement of 1930"

   Foreign Policy Reports, Vol. 7, No. 1, March 18, 1931, "Recent Balkan Alignments"

Fuchs, J., "Averescu: Rumania's Mussolini," *Nation,* 1926, CXXII, 526–28

Gauvain, A., "Les Projets de rapprochement Balkanique," *L'Esprit International,* 1927, I, 30–43

Gedye, G. E. R., "Ion Bratianu," *Contemporary Review,* 1928, CXIII, 35–38

Geöcze, Dr. Barthélemy de, "L'Article 250 du Traité de Trianon," *Revue de droit international de sciences diplomatiques et politiques,* 1929, VII, 61–69

Geurge, W., *Paneuropa und Mitteleuropa,* Berlin, 1929

Guest, Dr. L. H., *The Struggle for Power in Europe 1917–1921,* London, 1921

D. G. H., "The European Agrarian Bloc," *Bulletin of International News,* 1930, VII, 975–83; "The European Agrarian Movement," *ibid.,* 1183–90

Hajnal, H., "La Commission Européenne du Danube et le dernier avis consultatif de la cour," *Revue de droit international et de législation comparée,* 1928, IX, 588–645

   Le Droit du Danube international, La Haye, 1929

Hasas, E., *La Revision du Traité de Trianon,* Paris, 1928

Heathcote, D., "Bratianu and the New Roumania," *Fortnightly Review,* 1927, CXXII, 808–16

   "Hungary and the Peace Treaties," *ibid.,* pp. 217–26

   "The Hungarian-Roumanian Dispute," *ibid.,* 1928, CXXIX, 249–57

Iancovici, D., *Take Ionescu,* Paris, 1919

International Conciliation: No. 229, April 1927, J. T. Shotwell, "Locarno and the Balkans"; *ibid.,* D. Mitrany, "The Possibility of a Balkan Locarno"

   No. 244, November 1928, N. L. Hill, "Post-War Treaties of Security and Mutual Guarantee"

   No. 250, May 1929, P. Slosson, "The Problem of Austro-German Union"

   No. 252, September 1929, M. W. Graham, "The Soviet Security System"

No. 262, September 1930, "The Final Settlement of the Reparations Problem Growing Out of the World War: Protocol with Annexes, Approved at the Plenary Session of the Hague Conference, August 31, 1929, and Agreements Concluded at the Hague Conference, Jan. 1930"

Special Bulletin, June 1930, "Memorandum of the Organization of a Régime of European Federal Union. Addressed to Twenty-six Governments of Europe, by M. Briand, Foreign Minister of France, May 17, 1930"

No. 265, December 1930, "European Federal Union, Replies of Twenty-six Governments of Europe to M. Briand's Memorandum of May 17, 1930"

Ionescu, T., "The Future of the Little Entente," *Living Age,* 1921, CCCXI, 699–703

La Politique étrangère de la Roumanie, Bucarest, 1921

The Origins of the War; the Testimony of a Witness (translation by A. Zimmern. Council for the Study of International Relations, Foreign Series, No. 6), London, 1917

The Policy of National Instinct, London, 1916

Some Personal Impressions, London, 1919

Souvenirs, Paris, 1919

Iorga, N., *Partis politiques en Roumanie au 19ᵉ siècle,* Bucharest, 1900

"La Roumanie, les Balkans et l'Europe Centrale," *L'Esprit international,* 1928, II, 169–83

Cinq Conférences sur le Sud-est de l'Europe, Bucarest, 1924

Relations des Roumains avec les Tchécoslovaques, Prague, 1924

Jotzow, D., "Russian Policy in the Balkans," *Contemporary Review,* 1929, CXXXV, 64–72

Kelley, R. F., "Soviet Policy on the European Border," *Foreign Affairs,* 1924, III, 90–98

Kerner, R. J., *The Little Entente* (read before the annual meeting of the American Historical Society, Washington, D.C., December 1927)

Lapradelle, A. de, "Les Réformes agraires et le droit international," *L'Esprit international,* 1929, III, 433–59

Légrády, Dr. O., *Justice for Hungary,* Budapest, 1930

Lengyel, E., "Rumania's Revolution," *Nation,* 1929, CXXVIII, 27–28

"Rumania's Oil and Foreign Money," *ibid.,* 1924, CXIX, 296–97

"The Situation that Made Carol King of Rumania," *Current History,* 1930, XXXII, 1058–59

Lepper, G. H., "The New Régime in Roumania," *English Review,* 1929, XLVIII, 54–59

Lukacs, G., *Die Revision der Friedensverträge,* Berlin, 1928

Lupu, N., "Crushing the Rumanian Peasant," *Nation,* 1922, CXV, 724–26

"Rumania's Needs," *ibid.,* 1920, CX, 214–15

Lybyer, A. H., "The Balkan Situation," *Journal of International Relations,* 1919–1920, X, 404–24

Macartney, C. A., "Post-War Tangles in Southern Europe," *Current History,* 1930, XXXII, 534–39

Macartney, M. H. H., "Towards a Balkan Bloc," *Fortnightly Review,* 1928, CXXIX, 311–22

McDonald, J. G., *Rumania's Dynastic Crisis,* Foreign Policy Association, New York, June 30, 1930 (pamphlet)

Machray, R., *The Little Entente,* London, 1929

"The Peace of the Balkans," *Fortnightly Review,* 1929, CXXIX, 663–70

"Rumania and Her Problems: Some Personal Impressions," *Fortnightly Review,* 1926, CXXV, 667–77

"The Little Entente and Its Policies," *ibid.,* 1926, 764–74

Madgearu, V., "La Fusion de Parti Paysan avec le Parti National en Roumanie," Bureau International Agraire, *Bulletin,* 1926, No. 4, pp. 6–12

Malynski, E., *Les Problèmes de l'Est et la Petite Entente,* Paris, 1931

Marburg, E., *Der Rumänisch-Ungarische Optantenstreit vor dem Gemischten Schiedsgericht und dem Völkerbund,* Leipzig, 1928

Melville, C. F., "Italy, France and South-Eastern Europe," *Fortnightly Review,* 1928, CXXIX, 646–56

Mironesco, G. G., *La Politique de la paix,* Bucarest, 1929

Mitrany, D., *The Land and the Peasant in Rumania,* London and New Haven, 1930

Mowrer, P. S., *Balkanized Europe,* New York, 1920

Mousset, A., *La Petite Entente,* Paris, 1923

Okhotnikov, J., and Batchincsky, N., *La Bessarabie et la paix Européenne,* Paris, 1927

Pasvolsky, L., *Bulgaria's Economic Position,* Washington, D.C., 1930

Pavel, P., "La Résurrection d'un pays. La Transylvanie," *Revue mondiale,* 1929, CXCI, 173–78

Pekárek, J., *La Cooperation économique des états de la Petite Entente,* Prague (privately printed), 1930

Pernot, M., "La Conférence de la Haye et l'esprit international," *L'Esprit international,* 1929, III, 558–69

Politicus, "Roumanian Restoration," *English Review,* 1930, LI, 79–84

Popescu, A. I., "Parties and Politics in Rumania," *Nation,* 1927, CXXIV, 744–46

Rappard, W. E., *Uniting Europe,* New Haven, 1930

Rawson, C., "The Liberal Government at Bay in Rumania," *English Review,* 1928, XLVI, 538–45

Redlich, J., "Reconstruction in the Danube Countries," *Foreign Affairs,* 1922, I, 73–85

Research Center of International Affairs, *Bibliographical Bulletin on International Affairs* (since January 1, 1926), Paris, 1926—

Roth, K., *Bulgarien-Rumänien,* Berlin, 1922

Rouček, J. S., "New Tendencies of Roumanian Politics," *Social Science,* 1931, VI, 374–81

Roumanian Government, *Memoir Showing the Roumanian Government's Point of View regarding Germany's Obligation of Refunding the Security for the Bank Notes Issued by the "Banca Generala Romana,"* Bucharest, 1925

Sainte-Aulaire, Comte de, "Un Grand Latine—Jean Bratiano," *Revue Hebdomaire*, 1928, VIII, 5–26

Savadjian, L., *The Campaign against the Treaty of Trianon*, Paris (reprinted from the *Revue des Balkans*), 1929

Sebess, D. von, *Land Ownership Policy of New Roumania in Transylvania*, Budapest, 1921

Seton-Watson, R. W., "The Situation in Roumania," *Contemporary Review*, 1927, CXXXII, 151–58

"The Little Entente," *ibid.*, pp. 694–707

Simonds, F. H., "The Old Trouble in the Old Balkans," *American Review of Reviews*, 1927, LXXV, 494–502

Smogarzewski, C., "La Roumanie à la veille des elections," *Le Correspondant*, 1928, C, 641–56

La Roumanie à un tournant de son histoire. Le Cabinet Maniu, Paris (Extrait du *Le Correspondant*, Decembre 10, 1928), 1929

Spender, H. F., "The Situation in the Balkans," *Fortnightly Review*, 1925, CXXIII, 727–36

Szana, A., *Die Internationalisierung der Donau*, Wien, 1920

Tibal, A., "Bulgares et Roumains," *L'Esprit international*, 1928, III, 380–93

"Le Roi Charles II de Roumanie," *L'Europe Centrale*, 1930, V, 672–74

Titulesco, N., *Mémoire du Gouvernement Royal de Roumanie concernant la proposition du 9 mars 1928 dans l'affaire des optants Hongrois de Transylvanie*, Paris, 1928

Toporul, J., *Die Staats und Völkerrechtliche Stellung Bessarabiens und der Bukowina*, Vienna, 1925

Toynbee, A. J., *Survey of International Affairs, 1920–23*, London, 1925; also annually thereafter

Tyler, R., "The Eastern Reparations Settlement," *Foreign Affairs*, 1930, VIII, 106–17

Uhlig, C., *Die Bessarabische Frage: Eine Geopolitische Betrachtung*, Breslau, 1926

Vaida-Voevod, A., "Ten Years of Greater Roumania," *Slavonic Review*, 1928, VII, 261–67

Vallotton, J., *Le Régime juridique du Danube maritime devant le Cour Permanent de Justice Internationale*, Lausanne, 1928

Wheeler-Bennett, J. W., *Documents on International Affairs, 1928*, Oxford, 1929

Woods, H. C., "The New Régime in Roumania," *Fortnightly Review*, 1929, CXXVI, 378–87

World Peace Foundation, *Post-War Political Alignments*, Boston (League of Nations Publications, Vol. VI, No. 2), 1923

Wright, E. W., "Roumania," *English Review*, 1928, XLVII, 675–78

Xenopol, A. D., "Clouds over the Little Entente," *Living Age*, 1924, CCC, 209–11

Anonymous, "The Foreign Policy of the Little Entente," *Slavonic Review*, 1926–27, V, 523–36

F. Minorities

The American Committee on the Rights of Religious Minorities, *Roumania Ten Years After,* Boston, 1928

The American Jewish Committee, *Twenty-fourth Annual Report,* New York, 1931

American Unitarian Commission, *Transylvania under the Rule of Rumania,* Budapest, 1921

Andru, V., and Loewenfeld, E., *Die Rechtlichen Grundlagen des Ungarisch-Rumänischen Optanttenstreites,* Berlin, 1930

Arrowsmith, N., "National Minorities as a Current International Problem," *European Economic and Political Survey,* 1927, II, 454, 464 (Contains excellent bibliography)

Auerhan, J., *Die Sprachlichem Minderheiten in Europa,* Berlin, 1926

Balogh, A. de, *Les Droits des Minorités et la défense de ces droits en Roumanie,* Geneva, 1925

    Der Internationale Schutz der Minderheiten, Münich, 1928

Barta, Erwin, *Daus Auslandsdeutschtum,* Wien and Leipzig, 1930

Barthélemy, J., "La Procédure de l'appel des minorités à la Société des Nations," *L'Esprit international,* 1929, III, 416–32

Bell, K. (editor), *Das Deutschtum in Rumänischen Banat,* Dresden, 1926

Bernard, J., *Nationality, Its Nature and Problems,* London, 1929

Beyon, E. D., "Isolated Racial Groups of Hungary," *Geographical Review,* 1927, XVII, 586–604

Blaskovics, F., Bell, K., and Others, *Das Deutschtum in Rumänischen Banat,* Dresden, 1926

Brière, Yves de la, and Others, *La Réforme agraire en Roumanie et les Optants Hongrois de Transylvanie devant la Société des Nations,* Paris, 1928

Bruns, C. G., *Grundlagen un Entwicklung des Internationalen Minderheitenrechtes,* Berlin, 1929

Buday, L., *Dismembered Hungary,* Budapest, 1922

Budisteano, R., *Le Condition juridique des minorités éthniques selon les derniers Traités de Paix,* Paris, 1927

Buxton, N., and Conwil-Evans, T. P., *Oppressed Peoples and the League of Nations,* London, 1922

Cabot, J. M., *The Racial Conflict in Transylvania,* Boston, 1926

Ciats, L., *Das Minoritätenproblem in Grossrumänien,* Cluj, 1925

Cohen, I., "The Jews under the Minorities Treaties," *Contemporary Review,* 1929, CXXXV, 73–80

Cornish, L. C., *The Religious Minorities in Transylvania,* London, 1926

Deák, F., *The Hungarian-Roumanian Land Dispute: a Study of Hungarian Property Rights in Transylvania under the Treaty of Trianon,* New York, 1928

Detattre, P., "Le Catholicisme dans la Grande Roumanie," *Le Correspondant,* May 10, 1929, pp. 321–42

De Visscher, C., *The Stabilization of Europe* (chapter ii), Chicago, 1924

Dillon, E. J., "The Jews of Roumania," *Contemporary Review,* 1914, CV, 878–81

Dotation Carnegie pour la Paix Internationale, *Bulletin No. 2, 1929:* M. A. Tibal, "Le Problème des Minorités"; M. E. de Martonne, "La Répartition et le rôle des minorités nationales en Roumanie"; M. Bouglé, "Le Principe des nationalités et les minorités nationales." Paris, 1929

Dragomir, S., *The Ethnical Minorities in Transylvania,* Geneva, 1927

Eisenmann, L., Rappard, W. E., Harris, W. H., and Buell, R. L., "The Problem of Minorities," *International Conciliation,* No. 222, 1926

Evans, I. L., "The Protection of Minorities," *British Year Book of International Law, 1923–1924* (pp. 95–123), Oxford, 1924

Feller, F. M., *Antisemitismus. Eine Psychoanalytische Lösung des Problems,* Berlin, 1931

Foreign Policy Association, *Information Service,* "Protection of Minorities in Europe," Vol. II, No. 9, July 3, 1926

Foucques-Duparc, J., *La Protection des minorités de race, de langue et de religion,* Paris, 1922

Frankenberg, R., *Das Grenz- und Auslanddeutschtum in Geschichtsunterricht,* Berlin-Leipzig, 1930

Gouvernement Roumain, *Protection des minorités en Roumanie,* Genève, 1925

Grentrup, T., *Das Deutschtum an der Mittleren Donau in Rumänien und Jugoslavien,* 1930

Harris, H. W., "The League and the Minorities," *Contemporary Review,* 1929, CXXXV, 420–23

Iorga, N., "La Politique des Minorités en Roumanie," *Le Monde Slave,* Avril 1926, pp. 22–31

"Le Protestantisme Roumain," *Revue historique du Sud-Est Européen,* 1930, VII, 65–78

Kraus, Dr. H., *Das Recht der Minderheiten,* Berlin, 1927

Krstitch, D., *Les Minorités, l'état et la communauté internationale,* Paris, 1924

Krisztics, A., *Synopsis of the Legal Position of Nationalities in Europe before the War,* Budapest, 1923

Lazare, B., *Die Juden in Rumänien,* Berlin, 1902

League of Nations, League Information Handbook, *The League of Nations and the Protection of Minorities,* rev. ed., 1927

Protection of Linguistic, Racial or Religious Minorities by the League of Nations, Geneva, March 1931

Londrea, A., *The Jew Has Come Home* (translation by W. Staples), New York, 1931

Lucien-Brun, J., *Le Problème des minorités devant le droit international,* Paris, 1923

Luzzatti, L., *God in Freedom,* New York, 1930

Mair, L. P., *Protection of Minorities,* London, 1928

Mandelstam, A., "La Protection des minorités," Académie de droit international, *Recueil des Cours,* I, 362–519, Paris, 1925

Margolin, A. D., *The Jews of Eastern Europe,* New York, 1926

Meitani, R., *La Protection des minorités,* Paris, 1930

Newman, E. W. P., "The Melting Pot of Central Europe," *Nineteenth Century and After,* 1930, CVII, 577–90

Osuský, S., "Le Problème des minorités," *L'Esprit international,* 1929, III, 174–80

Plettner, H., *Das Problem des Schutzes Nationaler Minderheiten,* Berlin, 1927

Rappard, W. E., *International Relations Viewed from Geneva* (chapter ii), New Haven, 1925

Rauchberg, H., *Die Reform des Minderheitenschutzes,* Breslau, 1930

Reimesch, F. H., *Das Deutschtum in Grossrumänien,* Berlin, 1926

Robinson, J., *Das Minoritätenproblem und Seine Literatur,* Berlin, 1928

Rouček, J. S., *The Minority Principle as a Problem of Political Science,* Prague, 1928

    The Working of the Minorities System under the League of Nations, Prague, 1929

    "Procedure in Minorities Complaints," *American Journal of International Law,* 1929, XXIII, 538–551

Rudesco, C. A., *Étude sur la question des minorités de race, de langue et de religion,* Lausanne-Genève, 1929

Ruehlmann, P., *Das Schulrecht der Deutschen Minderheiten in Europa,* Breslau, 1926

Ruyssen, T., *Les Minorités nationales d'Europe et la Guerre Mondiale,* Paris, 1924

Sachar, A. L., *A History of the Jews,* New York, 1930

Schwarzfeld, Dr. E., "The Jews of Roumania," *American Jewish Year Book,* 5662 (1901–1902), pp. 25–87

    Les Juifs en Roumanie depuis le Traité de Berlin (1878) jusqu'à ce jour, Londres, 1901

Schwefelberg, A., "La Loi Roumaine du 23 Février 1924 sur l'acquisition et la perte de la nationalité Roumaine, par rapport aux Traités de Paix," *Journal du droit international,* Mars-Avril, 1926, 300–310

Schwicker, J. H., *Die Deutschen in Ungarn und Siebenbürgen,* Wien, 1881

    Die Nationalpolitischen Auspruche der Rumänen in Ungarn, Leipzig, 1894

Soubbotich, I. V., *Effets de la dissolution de l'Autriche-Hongrie sur la nationalité des ses ressortissants,* Paris, 1926

Stephens, J. S., *Danger Zones of Europe,* London, 1929

Stratton, G. M., *Social Psychology of International Conduct,* New York, 1929

Suciu, A., *De la nationalité en Roumanie,* Paris, 1906

Sunderland, J. T., *Three Centuries and a Half of Unitarianism in Hungary,* Boston, 1900

Szász, Z., *The Minorities in Roumanian Transylvania,* London, 1927

Szeptychyj, A., "Rumanian Catholics," *Commonweal,* 1930, XII, 258

Teodoresco, Dr. I., and Istrate, N., *Méthode pour la connaissance des minorités ethniques* (Reprint from *Les Annales économiques et statistiques*), Bucarest, 1928

Teutsch, F., *Die Siebenbürger Sachsen in Vergangenheit und Gegenwart,* Leipzig, 1916

Tibal, A., "Le Concordat et le régime des cultes en Roumanie," *L'Europe Centrale,* 1929, III, 821–23

Tichner, H. M., *Roumania and Her Religious Minorities,* London, 1927

Ullrich, K., *Die Volkswirtschaftliche Bedeutung der Siebenbürger Sachsen in Rumänien,* Leipzig, 1930

Visscher, Ch. de, "Unité d'état et revendications minoritaires," *Revue du droit international et de législation comparée,* 1930, XI, 326–60

Wallis, B. C., "Distribution of Nationalities in Hungary," *Geographical Journal,* 1916, XLVII, 176–88

"The Roumanians in Hungary," *Geographical Review,* 1918, VI, 156–71

Wertheimer, Fr., *Von Deutschen Parteien und Parteiführer im Ausland,* Berlin, 1927

G. Constitution and Administration

Andrews, A. I., "The New Constitution of Roumania," *Current History,* 1923, XVIII, 1017–24

Barasch, M. I., "La Protection légale des travailleurs en Roumanie," *Recueil de droit commercial et de droit de société,* 1929, I, 65–70

Blaramberg, N., *Essai comparé sur les institutions et les lois de la Roumanie, depuis les temps les plus réculés jusqu'à nos jours,* Bucharest, 1895

Boila, R., "Die Verfassung und Verwaltung Rumäniens Seit den Weltkriege," *Jahrbuch des Öffentlichen Rechts der Gegenwart,* 1930, XVIII, 324–54

Cohen, J. G., "La Nationalité des sociétés commerciales en Roumanie," *Revue de droit international privé,* 1926, XXI, 350–504

Colescu, L., *Geschichte des Rumänischen Staatswesens in der Periode der Fanarioten,* München, 1897

Constitution de 30 juin–12 juillet 1866 avec les modifications introduites en 1879, en 1884, Bucharest, 1884

La Constitution Roumaine promulgée le 28 Mars 1923 et publiée dans le Moniteur Officiel du 29 Mars 1923, Bucharest, 1928

Delpech, J., and Laferrière, J., *Les Constitutions modernes,* Paris, 1929, II, 351–79

Dimitru, C. D., *Le Problème administratif en Roumanie,* Bucharest, 1926

Dissescu, C. G., *Droit constitutionnel: droit administratif,* Bucharest, 1890–1892

Les Droits de la femme dans le prochain code civil, Bucharest, 1925

Egger, R. A., "Administrative Reorganization in Roumania," *National Municipal Review,* 1930, XIX, 724–25

Filotti, I. C., and Vrabiesco, G., "Le Conseil législatif de Roumanie," *Revue des sciences politiques,* 1929, LII, 481–98

Flournoy, R. W., and Hudson, M. O., *A Collection of Nationality Law of Various Countries as Contained in Constitutions, Statutes and Treaties* (Roumania, pp. 508–509), New York, 1929

Kauschansky, D. M., "Die Neue Rumänische Verfassung vom 28. März 1923," *Zeitschrift für Öffentliches Recht,* 1925, V, 117 ff.
"Grundzüge des Neuen Rumänischen Verfassungsrechts," *Archiv des Öffentlichen Rechts,* 1928, XIV, 112–20
Lehr, E., *La Nationalité dans les principaux états du globe,* Paris, 1909
Marcovici, J., "Das Verhaltniss Zwischen dem Normal Gesetz und der Verfassung in Rumänien," *Zeitschrift für Ostrecht,* 1929, III, 55–58
Meitani, G. G. G., *Le Pouvoir constituant en Roumanie,* Paris, 1901
Mirkine-Guetzevitch, B., *Les Constitutions de l'Europe Nouvelle,* Paris, 1928
"Les Tendances internationales des nouvelles constitutions Européennes," *L'Esprit international,* 1928, II, 531–46
Mitrany, D., "The New Rumanian Constitution," *Journal of Comparative Legislation and International Law,* 1924, VI, 110–19
"Democracy in the Villages," *Manchester Guardian,* November 28, 1929, p. 17
The Near East Year Book 1927, London, 1927
Oresco, V., *Le Contrôle de la constitutionalité des lois en Roumanie,* Paris, 1929
Popp, D. C., *De la condition juridique des sociétés étrangères en Roumanie,* Paris, 1929
Rey, V. F., "Un Aspect particulier de la question des minorités: Les Israélites de Roumanie," *Revue de droit international privé,* 1926, XXI, 461–64
Rouček, J. S., "Reorganization of the Governmental Structure of Roumania," *American Political Science Review,* 1931, XXV, 700–703
Roumania: Ministère des Affaires Étrangères, *Constitution,* Bucharest, 1923
Roumania (Imprimerie de l'état), *Le Problème administratif en Roumanie,* Bucarest, 1926
Tibal, A., "Le Projet de réforme administrative en Roumanie," *L'Europe Centrale,* 1929, III, 685–87
White, L. D. (editor), *The Civil Service in the Modern State,* Chicago, 1930

H. Art, Culture, Education, Language, and Literature

Ackerley, F. G., *A Roumanian Manual for Self-Tuition, Containing a Concise Grammar with Exercises, Reading Extracts, and a Select Vocabulary,* London, 1917
Alexi, H., *Rumänisch Deutsches Worterbuch,* Kronstadt, 1905
Alexics, G., *Geschichte der Rumänischen Litteratur,* Leipzig, 1906
Ancel, J., *L'Unité de la civilisation Balkanique,* Paris, 1927
Angelesco (le Dr. C.), *L'Enseignement primaire de l'état et l'enseignement normal primaire,* Bucarest, 1925
L'Enseignement particulier, Bucarest, 1925
Axelrad, P., *Complete Roumanian-English Dictionary,* New York, 1918
The Elements of Roumanian. A Complete Roumanian Grammar with Exercises, New York, 1919
Bals, G., *Un Ouvrage sur la peinture dans les monuments de l'art Roumain ancien,* Vălenii-de-Munte, 1929

Bengescu, G., *Bibliographie Franco-Romaine depuis le commencement de XIX*ᵉ *siècle jusqu'à nos jours,* Paris, 1907
Bercovici, K., *Ghitza and Other Romances,* New York, 1921
Beza, M., *Doda* (translated by Mrs. L. Byng), London, 1925
    Paganism in Roumanian Folk-Lore, London, 1928
    Papers on Roumanian People and Literature, London, 1920
    Rays of Memory (translated by Mrs. L. Byng), New York, 1929
    Roumanian Grammar, Bucarest, 1919
Bianu, I., *La Civilisation Roumaine au XIX*ᵉ *siècle,* Bucarest, 1891
Boutière, J., *La Vie et l'oeuvre de Ion Creanga,* Paris, 1930
Byng, L. (translator), *Roumanian Stories,* London, 1920 (and see under Beza, M., above)
Clark, C. U., *Greater Roumania,* New York, 1922
Condreá-Hecht, J. A., "Etymologies Romaines," *Romania,* 1902, XXXI, 296–314
Constantinesco, E., *De l'Esprit l'enseignement secondaire en Roumanie,* Paris, 1910
Damé, F., *Nouveau dictionnaire Roumain Français,* 2 vols., Bucharest, 1893–1895
Densușianu, O., *Histoire de la langue Roumaine,* 2 vols., Paris, 1901, 1914
    Un Essai de résurrection littéraire, Paris, 1899
Donici, H., *Chants Roumains,* 2 vols., Paris, 1922
Dotation Carnegie (editor), *Enquête sur les livres scolaire d'après guerre,* Vol. I, Paris, 1927
Eftimiu, V., *Contes Roumains* (Adaptation Française de Marc Varenne), Paris, 1918
    "Littérature Néo-Roumaine," *La Revue,* 1917, CXX, 578–95
Eliade, P., *De l'Influence Française sur l'esprit public en Roumanie,* Paris, 1898
    Causeries littéraires, 3 vols., Bucarest, 1903
Eminesco, M., *Quelques poésies de Michail Eminesco* (traduction de M. M.-V.), Genève
    Quelques poésies par Michail Eminesco (traduites en Français par Al. Gr. Soutzo), Iassy, 1911
Feraru, L., "The Development of the Rumanian Novel," *Romanic Review,* 1926, XVII, 291–302
Fischer, E., *Die Kulturarbeit des Deutschtums in Rumänien,* Hermannstadt, 1911
Fleury, V., *Anthologie générale de littérature étrangère,* Paris, 1927
Fotino, M., *L'Influence Française sur les grands orateurs politiques Roumains de la seconde moitié du XIX*ᵉ *siècle,* Bucarest, 1928
Galitzi, "Education in Roumania," Society of Friends of Roumania, *Bulletin,* October 18, 1926, pp. 89–95
    A Study of Assimilation among the Roumanians of the United States, New York, 1929
Gaster, M., *Geschichte der Rumänischen Literatur,* Strassbourg, 1901
Gerard, E., *The Land beyond the Forest,* New York, 1888

Graatia, J., "Roumanians in the United States and Their Relations to the Public Libraries," *Library Journal*, 1922, XLVII, 400–404

Graur, A., *Verbes Roumains d'origine Tsigane*, Paris, 1926

Grun, A., *Ballades et chants populaires de la Roumanie* (Recueilles et traduites par V. Alexandri), Paris, 1855

Gubernates, Comte Angelo de, *Dictionnaire international des écrivains du monde Latin*, Rome, 1905

Hasdeu, J. B. P., *Oeuvres posthumes*, Paris, 1889

Hommenau, V. O., *Literatur und Volkskunst der Rumaenen*, Timişoara (Roumania), 1928

Hušková-Flajšhancová, J., *Rumunští Prozaikové v Rámci Vývoje Jednotlivých Literárních Škol*, Praha (Czechoslovakia), 1927

Ioan, O. G., *L'Âme Roumaine*, Paris, 1928
    L'Influence étrangère chez les artistes Roumains, Bucarest, 1916

Iorga, N., *Art et littérature des Roumains*, Paris, 1929
    L'Art populaire en Roumanie, Paris, 1923
    Commémoration de deux cent cinquante ans de la fondation d'une faculté des lettres à Bucarest, Bucarest, 1928
    Contes Roumains, Paris, 1925
    Coup d'oeil sur l'art Roumain, Genève, 1925
    La Création religieuse du sud-est Européen, Paris, 1925
    Les Ecrivains réalistes en Roumanie, Paris, 1925
    Études Roumaines, Paris, 1923
    Formes Byzantines et réalités Balkaniques, Paris, 1922
    Geschichte der Rumänen und Ihre Kultur, Hermannstadt, 1929
    Histoire de l'art ancien, Paris, 1922
    Histoire des Roumains de Transylvanie et de Hongrie, 2 vols., Bucarest, 1916
    A History of Roumania, London, 1925
    Livres populaires dans le sud-est de l'Europe et surtout chez les Roumains, Bucarest, 1928
    La Littérature populaire, Paris, 1925

Iorga, N., and Gorceix, S., *Anthologie de la littérature Roumaine*, Paris, 1922

Istrati, P., *The Thistles of the Baragan*, New York, 1930

Jarnik, Jean-Urbain, *Glossaire des chansons populaires Roumaines de Transylvanie*, Bucarest, 1885

Kanner, B., *La Société littéraire junimea de Iasy et son influence sur le movement intellectuel en Roumanie*, Paris, 1906

Kerner, R. J., *Social Sciences in the Balkans and Turkey*, Berkeley (California), 1930

Klein, Dr. K. K., *Rumänische-Deutsche Literaturbeziehungen*, Heidelberg, 1929

Lahovary, J., *Carnet d'un égoiste*, Paris, 1927

Lévèque, L., *Précis de grammaire Roumaine à l'usage des étrangers*, Bucarest, 1922

Littlefield, W., "New Aspects of Roumanian Literature," Society of Friends of Roumania, *Bulletin*, October 18, 1926, pp. 70–74

Mangiuca, S., *Daco-Romänische Sprache und Geschichtsforschung,* Wien, 1891

Marie, Queen of Roumania, *The Country That I Love,* London, 1925
The Magic Doll of Roumania, New York, 1929

Mehendinți, S., *L'École de la paix. L'esprit pacifique de l'école Roumaine,* Bucarest, 1928

Meillet, A., *Les Langues dans l'Europe Nouvelle,* Paris, 1928

Miller-Verghi, M., *Motifs anciens de décoration Roumaine,* București, 1911

Murray, E. C. G., *Doine: Or the National Songs and Legends of Roumania,* Bucharest, 1928

Nanu, D. A., *Le Poète Eminescu et la poésie lyrique Française,* Paris, 1930

Nistor, I., *Zur Geschichte des Schulwesens in der Bukovina,* Czernowitz, 1912

Notice sur l'histoire de l'enseignement secondaire et sur la situation actuelle de l'enseignement en Roumanie, Bucarest, 1928

Olszewski, G., *Vieux Tapis Roumains,* Bucarest, 1926

Oprescu, G., *Peasant Art in Roumania* (Special Autumn Number of *The Studio*), London, 1929

Orendi-Hommenau, V., *Literatur und Volkskunst der Rumänen,* Timișoara, 1928

Pankhurst, E. S., and Stefanovici, I. O., *Poems of Mihail Eminescu,* London, 1930

Pârvan, V., *Dacia. An Outline of the Early Civilization of the Carpatho-Danubian Countries,* Cambridge, 1928

Pascu, G., *Beiträge zur Geschichte der Rumänischen Philologie,* Leipzig, 1920
Dictionnaire Etymologique Macédoroumain, 2 vols., Iași, 1925

Patterson, R. S., *Roumanian Songs and Ballads,* London, 1917

Poisson, G., "L'Origine Latine des Roumains," *Revue Anthropologique,* 1917, XXVII, 355–79

Rebreanu, L., *Ciuleandra* (traduit du Roumain par B. Madeleine et Marina Bousquet), Paris, 1929
The Forest of the Hanged, New York, 1930

Romstorfer, K. A., *Die Moldauisch-Byzantische Baukunst,* Wien, 1896

Roques, M., *Les Premières Traductions Roumaines de l'Ancien Testament,* Paris, 1925

Rosetti, A., *Lettres Roumaines de la fin du XVIᵉ et du début du XVIIᵉ siècle, Tirées des archives de Bistritza,* Bucarest, 1926

Rouček, J. S., "The People's University—Professor Iorga's Experiment at Valenii-de-Munte, Roumania," *School and Society,* 1931, XXXIV, 199–200
"Recent Tendencies of the Roumanian Educational System," *ibid.,* 1931, 373–75

Roumania: Ministère des Cultes et des Beaux-Arts, *La Dobrodja,* Bucarest, 1928

Roumania: Ministère de l'Instruction Publique et des Cultes, *L'Enseignement public en Roumanie,* Bucarest, 1900

Rudow, W., *Geschichte der Rumänischen Schriftums,* Wernigerode, 1892

Das Rumänische Sozialinstitut 1921–1926, Bukarest, 1927

Russo, A., *La Pierre de Tilleul* (Manuscript publié par P. V. Haneş), Bucarest, 1908

Saineanu, L., *L'Influence orientale sur la langue et la littérature Roumaines,* Paris, 1902
  "Les Éléments orientaux au Roumain," *Romania,* 1901–1902, XXX, 539–66; XXXI, 82–99, 557–89

Samurgas, A. T., *Tapis Roumains,* Paris, 1924

Schedulenko, D., "Nordslavische Elemente in Rumänischen," *Balkan Archiv,* Bd. 1, pp. 153–72, Leipzig, 1925

School and Society, 1928, XXXVIII, 474–75, "Financial Support of Education in Roumania"

Serboianu, C. J. Popp, *Les Tsiganes. Histoire, Ethnographie, Linguistique, Grammaire, Dictionnaire,* Paris, 1931

Spaul, H., *Peeps at Many Lands—Roumania,* London, 1930

Ştefanescu, I. D., *L'Évolution de la peinture religieuse en Bucovine et en Moldavie depuis les origines jusqu'à XIXᵉ siècle,* Paris, 1928
  Contribution à l'étude des peintures murales Valaques, Transylvanie, district de Valcea, Targoviste et région de Bucarest, Paris, 1928

Sterian, G., *Notes de littérature populaire Roumaine,* Paris, 1889

Sturdza, D. A., *L'Activité de l'Académie Roumaine de 1884 à 1905,* Bucarest, 1905

Thévenin, L., "Le Movement littéraire en Roumanie," *Vie des Peuples,* 1924, XIV, 385–94

Ţigara-Samurcaş, A., *Rumänische Volkskunst,* Bukarest, 1910
  Esquisse sur l'Art Roumain, Paris, 1914

Tzigara-Samurgas, A., *Tapis Roumains,* Paris, 1928

Ureache, G., *Chronique* (Édition critique par J. N. Popovici), Bucarest, 1911

Urechea, V. A., *La Ligue pour l'unité culturale des Roumains,* Naples, 1901

Vizanti, A., *La Réforme de l'enseignement public en Roumanie,* Bucarest, 1887

Vladescu, R., *La Sociologie en Roumanie,* Paris, 1929

Vlahoutza, A., *N. I. Grigoresco. Sa vie et son oeuvre* (traduit du Roumain par L. Bachelin), Bucarest, 1911

Vulpesco, M., *Doinas de Roumanie,* Paris, 1917
  Les Coutumes Roumaines périodiques, Paris, 1927

Wace, A. J. B., and Thompson, M. S., *The Nomads of the Balkans,* London, 1914

Weigand, G., *Die Aromunen. Ethnographisch-Philologisch-Historische Untersuchingen über das Volk der Sagennanten Makedo-Romanen oder Zingaren,* Leipzig, 1894–1895

Zamfiresco, D., *Temps de Guerre* (traduit du Romain), Paris, 1900

I. Economic Roumania and Agrarian Reform

Amiable, L., *La Question des paysans en Roumanie,* Paris, 1861

Antonescu, C. G., *Die Rumänische Handelspolitik von 1875–1915,* Leipzig, 1915

Anninos, E. G., *Der Wirtschaftliche Einfluss Deutschlands auf die Petroleum Industrie Rumäniens und Ihre Bedeutung für die Internationale Wirtschaft,* Darmstadt, 1927

Axente, T., *Le Mouvement coopératif de crédit en Roumanie à la fin de l'année 1925,* Bucarest, 1926

Badulescu, V. V., *Les Finances publiques de la Roumanie,* Paris, 1923

Baicoianu, C. J., *Le Danube: aperçu historique, économique et politique,* Paris, 1917
    Histoire de la politique Douanière de la Roumanie de 1803 à 1903, Bucarest, 1904

Banker's Magazine, 1925, CX, 90–99, "Survey of the Present Situation of Roumania. Prospective Program within the Scope of the New Economic Law"

Banque Marmorosch Blank et Cie, *Les Forces économiques de la Roumanie en 1929 (1930),* Bucarest, 1930 (1931)

Bercaru, V., *La Réforme agraire en Roumanie,* Paris, 1928

Blank, A., "The Public Finances of Roumania," *Banker's Magazine,* 1922, CV, 617–30

Boncescu, G., "Roumania and Foreign Investments," *International Communications Review,* 1930, VI, 15–22

Bungetianu, C., *La Richesse forestrière de la Roumanie. L'industrie et le commerce du bois,* Bucarest, 1927

Child, J. R., "Development and Organization of the Roumanian Oil Industry," *Commerce Reports,* No. 37, September 15, 1930, pp. 677–79

Cioriceanu, G. D., *La Dette publique de la Roumanie,* Paris, 1927
    Le Problème monétaire Roumaine, Paris, 1925
    Les grands ports de Roumanie, Paris, 1928
    La Roumanie économique et ses rapports avec l'étranger de 1860 à 1915, Paris, 1928

Coffey, D., *The Co-operative Movement in Jugoslavia, Rumania, and North Italy during and after the World War,* New York, 1922

Conacher, H. M., "Agrarian Reform in Eastern Europe," *International Review of Agricultural Economics,* 1923 (New Series), I, 3–38

XIVᵉ Congrès International d'Agriculture (Bucarest, 7, 8, et 10 Juin, 1929), *La Roumanie agricole,* Bucarest, 1929

Constantinesco, M., *L'Évolution de la propriété rurale à la réforme agraire en Roumanie,* Bucarest, 1925

Day, C., "The Pre-War Commerce and the Commercial Approaches of the Balkan Peninsula," *Geographical Review,* 1920, IX, 277–98

Decoudu, H., *La Partage de dettes publiques Autrichiennes et Hongroises, 1918–1926,* Paris, 1926

Delaisi, F., *Oil and Its Influences on Politics,* London, 1922

Denny, L., *We Fight for Oil,* New York, 1928

Dobrin, C. J., *Les Optants Hongrois et la réforme agraire Roumaine,* Paris, 1929

Dragu, T., *La Politique Roumaine après les troubles agraires de 1907,* Paris, 1908

Dunn, R. W., *American Foreign Investments,* New York, 1926

The Economist, Roumanian Supplement, July 20, 1929

Einzig, P., "Notes on Recent Currency Events in Roumania," *Economic Journal,* 1920, XXX, 556–59

Emilien, S. D., *L'Industrie en Roumanie,* Bucarest, 1919

L'Espagnol de la Tramerye, *The World Struggle for Oil,* New York, 1924

European Economic and Political Survey, December 15, 1927, III, 210–14, "Roumanian Petroleum"

Evans, I. L., *The Agrarian Revolution in Roumania,* Cambridge, 1924

Feis, H., *Europe the World's Banker 1870–1914,* New Haven, 1930

Fischer, L., *Oil Imperialism,* New York, 1926

Gane, A., *Les Solutions économiques Roumaines,* Paris, 1924

Graf, Dr. O., *Die Industriepolitik Alt-Rumäniens und die Grundlagen der Industrialisierung Gross-Rumäniens,* Bukarest, 1927

Gross, H., *Deutsch-Rumänische Wirtschaftsbeziehungen,* Berlin, 1929

Hallunga, A., *L'Évolution et la révision récente du tarif dounanier en Roumanie,* Paris, 1927

Iangulescu, A. P., *La Richesse minière de la nouvelle Roumanie,* Paris, 1928

International Institute of Agriculture, "Co-operative Movement in Roumania," *International Review of Agricultural Economics,* October–December 1924, pp. 569–94

Institute of International Finance, "Credit Position of Roumania," *Bulletin,* No. 17, July 31, 1928

Ionescu-Sisesti, G., *Structure agraire et production agricole de la Roumanie,* Bucarest, 1924

   L'Agriculture de la Roumanie pendant la guerre, Paris, 1929

Juvàra, *Le Problème du credit agricole en Roumanie,* Paris, 1929

Kastric, D., *Les Capitaux étrangers dans la finance Roumanie,* Paris, 1921

Knight, M. M., "Peasant Co-operation in Roumania," *Political Science Quarterly,* 1920, XXXV, 1–29

Kolaroff, I., *La Loi Roumaine pour la nouvelle Dobroudja,* Sofia, 1928

Leonhardt, G. (editor), *Compass Finanzielles Jahrbuch, 1930,* "Rumanien," Wien, 1930

Madgearu, V., *Roumania's New Economic Policy,* London, 1930

Michael, L. G., *Agricultural Survey of Europe: The Danube Basin* (United States Agricultural Department, Technical Bulletin 126), Washington, D.C., 1924

Michell, M. S., "On the Oil Fields of Rumania," *English Review,* 1927, XLV, 302–307

Mitrany, D., *The Land and the Peasant in Rumania,* New Haven, 1930

Mrazec, L., *L'Industrie du pétrole en Roumanie,* Bucarest, 1910

Naumann, F., *Central Europe,* London, 1916

Netta, X., *Die Rumänische Nationalbank; Vorgeschichte, Entstehung, Organisation, Tätigkeit, Kredit- und Wahrungspolitik,* Leipzig, 1929

Ogg, F. A., "Rebuilding the Economic Life of Rumania," *Current History,* 1930, XXXII, 725–31

Pasvolsky, L., *Economic Nationalism of the Danubian States,* New York, 1928

Penacoff, D. I., *La Législation sur la proptiété rurale dans la Dobroudja du Sud* (Extrait de la *Revue Bulgare*), Sofia, 1929

Petrescu, N., "Roumania's Economic and Financial Situation," *Banker's Magazine,* 1924, CIX, 49–60

Pizanty, M., *Petroleum in Roumania,* Bucharest, 1930

    Les Problèmes actuels de l'industrie pétrolière Roumaine, Bucarest, 1929

Popescu, G., *La Navigation et la politique commerciale,* Bucarest, 1926

Radulescu, S., *La Politique financière de la Roumanie de 1914 à 1922,* Paris, 1925

Ravard, R., *La Danube maritime et le Port Galatz,* Paris, 1930

Revue Internationale du Travail, September 1926, pp. 367–80, "Le Mouvement Syndical dans les Pays Balkaniques"

Rommenhoeller, C. G., *La Grande-Roumanie,* La Haye, 1926

Rouček, J. S., "Economic Geography of Roumania," *Economic Geography,* 1931, VII, 390–99

Rumer, W., *Die Agrarreformen der Donau-Staaten,* Innsbruck, 1927

Scarlatesco, V., *La Problème monétaire en Roumanie,* Paris, 1928

Schlesinger, K., "The Disintegration of the Austro-Hungarian Currency," *Economic Journal,* 1920, XXX, 26–38

Sering, M., *Agrarrenrevolution und Agrarreform in Ost- und Mitteleuropa,* Berlin, 1929

Sisesti, G. J., "Share Tenancy in Rumania," *International Review of Economics* (New Series), 1923, I, 210–26

Sterian, P., *La Roumanie et la réparation des dommages de guerre,* Paris, 1929

Tatarano, C., *Les nouvelles tendances économiques de la Roumanie d'après la littérature économique et les discussions parlementaires,* Paris, 1922

Tibal, A., "La nouvelle législation économique en Roumanie," *L'Europe Centrale,* 1929, III, 606–608

United States Department of Commerce, Bureau of Foreign and Domestic Commerce, Special Agents Series, No. 222, *Rumania: An Economic Handbook,* Washington, D.C., 1924

United States Department of Commerce, *Commerce Yearbook 1930,* Vol. II, Washington, D.C., 1931

United States Labor Statistics Bureau, "Labor Conditions in Rumania," *Monthly Review,* 1929, XXVIII, 487–90

Woods, H. C., "Communications in the Balkans," *Geographical Review,* 1916, XLVII, 265–92

Zeciu, F., *Die Landwirtschaft in der Dobrudscha,* Leipzig, 1919

INDEX

Academy, Roumania, 378–79

Administration, changed by the Constitution of 1923, 223; local government, 238 ff.; ministries, 237–38; opposition of Liberals to reforms of, 123, 243; reform bill of Maniu, 121–22; reform of 1918, 221; reform of 1925, 110, 238 ff.; reorganized by the National-Peasant Government, 241 ff.; under the Constitution of 1866, 220–21; *see also* Constitution

Adult education, 379 ff.

Agrarian policy, 257, 307 ff.

Agrarian reform: Averescu's measures of, 106; background of, 293 ff.; constitutional amendment in favor of, 43–44, 219, 301 and n.; by Prince A. I. I. Cuza, 21; effects of, 305–06; Iorga collaborates in proclamation of, 81 n.; law of settlement drafted, 104; optants' question, 158 ff.; results of, 257, 303 ff.; in Wallachia, 18; *see also* Bessarabia, Bukovina, Dobrogea, Ferdinand, Transylvania

Agriculture: character of Roumanian, 251; conferences on, 165 ff.; credit, 321 ff., 342; crisis of, in Little Entente states, 164 ff.; debts of, 323; favored by National-Peasant Party, 312 ff., 320 ff.; Madgearu on deterioration of, 321; maize and wheat production, 255–56; Mihalache on, 307; overproduction, 333; policy of government, as to, 307 ff.; production of, in Roumania, 252 ff., 309 ff.; and tariffs, 331–32; utilization of land, 253–54

Amendments, constitutional, *see* Constitution

American Committee on the Rights of Religious Minorities, 186, 203

Andreaş II, privileges to Germans granted by, 5

Andrews, Professor A. I., on impress of alien control upon Roumania, 62

Angelescu, Dr. C., 76, 129

Apponyi, Count Albert, 152

Argetoianu, Dr. C.: biography of, 76; joins Averescu's Government, 106; joins Brătianu's Government, 114; joins Iorga's Government, 130 ff.; organizes Averescu's party, 82–83; program of, 133

Armenian minorities in Roumania, 194

Austria (Austria-Hungary): Austro-German customs union, *see* Little Entente; concludes commercial treaty with Roumania, 24, 329–30; custom war with Roumania, 29–30; Danube diplomacy of, 29, 34; diplomacy in Balkan wars, 35–36; encroaching upon the principalities, 10; investments in Roumania, 34, 38; occupation of Roumania, 309; opposition to Roumanian union, 20; repressive measures of, 18

Averescu, General (Marshal): biography of, 83–84; founds his "People's League," 82–83; participates in Vaida-Voevod's cabinet, 56; program of People's Party, 84

Balkans: Balkan wars, 34; Mowrer on the "Balkanization" of Europe, 142; objections of Roumania to being included in, 170 n.

Banat, ceded to Austria, 10; German minority of, 190–91

Bank of Roumania, *see* National Bank

Banks, 345 ff.; encouraged by Liberals, 311; popular, 321 ff.; in provinces, 346–47; Willis on development of, 352; *see also* Co-operatives, National Bank

Basarab, 6

Beneš, Dr. E.: on contacts with Roumanians during the war, 137; co-operates with Roumanians in Paris, 138; on economic co-operation of Little Entente, 143 n.; emphasizes possibility

413